THE EVOLUTION OF LAW AND ORDER

THE EVOLUTION OF LAW AND ORDER

BY

A. S. DIAMOND, M.A., LL.D.

Barrister-at-Law
Author of *Primitive Law*

GREENWOOD PRESS, PUBLISHERS
WESTPORT, CONNECTICUT

The Library of Congress has catalogued this publication as follows:

Library of Congress Cataloging in Publication Data

Diamond, Arthur Sigismund.
  The evolution of law and order.

  Reprint of the 1951 ed.
  Bibliography: p.
  1. Law, Primitive. 2. Law--History and criticism.
3. Civilization--History. 4. Society, Primitive.
I. Title.
LAW   340'.09   72-9372
ISBN 0-8371-6580-6

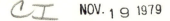 NOV. 1 9 1979

Originally published in 1951 by Watts & Co., London

Reprinted with the permission of Sir Isaac Pitman and Sons, Ltd.

Reprinted in 1973 by Greenwood Press, Inc., 51 Riverside Avenue,
Westport, Conn. 06880

Library of Congress catalog card number 72-9372
ISBN 0-8371-6580-6

Printed in the United States of America

10 9 8 7 6 5 4 3

PREFACE

WHEN this title was suggested to me it seemed at first wholly inappropriate. Is it to be said that there is more disorder in the simpler societies than in those in which we live? Indeed, such a title may seem to some ironical in the light of the present condition of the world. But plainly there has been at least a growth in the scale of social, political, and economic organization, and in this sense (among others) we may speak of an " evolution of order." On the other hand, the title is appropriate as indicating that the law is only part of a wider series of phenomena, and that the history of the whole is properly one history.

As far as can be avoided, this book contains no theories. It implies no knowledge of law or anthropology on the part of the reader, and an endeavour has been made to treat of its subject in the simplest terms. Yet it is hoped that the book contains a good deal of matter new both to lawyers and anthropologists.

Among the books which have taught me much is Hobhouse, Wheeler, and Ginsberg's *The Material Culture and Social Institutions of the Simpler Peoples*. For the earliest stages of economic progress (that is to say, up to the Second Agricultural Grade) I have to a large extent adopted the same classification as theirs, but above that grade—that is to say, from the point where law, properly so called, first appears— I have followed the classification that I adopted in *Primitive Law*, but with some simplifications.

The citation of references has given me some anxiety. To do justice to the mass of evidence on which many statements in the text are based would have required the citation of so many instances as to increase the size of the book far beyond what was practicable. The book is in substance a collation of the best information available as to several thousand tribes and nations, its arrangement according to grades of economic progress, and a statement of features of importance, especially the common features in each grade. I have usually contented myself with citing a few instances where thought apposite, but have sometimes referred (for example, in the form of a percentage) to peoples not named. I have often referred to a people in the present tense, whether it still survives or not.

I am grateful to George Allen and Unwin, Ltd., for their kind permission to make use in Book I, Chapter VI, of material from Volume I of Malinowski's *Coral Gardens and their Magic* (1935).

By far the most important accretions to the known legal relics of the ancient world are the copies of a code of laws of the feudal city-state of Eshnunna, discovered at Tell Harmal in 1947, and published and translated by Dr. Albrecht Goetze in 1948. They are copies of a code some 200 years earlier than Hammurabi's, and the oldest we possess. I gave reasons in *Primitive Law* (1935) for saying that the principle of the *talio*, or " an eye for an eye and a tooth for a tooth," is a late development which appears at a stage shortly before that represented in the Code of Hammurabi, where it is at its height. The Eshnunna laws contain no trace of such a rule: the sanctions for wounds are all pecuniary.

A. S. D.

March 1951.

CONTENTS

Book I
SAVAGERY

Book II
BARBARISM

Book III
EARLY CIVILIZATION

BOOK I

SAVAGERY

CHAPTER I

INTRODUCTORY

IN this "age of the common man" the historian is busy recording much of his manner of life. At some periods of history the impression may be derived that the destiny of man is forged by the will, the capacity, and the caprice of eminent individuals. But this is only a part of the story: as well endeavour to explain the movements of ocean by tracing the course and fate of the crests of the waves. Yet individuals, be they kings, poets, philosophers, or scientists, have great influence over the course of events, as, for example, by propagating ideas that move men to action or change their manner of life. Whence come these ideas? And why are they accepted by others? Are they independently evolved in different times and places? What is the part played by the common man and the common environment in their production and acceptance? And what was the course of events before the dawn of history? These questions are too large and too vague to be capable of an answer.

But there is one body of ideas in regard to which some precise answers can be given. These are among the most important and fundamental of all ideas outside the relations between the members of the family. They are the body of ideas represented by the word "law." Their history is the history of those concepts of right conduct between man and man that must be obeyed in a community. Are such ideas independently evolved in different lands and ages; or are they obtained wholly or mainly by diffusion from one source? To what extent are their origin and their acceptance determined by the environment and the views of the common man, and to what extent by original thinkers? To what extent are the views of the common man determined by his environment? And—more important—what was the history of these ideas, and what changes did they undergo? Did they take one course in history, or several independent courses?

And what was their course in the long ages before history begins? This is the subject-matter of the present book.

To trace a history we must order our facts in accordance with some principle of arrangement. We cannot choose a chronological order of events, for we do not directly know enough of the ideas of man on this subject in prehistoric times. We shall arrange our facts in accordance with stages of economic development of the societies in which they appear, and shall presently see what results we obtain thereby and to what extent the economic order of events is also a chronological order. In the absence of dates it is necessary to define our economic stages as precisely as possible, and not least in order to appreciate the functional importance of these ideas of right— that is to say, how, in their working, they are part of the whole working of a society. Our stages must be fundamental stages, and therefore must be based on the degree of control of a society over its environment.

Accordingly, our first stage is that of the Food-Gatherers. They live mainly by gathering their food, whether it be roots or fruits, honey, game, insects, vermin, or fish. They live in the Palæolithic Age, their stonework is of the crudest, and they have no metals. They have no permanent houses, and no spinning or pottery. They have no domestic animals except the dog. Many of these peoples are still to be found in the world today.

Our second stage we call the First Agricultural Grade. These peoples, too, still subsist mainly by gathering or hunting their food, but have added a rudimentary agriculture as a secondary means of livelihood. The field work is mainly done by the women and by means of the digging-stick. The more advanced of them have substantial houses. They still have no metals, but they have rudimentary pottery, spinning, and weaving, and they domesticate an occasional pig or some poultry in addition to the dog. They engage in a little barter of natural products.

Our Second Agricultural Grade is that of the peoples among whom agriculture (or rather horticulture) is the main means of subsistence. Their chief implement is still the digging-stick. They are of the Neolithic Age, and possess neither metals nor plough. They keep no cattle. They occupy substantial wooden huts and have skill in several arts. Trade includes the barter of a few manufactured products.

The Third Agricultural Grade is that of the peoples who combine with agriculture the keeping of large cattle. They are no longer of the Stone Age, and possess and work metals. They have law and courts of law. This grade we subdivide into several stages, in a way which will be later defined.

But though this is the broad highway of economic progress, all peoples do not so readily take to agriculture or cattle-keeping.

There is, first of all, parallel to the First and Second Agricultural Grades, the grade of those who, no less advanced economically in other respects, develop a specialized and advanced hunting way of life and do not cultivate the land. These we call the Hunters.

There are also the early cattle-keepers, who, no less advanced in other respects than the First and Second Agricultural Grades, domesticate cattle without cultivating the land. Of these, too, we shall say something.

This is our general scheme of arrangement, and we shall see what results it produces.

CHAPTER II

THE FOOD-GATHERERS

We described the Food-Gatherers as comprising those peoples who live mainly by gathering their food, whether it be roots or fruits, honey, game, insects, vermin, or fish. They live in the Palæolithic Age, their stonework is of the crudest, and they have no spinning, pottery, or metal, and only rudimentary weaving in the form of plaiting, and some simple woodwork. Those who live by the sea have poor canoes or rafts. They have no permanent dwellings, and commonly live in caves, rock-shelters, or holes or protect themselves by the erection of windbreaks or rude shelters of branches or thatch. Their only domestic animal is the dog, which in most places the white man has taught them to domesticate.[1] They know how to make fire. This is the type of the Food-Gatherers, but some of them are in some respects more advanced and in some more backward.[2]

The less advanced of the folk of this grade include such of the Veddas of Ceylon, Sakai of Malaya, and Kubu of Sumatra as may still be called wild; the bulk of the Negritos (including the Semang of Malaya and the Andaman Islanders); the Bushmen (now mainly confined to the Central and Northern Kalahari Desert and northern half of South-West Africa); and the Pygmies of Central Africa. There are also in South America the Chono, Alacaluf, and Yahgan of the South Chilean Archipelago, and the Ona of the large island of Tierra del Fuego;[3] the Guayaki of the forest of Eastern Paraguay,[4]

---

[1] In Australia the dog took the place of the half-domesticated dingo. Mesolithic man had the dog.

[2] For example, the Andaman Islanders have pottery, and acquired iron from shipwrecks as long ago as the eighteenth century, and work it cold. On the other hand, they have no stonework except a simple method of flaking, and (perhaps alone of all peoples) cannot make fire. They carry fire with them (as do also the Alacaluf).

[3] See Cooper, *The Chono*; Bird, *The Alacaluf*; Cooper, *The Yahgan* and *The Ona*.   [4] Métraux and Baldus, *The Guayaki*.

the Puri, Botocudo, and Patasho of Eastern Brazil,[1] and Guaja of North-East Brazil;[2] and the Yaruro, Guahibo, Chiricoa and Guamontey of the Venezuelan Llanos.[3] In North America there are a number of peoples, including the Lower Californians and some Shoshoneans.[4] There are also the Tasmanians, and the most forward peoples among the Food-Gatherers are the Australian aborigines. On the whole, they must be included in this group and not in the Hunters, in spite of their knowledge and use of spears, clubs and boomerangs, dams for catching fish, and hunters' traps and fences.

Food-Gatherers require a vast territory within which to find sufficient food for their sustenance. Indeed, territory occupied by them hardly seems to be inhabited. J. Baegert said of the inhabitants of Lower California in the late eighteenth century, "There are very few Californians, and in proportion to the extent of the country almost as few as if there were none at all. . . . A person may travel in different parts four and more days without seeing a single human being."[5] In the favoured conditions of the Andaman Islands, where few places are farther than some 10 miles from the sea, with its rich sources of turtle and fish, the density of population was about two persons per square mile,[6] mainly concentrated (as is the population in Tierra del Fuego) by the shore. In Tierra del Fuego the density of population among the Ona was about one person per 8 square miles, and Steward calculates the average density of population of the whole South Chilean Archipelago at one per 4 square miles, and among the Botocudo at about one per 3 square miles.[7] In the most densely populated part of Australia E. J. Eyre found three or four natives to every mile of the Murray River. The Aranda of Central

[1] Métraux and Nimuendajú, *The Mashacali*, etc.; Métraux, *The Puri and The Botocudo*.

[2] Nimuendajú, *The Guaja*.

[3] Kirchhoff, *Venezuelan Llanos*.

[4] Also in Europe the Finns (Fenni) in the time of Tacitus (*Germania*, c. 46); and everywhere the peoples of the late Palæolithic Age.

[5] Cited Krzywicki, p. 2.

[6] 5,500 persons occupying 2,500 square miles in 1858, Radcliffe-Brown, pp. 15–18.

[7] Steward, *Native Population of South America*.

Australia represented a density of about one person per 25 square miles,[1] and, to take an extreme case, among the Yanda, E. M. Curr found one native to every 250 square miles. Among the Food-Gatherers a rate of one person to every 7 square miles may be taken to represent an average density of population.[2]

The unit of population is a small band of persons—in this book we shall call it a local group—which lives a semi-nomadic life, roving about mainly as a group, gathering its food within a delimited territory, and economically self-sufficient. Here and there within that territory are favourite and traditional camping-places where the group lodges at different seasons and from which it scours the countryside for food. Everywhere [3] the women (assisted by the girls and younger boys of the family) are commonly at work near the camp with the digging-stick (the woman's implement) [4] grubbing up yams, roots, witchetty grubs, or reptiles, or collecting plants or shellfish, while the men are hunting farther afield. Among the most backward of the Food-Gatherers (the Veddas, Bushmen, Pygmies, Alacaluf, Yahgan, Ona, Guayaki, and Tasmanians) the average size of this local group is between ten and twenty persons. Among the Andamanese it is about twenty-five persons, and in Australia it has increased to between twenty-five and thirty.[5]

In the neighbourhood of each of these local groups are

[1] 2,000 persons with a territory of about 50,000 square miles.

[2] For a number of references on this topic, see Krzywicki, p. 4. For Tasmania, see Roth, pp. 163 f. There the density of population at the coming of the white man was about one person per 7 square miles. Over the whole of Australia the average density was about one person per 12 square miles. A density of one per 7 square miles would produce the reasonable estimate of a population of about 10,000 in Britain in a warmer period of the late Palæolithic Age.

[3] E.g., among the Semang (see I. H. N. Evans, The Negritos of Malaya, 1937, p. 60); Andamanese (Radcliffe-Brown, pp. 43–4); Aranda (Spencer and Gillen, p. 1927); Seligman, Veddas, p. 91; Bushmen (Schapera, Khoisan, p. 117).

[4] For example, among the Aranda no man is permitted to touch one.

[5] See some references in Krzywicki, pp. 4–9, and, in regard to the Bushmen, Schapera, Khoisan, p. 78.

similar groups speaking the same language and sometimes the same dialect. There are usually some social relations between the groups, and if their marriage customs are exogamous they may freely intermarry. They usually recognize one another as kindred (as they in fact are), and may call one another, as we call them, by a common name. Together they constitute what we call in this book a " tribe." In Australia Howitt defines the tribe as " a larger or smaller aggregate of people who occupy a certain tract of hunting and food ground in common, who speak the same language with dialectical differences, who acknowledge a common relatedness and who deny that relatedness to all other surrounding tribes." [1] Among the least advanced of the Food-Gatherers (for example, the Ai-San Bushmen and the Bushmen of the Kalahari) the average size of the tribe is between 300 and 400 persons. In the Andamans the figure was 400 to 450; and Krzywicki [2] calculates the average size of 123 Australian tribes as between 300 and 600 souls.

These tribes have so long lived in isolation from other tribes that as a general rule each possesses a distinct language, unintelligible to the members of any other tribe, and commonly divided into, say, three or four dialects. Such is the sparseness of population and the extent of isolation of human beings at this stage of economic progress. The population of Australia when the white man came—according to the best estimates some 250,000 in number—spoke about 500 different languages, according to E. M. Curr. [3] The Alacaluf, Yahgan, and Ona spoke unrelated languages. If we imagine a substantial block of London flats, or a street of modest size, containing 400 occupants, they would in an average food-gathering community represent a whole tribe in sole occupation of an area of some 3,000 square miles, speaking a separate and distinct language of its own divided into some three distinct dialects, and this tribe would consist of about twenty local groups, each of twenty persons, and each roving over and feeding

---

[1] A. W. Howitt, *Australian Group Relations*, Annual Reports of the Smithsonian Institution (1883), p. 799.

[2] Pp. 58–64. For figures relating to the Tasmanians, see Roth, pp. 163 f.

[3] E. M. Curr, vol. i, pp. 12–15.

upon an area of about 150 square miles.[1] Normally each such local group lives its life separate and distinct from others, supported by the scanty or adequate provision of Nature, and visiting other local groups upon occasion; but perhaps once a year, and perhaps more rarely, will occur either a seasonal migration of game or fish, or a seasonal harvest of nuts, or the stranding of a whale, or other glut of food, and the whole tribe will congregate to it, and a sentiment of tribal solidarity will for the time being be felt. Then there will be the excitement of abundant food and dancing and other licensed pleasures of social life, and advantage will be taken of such occasions, especially in Australia, to perform the great and solemn ceremonies of initiation (for example, the circumcision of the males) or other important social events, and there may be some barter or exchange of ochre or other articles of adornment or use. Some tribes may become too small to hold an initiation alone, and for this or other reasons a group of tribes may meet on similar occasions and may come to feel a certain tie between them, and even be known by a common name. Such a group of tribes—sometimes misnamed a nation—is exemplified by the Australian Kamilaroi, Wiradjuri, and Narrinyeri, which were among the largest of these groups, each containing a population of some 3,000–5,000 persons. In some cases (for example, among the Narrinyeri) the whole group of tribes spoke dialects of the same language. These are isolated phenomena found only among the most advanced of the Food-Gatherers. Commonly no tribe knows anything of a tribe 20 to 50 miles outside its territory. But the tribes extending far beyond that territory are all of the same race—the Australians all of one distinct and separate race, the Bushmen of another, the Pygmies of another, the Negritos of the Andamans, and indeed of Malaya and the Philippines all of another. New races form themselves more slowly than languages—if indeed they ever do—and all these facts show

---

[1] In the favoured conditions of the Andamans the average territory of a local group was about 15 square miles, or 10 miles by the shore. Towards the other extreme, Seiner (*Ergebnisse einer Bereisung der Omaheke*, 1913) estimates the average territory of a Bushman local group in a district of South-West Africa at about 300 square miles.

that there is little movement of populations throughout the territory occupied by the race, and right up to the borders. These tenuous populations, so far as can be seen and surmised, have remained fairly constant in numbers over a vast period of time in each area, subject to temporary rises and falls by reason of epidemics and seasonal famines. The limiting factor is the food supply available to the stage of food-getting technique of the inhabitants, and in particular the impossibility of feeding a child except by the mother's milk. In the result the child is suckled for an average period of two to three years (as indeed it is throughout the primitive period).[1] The woman has not the strength to carry more than one child upon her back, nor to bring another to birth while she is suckling, and generally [2] intercourse between the sexes is prohibited by tribal custom till the child is weaned. Accordingly (since all marry and practically none are barren) on the average the woman bears altogether some four to five children in the course of her life, of whom only half reach maturity, whether in such a favoured terrain as the Andamans or the torrid Australian or desert African landscape.[3] In Australia, because of the shortage of food and the mother's difficulty in carrying a child over long distances and keeping up with the group, or because the child is weak, or cries too much, or is unusual in some way, children are often killed or abandoned, and sometimes even stolen and eaten; and indeed in some tribes it is not customary to rear the first child or two, on the ground that they are thought not to be strong. In short, the population remains fairly stationary, so far as can be seen or surmised, over the long millennia.

Accordingly, it rarely if ever happens that a growth of population in one local group or tribe makes its wide territory no longer sufficient and causes it to demand a portion of its neighbour's territory, and that the latter refuses, and the groups fight it out. Such incidents may have occurred,[4] but

---

[1] That is, the period up to the Late Codes, and covered by Books 1, 2 and 3 of the present work.

[2] Except in parts of South America.

[3] See, e.g., Spencer and Gillen, *The Arunta*, vol. i, pp. 39–40, 221; Krzywicki, pp. 271–6; Schapera, *Khoisan*, p. 116.

[4] See, for example, Krzywicki, p. 281; Schapera, *Khoisan*, pp. 156–7.

such fighting as takes place between groups or tribes is rarely caused in this way. Among the most backward of the Food-Gatherers, such as the forest tribes of Asia, there is very little contact between the local family groups, and although there is an instinctive embarrassment, mistrust, dislike, and fear at meeting with strangers, there is nothing of violence between groups, except a rare fight at a boundary over a matter of food.[1] Among the bulk of the rest—for example, the Andamanese, Bushmen, South Americans, and Australians—whatever fighting takes place consists of small raids. If an attack is to be made on another local group of the same or another tribe, the raiding party (which may be drawn from one or two local groups) puts on its ornamental paint, and after celebrating the emotional significance of the occasion by a dance, sets out for the neighbouring encampment, with a view to attack it by surprise in the early morning. The camp is rushed and as many men as possible are shot, and then the one party or the other takes to flight. Usually there is no lasting feud : memories are short and peace is soon made.[2] There are no specialized weapons for fighting : they use their weapons of the chase, the bow and arrow,[3] or the wooden spear,[4] club, stick or boomerang,[5] and stones. Some Australians use a wooden shield.

[1] See, e.g., Seligman, *Veddas*, p. 7.
[2] See, for the Andamans, Radcliffe-Brown, p. 85, and for the Bushmen, Schapera, *Khoisan*, p. 158.
[3] E.g., Negritos of the Andamans and Malaya, the Bushmen, and the Guahibo, Chiricoa, Guamontey, and Botocudo.
[4] Southern South Americans, Tasmanians, and Australians.
[5] Some Australians.

CHAPTER III

THE FOOD-GATHERERS (*Continued*)

AMONG the least advanced of these peoples, though information is scanty, it appears that the local group commonly consists of one or two families, and that whatever influence is exercised upon the members is that of the older upon the younger.[1] Among the most advanced—that is to say, in Australia—the local group is larger, and as a rule includes more than two families. In about half the latter communities there is something that can be called by the grandiloquent name of a primitive organ of government of the local group—namely, the restraint and guidance exercised by the old men—and in a third of them there is also a leading man or headman.[2] The latter as often as not holds a hereditary position, but his power or influence is slight, and beyond the local group it is only in about a quarter of the communities that there is a headman exercising influence over a tribe. Sometimes even this influence is found only among those temporary gatherings that we spoke of, in times and places of abundant food. It is already apparent that, to enable the little society to grow, it must obtain restraints, guidance, and cohesion, and the greater size of these communities and a certain occasional freedom from the preoccupation of finding sustenance and a growing intelligence and organizing capacity allow this to be provided.

[1] See, for the Bushmen, Schapera, *Khoisan*, pp. 81-3; for the Alacaluf, Bird, p. 71; and, for the Ona, Cooper, *The Ona*, p. 116.

[2] In the Andamans there are usually only two or three leading men in a tribe, with local influence based on respect for their personal qualities; i.e., hunting prowess or generosity (Radcliffe-Brown, pp. 45-7). There are no chiefs among the smaller family groups of the Cape and Namib Bushmen; but there are chiefs among the larger local groups of the more advanced Bushmen of the North-West (see Schapera, *Khoisan*, pp. 149, 150). There are no chiefs among the Alacaluf, Ona, or Yahgan. The Tasmanians seem to have had a few leading men here and there, with very slight influence (see Roth, pp. 57 *et seq.*). They were heads of families with some reputation for prowess.

The constitution of the local group is also becoming more complex. Even among the Tasmanians, Pygmies, Andamanese, Bushmen, Alacaluf, and Yahgan there are still no clans and no totems.[1] In Australia the constitution of the local group differs much from tribe to tribe, and the relations of the parts of the tribe to one another are so various and complex that no detailed account can be given here. Sometimes, indeed, there are no distinct local groups, apart from the clans or totemic[2] groups, which are found throughout the territory of the tribe and have an organization of their own. Where, as usual, there is a distinct and separate local group, it is generally not one purely kinship or totemic group, but includes some members of more than one clan or totemic group. Members of the same clan or totemic group are usually also found in other local groups of the tribe. Again, Australian tribes are often divided into two moieties, which are exogamous[3] intermarrying units and which are often at the same time totemic groups. These moieties are each subdivided into two sections, and often each section is again divided into two sub-sections. Usually a member of one moiety can only marry a member of a particular section (or sub-section) of the other moiety. In short, the rules of marriage have become complex, and where the population of a tribe is reduced in numbers it may even be difficult or impossible for a man to find a woman whom he can marry with strict adherence to custom.

Marriage is the first institution to evolve. Among the less advanced of the Food-Gatherers (for example, the Veddas,

---

[1] See, for the Bushmen, Schapera, *Khoisan*, p. 85. A clan is a group of persons, intermediate in size between the family and the tribe, whose members are (or are thought to be) related to one another through male or female parents, according as the descent in that tribe is traced through males or females. In the former case it is a patrilineal clan, in the latter case matrilineal. In the Andamans marriage is prohibited only between close blood relations.

[2] A totemic group consists of persons possessing a common totem—that is to say, considered to stand in a special relation to an animal, plant, or other natural object or phenomenon. It is not necessarily a kinship group.

[3] An exogamous group is one between whose members marriage is prohibited.

Semang, and Andamanese) the status of the sexes is almost equal—a thing never found again. Monogamy is in force; the standard of marital fidelity is very high; marriage is for life, and divorce is, generally speaking, unknown.[1] The young people marry very early—the girls about puberty—with little outside interference except a certain amount of arranging on the part of parents and expressed approval by local elders (assuming always that the marriage is between a pair who may marry one another). At the time of marriage, among some tribes,[2] the young man gives presents to the girl's parents in return for their consent to the marriage—for example, among the Bushmen, to show his prowess, he presents the girl's mother with the carcase of an animal which he has hunted, or with skins or vegetable food;[3] and the Vedda youth gives to his future father-in-law presents of food. There are also, more rarely, return gifts. Marriage is generally matrilocal —that is to say, the young couple take up their residence with the young woman's group. Descent is matrilineal—that is to say, reckoned in the female line. This is not surprising, for any of these peoples who believe that sexual intercourse is necessary to conception (and they are very few)[4] may still reasonably believe that a child is born of its female ancestors. Indeed, some peoples (for example, the Andamanese) believe that a child is born by reason of a spirit child (which need not be the spirit of an ancestor) entering the mother's body. Inheritance, in so far as there is anything to inherit—and there is practically nothing, even if the goods of the deceased are not buried or burnt with him—goes with descent and is matrilineal. Among a few tribes, however, as among modern peoples, descent is reckoned both in the male and the female line.[5] There are also, even at this stage, traces of the beginning of the practice which we later know as the levirate. Among the Andamanese, custom already almost compels a

[1] See, e.g., *Veddas*, pp. 87-8. This is particularly striking when compared with the habits of the more advanced peoples around them.
[2] Veddas, Bushmen, Botocudo, Yahgan.
[3] Schapera, *Khoisan*, p. 106.   [4] They include the Ona.
[5] So among the Andamanese. Here what the deceased leaves is generally taken possession of by the family and divided among friends and relatives in token of their affection for him.

bachelor or widower to propose marriage to the childless widow of his elder brother or cousin (if she is not past her prime), and gives her no choice except to marry him or remain single; [1] and among the Veddas and the Yahgan, too, a widow usually marries the unmarried brother of her deceased husband.[2]

By the time we reach the Tasmanians and the Australians all this has changed. One result of the developing intelligence is that the status of the weaker sex has begun to fall *vis-à-vis* the man. There are now few, if any, tribes among whom polygamy is prohibited. The great bulk of men still take only one wife, but some of the elders are in a position to have two or three or more. We shall see the extent of polygamy slowly spreading through the grades with the increase in wealth. In part, polygamy is made possible by the increase in fighting already referred to, for this has the result that, although more males may be born than females, among the elderly folk the women considerably outnumber the men, and more so than in modern Europe.

The fundamental and permanent physiological, psychological, social, and economic factors, which come into play in relation to marriage, take shape in a variety of the methods by which a wife is obtained, and the custom of a particular tribe stresses one method more than another. The man is the active seeker-out. The girl's family are loth to lose her and her work. She is influenced by their wishes, and she is coy and anxious to be sought after and appreciates a certain show of force. The community has an interest to see that marriage is contracted only between persons who are entitled to marry, and that its obligations are observed. In some cases in Australia wives are obtained with the aid of gifts to secure the consent of their fathers, but property is too little for the purpose. More commonly marriage takes place by arrangement between the couple, or by betrothal arranged between the parents (the latter sometimes even before the girl is born, and perhaps because she will be the only person in the group belonging to a class with which he can intermarry). In about half of the

---

[1] Radcliffe-Brown, p. 75.
[2] Seligman, *Veddas*, pp. 33, 69; Cooper, *Yahgan*, p. 92.

Australian communities a wife is sometimes obtained by an exchange of women (not necessarily contemporaneous). We must not be surprised if women are not " given away " in marriage for nothing, nor hastily dub the match a commercial transaction. In these days, before the rule of trade has created a distinction between "commercial" and " friendly " transactions, there is a reciprocity in social acts which is relied upon by the members of the society to an extent difficult for us to follow. We shall see more of this later. And we must not overlook the importance of the transaction of marriage to the families concerned. To hand over a woman to a stranger —especially in the higher grades, to which we shall come—is to deliver up part of the wealth of the group—that is to say, its wealth in personnel. The woman given in exchange by the bridegroom or his relatives is a woman belonging to their family, who is herself given in marriage, and may be a sister or wife of the bridegroom. Capture of wives is a less common institution. In some communities it is only an occasional phenomenon; in some it is mere play-acting; in others it is a general practice, found as such in some fifth part of the Australian tribes. Imperceptibly it shades into elopement. The girl has little to say in most of these various arrangements.

Marriage is still matrilocal, and descent and inheritance matrilineal, in some two-thirds of the cases in Australia, but there is also now a minority of about one tribe in three which trace descent through males, while a few trace through both parents.

Even among the Australians, goods are still extremely scarce—a few articles of adornment and a few weapons. These things, among all Food-Gatherers, are considered to belong to the person who uses them, for that which happens is, in their minds, as in the minds of the bulk of mankind, that which ought to happen. He, therefore, who exclusively uses a certain article is alone thought entitled to use it. This is practically the sum total of the notions of the Food-Gatherers on the subject of property in goods.[1] Commonly the only other goods found among

---

[1] Among the Andamans a tree belongs to the first man who notices it as being suitable for making a canoe and announces the fact; certain fruit-trees to the first who finds them; a pig to the first man whose arrow strikes it (Radcliffe-Brown, p. 41). Compare Schapera, *Khoisan*, p. 127.

them are the articles of food which they have gathered. There are in many of these tribes—and especially the more advanced of them [1]—practices defining the persons to whom and the manner in which such articles should be distributed among the group; often, for example, assigning a particular part of the kangaroo or other prize to a particular relative, and sometimes a smaller share to the hunter. These practices have grown in much the same way as other human practices evolve—from the natural act of giving for the sustenance of members of the family or kinship group, and each person's (including the hunter's) natural act of taking; from the hunter's expectation of a return gift; and from his desire for general approval and the satisfaction he gets by the display of his generosity (the greatest of all virtues in their eyes), and his prowess as a hunter. The practice survives because it is easier to do what has been done rather than something different; and since the practice benefits the group—for by its means the group is helped to survive—the practice survives with it. Because that which is done ought to be done, and the practice concerns a matter fundamental to their way of life, it becomes in the minds of the community a binding practice, and the longer it is in use the more definite and detailed its "rules" become. And yet, like all other binding practices, it is sometimes broken. As for the expectation of a return gift, primitive men, like children, are prone to make gifts, gaining a sense of confidence and power thereby, and often indicating what they would like in return. But there is also an important economic aspect involved here. Firstly, it is in the interests of each that all shall be fed. Secondly, at this stage of material progress and in these climates there is no question of storing a temporary surplus of food for more than a few hours. The better alternative is to give the surplus, and thereby get the customary return gift of food at a time when it may be needed, and incidentally to add variety to one's diet. Quarrels at the failure to make a return gift are not unknown.[2]

As for property in land, this is a more difficult notion to acquire than that of property in movables, and seems to arise later. The notion of an area of land as a separate and distinct

---

[1] But see already Seligman, *Veddas*, pp. 66–7.
[2] See, e.g., for the Andamans, Radcliffe-Brown, pp. 42, 83.

thing is a more difficult conception than that in regard to an article which moves or is moved, and thereby attracts attention. Among the simplest peoples (the Kubu and Sakai, the Negritos of Malaya and the Andamans and the Alacaluf) there appears to be no notion of property in land. The Veddas have notions of the land as being the property of local groups, and, at the same time, of portions of that land as the property of individual males. The Australians have widespread if vague ideas on this topic. The origin of these ideas is the same as that of rights in goods—namely, that whatever is customary ought to be done, and therefore whoever is accustomed to use a thing becomes entitled to use it. Among the Australians these ideas, according to the accounts of observers, are of every kind. The most common notion, as is to be expected, is the notion that the land belongs to the members of the local unit—the local group or clan.[1]   Somewhat less prominent is the notion that it belongs to the tribe (for the tribe is a comparatively hazy and distant unit), and also to the families or individuals who compose it. We are told, for example, of the Kurnai, Yuin, Wolgal, Theddora, and other tribes, that the country in which the tribe moved belonged to each person who was born in it, and indeed among the Yuin if a child was born there to a father who belonged elsewhere, he was thought to confer the same right upon his father.[2] These ideas are obviously remote from the conceptions of modern law. They are vague and popular, and still amount in all to little more than the notion, to which we have already referred, that whoever customarily uses a thing is entitled to use it, and a resentment at the presence of interlopers.[3]

[1] Among the Bushmen the land is generally considered to belong to the local group and all its members, Schapera, *Khoisan*, p. 127; among the Ona to the extended family and all its members.

[2] Howitt, *The Native Tribes of South-East Australia* (1904), p. 83.

[3] According to various accounts of observers, of these ideas some 43 per cent. are cases of ideas of family or individual rights, and 57 per cent. ideas of community rights (including both rights of local groups and clans, and of tribes). These two figures can be further subdivided as follows: of the total for family and individual rights, 32 per cent. are cases of individual rights and 68 per cent. of family rights—that is to say, individual rights are 14 per cent. and family rights 29 per cent. of the whole. Of the community rights, 57 per cent. (33 per cent. of the whole) are rights of local

Among the least advanced of the Food-Gatherers, these local groups (some fifteen to twenty persons in number) are so small that serious offences against good order, or what passes for good order, are in most groups uncommon and in many rare, and in all too rare to have given rise to any customary way of handling them. When we hear of such offences —and our information is necessarily scanty—they seem to arise out of a variety of incidents. It may be a mere running amok by some individual and a venting of his wrath or frenzy on some near-by persons or goods; or more often a fight over a woman, or a rare murder. Such incidents are treated as the affair of the parties. But from the commencement we can see signs that in addition to such private wrongs there are in their minds a class of public wrongs—offences so outrageous that whether or not some individual is hurt, they are a matter of public concern and their punishment a matter for public action.[1] At this stage there is little or nothing to be seen of such offences except incest, which is marriage with a person with whom it is not permitted. For example, among the Kalahari Bushmen and the Veddas it is punishable with death. As for private wrongs, and sanctions for private wrongs, we may take the Andaman Islanders as an example. Among them, we are told, an aggrieved party, when sufficiently provoked, usually gives vent to his resentment by a physical reaction of some sort, as by flinging a burning faggot or shooting an arrow. Thereupon everyone else will run away till the quarrel is composed, though friends may forcibly intervene and take sides. If one man kills another, nothing is necessarily said or done to him. A friend of the slain man or one of his family may avenge him in some way or other, but more commonly everyone is so much afraid of the slayer that no one

---

groups and clans, and 43 per cent. (23 per cent. of the whole) are rights of tribes. These figures mark the importance of the family in the public mind, as compared with the individual, and of the local group (or the clan) as against the tribe, at this early stage of economic advance. But it also shows that a process of change has begun. We started with the family. Now the place of the family in the public mind begins to be taken, on the one side, by the local group, clan, and tribe, and, on the other side, by the individual male head of the family.

[1] See, e.g., for the Andamans, Radcliffe-Brown, p. 48.

will touch him or criticize him in his presence. He will often, however, keep away till he is assured that the grief and indignation of the family and friends of the dead man have abated.[1] In other words, even homicide among these peoples is an affair of the individuals concerned, and not of the group.

When we reach the Australians the local groups are a little larger, and therefore offences against order are more common in a group, and it is apparent that some progress has been made. Public offences now consist mainly of incest, murder by magic, and a few sacral offences. Incest is sexual intercourse with persons with whom marriage is forbidden. Accusations of murder by magic are the main disturbers of the peace.[2] Magic (of which little has been hitherto seen)[3] is the mechanical application of supernatural (or secret) power. It is to be distinguished from religion, which embodies an appeal to the will of supernatural beings. Religion hardly exists at this stage.[4] Magic is commonly employed for private ends of various kinds, and the belief in its potency is so great, and its use is so dreaded, that the mere thought that others are attempting his death by this means is often enough to cause a man to pine and perish. In the prevailing ignorance of the causes of death, the demise of a young or apparently healthy person is usually attributed to magic, and the sole question is, Who is the guilty person? In the inevitable absence of evidence, the question is answered by observing an alleged movement of the corpse, or the fact that it points in a certain direction, or by consulting a local magician; and the guilt is commonly fastened upon an unpopular member of the community, or, still more often, upon another community, for the unfamiliar is feared and disliked. There is no such thing as a trial, but there is sometimes a consultation of elders. As an example of

[1] Man, p. 42; Temple, p. 81; Radcliffe-Brown, pp. 48–9. A man is just as likely to vent his irritation on anyone who may be in the neighbourhood—see, e.g., among the Tasmanians, G. W. Walker, pp. 101–3, where a man who had a quarrel with his wife, instead of retaliating physically upon her, cut the feet of seven women lying near him asleep.

[2] As among the Ona (Cooper, The Ona, p. 117).

[3] See, e.g., Schapera, Veddas, p. 190.

[4] See more fully on this topic, post, pp. 81–7. The Andaman Islanders and some others possess a primitive religion.

a sacral offence may be taken the offence committed among
the Aranda by a woman or uninitiated man who looks upon
one of the sacred *churinga*, and thereby merits the penalty of
death or blinding or other severe punishment. Similarly, in
modern communities there is a meeting-place between the
criminal law and religion, for sacrilege and blasphemy are
commonly criminal offences. The general punishment in
Australia for all public offences is death.

The second class of offences—those thought to concern
merely the injured person, his relatives and friends—consist
mainly of homicide, wounding, adultery and wife-stealing, and
theft. Theft is unimportant : there is hardly anything to steal,
and in many places a man is permitted to take food and goods
of certain kinds of which he stands in need. Such and the
like trivial matters and small quarrels are disposed of, as
among the Andamanese, by irregular retaliation or by being
forgotten. But homicide, adultery with a wife, and the
stealing of a wife (including the capture or elopement of a
bride) commonly rouse fierce passions, and might lead to the
murder of the offender or his friends by an aggrieved person
or his friends, or to fights or feuds between two kinship or
local groups. To avoid such a result is the object of the old
men. It cannot be achieved by an offer of compensation in
goods, for hardly any such exists, and the purpose is effected by
attempts to limit disorder and make peace. The operative
factors in such a situation are the anger of the avengers and their
demand for satisfaction, the offender's fear of being handed
over by his group to avoid feud or disorder, the desire for
peace of the group to which the offender belongs, and at the
same time the pride, sensitiveness, and solidarity of that group.
By custom this limiting of disorder and vengeance takes the
form, among many tribes, of the voluntary submission of
himself by the offender to the throwing of spears or hacking
with knives or other regulated fight. As an example may be
taken Howitt's vivid account [1] of an occurrence among the
Mukjarawaint tribe, where two men of the Garchuka totem,

[1] *Native Tribes of South-East Australia*, p. 335. Compare the account of
similar incidents among the Tasmanians, Davies, " On the Aborigines of
Van Diemen's Land " (*Tasmanian Journ. Science*, vol. ii, p. 419).

for some affront, had killed a man of the Wulernunt, or black snake, totem, spearing him at night when asleep in his camp. They escaped, but were seen and recognized by the victim's wife, and his relatives sent a Wirri-gir, or messenger, to the offenders telling them to look out for themselves and be prepared for revenge. In reply a message was sent saying that the relatives should come with their friends, and the offenders would be prepared to stand out and have spears thrown at them. A grand meeting of the two totems then gathered at a fixed time and place, and the headman of the Garchukas stood out between the two groups and addressed them, calling upon his men not to take any undue advantage in the encounter. Then he fixed a spot near at hand for the expiatory encounter to take place that afternoon, it being agreed that as soon as the offenders had been struck by a spear, the combat should cease. The offenders stood out, armed with shields, and received the spears thrown at them by the kinsmen of the deceased, until at last one of them was wounded, when the Garchuka headman threw into the air a lighted piece of bark which he held, and the fight ceased. Had it continued, says Howitt, there would have been a general fight between the two totems.

This is an example of the phenomenon in its more organized form, but the same factors operate frequently in other cases. For example, even among tribes where marriage by elopement or capture is common usage, or where one man carries off another's wife, the pair will be exposed to spears or hacking by knives if caught before the memory of the incident has entirely faded. The difference between this proceeding and a fight is well brought out among the Aranda. There, when the wife of A has run off with another man (B), and the couple have hidden themselves far away for some months, and when at last they return to the local group with some of B's friends, one of two incidents may take place. The two men may fight for the woman, both freely using their weapons. Or, after long discussion in the men's camp, the local women having also assembled, B may walk out to a clear space and call out to A : " I took your woman—come and growl." [1] Then A will

[1] The same expression " growling " was used in Tasmania, see G. W. Walker, p. 101.

throw spears and boomerangs at B, who guards himself with a shield but makes no attempt to retaliate. A, having thrown everything, may rush in to close quarters and try to cut B with a stone knife, B guarding himself but still not retaliating. After a time the onlookers will call out, " Enough, leave him," and drag them apart. A then, having cut his wife about with the knife, will wave it in the air and shout, "You keep altogether, I throw away," and in this way she is abandoned to B.[1] In South America the practice is slightly different : the two sides pair off, and each man of the pair assaults the other in turn until resentments are assuaged.[2]

It is obvious that these various acts of disorder are treated as the concern of the parties, and that the intervention of the old men or the group is for the purpose of preventing the extension of the quarrel into feud or war, and limiting the disorder as far as possible. They intervene for the purpose of peace-making. So, too, in modern Europe the action of the State in regard to private wrongs is for the purpose of peace-making, of preventing the recourse to revenge and the spread of the dispute. This it does by the provision of courts for the decision of disputes between individuals should they choose not to settle their differences between themselves. But if the injured person chooses to suffer wrong in silence, the State will not frown so long as the peace is not broken. In modern Europe the courts award compensation in money to the wronged party for the injury to his feelings and the damage to his property. In Australia there is no money, and there can hardly be damage to property but only injury to the feelings. While the old men in Australia are making peace the offender is buying peace. In Europe he does this by paying compensation, either by consent out of court or under a judgment of the court. In Australia there is no property wherewith to pay compensation, and he gives satisfaction by exposure of his body. These special factors, added to the solidarity of the kinship groups in Australia, are sufficient to produce

[1] Spencer and Gillen, pp. 468-9.
[2] The Ona use arrows, first rendered harmless (L. Bridges, *Man*, Vol. 38, pp. 4-7); the Botocudo use long sticks (Métraux, *The Botocudo*, p. 536).

the differences between the practices in Australia and in
Europe.

These are the two classes into which offences among the
Australians may be divided—namely, public (or criminal) and
private (or civil) offences. But the dividing line is more
blurred than might appear from the above account. There is
sometimes not a large difference between the " community "
which is concerned to punish a public or criminal offence
and the injured party and his clan or totemic group or friends
who are concerned to obtain satisfaction for a private wrong.
The action taken upon a criminal wrong may be by only one
or two members of the group—for example, friends of the
deceased, who may kill the supposed offender, having sometimes consulted and obtained the approval of others, and
sometimes not. The community's reaction is partial, fitful,
and irregular. In regard to incest nothing may be done until
the matter becomes a public scandal; and even then a man of
influence, or one who knows how to use his weapons, may
escape punishment (just as the perpetrator of the private offence
of homicide may be strong enough to avoid all inducements to
expose himself to be speared). And if the murderer by magic
is a member of another tribe, what follows may as well be
called war as the punishment of a crime. Again, in the prevailing ignorance of the causes of death, the boundary between
killing by magic and mere homicide is vague indeed. Even
the offence of adultery by a married woman, although a
private offence, stands near the borderline between crime and
private wrong, for it tends to be coloured by its close association with marriage and the rules of marriage.[1] As an extreme
case of the interference of the council of elders to prevent
disorder, we may take the example of North-West Central
Queensland, where, according to W. E. Roth, when a man has
been killed there is some kind of inquiry by the camp council
as to whether he deserved his fate, and, if not, the killer is put
to death. We are also told in more than one place in Australia

---

[1] Even among the Bushmen, Veddas, and Semang, adultery is avenged by
the husband or relatives with death. See Schapera, *Khoisan*, pp. 108,
152 *et seq.*; Seligman, *Veddas*, p. 96; Schebesta, *Among the Forest Dwarfs
of Malaya* (trans. by Chambers, 1929), p. 280.

that the camp council will interfere and punish a man who, in avenging his wrongs, causes excessive injury to the offender.

Nevertheless, the distinction between public and private wrongs is real; and the reference just made to marriage serves to call to mind that in the rules of marriage, or at least the rules prescribing with whom it may or may not take place, we have reached a vague beginning of law. There are not as yet courts or trials, but these rules are in the minds of the community compulsory and binding, and a breach may be punished by action of the community or its members.

CHAPTER IV

THE FIRST AGRICULTURAL GRADE

IT was noticed that those Food-Gatherers whose supply of food was more plentiful—for example, the Andaman Islanders by the coast—required a smaller territory for their needs, and therefore used fewer camping places, and were less nomadic. It was also said that the women, assisted by the girls and small boys, wielded the digging-stick in the neighbourhood of the camp, searching for grubs, roots, and reptiles, while the men hunted further afield. Some of the Food-Gatherers discovered, for example, that the crowns of yams, after removal of the tubers for eating, would grow again when put back in the earth. Some of the North and South American Indians learned to tend and gather the wild rice in the margins of lakes and marshes. Our First Agricultural Grade [1] consists of peoples who still subsist mainly by food-gathering or hunting, but have added a rudimentary agriculture as a subordinate means of livelihood. The field work is done mainly by the women and by means of the digging-stick, the men wandering further afield to hunt for food or attack their enemies. No domestic animals are kept save the dog, as before, with the addition of birds or an occasional pig. These peoples are still of the Stone Age: their pottery, spinning and weaving are rudimentary. Some substantial houses are to be found among the more advanced of them, and they have a little trade, but only in the barter of a few natural products. The peoples of this grade are to be found chiefly in South and North America. The former, who are, on the whole, the more backward, are mainly hinterland tribes around the periphery of the Amazon basin—that is to say, they include the following tribes of the South Amazon periphery, namely, the Tapirapé, tribes of the Upper Xingu, Nambucuara, Siriono, Bororo, Guato, and Mura; in Eastern Brazil the Caingang, North-Western and Central Ge, and Guaitaca;

[1] Sometimes referred to in this book as Grade A1.

the Guana of North-Western Chaco; and Mayoruna of the Peruvian and Ecuadorian Montana.[1] The North American Indians of this grade include, apart from smaller tribes, Dakotas and other Siouan peoples, and members of the Iroquois, Delaware, and Abnaki confederacies, who stand near the border of the Second Agricultural Grade.

The peoples of the First Agricultural Grade are still scattered thinly about the territory they cover, but not so thinly as the Food-Gatherers. The density of the South American tribes mentioned above appears to have been about one person per 2 square miles.[2] Moreover, the population of the whole of Brazil at the coming of the European has been estimated at between 1 and 1½ million persons;[3] and this is equivalent to a rate of about one person to 2 square miles. The native population of the State of California, a less inhospitable territory, has been estimated at 133,000 souls—namely, at a rate of one person per square mile.[4] The population of native America north of Mexico is generally estimated at 1 million,[5] and this represents a density of about one person per 4 square miles. These lands were occupied by persons of higher and lower grade than the First Agricultural Grade, but an overall density in this grade of one person per 2 square miles cannot be very far from the truth.

The local group has now become the village, from which the half-settled community covers its territory. The smallest of the local groups are of much the same size as among the Food-Gatherers, but the largest have vastly increased. The available information as to the state of these tribes when the white man reached them comes from various dates between the sixteenth and nineteenth centuries, and much of it, especially in regard to South America, is lacking in accuracy and detail. Nothing

[1] See J. H. Steward in *H.S.A.*, vol. iii, pp. 896 ff. ("The Marginal Cultures"). In the Amazon basin itself are the more advanced tribes of the following, the Second Agricultural Grade.

[2] Steward's estimates as to most of these tribes are to be found in *Native Population of South America*, p. 661.

[3] Von Martius, *Beiträge zur Ethnographie und Sprachenkunde Amerikas, zumal Brasiliens* (1867), vol. i, p. 53.

[4] A. L. Kroeber, B.A.E., Bulletin 78, p. 882.

[5] By Kroeber (ibid. p. 884), Rosenblat, and Steward (op. cit., p. 656).

more than a guess—a figure of 300 persons—can be hazarded as to the average size of the villages, but at the upper extreme, among the most advanced of the North American Indians of this grade, the figure is much larger.[1] A tribe consists of few villages—sometimes, especially in winter quarters in North America, of only one.

The average size of the tribe of this grade is some 1,500 persons as against the Australian 450.[2] But the most advanced of these peoples in North America formed confederacies of tribes who considered themselves to be of the same racial stock and felt a social tie between them, the Abnaki (of 3,000 persons), the Tuscarora (of 6,000), the Iroquois (of 25,000), the Delaware (of 8,000), and the Dakota (of 25,000).[3] These tribes, especially in South America, where they were smaller, spoke a portentous number of languages, and usually each tribe spoke a language of its own; but in California and elsewhere in North America we find not merely languages but families of kindred languages,[4] and finally we reach such linguistic families as the Siouan, Iroquoian, and Algonkian, which have stretched forward over great areas of the continent, leaving islands of foreign tongues behind them.

In short, these populations of the First Agricultural Grade are on the move; and whereas among the Food-Gatherers it was rare to find any tribe who possessed a tradition of migration from elsewhere, we see plain evidence here both in tradition and the observations of eye-witnesses. The fundamental reason for this is a natural increase of population, of which we have already remarked certain results. It requires only a slight change in vital statistics to produce it. A child is still suckled for about three years. The burden upon the woman is still

[1] A combination of hunting and subsidiary agriculture makes for large villages. We shall see this position again later in the Congo.

[2] See Krzywicki, pp. 71–6. He there deals with North American and South American tribes generally, but the figure for the First Agricultural Grade is probably a little smaller.

[3] Figures of estimates by J. Mooney, *The Aboriginal Population of America North of Mexico* (Smithsonian Misc. Coll., vol. 80, No. 7). See also figures and references in Krzywicki, Appendix II.

[4] See J. W. Powell, *Indian Linguistic Families of America North of Mexico*, Washington, 1891; and Meillet et Cohen, *Les Langues du Monde*.

heavy, for though she has now smaller distances to travel, the field work falls to her lot. There are, as a rule, no marital relations while a child is suckled, for a woman cannot suckle two at a time, and accordingly she has a child every three years, and rarely more than five in all. Infant mortality is still extremely high, but a certain tempering of the harsh conditions of livelihood and a surer food supply has produced a slight but all-important improvement.

In South America there is very little change from the practices of Australia. Infanticide is almost as rife as before, and children are even known to be eaten. But abortion is also widespread, and more so than in Australia, and often only one child in two or three is reared. The Guana,[1] and the Indians of the Xingu basin, rear few children. Among the more advanced tribes—namely, the North American Indians—infanticide has dropped to an insignificant part of what it was among the Food-Gatherers, though there is a great deal of abortion, which has taken its place to some extent. Nevertheless, a new feature begins to appear here and there—namely, a feeling that abortion does not suit the interest of the tribe. The growth of population is sufficiently checked by war.

Among the Food-Gatherers of the Asiatic forests, the wild Negritos and Sakai of Malaya, and Kubu of Sumatra, as well as the Punan of Borneo, war is said to be unknown. Among such intermediate peoples as the Fuegians and Bushmen there is great distrust, fear, and hatred between tribes; and in Australia war in the form of raids between neighbouring groups is known practically everywhere and is, in some areas, frequent, though the cause is generally not the desire for territory but a quarrel arising from distrust, as, for example, when a death is attributed to the sorcery of a foreigner. Among the South Americans of the First Agricultural Grade the position shows little change;[2] but in North America, and especially among the most advanced peoples, the transformation is complete. It is no longer a matter of a local quarrel or a feud; a state of war

---

[1] Fr. Azara, *Geografia fisica y esterica de las provincias del Paraguay y missiones guaranies* (1904), pp. 384–5.

[2] See Steward in *H.S.A.*, vol. iii, pp. 897, 899; and contrast with the A2 tribes at pp. 886–95.

may almost be said to be the normal condition between tribes speaking different languages. The adult men of the tribe, among the more advanced peoples of this grade, must now be called the warriors. "They are early possessed with a notion that war ought to be the chief business of their lives, that there is nothing more desirable than the reputation of being the great warrior, and that the scalps of their enemies or a number of prisoners are alone to be esteemed valuable."[1] Among several of the confederacies a large number of the warriors leave their villages for months or even years at a time, tenanted by little more than women and children, in pursuit of the scalps of an enemy, sometimes seeking him hundreds of miles away, whither he had removed to escape them. It was not uncommon that the menfolk in a tribe, reduced by length of war, numbered only 60 per cent. of the women, and such peoples as the Iroquois filled up their losses, so long as they could, by forcibly incorporating and adopting the remnants of their adversaries, till they contained more foreigners than natives. Tribes extruded from their territory attacked their nearest neighbours to find a home. Such are the results of the increase and movement of populations who enjoy some improvement in combination and mental initiative. Their hostilities were mainly a succession of mere raids, and their weapons were crude, but endemic war made up for these shortcomings by length of time. As for their treatment of the vanquished, in Australia the bulk were slain and a few were eaten, but women were often carried off forcibly as wives. Among the peoples of the First Agricultural Grade, while the majority of the vanquished (and the great bulk of the adult males) are still slain, and a few are eaten, there is also, both in South and North America, a widespread practice, already noticed, to adopt and absorb prisoners (mostly women and children). In addition, a practice of making the captives slaves (of which there was hardly a trace in the Food-Gatherers) now makes its appearance, and we hear of it in 23 per cent. of the tribes. In this stage of economic progress a captive's labour is of use in the fields. The institution of slavery, which is relatively very mild, varies much in frequency and extent

[1] J. Carver, *Travels through the Interior Parts of North America in* 1766-8.

between one people and another. Among the North American Indians of the First Agricultural Grade it is hardly to be found, though we shall see much of it among the more advanced American hunting peoples of the North Pacific coast.

One of the first results when a nomad people adds agriculture to its hunt for food, and becomes half-settled in a number of villages, is that there is an increase in cohesion in the local group, as compared with the Food-Gatherers, but a temporary loss of cohesion in the growing tribe. In South America a third of the local groups have practically nothing in the way of the guidance and restraint of a chief or elders, but in North America there are chiefs or elders exercising influence in almost all villages, and over the whole of the First Agricultural Grade there are chiefs or elders exercising influence in three-quarters of the villages, and in a half of the villages there is a local chief or headman. In the tribe, on the other hand, there is even less authority than there was in Australia: only in approximately one-fifth of the tribes (instead of one-fourth) is there found a chief exercising any authority over a tribe. Indeed, it is easy to exaggerate the strength of chieftainship, wherever it is found, whether in tribe or village, and where it exists (and especially in the tribe) it is better called influence than authority. For example, among the Karayaki and the Caingang we are told that if the conduct of a chief is overbearing or miserly they merely leave him.[1] In South America generally the function of a chief is mainly to give generously, make suggestions as to migration, the allocation of work, or siting of huts, organize gangs for fishing, hunting, or tillage, and deliver harangues. His suggestions need not be followed and his authority depends on the goodwill of the heads of families. He may lead in war.[2] Among the Ojibway of Lake Superior in 1800 we learn that the influence of chiefs was uncertain, and no one would acknowledge any authority as superior to his own will.[3] A chief received deference,

[1] Krause, *In den Wildnissen Brasiliens* (1911), p. 321; Métraux, "The Caingang," in *H.S.A.*, vol. i, p. 446.
[2] See *H.S.A.*, vol. i, pp. 427, 463, 489; vol. ii, pp. 186, 336, 367, 459.
[3] Tanner, *An Indian Captivity* (1789–1822).

indeed, but not obedience from those of other views. Among
the Teton (the main Dakota tribe) no chief at that date,
according to a trader, could carry his will against a single
dissentient.[1] These instances are typical of many other
cases.

Among the Food-Gatherers, from the forest tribes of Asia
to the Australians, the position of the woman was falling in
relation to the man, but the agricultural way of life, under
which she begins to perform a more important economic
function in the community, and thereby to obtain for herself
a certain economic independence, raises her status to an
appreciable degree. For example, the extent of polygamy
diminishes. The number of tribes among whom polygamy is
the rule shrinks from 35 per cent. among the Food-Gatherers
to 21 per cent. in this grade. There is also a somewhat
increased proportion (16 per cent.) of tribes who practice
monogamy. The woman is to a less extent than in Australia
married and divorced without her consent, and she is occasionally even found taking a part in public affairs.

The goods available at this stage of advance are still mainly
food, with the addition of dogs, a few birds, and weapons of
the chase and of war. But they have increased sufficiently
to cause a significant change in marriage custom. As compared
with Australia, the exchange of women diminishes in importance, and capture of brides survives only to a slight extent in
South America, and even less in North America. Elopement
wanes, and even in some North American peoples where it
survives is regarded as an irregular and less honourable form
of marriage. The place of these practices begins to be taken
by the growing custom of making a present of goods to the
father or other near male relative of a girl, or performing
labour for him, in order to secure his consent to the marriage.
Among the Food-Gatherers there were practically no goods
available for the purpose, and before the rise of agriculture no
services were of use. The new practice is seen in a number of
cases in South America, and over the whole grade the giving
of goods or services to obtain a wife is in practice in 34 per

[1] Lowie, *Some Aspects of Political Organization among the American
Aborigines* (1948), p. 5.

cent. of the tribes. Later this custom will develop into one of the chief social institutions of primitive life.

The diminution that we perceived, in the previous chapter, in the sway of the maternal principle—if we may call it so—continues in marriage and inheritance, but the fall is far less steep. In the present grade cases of matrilocal marriage and matrilineal inheritance still exceed the total of patrilocal and patrilineal cases, but the proportion has decreased to 58 per cent. of all cases, as against 66 per cent. in Australia.

With the introduction of agriculture the notions of these peoples on the subject of property in land have achieved a palpable advance. As in Australia, ideas of communal property in land—that is to say, notions that land is held by tribes or local groups or clans—are more frequent than ideas of family or individual rights; but ideas of tribal property increase as against ideas of the property of clans and local groups, and individual as against family property, and these various notions of property are less vaguely held.[1]

As regards offences, there is little to be said of crime: the main criminal offences continue to be incest and murder by magic, but the latter offence shows signs of growing wider to include the practising of witchcraft generally. As the influence of local chiefs and elders increases, they take a more definite and conspicuous part in discussing the guilt of the offender and arranging action against him. In a number of advanced peoples we even find something approaching a primitive kind of trial for crime, but it remains always true that the condemnation of a witch is not a matter of evidence.

In regard to private offences, the position as we left it among the Australians was that homicide, wounding, and adultery (or wife-stealing) gave rise to violent revenge on the part of the injured man, his clan, or his friends; or possibly, if he were thought to have deserved his fate, no action might be taken.

[1] The proportion of communal to (family and individual) ownership is in Grade A1, as in Australia, constant at 57 per cent. to 43 per cent. But in Australia the 57 per cent. is split into 33 per cent. (clans and local groups) and 24 per cent. (tribal). In Grade A1 it is 11 per cent. (clans and local groups) and 46 per cent. (tribal). In Australia the 43 per cent. is split into 30 per cent. family ownership and 13 per cent. individual. In Grade A1 it is 21 per cent. family ownership and 21 per cent. individual.

The further spread of disorder was prevented so far as possible by the voluntary exposure of the offender to spears or knives, or some other form of regulated fight. The main change that now occurs in the First Agricultural Grade—and it is of profound subsequent importance—is that the slight increase in goods which has been attained enables peace to be purchased by its means; and such a practice, as an occasionally used alternative to violence, is general among the North American peoples of the Grade. The system of maintaining peace by some form of regulated fight now survives only to a small extent, and that mainly in South America.[1] But chiefs and elders continue their efforts to check the spread of disorder, not by arranging an exposure to spears, but by peaceful suasion. The peacemaker may be self-appointed, or hold a kind of office as such, or he may be an elder in whom the rest have confidence. It would be a misuse of language to call him an arbitrator. There is no authority sufficient to carry out decisions, nor are decisions made. To take an extreme case, among the Winnebago " if necessary the chief would mortify himself, and with skewers inserted in his back have himself led through the village to the home of the nearest kinsman of the murdered person." [2] In this way he sought to show sympathy, give satisfaction to outraged feelings, arouse pity, and prevent the spread of violence.

One result of the increase in goods is that we hear more of theft, but the degree of seriousness with which it is regarded varies much. Sometimes it is a heinous offence, sometimes an amusing or contemptible peccadillo, sometimes only a curious or irritating idiosyncrasy.

[1] See, e.g., Métraux, *The Caingang*, p. 467.
[2] Paul Radin, *The Winnebago Tribe* (1923), *B.A.E.R.*, vol. 37, p. 209.

CHAPTER V

THE SECOND AGRICULTURAL GRADE

As distinct from the First Agricultural Grade, in which a rudimentary agriculture is only a subordinate means of livelihood, the Second Agricultural Grade [1] consists of peoples among whom agriculture (or, as it is better called at this stage, horticulture) has become the main means of subsistence. On the other hand, as compared with the tribes of the Third Agricultural Grade, these peoples do not possess herds or flocks. They do not work in metals, and they have not the plough. Their main implement is still the digging-stick. They occupy substantial wooden huts, and have skill in woodworking, spinning and weaving, and some pottery. Trade is slowly advancing, and now includes a few manufactured objects as well as agricultural and other natural products. The tribes of this grade include a great number of peoples scattered about Asia, and practically the whole of the Melanesians and Polynesians of Oceania; but there is also a small number of tribes in North America (for example, the Natchez and the Seminole; the Powhatan, Pawnee, Creek, and Illinois confederacies). In South America there is the great majority of the Tropical Forest tribes, or in other words the tribes in the basin of the Amazon and its tributaries, living in areas accessible by water.[2] The most advanced of the peoples whom we have chosen are in Polynesia and in Asia.

The folk of the Second Agricultural Grade require a smaller area than before for their maintenance. The density of population in the areas least favourable to habitation is almost

---

[1] Also briefly referred to in this book as Grade A2.
[2] These are described in *H.S.A.*, vol. iii, " The Tropical Forest Tribes." In defining the characteristics of this grade, there is great difficulty in setting a precise upper limit in Polynesia and America, for no herds of cattle were kept in either region before the coming of the European. See further, upon this topic, *post*, p. 200.

as low as we found it in the lower grades,[1] but in the most favoured situations it is vastly higher than before, so that the average density is increased. A large part of these peoples are islanders, and the sea is so rich a source of additional food that the density of population (other things being equal) tends to vary inversely to the distance from the sea. Accordingly, in New Zealand, for example, with its wide extent of some 100,000 square miles and a proportion of unfavourable land, the Maori population at the coming of the Europeans probably averaged little more than one person per square mile. The large island of New Caledonia, about one-tenth that size, had a density of something over eight per square mile. Smaller islands of about 300 square miles, such as Tanna in the New Hebrides, George Rook Island, and Normanby Island among the D'Entrecasteaux group, have a density of about thirty per square mile; and at the other extreme we find a small islet like Tikopia, in the Polynesian fringe of the Solomons, with an area of 3 square miles and a density of 400 persons per square mile. If there can be such a thing as an average density in this increasing variety of conditions, it is now of the order of between five and ten persons per square mile.

The size of the village has not increased. The average village in North America and Melanesia appears to consist of approximately 200 persons, though several can be named with a population of 600 and more. The largest Polynesian villages are much larger, but the variety is great. For example, in Tikopia the average village consists of only forty-eight persons. Over the whole grade the average village is of the order of about 250 persons.

The size of the tribes also varies within wide limits. The smallest tribes are no larger than about 400 persons, and there are many such in New Guinea. The hundreds of tribes of New Guinea, New Caledonia, and Melanesia generally appear to vary from 400 to 2,000 souls, and to be of an average size of about 1,200 to 1,500. The South American and Polynesian tribes are much larger, and the average size of a Maori tribe

[1] Steward gives calculations of the density of population of South American Tropical Forest tribes, showing an average of a little over one person per square mile (H.S.A., vol. v, pp. 662–3).

was apparently over 4,000. The Natchez in 1650 numbered about 4,500. None of these figures is of statistical value, or is intended to do more than indicate the type of change that is continuing : the largest is increasing, and the average is consequently rising.

The linguistic phenomena are of a piece with these changes. In New Guinea and Melanesia the number of languages spoken is hardly to be believed.[1]   A land journey of 5 miles generally brings a new dialect.[2]   A small tribe of 500 inhabitants such as the Manumbo of New Guinea normally has its own language.[3]   The island of Tamara has its separate tongue, which is used by some 250 persons, and is divided into two dialects.[4] And at the other extreme the whole vast oceanic expanse and innumerable islands of Polynesia are peopled by tribes all speaking languages which belong to one linguistic family and once formed a single tongue.   These facts speak eloquently of increasing movement and communication and a surplus of population as we ascend the grades of economic progress.

There is no great difference to be observed in vital statistics as against the First Agricultural Grade. Women continue to suckle their children for about three years, and give birth to much the same number of children. The fertility of the sexes is low, and we have not reached economic stages where a large family is sought after or considered a blessing. Infanticide is as widespread as before, and abortion is high. In many islands there is a set practice of rearing only one male and one female child to each married couple, and over the whole grade the average number of children reared is little more than this ; but even this number, where the generations succeed one another more quickly than with us, is enough to create a certain surplus of population unless checked by war and cannibalism. The extent of war and the devotion to the practice of war, while they vary from place to place, are considerable. War is the general condition of things between neighbouring tribes speaking different languages and is com-

---

[1] See a great many references in Krzywicki, pp. 20–8.
[2] G. Turner, *Samoa A Hundred Years Ago* (1884), pp. 15, 82.
[3] Fr. Vormanes, in *Anthropos*, vol. iv (1909), p. 661.
[4] M. Krieger, *New Guinea*, p. 209.

mon between others.   In the most primitive tribes of the grade
it is still largely caused by the murder of individuals or their
death by the reputed sorcery of neighbours, but in the more
forward peoples war often affords an ideal which is fundamental to their way of life, and, being removed by the advent
of the white man, has left nothing in its place to live for.
But the scale of war is small: for the most part its practice
consists of small raids.   One form of raid, at least as effective
as other forms to check the growth of population, is the raid
of the head-hunter.   Among the Dyaks and some other
peoples head-hunting forms one of the chief social institutions
and mainsprings of existence.   A youth will not secure his
bride without heads to show for his manliness, and the number
of heads taken by a family is a common standard of its social
worth and influence.   There are substantially no peoples in
this grade among whom war is unknown.   One of the objects
of warfare is the obtaining of human flesh.   Among the lowest
Food-Gatherers cannibalism was unknown, and it was hardly
to be seen in the First Agricultural Grade; but it has increased
to appalling proportions among the most advanced peoples of
this grade.[1]   While this practice of eating captives is becoming
widespread, the practice of taking them as slaves shows also
a great increase among the more forward tribes of the grade,
no doubt owing to the increased extent of agriculture as well
as of war.   The taking of prisoners as slaves is often a major
object of warfare.   Altogether we hear of it in 41 per cent.
of the cases, as against 23 per cent. among the peoples of the
grade below.   The bulk, however, of male prisoners of war
are still slain (whether eaten or not).   The women and children are usually assimilated into the community.

Among the folk of the Second Agricultural Grade organs of
government have made some advance.   In the local groups
there are still a handful of peoples of whom we hear nothing
of organs of restraint or influence outside the family, but in all
the remaining cases elders exercise some functions of this kind,
and in nearly a half of the cases there is also a headman of the
local group.   In a third of the tribes we also hear of a chief
(sometimes with a council) exercising authority over the tribe,

[1] See, for a nauseous example, Métraux, *The Tupinamba*, p. 119.

as against a fifth of the cases in the grade below. The peoples among whom there are no chiefs or headmen of the tribe or local group are the least advanced of the grade. For example, in Melanesia, at the present time at any rate, they are hardly to be found outside the Trobriand. Among many of the more backward peoples, in North America and in New Guinea, the main function of a chief (apart from a certain capacity for leadership and oratorical ability) and his main claim to authority among his followers is that he should display a generous hospitality towards them. Among the most advanced folk of the grade the position of the chief has strengthened much, in spite of the absence of an organized administration. In Tikopia, for example, Professor Firth tells us that if a man fell foul of the chief of his clan and could not make his peace with him, there would be nothing for it but to take a boat out into exile and certain death on the high seas. Among some of the more advanced peoples the chief thrashes the trouble-makers and the disobedient.[1] He has often more influence in war than in peace, and his position is now usually hereditary. Among the most developed of the Polynesian communities, the villages with their headmen are grouped together under chiefs of greater prestige, and these perhaps under a paramount chief. In return for his favour and generosity, the chief (in the Trobriand and in Polynesia) is possessed of privileges and monopolies and receives tribute, and there is a tendency for a growing share of the wealth of the community to find its way into his hands. In a small proportion (14 per cent.) of peoples we also meet for the first time families who have acquired such prestige in one way or another that their heads may be described as nobles, commonly holding their position by hereditary right. Nobles are hardly to be found in the more backward peoples of the grade, but among the tribes of Asia and Oceania they are to be seen in at least a quarter of the cases, and they are almost everywhere in Polynesia.

We see in this grade a continuation of the improvement, which we noted in the previous grade, of the status of the woman. Agriculture began in the previous grade as part of

[1] See, for the Manasi and the Mojo, Métraux, in *H.S.A.*, vol. iii, pp. 389, 419.

the wife's domain, and it often still remains so.   It has become
the main method of subsistence, but she takes at least a full
share in the work, and the economic independence of the
family depends in large measure on her labours.   Hence the
continued improvement in her status, which is less unequal
than at any time since our story began among the forest tribes
of the early Food-Gatherers.   She takes a part in public ceremonies of various kinds, and even in government.   The
man is not free to divorce her at will, and she is rarely married
without her consent.   In spite of the increase in wealth, the
number of tribes among whom polygamy is the rule shows
hardly any increase—only from 21 per cent. to 28 per cent. of
the tribes—nor is there any substantial increase in the extent of
polygamy among such tribes; and, on the other hand, there is
a real increase in the proportion of tribes among whom polygamy is forbidden (from 16 per cent. to 25 per cent.).   There
is even a certain increase in the ratio of cases of matrilineal to
patrilineal descent, although (with the rising degree of organization of society) there is an increase in the proportion of patrilocal to matrilocal marriage; so that altogether the proportion
of sway of the maternal principle (if we may use such an
expression) remains almost unchanged, falling only from 58
per cent. in the previous grade to 52 per cent. in the present.
It is characteristic of the present stage of economic progress
that there occurs a sprinkling of tribes among whom there is
matrilineal descent, though there is patrilocal marriage.

As regards the methods of marriage, the still-widening use
of goods makes the giving of presents to the girl's relatives to
secure their consent to the marriage the general method; less
so among the more backward peoples (of South and North
America), where we hear of it in only one case in three.
Among the more advanced peoples (in Asia and Polynesia) it
is found in 70 per cent. of the cases, and 60 per cent. over the
whole grade.   The giving of service for the bride is widespread in South America.   Other methods correspondingly
decrease, but may be combined with the giving of presents, as
in the case of marriage by capture in Tikopia.[1]

[1] *We the Tikopia*, by Prof. Raymond Firth (1936), pp. 531–74.   Marriage
by exchange of women still survives in Melanesia.

When we turn to consider ideas of right in regard to land, we see the same processes of change that we saw in the previous grade, together with new changes which result from factors that we have just considered. Both the rights attributed to communities and the rights attributed to families and individuals are gradually becoming more specific and concrete, and are changing from mere rights to occupy (in North and South America) towards something more of the nature of ownership in Asia and the South Seas. Among the most forward of the peoples of the South Seas (for example, in Samoa, Hawaii, Tahiti, and Tonga) there is a beginning of ownership of the land by chiefs. This is an aspect of the organization of the tribal group in the person of the chief, and hence community rights in land are beginning to turn into chiefs' rights. Among the same advanced peoples we begin to see property vested in nobles, and we are on the threshold of feudalism. As regards family and individual rights in the land, in Asia and the South Seas the latter continue to gain at the expense of the former, for the family is being organized in the person of the male head just as the tribe is being organized in the person of the chief: so that whereas in the First Agricultural Grade and in the less advanced peoples of the present grade the cases of individual and of family rights in land were approximately equal, in the present grade taken as a whole there are two cases of the former to each case of the latter.

As to offences against order, there is little increase in the list of public or private offences, though both types of offence are more commonly perpetrated in the community, for the community is larger. Nor is there any great change in the sanctions applied to private offences. In most tribes the injured person or his clan or other relatives or friends either wreak revenge, or are bought off, or take no action, according to circumstances, but among the more forward tribes composition—that is to say, the payment of compensation in goods—plays a slightly increased part.

There is, however, a continuing advance towards the administration of justice. In the First Agricultural Grade we saw that the functioning of whatever authority there was took the form of an ill-defined and irregular punishment of public offences, preceded sometimes by an informal discussion of the matter between individuals; and in regard to civil wrongs there was a peace-making activity on the part of persons of influence, who might be the chief or headman or an elder of influence or known impartiality, or a more or less official peacemaker. Among the more advanced peoples of the present grade (that is to say, in Asia and Polynesia) this peace-making activity has become somewhat more pronounced and characteristic.[1] At the same time, as the authority of the chiefs and elders increases, the peace-making activity is more and more exercised by the chief, with the assistance of his elders, and so we reach the threshold of a system of courts of trial.

At the close, then, of the Second Agricultural Grade, among the advanced peoples of Polynesia, we see the evolution of a real governmental authority and of ranks in society, a developed religious system supporting both, general slavery, human sacrifice, a great increase in the extent of cannibalism and of war, an approach to feudalism, and a beginning of the administration of justice. We may say, then, that we have now reached a first stage in the development of civilization. This stage properly belongs to the beginning of the Third Agricultural Grade, where we shall examine the course of its history in some detail.

[1] Among the Caraja the chief's main function is said to be that of a peace-maker (Lipkind, p. 186).

CHAPTER VI

LAW BEFORE THE EVOLUTION OF COURTS

THE stage of advance represented by the tribes of the Second Agricultural Grade is an important stage in our story of development, because this is the point immediately before we find courts and trials in operation. In the Third Agricultural Grade we shall find that because there are courts and trials there are rules enforced by courts, and such rules are "law" by any definition of the word. At this point, therefore, in our progress it is convenient and important to pause and consider whether there has hitherto been anything that we can appropriately call law; and if not, what has taken the place of law; and, in the absence of courts, by what means the orderly activity of the community has been maintained. We meet here the chief problem in the early history of law, and the one that has been most debated.

For the purpose of this inquiry it is not sufficient to examine the few characteristic features, noted in the last chapter, of an average community of the Second Agricultural Grade. The skeleton must be clothed with some flesh and blood, and an attempt made to portray it in life. As an example of a people of this grade, of a medium degree of advance, let us take the inhabitants of the Trobriand Archipelago, a Melanesian people who have been described as thoroughly as any other primitive folk, and with outstanding brilliance by Malinowski.[1]

The main occupation of the inland villages of the Trobriand is horticulture, and especially the culture of their staple yam, the *taytu*. They have no cattle, sheep, or goats. The main occupation of the villagers by the sea and on the lagoon is fishing; and in some villages there is the despised community

---

[1] The reader is referred in particular to his *Crime and Custom in Savage Society* (1926), *Argonauts of the Western Pacific* (1922), *Coral Gardens and their Magic* (1935), vol. 1.

of craftsmen and traders, highly skilled in wood-carving and basketry, and also reputed to possess the greatest efficiency in sorcery—that is, the killing or injuring of persons by means of magic. The average village is of some 200 inhabitants.

Among the Trobrianders the position of women is far higher, and nearer to that of the men, than among the bulk of primitive peoples. Descent and inheritance are matrilineal, but marriage is patrilocal. Marriage is exogamous : it is not permitted with a member of the same sub-clan or clan. It is the culminating point of an intrigue between a boy and a girl, an intrigue in this case which takes a permanent form, being accepted by the girl's family and evidenced by the fact that the pair publicly live and feed together. At the time of the marriage there is an exchange of gifts between the bridegroom and the bride's family, and on marriage the pair go to live together in a hut in the bridegroom's village. The sons of the marriage, when they reach maturity—that is to say, at some time between the ages of eighteen and twenty-two —will return to live in their mother's village, to which they are considered to belong, as being descended from their mother's family. Indeed, the birth of children, and especially of the first child, often takes place in her parents' hut. The daughters live with their parents until they marry.

The physiological part of the father in the birth of a child, if it is known to the natives (and this is very doubtful) is ignored by them. They ascribe the birth to the wife's deceased ancestors. The father is called a stranger, an outsider; but an adult man, in their view, needs a woman with whom to live sexually, and without a woman he has no household and no place in society; and, on the other hand, a woman needs a man to look after the workings of her sexual and reproductive processes and render them honourable, and to render her children respectable and give them a place in society. A woman is not supposed to have children before marriage, though sexual intrigues between the young folk are looked on with an understanding and forgiving eye.

Her brother is under a rigid taboo which prevents any intimacy, even any friendly intimacy with her, and indeed after her marriage they never see one another. At the first harvest after her marriage her brother—that is to say, if there are several brothers and sisters, one particular brother who is paired off with her; and if there is only one sister, all her brothers—make a gift of *taytu* to the married household by virtue of the brother's obligation to support his sister and her offspring. This harvest gift, the *urigubu*, is repeated at every harvest as long as the marriage lasts. It is very large, and may perhaps, on the average, be a half of what the donee's household consumes, though it will vary according to circumstances, and in particular according to the rank of the sister's husband. If he is, for example, a chief, its proportions will be very great. The husband makes return gifts from time to time, but of lesser amounts.

The son of the marriage is the heir to the possessions of his maternal uncle, and succeeds to his honours and status, including the membership of his clan and sub-clan; and a younger brother succeeds to an older brother. Yet the father, though a stranger in blood to his son, has a natural affection for his child and his wife's child, and he shows this in various gifts, attentions, and favours. Often he seeks to benefit his son at the expense of his own matrilineal nephew—for example, to retain him in the village after his maturity. If the father is a chief, and seeks to hand over the rights of chieftainship to his son at the expense of his sister's son, there is likely to be a revolt of the population—at any rate, unless the son's rank (that is to say, the rank of the sub-clan to which he belongs through his mother) is higher than that of his father, in which case the honoured village may be willing that he should stay. In the ordinary way, however, this would be outside the father's right, and a violation of the right of his nephew. The father's position is well understood: he is a stranger to his sons, and has no power over them. He very properly renders sundry attentions to his wife and her children, but they are return gifts for the services her family render to him, including her own sexual services. Indeed, all sexual favours by a woman to a man call for return gifts by the man, and these gifts have a special name of their own. The son, for his part, while he lives in his father's village, helps to fill his father's yam-house with produce, but he is thought to do so as representing his uncle and as helping to perform his uncle's obligation to support his sister's household.

Every village is connected with one or more sub-clans, whose earliest ancestress emerged from a hole in the ground in that area. Each village has a headman, who is the eldest male in the senior lineage of the local sub-clan of highest rank. The headman, or rather chief, of a village of high rank is a person of great prestige, and the headman of a village which is the capital of its district is also the chief of that district; and at the capital village of Omarakana is the paramount chief of the whole territory. But government is by no means organized in the sense that one ruler is in all things subject to a higher ruler or represents him. The paramount chief is surrounded by an aura of the highest dignity and prestige, and he wields the rain and sunshine magic—that is to say, he controls the fertility of the tribe. But on occasion the great military chief, the chief of the province of Tilataula, could drive him out of his home.

The headman of each village possesses all the local ceremonial functions and powers vested in the local community as a whole; and in particular he is the wielder of its magic (unless he delegates it to a deputy) and the master of all its fields. Each of the sub-clans in the village also owns or is master of a portion of its land; and each citizen of the village is master or owner of one or more plots in the cultivable fields, and is entitled to have these allotted to him by the administrative body called the Garden Council (unless he allows some other person, in return for a gift called the *kayeda*, to cultivate one or more of them for the season). On the garden plot works the family—husband, wife, and children, the basic economic unit in Trobriand society. The number of the plots they till depends on the husband's needs, and in particular on the size of the *urigubu* which he gives to his sister's household. But the family is not the only unit of production. The gardening team, which consists of the heads of families and their dependants, carry out work on all the plots of the village at certain stages in the annual cycle of work.

The *urigubu* is the central social-economic institution. It has the effect that everyone is working for someone else in another village. But it is not a commercial institution, though the need to produce it is one of the chief incentives to industry. It is a gift in which the giver finds the greatest pride and satisfaction. Indeed, when the sister's husband is a chief, it largely supplies the place of tribute. Not only is each gift to a chief large, but it comes from the brother of each of his wives—in the case of the paramount chief each of his fifty or so wives—and, in addition, all the kinsmen of his brother-in-law—that is to say, all the members of the same sub-clan—will make similar gifts. The paramount chief therefore, and to a lesser degree the inferior chiefs and headmen, have in their hands a large part of the wealth of the community. They have the *urigubu*, they have the most productive gardens, and they have certain monopolies. For example, the paramount chief is the titular owner of all the coconut and betel-nut palms in the district, and the only person entitled to keep pigs, and he therefore receives a proportion of the yield of the trees and a portion of the carcase of the animal when slain. This concentration of wealth the chiefs use—and this means that they are considered to have the right and the duty to use it—in furtherance of the activities of the community in large enterprises. A feast, to usher in the commencement of such a work as the building of a canoe or storehouse, is given to the men who will do the work, and further gifts or feasts are given in the course of the work. Or the chief's wealth may be used to pay a sorcerer for killing a man by witchcraft, or to pay someone for spearing a man who has offended against him. But there are no courts and no hearings of private disputes and nothing like a formal hearing of a criminal offence.

The bulk of economic transactions in the Trobriand are not of a commercial nature. They are not *gimwali* (barter) but *kula* (the exchange of gifts). Commerce is still in its infancy, and has not yet contributed its peculiar spirit and atmosphere to the transactions that take place in the community. *Gimwali* occurs only with members of the despised community of craftsmen and traders. The bulk of the other transactions consist of mutual acts or gifts, not regarded as being of a commercial nature. We have mentioned the building of canoes or large storehouses, preceded by initial feasts or gifts of food to the workers, which are repeated in the course of the enterprise and at its end. Again, the owner of a canoe keeps (and therefore must keep) it in repair, and in the work of repair the members of the crew must assist. When the community goes fishing, the owner, it is thought, must allow his canoe to be used, and take part in the expedition or allow someone to do so in his place. Each member of the crew performs his customary part of the work and receives his customary share of the catch. If on occasion the owner or a member of the crew surrenders his place to someone else, it is in return for a payment of some kind. Each member takes a place for which a combination of rank, age, and personal ability fits him, each canoe has its place in the village fleet, and the owner represents the interests of the men in the village. The owner and crew are all members of the same sub-clan.

On frequent occasions an inland village requires fish, and a coastal village agricultural produce. The exchange takes place in various ways, but it is done with some ceremonial display and between whole village-groups, though each fisherman and each cultivator conducts the exchange with his opposite number. Commonly the inland village brings the vegetable food into the coastal village in receptacles elaborately decorated, and the fishermen must return an equivalent quantity of fish when a spell of good weather presents itself. There is a permanent relation between two communities for the purpose of such exchanges, and a permanent relationship between opposite numbers.

As compared with the ceremonial gift-exchange, or *kula*, *gimwali* (or barter with bargaining) has no ceremony or magic, and no permanent personal relationships, and, as has been said, only takes place with a member of the industrial community. But even the commercial character of *gimwali* may easily be exaggerated. In one of its common forms it consists of hiring the services of a craftsman to make and supply some article. The person ordering the goods gives an initial gift of *taytu*, and later the craftsman will bring the unfinished article to see if it is in accordance with the other's wishes, and will receive another basket of yams, and there will be a final gift when the work is done.

Serious offences against order, especially murders, are rare; and there are no recognized sanctions even for murder, except that where the murderer and the victim are of different sub-clans there is considered to be a duty to take life in retaliation. In practice, however, this takes place only where the victim was a male adult of rank or importance, and not even then if he was thought to deserve his fate. In other cases satisfaction may commonly be given by payment of blood-money (as it is by one side to the other at the conclusion of a war), but there are no recognized sanctions either for homicide or for wounding. Vengeance is irregular and fitful; chance and emotion largely determine the action taken. Theft is rare. The valuables and other objects of personal use in the community are too easily recognized, and their owner too well known; and theft of food is too dangerous in another way, for in the Trobriand (as in many other places in Melanesia) it is vital to the self-respect of a native that he should be reputed a good gardener and well supplied with food, and the shame and ridicule attaching to a theft of vegetables would make life insupportable. As for criminal offences, as elsewhere there is witchcraft, and there is incest—that is to say, marriage or sexual intercourse in breach of the law of exogamy: but though this is held to be the most heinous of offences, no action is taken unless the relationship becomes a scandal, in which case one or other of the pair may by ostracism or insult be driven to suicide.

The above scanty description serves to show to what extent native ideas are shaped by a combination of human nature and economic circumstances, as, for example, in their estimate of the relation between a father and his son. But our primary concern at this moment is to answer the problem: By what means, in the absence of courts, is the orderly activity of the community maintained?

But firstly, is there a problem at all?—that is to say, are courts necessary for the maintenance of orderly activity in a community? The answer depends in part on the size of the community and in part on the existing standard of social conscience. Modern courts exist, in the first place, to ascertain the facts of a dispute; and, secondly, to determine what compensation or other remedy to the aggrieved person, or punishment to the wrongdoer and deterrent to others of like mind, is appropriate; and if necessary, the power of the State carries out the court's decision. When a community is small, public opinion has a strength which it does not possess in a more advanced stage, for it can reach all where each relies on the goodwill and support of the rest. Accordingly, where a community is sufficiently small, public opinion has a powerful effect in deterring a would-be offender from breaches of good order. Something of this can still be seen in a modern village as compared with the circumstances of a city. Public opinion will also, in a small community, perform something of the fact-finding function of courts, which, when they arise, are but, as it were, the public opinion of the State's specialized agents. When a community is small enough, it knows the facts of a dispute fairly well, having ascertained them by inquiry much as a court does; or at any rate it thinks it knows the facts, and that is sufficient to satisfy it. As for the question what remedy is appropriate, the community at this stage is not directly interested. If the small group produces an occasional wrongdoer, so long as only an occasional individual is wronged, there is no necessity for action by the general body —and indeed the individual has the assistance of his friends, his family, or his clan to gain him satisfaction. But if the offender becomes a general nuisance, he will be got rid of by violent means at the hands of an agent of the chief, or one or more persons who have gained the consent of the rest—if he has not already found himself outside the pale. And so in the Trobriand. Accordingly, we must not exaggerate the seriousness of the problem by what means, in the absence of Courts, is the orderly activity of the community maintained?

Malinowski, in his answer to the problem how it is maintained in the Trobriand, lays chief stress on the factor of reciprocity.[1] Instances are set out above of gifts or services

---

[1] William Seagle forcefully criticizes Malinowski's analysis in " Primitive Law and Professor Malinowski " (*American Anthropologist*, vol. 39, No. 2, 1937).

which are thought to call for a compulsory counter-gift or service. Even acts of piety towards a deceased person entitle the doer to a customary gift in season from the relatives. It is not without significance that Malinowski is writing of the Trobriand, which represents the most advanced economic stage before courts appear, and a stage therefore at which the factor of reciprocity can best be seen at work. But it is in some degree everywhere. Instances come to mind among the lowest communities, where, for example, a woman may not be given in marriage without the counter-gift of another woman. It continues to be important in far higher stages of advance—for example, where we find in Ashanti and elsewhere that no one acts as a witness of a legal transaction without a payment. In our modern civilization the spread of commercial transactions makes it difficult to appreciate what happens among primitive peoples. With us business is business and gifts are gifts. In the former case the consideration for a transfer is a matter of agreement and is arrived at by a fine ascertainment of values. In the other case a gift needs no return. There are, of course, such gifts among early folk too, but only upon unimportant matters. For the rest, trade has not yet arrived to an extent sufficient to turn counter-gifts, compulsory (as it were) by custom, into commercial transactions compulsory by agreement enforceable in court.

Reciprocity, therefore, and the effect of public opinion are all-important factors which maintain orderly communal life. But we must add the natural reactions of a man towards those whom he loves, and the sense of gratification and power which (like a modern child) he feels when he has been generous to others—and especially when the whole community knows of it. Generosity is held to be one of the greatest virtues among simple peoples.

The orderly activity of the community is not greatly maintained by religion, that is plain. In the first place, the field of the supernatural chiefly belongs to magic, not religion, in the Trobriand. In all activities, the outcome of which is attended by uncertainty—above all, in tilling and planting and all the other stages in the annual cycle of horticulture, and equally in fishing in those places and for those kinds of fish where the outcome is attended by chance—magic is almost invariably employed. It consists commonly of simple acts or rites by the appropriate magician, accompanied by a customary formula of words—usually an exhortation to the earth or tuber to swell, or the plant to shoot or blossom, or a narrative of the desired event as though it were already taking place. There is commonly little ceremonial, and apart from the fact that the words are chanted by the magician, it would seem to the onlooker that here is a man working at his garden. A visitor might live a long time in the Trobriand, says Malinowski, before he discovered the existence of magic. The native knows that successful horticulture demands skilled work, but he believes that it also demands magic, the mechanical employment of some kind of occult power. Magic is as near to primitive science as to primitive religion. And on the other hand, in processess not attended by chance, magic is not employed. It is not employed by the craftsman at work on the wooden articles he makes, or in the building of dwelling-huts or storehouses, and it is not used in the lucrative and simple method of fishing by poison. These considerations enable us to see that, apart from ignorance, the main support of the institution of magic is psychological: it serves to give man confidence that he can overcome the hazards of his daily life. So far as it helps to maintain the orderly activity of the community, its effect is indirect. It does not take the place of law.

Compared with magic, religion plays a small part indeed among peoples at this stage of economic progress. It is not true to say that the Trobrianders have a belief in a god or gods. Except for the sceptics among them, they have a vague belief in spirits—spirits of the departed, ancestral spirits, including a few mythological heroes, who return annually to the village and are mentioned in certain formulæ of magic. There is also a belief, says Malinowski, that if custom is not obeyed and tradition observed, these spirits will be displeased and may bring some form of bad luck upon the natives. But the main part of the religious phenomena among them—if such they may be called—consist in mere ceremonies, the washing and adorning of a father's corpse, the mourning of a widow for her husband, the display of the first-fruits of the garden on the graves of the recently deceased.

Magic, therefore, plays but a small part in maintaining orderly activity in the community, and religion even less. Such as it is, their part is to stabilize and conserve. They do no more than help to retain and reinforce the devotion of a society to its traditional norms of behaviour,[1] playing in that respect much the same part as religion in modern times. Indeed, even the sorcerer may be said to perform a similar function, for his victims tend to be those who offend against the community's canons of good behaviour, and when the European comes upon the scene he is the head of the resistance offered by the old system of things. This thought reminds us that traditional norms of behaviour have a force of their own that makes for the maintenance of orderly activity in a community. We have noticed more than once that one of the chief sources of ideas of right is the notion that what is usually or customarily done ought to be done, and accordingly the mere fact that a thing is customary is a good reason why it should continue to be done. This notion is embodied in the ancient and modern legal doctrine of the binding nature of precedent.

We have still not answered one question which we set out to answer—namely, whether there is anything in this community that we can appropriately call law. Malinowski says Yes. "There must," he urges, "be in all societies a class of rules too practical to be backed up by religious sanctions, too burdensome to be left to mere goodwill, too personally vital to individuals to be enforced by any abstract agency. This is the domain of legal rules, and I venture to foretell that reciprocity, systematic incidence, publicity, and ambition will be found to be the main factors in the binding machinery of primitive law."[2] "There is no religious sanction," he says, "to these rules; no fear or superstition enforces them, no tribal punishment visits their breach, not even the stigma of

---

[1] Compare the views of Durkheim in *Les formes élementaires de la vie religieuse* (1912), pp. 323, 497; of A. R. Radcliffe-Brown in *Religion and Society* (1945), *J.R.A.I.*, vol. lxxv, p. 33; also the present author's *Primitive Law*.

[2] *Crime and Custom*, pp. 67-8.

public opinion or moral blame." [1] He cites all those cases—some of which are instanced above—in which a gift-payment or service is always followed by a counter gift-payment or service, and distinguishes the many cases in which gift or service is not considered necessarily to call for a corresponding gift or service.

But looking at the matter generally, we must, I think, answer (though not without some doubt) that these things are not law. The question is partly one of language. [2] If these " rules " of behaviour are sufficiently different from law, in the sense in which the term is commonly or properly used, they should be given a different name, to avoid confusion. If historically they are law in its infancy, the use of the same term would be justified. But they are different from law and never become law. The question is also partly one of the attitude of the native. There is no word for " law " in the language of the Trobriand or other peoples of the same economic grade. Nor is there any conception of " law." There is not indeed, in Melanesia, so far as I am aware, any word signifying " right " in the simple sense of the expression " it is right to do this " and " it is not right to do that." Their nearest expressions are words signifying " customary." As for gifts to which the receiver " must " make a corresponding gift, it is to be doubted even whether these peoples have words signifying " must." They are certainly aware that certain gifts call for corresponding counter-gifts and others do not. But there is no gift, payment, or service of which it can be said that a return payment or service is always made. All rules are liable to be broken, just as all modern laws are broken. In a civilized community we nevertheless recognize these as laws, though they are broken, because courts will enforce them. In the Trobriand there are no courts to enforce them, and no notion of law. Reciprocity itself is not, of course, a law, but a social relation which weakens to some extent as law grows and, to that extent, takes its place and its function.

[1] Ibid., p. 66.
[2] A view with which Malinowski forcefully disagreed in conversation with the present author.

This is the answer we give looking at the matter generally. In detail, as we have seen, there are a few rules which lie in the direct ancestry of law, and merit the use of the term "primitive law" to the extent that there is some means of enforcing them. First and foremost there are rules of marriage prescribing between what persons it may take place, and as their breach is incest, and is visited by criminal sanctions, albeit fitful and irregular, we may call these rules of marriage a beginning of law. The same applies to other criminal offences, irregularly as they are punished. Bound up with the rules of marriage are a few rules of descent and inheritance, and yet in the Trobriand the young man partly earns his inheritance from his maternal uncle by a series of gifts and services. As for rules of the ownership of land, all is too vague and popular. There is no Trobriand word for ownership, and the ownership of any particular plot of land is hard to find. It is part of the fields which belong to a local sub-clan, and of which the local headman is master; it is one of the plots in those fields which are allotted to the local inhabitants by the Garden Council of the village; it is a plot which a certain individual is entitled to have allotted to him by the Council and which he works with his family. As for civil wrongs, there is nothing so definite that it can be called a rule, and there is no court to enforce it.

It is true to say, in short, that as yet there is no law in this community, except perhaps rules relating to marriage, and a few other incipient rules of criminal law.

CHAPTER VII

THE HUNTERS

BEFORE we proceed to the description of the tribes of the Third Agricultural Grade, this is perhaps the most convenient point at which to retrace our steps for a while and consider a type of material culture which stands, as it were, on a by-path or parallel minor road to the main highway of human economic advance. This is the culture of the Hunters (or, as they may be called in relation to the Food-Gatherers, the Higher Hunters). Their study is of importance because it shows these peoples, in the course of their development, producing the same stages of advance that we witnessed in the First and Second Agricultural Grades, except in so far as they are affected by the conditions of their own specialized hunting way of life. Their study is of value as confirming our plotting of the general direction of human progress, and the relation between economic and legal advance. At various points such peoples have been seen to rejoin the main highway.

We return, then, to the point reached at the close of our third chapter, when we had described the Food-Gatherers (or Lower Hunters). These were defined as consisting of those peoples who live mainly by gathering their food, whether it be roots or fruits, game, insects, reptiles, or fish, even though they may also hunt the larger animals, such as the kangaroo. They have no arts of spinning, pottery, or metal-work, and no permanent dwellings, and commonly live in caves or holes or protect themselves by the erection of windbreaks. They have no domestic animal save the dog.

The Hunters consist of all hunting peoples except the Food-Gatherers. Taken as a whole, they find their sustenance by hunting rather than by gathering their food; know something of the arts of spinning, weaving, and pottery; build good canoes; have often well-made dwellings, whether they be tents or substantial wooden houses, and besides the dog have now the horse or other domestic animals introduced by the

Europeans. In addition to a few Asiatic peoples, they comprise mainly North American Indians, the bulk of whom belong to this grade, the Eskimo, and a considerable number of South American tribes.[1] As examples representing the least advanced of the Hunters may be instanced the Eskimo. They are as remote in space from the Australians, and their climate is as different as it is possible to be, and yet, as will be seen, they share with them a large number of fundamental characteristics created by their close nearness in stage of economic development, for both stand near the boundary between the Food-Gatherers and the Hunters. Only a little more advanced are some of the North American Indians—namely, such Athapascan tribes as the Tsattine, Tsilkotin, Takulli, Kutchin, and Loucheux, as well as Nahane, and the bulk of the South American Hunters. At the other extreme stand the fishing peoples of the coast of British Columbia and Haida of Queen Charlotte Islands, the most advanced folk of this grade, with their skilled metal-work. The Hunters cover a wide range, standing at various points at the levels of the First and Second Agricultural Grades, and on the average their stage of advance is at a level midway between these two grades.

The size of the local group is much the same among the Hunters as in those grades. For example, the largest settlements among the Caribou Eskimo, as in Australia, contain a population of about fifty persons. Among such intermediate peoples as the Yurok of North-West California the local group is of an average size of fifty souls, and in Patagonia, the Pampa and Chaco about 100, and it rises to about 200 among the Haida and other tribes of the North Pacific coast. In regard to the size of the tribe the picture is much the same. Among the Caribou Eskimo in 1900 the largest tribe was under 200 souls in number. Krzywicki[2] calculates the average size of twenty-four Athapascan and Tlingit tribes at 700 persons, and of twenty tribes of Indians of the Plains at 3,000.

[1] These are mainly the tribes of Patagonia, east of the Cordillera, and the Argentine Pampa (i.e., the Tehuelche and Puelche) and farther north the Querandi and Charrua; and in the Gran Chaco the Abipon, Mocovi, Mbaya, Lengua, Toba, and Vilela.
[2] P. 72. For California, see B.A.E., Bulletin 78, pp. 16 et seq., 883.

The density of population develops accordingly. Among the South American Hunters of Patagonia and the Pampa, and the Querandi and the Charrua, it is estimated at only one person per 2 square miles. In the Western Chaco it has increased to one per square mile, and on the North Pacific coast of North America the population was one of the densest of the continent.

In the local group government increases to much the same extent as in the first two agricultural grades. Among the Eskimo there are few chiefs indeed, and it is only in one-fifth of the cases that authority is exercised by chiefs or councils of elders in the local groups. Much the same picture is seen among the rest of the most backward peoples of the grade—for example, the Tsilkotin, Takulli, and East Nahane. Taking the Hunters as a whole, we find chiefs or councils of elders exercising authority in the local groups in three-quarters of the cases, and in the bulk of these cases there are chiefs. When we turn to the government of the tribe the position remains much the same among the Eskimo and other less-advanced tribes; but over the Hunters, taken as a whole, there are chiefs or councils of elders exercising authority in one-third of the tribes, and there are chiefs in almost all these cases. Among the advanced peoples of the North Pacific coast there appear to be chiefs in all tribes.[1] There the position of the *shaman* or other ruler is commonly fortified by mythology and tradition, and his authority and reputation for magical power have grown a good deal.

Yet it would be easy to exaggerate the extent of this authority in any hunting people. In South America the headman's chief function is to harangue the band, make suggestions as to the day's programme of hunting and travelling, and voice the views of the majority. No one pays any great attention, nor would an order be obeyed if it were given.[2] Among the bulk of intermediate peoples (for example, Assiniboine and Crees) a chief was entitled to deference only, not obedience, and any

[1] Though even here there is hardly a tribal chief among the Nootka, and the chief of each sept is the real ruler.
[2] See Cooper, *H.S.A.*, vol. i, p. 194; Serrano, ibid., p. 194; Métraux, ibid., pp. 363 f.

man might carry the Council in a sense opposite to his views. Even in British Columbia the Tsimshian chief compensated the relatives of a man killed in battle, and the authority of a Haida chief was mainly limited to the arranging of *potlaches* or feasts.[1] As in the Second Agricultural Grade (for example, in Melanesia), the position of the chief among the more advanced of the Hunters largely depends on the extent of his generosity and munificence, and the title is often given to the man who is most lavish in his feasts or donates a public building.

Among the rudest of the Hunters the clan organization is absent.[2] From the lowest to the highest of the Hunters society tends to lose its uniformity and crystallize into ranks. Nobility, which was not to be found in the First Agricultural Grade but is mentioned in 14 per cent. of tribes in the Second, is similarly unknown among the most backward of the Hunters, but is common on the coast of British Columbia and is found in about 10 per cent. of tribes in the whole grade.[3] Slavery (found in about 23 per cent. of the peoples of the First Agricultural Grade and 41 per cent. of the Second) is mentioned among approximately 32 per cent. of the Hunters, where it is mainly confined to the North Pacific coast in America. The chief source of slavery is warfare, which increases in scale and frequency among the Hunters as in the two agricultural grades. War is still a matter of raids at dawn, and the attackers fly if they suffer a few losses.[4] Among the bulk of the Eskimo slavery and war are both unknown.

In the forms of marriage, too, the same changes occur as in the two agricultural grades. Except among the Eskimo there is little to be seen of the capture of brides or exchange or lending of wives, so frequently found in Australia. Just as in the two agricultural grades, the increase in the quantity of available goods introduces a growing practice of giving to the relatives of the bride movables of some kind as a compensatory

---

[1] R. M. Lowie, *Some Aspects of Political Organization among the American Aborigines* (Huxley Memorial Lecture, 1948), p. 5.

[2] For example, the Eskimo; the bulk of the Athapascan, interior Salish and Californian tribes; Tehuelche and Puelche.

[3] See, for example, Métraux, *H.S.A.*, vol. i, pp. 304–5 (Chaco).

[4] Métraux, ibid., p. 314 (Chaco).

gift-payment to secure their consent to the marriage.[1] In the First Agricultural Grade we found this practice among 34 per cent. of the tribes, and in the Second among 59 per cent., and over the whole of the Hunters the figure is again midway—namely, about 42 per cent. Among peoples with whom the position of woman is low, the gift already begins to assume the appearance of a purchase-price for the bride; and the position of the woman remains as low among the Hunters as it was in Australia, for we miss the ameliorating effect of the introduction of agriculture. Apart from gifts, and chiefly among a few of the least advanced of the Hunters, in place of goods the man gives his service for a period in return for his bride.

The cases in which marriage is matrilocal, or descent and inheritance matrilineal, still number the majority (about 60 per cent.) of the Hunters. Among the Eskimo and the other backward tribes referred to the proportion is about 75 per cent., but at the other extreme there is a minority of such cases (about 40 per cent.) among the peoples of the North Pacific coast. There, as in the Second Agricultural Grade, we see the same sprinkling of peoples among whom marriage is patrilocal and inheritance and descent are matrilineal.

It is in regard to ideas on the subject of property in land that the specialized hunting way of life has its effect. Hunting[2] involves movement over a comparatively large tract of land, and the same tract can be efficiently hunted by different persons at the same or different times. Horticulture is sedentary over a small territory, and efficiency demands that he who sows shall reap. While, as among the Australians, ideas of family property among the Hunters are approximately twice as frequent as ideas of individual property, both have a much-reduced sway.[3] Rights of local groups and clans (36 per cent.) remain at much the same figure as among the Australians, but ideas of tribal rights spread fast,[4] and there is now also a total of about 10 per cent. of cases (confined to the more forward

---

[1] As early as the Tehuelche and Puelche.   [2] Except fishing.
[3] Among the Australians family rights 29 per cent. and individual rights 14 per cent. Among the Hunters family rights 9 per cent. and individual rights 5 per cent.
[4] Among the Australians 23 per cent., among the Hunters 40 per cent.

tribes) where the land is considered in some sense to belong to the chief. In other words, the proportion of ideas of community or public rights to private rights shows a great increase.

As regards movable property, we found that customary rules governing the distribution of food acquired in the hunt were general among the Food-Gatherers. They are also general among the Eskimo and less advanced Hunters,[1] but decrease among the rest of the Hunters, and practically disappear on the North Pacific coast. The notion of the individual right to movables is everywhere well developed.

In regard to offences against good order, the public or criminal offences remain what they were—namely, witchcraft, incest, and sacral offences. The latter are few among the more backward of these peoples, but receive notable additions among the more advanced. They are mainly acts which are thought to imperil the success of the hunt (for the outcome of a hunt is much a matter of uncertainty), and are therefore considered to affect the whole community among a hunting people. The Omaha, indeed, punished offences against good order in the hunt by a special hunt police. Among the tribes of the coast of British Columbia some kind of trial for all these criminal offences takes place before the leading men of the village.[2]

In regard to private offences the picture is much the same as in the two agricultural grades. Among the most backward Hunters, private wrongs give rise to irregular retaliatory violence on the part of the individual or his clan or friends, or, if he is thought to have deserved what he suffered, no action may be taken. Though the wrong is considered an affair of individuals, the community has an interest in the early termination or prevention of feuds or other disorder. There were noticed among the Australians widespread practices of giving satisfaction for a private wrong by self-exposure to weapons or other forms of regulated fight. Exposure to weapons is not a frequent practice elsewhere, but it is found, for example, among the Ghiliaks of Asia,[3] and regulated fights of various kinds are common among the Eskimo and in the extreme

---

[1] E.g., Tehuelche (Cooper, *H.S.A.*, vol. i, p. 153).

[2] Niblack, *Smithsonian Reports* (1888), p. 252.

[3] Deniker, *Revue d'Ethnographie*, vol. 2, p. 309.

south of America.[1]   For example, among the Central Eskimo we are told that a murderer goes to live with the relatives of his victim, and after a few weeks is challenged by one of them to a bout of wrestling.   If defeated he is put to death, and if victorious may kill one of the relatives.[2]   In this way, as by exposure to spears or knives in Australia, the feud may be avoided.   Among the Western and other Eskimo minor wrongs may be settled by a boxing-match.   Something of the like nature, which further illustrates the public interest in private disputes, may be seen in the practice—found as far apart as Greenland and the Trobriand—in which the two parties to a quarrel, accompanied by their respective relatives and friends, will assemble in the presence of an interested and amused audience, and hurl at one another taunts and satirical songs.   The winners are the party who can secure the laughter of the audience on their side, and the losing party may even be driven by these means from the community.[3]   These various methods are not to be seen to any extent among more advanced Hunters, and for the most part private wrongs continue to be followed by violence, if anything.   But the increase of goods (as in the agricultural grades) brings about a spreading practice of purchasing peace by compensation in this form.   Among the least advanced of the tribes of the grade, who have been instanced above, it is only to be seen in about 18 per cent. of the cases; but among the peoples of the North Pacific coast of America this practice is found everywhere. Yet even here a common result of a serious offence is physical retaliation by the clan of the wronged man.[4]   There is also in this grade, wherever there is government of chiefs or elders, a practice of endeavouring to avoid resulting disorder by peace-making, and among some tribes elders are to be found who hold an official position as peace-makers.   The public retains in the last resort an interest in the preservation of peace,

[1] E.g., Tehuelche (Cooper, *H.S.A.*, vol. v, p. 152); Charrua (Serrano, *H.S.A.*, vol. i, p. 194).

[2] Boas, *Smithsonian Reports* (1884–5), p. 582.

[3] See Rink, *Eskimo Tribes*, p. 24; idem, *Greenland*, pp. 141, 150; Nansen, *First Crossing of Greenland*, vol. ii, p. 328; Malinowski, *Crime and Custom*, p. 60.   Compare the public jeering among the Tasmanians, Davies, p. 419; Roth, p. 59.   [4] Niblack, loc. cit.

and in a number of the Hunters (including even Eskimo) there is a practice, which we shall still find as late as the early Third Agricultural Grade, that a person who by repeated offences against his fellow-man makes himself a public nuisance, will be murdered by one or more with the consent or at the instance of his neighbours.[1]

[1] See, e.g., Boas, loc. cit.; Turner, *Smithsonian Reports*, vol. ii, p. 186.

BOOK II

BARBARISM

CHAPTER I

INTRODUCTORY

THE steps described in the previous chapters have brought us to the Third Agricultural Grade, which can be briefly described as the grade of economic advance reached by those peoples who add the pastoral way of life to the practice of agriculture.[1] It marks also the beginning of law in the proper sense of the term. As we trace stages [2] of economic and legal development among the innumerable peoples of the Third Agricultural Grade, we shall find that, watching the developing law, we can separate the steps of advance both of law and of economics with far more precision than anything hitherto possible.

A new situation will presently arise as we make this analysis. We shall soon be concerned not merely with the primitive peoples of the world around us, or those described by observers during the last three centuries, but also with the primitive peoples of the ancient world, and we shall be able to take our instances from ages covering a period of over 4,000 years. The modern peoples of the Third Agricultural Grade are to be found mainly in Africa and Asia; the peoples of the ancient world in Babylon and Assyria, in Egypt, China, and the Hittite Empire, in India, Palestine, Greece, and Rome, in Western Europe, and not least in England. The evidence from the peoples of the past is certainly no less credible and cogent than the reports of observers of present-day tribes, for they have left us their written accounts of their own rules of law; and these, if we can read them aright, are no less valuable than many opinions of foreign observers and travellers, or traditions of native peoples. Accordingly, as each stage is

---

[1] There continue to be many peoples, pursuing a parallel path of progress, who are agriculturists or hunters and do not keep cattle. We shall say something of them in Book III, Chap. IV.

[2] We shall now use the word " stage " only as signifying each of the divisions of the Third Agricultural Grade.

described, we shall take our instances both from latter-day tribes (chiefly of Africa) and from peoples of various sundered ages in the past from the third millennium B.C. and onwards. There are in the civilized world few agricultural nations wihch do not also practise the keeping of herds, so that in a sense the bulk of peoples beyond the stage which we have now reached might be assigned to the Third Agricultural Grade; but for many reasons of convenience we end our grade, among the peoples of the past, with the stage reached by the Code of Hammurabi (which is also one of the earliest codes of law that we possess), and we end our grade, among the peoples of the present, with Abyssinia—the most advanced of the native nations of Africa, excluding the Mediterranean coast—as it existed in 1935 immediately before its conquest by Italy, and with China as it existed till the nineteenth century.

There is a second great change in the evidence at our disposal. Hitherto we have collated the peoples of each economic grade and described their common features of interest, and it was a matter of inference that this was a description of the general history of human advance. Progress was slow, and it was only occasionally and for short periods that we were able to witness a change from step to step in the same people and country. For example, reason told us that before man tilled the ground he must, like the other animals, have taken his food growing wild where he found it. Archæology informed us that this was indeed the fact, but could tell us little about man's social organization and nothing of his legal ideas at that level of culture. But presently we shall be able to witness the changes that now progressively show themselves in the Third Agricultural Grade as they appear over many centuries and in the same country; and in England we shall see all these stages (except for the first) in a period of only some 700 years, ending with a date of about A.D. 1300—on the continent of Europe it is a little earlier—when law and economics had reached the stage of development of the Code of Hammurabi. This is rapid progress. At the close of the grade, and yet at the earliest point of time after the dawn of history,[1] we see in

[1] The word "history" is used as referring to the period covered by contemporary written records.

Babylonia the passage of two millennia with little of legal or economic progress.[1] In Western Europe, on the other hand, we are fortunate in that history dawns when conditions are far more primitive and advance is far more rapid. This is not surprising. The peoples of Babylonia and China and Egypt had to achieve their own progress and to discover for themselves the use of writing. Civilization is built up by painful labour, inspiration, and error over long ages, though we have seen it—especially in Western Europe 1,500 years ago—destroyed in a day. Each successive people found the torch ready to its hand, and was able to add to its own stock of vitality and ideas the achievements of its predecessors. In Western Europe the missionary and the trader brought to the Germanic barbarians writing and trade (just as they bring them now to backward peoples), and the record of history began in a more primitive age, and the progress was faster. Since then we have seen it moving even faster in Japan, in Africa, and elsewhere. But the legal ideas of the nations of the past mean nothing to a people who have not reached the grade of economic advance to which those ideas belong, and law and the rest of material culture must still advance hand in hand.

Accordingly our evidence for the changes in the Third Agricultural Grade is taken in the main from various parts of modern Africa; from tribes and nations of past ages during the last 4,000 years, irrespective of time and place; and from progressive stages of advance appearing in the course of time in the same country.

For important reasons we divide the Third Agricultural Grade into the following main stages. The first is that represented by the peoples of the past and present who combine cattle-keeping with some agriculture, but have not yet reached the legal and economic stage at which the most primitive written Codes of the law appear. The present peoples of this stage have no writing, nor had the peoples of this stage in the past. The law that follows—namely, that represented in the Codes of the past and the law of the corresponding peoples of today, we divide into three stages: the Early Codes, the

[1] In China the last three millennia up to 1900 have produced even less economic and legal progress.

Central Codes, and the Late Codes, according to their degree of development. In other words, we separate the Central Codes from the rest. It is important to do so, for among them there appear phenomena of a religious nature which are of the greatest interest and importance, and this stage may be said also to mark the beginning of civilization. Accordingly our second stage in the Third Agricultural Grade is that of the Early Codes, our third that of the Central Codes, and our fourth that of the Late Codes. This is the stage already reached in Babylonia at the dawn of history and before 2000 B.C., in England about A.D. 1300, and in Abyssinia before A.D. 1935.

All these various stages are also to be observed in modern Africa, in circumstances which show that they are stages not only in economic progress but also in history. Here on the fringe of the Bantu world, in Eastern and South-Eastern Africa, are the most backward of our peoples. Travelling thence towards Central Africa, we watch continuous advances in culture, and finally in West Africa meet with a vast number of peoples of the Late Codes. This is the broad continental picture, and a traveller pursuing this route passes a living panorama of many centuries of the history of law; but here and there are other peoples of the Late Codes—for example, the peoples of Bechuanaland—and, above all, isolated in the lofty highlands of Ethiopia, the Abyssinians, a colonizing offshoot of the Semitic world. Apart from the effects of local varieties in soil, climate, and supplies of water—and apart, in particular, from the incredible fertility of the shores of Victoria Nyanza—there goes, among all these peoples, a corresponding increase in the size of tribes and of States and in the density of populations, until in West Africa and Abyssinia we find the densest populations of all native Africa south of the Mediterranean littoral.

It was noticed in regard to the lowest grades of culture that the lack of movement was such that few tribes possessed a tradition of movement from elsewhere, and the extent of isolation was such that commonly a tribe of a few hundreds spoke a language distinct from all other tribes, and often a language bearing no˙ detectable relationship to any other known tongue. In subsequent grades we saw, on the whole, steady and progressive changes, and we shall see the process continuing. In East Africa most tribes have come to their present territory in recent centuries; and in South Africa few have occupied their present home for more than 200 years, and some for no more than fifty or a hundred. In Nigeria it was only the British occupation of a century ago that stayed a process of widespread invasion and migration. The position is much the same in regard to language. The whole of the peoples occupying the southern third of Africa (excluding the few Bushmen and Hottentots) speak languages of the Bantu family, either derived from one language that has spread over that vast area, or acquiring common characteristics by the communications and movements of peoples. So, too, during the period of the Third Agricultural Grade, Aryan languages have embraced almost the whole of Europe and extended over a large part of India, all being but the slowly widening dialects of one early language, as its speakers, under the pressure of growing populations, spread far and wide over seas, rivers, and mountain ranges, and handed it on to others.

CHAPTER II

THE LEGAL RELICS OF THE PAST

THE evidence from the past, embodying the law of the
Third Agricultural Grade, begins in point of time with
Babylonia, for of the law of ancient Egypt little is
known. So far as the evidence shows, civilization first emerged
in a number of places in the world where the natural conditions
were very much alike. It was alongside great and permanent
rivers, most of which spread water and silt in seasonal flooding;
in latitudes where there was no great winter cold, the climate
was mild and sunny, and the fertile and well-watered soil
could produce more than one crop a year. This meant a
latitude, at low altitudes, of between 25° and 35°, or, at greater
heights, a lower latitude. These regions were semi-arid, and
therefore free of rain-forest, which could not have been cut
down with the available tools of stone or bronze; and for this
reason, too, these homes of civilization were in river-valleys.
Here was a substantial source of food in the rivers, and a water-
way for trade and communications, and here were the chief
concentrations of population in a world of which the total of
human inhabitants was an insignificant fraction of what it is
today. In the absence of rain-forest and tsetse fly, it was also
possible to rear cattle, if they were to be found in those
areas.

These sites consisted of the northern part of the valley of the
Nile, Southern Mesopotamia, and the southern Indus valley
(all between 25° and 35° north), and in China the valley of
the Yellow River at its great eastern bend between Shensi,
Shansi, and Honan (about 35° north), where it descends from
the dry highlands towards the plain. The corresponding sites
in America were, for reasons of geography, nearer the equator,
and at correspondingly higher altitudes—namely, the valley of
Mexico, with its five lakes, at a latitude of 18° north and a height
of some 7,500 feet, and the Guatemala tableland; and, in the
Central Andes, the valley of Cuzco and Lake Titicaca and the

river-basins of that region, all at an average height of some 11,500 feet and a latitude of about 13° south. These American areas were also semi-arid, but both somewhat less favourable than those in the East, and gave rise to their independent civilizations at later dates.[1]

In the latter part of the third millennium B.C. Babylonia, in Southern Mesopotamia, was economically and legally in advance of the rest of the world. The southern portion was mainly occupied by persons speaking the Sumerian language, and the northern part, Accad, by peoples of Semitic tongue. From the great Third Dynasty of Ur survive many private legal documents in the form of clay tablets, for all important trans-actions were already recorded in writing. This was the last great Sumerian power, and when that dynasty fell shortly before 2000 B.C., it left several of the city-states of Southern Babylonia, especially Isin and Larsa, to struggle for the mastery. Their rulers were mainly Semites, holding sway over mixed Semitic and Sumerian populations, and in these centuries several of them appear to have promulgated written codes of law to meet the changed circumstances of the region and to apply both to Semite and Sumerian subjects. A smaller feudal State, Eshnunna, situated on the east bank of the Tigris on both sides of the River Dyala, and stretching to the Persian foothills, has left us copies of a very valuable code of law of King Bilalama, who reigned in 2000 B.C. or very soon after. They were discovered in the year A.D. 1947,[2] and are written in the Accadian (that is to say, Semitic) language, and constitute our earliest extant code of laws. A little later, from the city-state of Isin, survives a less important and mutilated part of a code of Lipit Ishtar (fifth king of the Isin dynasty) dating from about 1920 B.C.[3] It is in the Sumerian tongue. Not long afterwards a Semitic dynasty, the first dynasty of Babylon, gained control of all Mesopotamia. About 1750 B.C., at the close of his long reign, Hammurabi, third king of that dynasty,

---

[1] See, further, as to China, Mexico, and Peru, *post*, Book III, Chapter V.

[2] Found at Tell Harmal (a provincial centre of the State); published and translated by A. Goetze in *Sumer*, vol. iv, No. II, pp. 63 f. (Sept. 1948).

[3] Translated by F. R. Steele, *American Journal of Archæology*, vol. 51 (1947), pp. 158–64; vol. 52 (1948), pp. 426 f.

promulgated a code of laws [1] for all his subjects, Sumerian and
Semitic. He drew upon the common legal ideas of the
civilization of the country, and utilized the work of his
predecessors in both Sumer and Accad, reconciling their
divergencies and improving upon their codes. The Code of
Hammurabi is one of the world's great legal landmarks, and
the Code and copies of it were studied and admired from Elam
to the Syrian coast for some 2,000 years thereafter. We are
indeed fortunate that, almost alone of all ancient codes, it
survives upon the very stone on which it was published—a
stele of black diorite which was carried away to Susa in the
twelfth century B.C. and was there discovered in A.D. 1902.
It is a long compilation of about 282 clauses.

When Hammurabi's dynasty fell, an invasion of Cassite
mountaineers from the north-east ended what is known as the
Old Babylonian period, and little survives from the simpler
age of the next 1,000 years, though such documents as do
survive betoken some general continuity. This Middle Period
includes the time of supremacy of another Semitic power—
that of Assyria in Northern Mesopotamia. In addition to some
laws and legal documents hailing from Cappadocia and dating
from the Old Period, Assyria has left us, from the Middle
Period, an important code of laws of some fifty-nine sections—
namely, a collection of laws relating to women, of a date not
long after 1500 B.C. It was probably a collection, and not
an enactment, but it is of the highest value. Assyria has also
left us some smaller fragments of laws, as well as a large number of clay contract-tablets.

There follows a substantial gap in the records until we
reach the Neo-Assyrian Period of 750 to 700 B.C., which
produces a plentiful number of contracts and other private-
law documents. The Neo-Babylonian supremacy that follows
the fall of Assyria extends from the end of the eighth century
B.C. to the end of the sixth, and embraces, among other
events, the fall of little Jerusalem in 587 B.C. and the capture
of Babylon by the Persian Cyrus in 539 B.C. So numerous

---

[1] Translated into English by R. W. Rogers, *Cuneiform Parallels to the
Old Testament* (2nd ed., 1916); Chilperic Edwards, *The World's Earliest
Laws* (Thinker's Library, 1934).

are the contracts and other private documents of this period that we even obtain from them a detailed knowledge of the important families and industrial houses of Babylon, and there are also fragments of a code.

The Code of Hammurabi and the Assyrian Code and the whole law of this Mesopotamian field (at any rate up to the Neo-Assyrian and Neo-Babylonian periods, which are more advanced) belong to the stage of our Late Codes. With her relatively dense population and great wealth, Mesopotamia was the economic centre of her world, radiating material progress to the countries on her outskirts by means of mutual trade and contact in a degree roughly proportionate to their nearness to her and the relative ease of communications. In the Middle Babylonian Period, on the northern outskirts of that world, there flourished in Central and South-Eastern Asia Minor the empire of the Hittites, and from here survives an important Hittite Code of some 187 clauses—again, not an enactment but a collection—found at the palace of the Kings of Hatti at Boghazkoi. Hittite material culture was simpler than that of Babylon, and the code is one of our Central Codes. Beyond the Hittites stretched the sparsely populated world of barbarism and savagery.

Farther south, and dating from a later age, on the outskirts of both the Babylonian and Egyptian spheres of influence, a Hebrew code of law [1] survives.   It is embedded in the Pentateuch, a religious history of Israel and Judah which was compiled by the priests from earlier materials and published about 375 B.C.   The Code is the oldest document in the Old Testament and is generally attributed to the ninth century B.C.   It is a document of the highest value and interest, although in its present form it has in places been brought up to date to correspond with the contemporary law of the fourth century. In our classification it is one of the Late Codes, coming midway in development between the Hittite and Mesopotamian codes.

Little remains of the laws and contracts of early Egypt.   The material used for the contracts—namely, papyrus—was not so

---

[1] Exodus 21[2] to 22[17].

well preserved as the clay tablet, which is in those climates well-nigh indestructible by time. But the absence is better explained by the fact that the Egyptians were less advanced economically than the Babylonians, and had not the same interest in and genius for law. When civilization and material advance started or continued on their journey north and west, and passed via Crete and Asia Minor to Greece, there, too, the law found a people with little interest and no genius for it. Most of the city-states had their legislators, and their names and the dates when they lived are known, but practically nothing of their work survives, at any rate until we reach a period of greater advance. Zaleucus, of the Greek colony of Locri in Italy, is said to have produced the first written code of laws about 660 B.C.

The march of civilization continued to the north-west, for the forests of Central and Southern Europe formed an effective barrier against trade and communications directly to the north, and the peoples of Germany, Poland, and Russia were as yet too backward, their climate too inhospitable, and their populations too scanty and too distant to be influenced to any great degree. Civilization soon reached Central Italy, and the second of the world's great legal influences came to birth. The fountain-head of the Roman law, according to tradition, was a code of 450 B.C. known as the Twelve Tables; but the story of its compilation is not historical or credible, and there is no reliable evidence as to what it contained. Certainly Roman law had its origin in a system of rules characteristic of the stage of the Late Codes, for the principles of the classical Roman law are plainly derived from the circumstances of that stage of economic progress. As late as 350 B.C. Rome was in severe military and financial straits, engaged within the limits of the town in a struggle for life against neighbouring Latins and invading Gauls. Yet by 265 B.C. it was supreme in Italy, and by 250 B.C. it had also taken to the sea, acquired a fleet, defeated the Carthaginians, and become a Mediterranean —that is to say, a world-power. In the ensuing four centuries, as the Roman empire grew to an extent hitherto undreamed of, the booty of war, the profits of world trade, and streams of free foreigners and slaves poured into the capital in an ever-increasing flow, and the population of Italy and the empire grew ever denser. At the same time the organs of government and the authority of the State became ever more powerful, and, keeping pace with these changes, Roman law attained a degree of development and underwent a change in character not previously witnessed in the world's history.

But the Roman republic had given place to a despotism, and the Roman citizen was fast losing his freedom, and the main source of development of the law was now the process of legislation. From A.D. 250 onwards civil strife and external war imposed an intolerable strain on a falling population, and helped to bring a progressive deterioration in wealth and government. Tribute ceased to flow. The prosperity of the Empire had been built up largely upon slave labour, and from the latter part of the third century A.D. there were not sufficient slaves to maintain its trade, its crafts, and its roads. The currency became debased and the well-to-do townsman all over Europe was crushed by intolerable fiscal burdens. Towns decayed and were deserted, especially in Britain and other outlying parts of the Empire. Legislation lessened as the power of Rome to govern its far-flung territories diminished. It was necessary to sub-divide the Empire, and claimants to the various divisions fought one another. The barbarian [1] tribes of Northern and Central Europe, rising in material culture and now better organized and equipped, were pressing at the frontiers in search of booty or driven by those behind. The Empire could not for ever hold back the weight of these increasing populations. Britain, for long raided and ravaged by Frankish and Saxon pirates, was abandoned. From time to time whole Teutonic peoples, under the name of *foederati* or allies, were settled by the Emperors in this or that Roman province, and were presented with part of the lands and serfs of the provincials. The Roman colonials continued to live under the Roman law of the province; the barbarians ruled their subjects of their own race under native rules. But the prestige of Rome was still indisputable, and barbarian chieftains were often content to acknowledge her as their over-

[1] The term is again used as signifying peoples of the early Third Agricultural Grade.

lord.   From time to time, however, they waged war against
her, and were sometimes resettled, as the price of peace, in
a larger portion of the same or another province of the
Empire.

In the latter half of the fifth century A.D. the West Goths
and the Burgundians, who had settled themselves or been
settled as *foederati* within the Empire (the former in Southern
France and in Spain, the latter in Eastern France and Upper
Germany) emerged as independent States.   They had assimilated something of Roman civilization and culture, and
adopted from her Christianity; and when they legislated for
their subjects it was legislation of the stage of the Central
Codes.   There survives an impressive fragment of a code of
laws of Euric (King of the West Goths in A.D. 466–85).
Among the Burgundians King Gundobald legislated at the
beginning of the sixth century, and a ninth-century edition
survives of an excellent code of his laws together with
later additions.   This legislation, both of the West Goths and
the Burgundians, was in force between Teuton and Teuton
subject, or between Teuton and Roman provincial.   In both
kingdoms codes of Roman law were promulgated by the rulers
for disputes between their Roman subjects.

The Salic Franks were far more primitive.   Though they
had lived for a time on the border of the Empire, on the
northern coast between the Meuse and the Scheldt, and for a
brief period had acknowledged themselves as Roman allies,
they had received little of Roman material or other culture.
It was not till the latter part of the fifth century that they
adopted Christianity.   By then, under Clovis, who ruled
about A.D. 480–510, they had made the whole of Gaul, except
Burgundy and the extreme south, a Frankish kingdom.   In
the middle of the fifth century the Ripuarian Franks—a
kindred tribe standing at a similar stage of progress—occupied
part of the left bank of the Rhine.   From there they spread
southwards, and when they chose Clovis as their King the
territories of the Salic and Ripuarian Franks were united.
Towards the end of the century Clovis appears to have
produced some primitive legislation, belonging to the stage
of the Early Codes.   This is now represented in the Salic

Law, a compilation of the eighth century which includes some later accretions and is couched in a barbarous Latin.

At the same period, within the shrunken Roman empire, the old glories of the classical Roman law were the subject of a new and intense study. In 527 and the following years, under the Emperor Justinian, there was produced a Code of Imperial Legislation; a text-book for students, namely the Institutes; and, above all, the Digest of Roman law. But this great compilation was made within an empire that had already lost Italy to the barbarians. There Theodoric, King of the Ostrogoths from 493 to 526, issued law to his native subjects (the so-called Edictum Theodorici). In 552 Justinian recovered Rome for a brief spell; but soon the Lombard was in the land, and from Rothar onwards Lombard rulers produced a continuous flow of native legislation.

The Germanic invaders who spread over England in the fifth and sixth centuries had also come from beyond the confines of the Roman empire, and were not directly affected by its civilization. According to tradition (which there is no reason to doubt) the enactment of written law commenced under Æthelberht, King of Kent, soon after his conversion to Christianity in A.D. 597, and before the death of Augustine (about 604). The laws of Hlothhere and Eadric followed. The laws of these three kings, which are of the stage of the Early Codes, and survive with others in a text of the twelfth century, begin the series of the Anglo-Saxon laws.

The subsequent Leges Barbarorum, or laws of the barbarian peoples of the continent of Europe, and the subsequent Anglo-Saxon laws of England, which appeared in the eighth and following centuries, belong to the periods of the Early and Central Codes, and we shall refer to them in that place. England during those centuries was uniformly more than a century behind the bulk of the Continent in economic advance, and the same difference appears in their laws as they develop. In some ways it was—at any rate superficially—a strange and abnormal development. It was not till the eleventh century, when the Continent as a whole was reaching the economic stage of the Late Codes, that men became conscious of the compilation of the Roman law, though it had been available for study for five centuries. And it was largely because the Roman law consisted of a body of principles born out of the economic conditions of the early days of Rome, when she also stood at the stage of the Late Codes, that that law now had meaning for the peoples of Western Europe. The effect was startling. At first in Bologna, where Irnerius taught students from France and Germany and Italy, and somewhat later and to a lesser degree in distant and backward and insular England, where indeed philosophy, logic, and principle have never found fertile ground, there blazed out a passionate devotion to the study of the law. So began the revival of learning, and the first step was taken towards the closing of the gates of the Middle Ages and the opening up of the modern world. And so, as in the other lands which we have named in this chapter—in Babylon, Jerusalem, Rome, and the barbarian States—as well as in many other realms, we see the universal phenomenon of law and legal writings ushering in the civilization and literature of every land.

CHAPTER III

RELIGION

IN the course of the Third Agricultural Grade the development of organized religion will give rise to certain conspicuous phenomena in our legal institutions, and it will be necessary and important properly to appraise them. Reluctantly, therefore, we are driven to consider this development in a little detail in the present book, and to offer some introductory observations at this point.

Magic may be defined as the art or power of influencing the course of nature by occult natural means: religion as a "belief in and a regardful attitude towards a supernatural being on whom man feels himself dependent and to whose will he makes an appeal in his worship."[1] If we use the terms "magic" and "religion" with these meanings, we must acknowledge that the importance of magic lessens as humanity progresses. Looking broadly at the course of history we see the sway of magic diminishing until among modern European nations it has almost disappeared. Religion, of which little or nothing is seen among the peoples of the least advanced of our grades, survives almost alone in civilized peoples. But the two definitions suggested above mark merely, as it were, two peaks, between which lies a wide connecting plain out of which both rise. In the first place, we have noticed one characteristic function of magic: that it is largely employed, when other more mundane methods fail, to give man confidence to meet the hazards of life. The same may equally be said of religion, especially among simpler minds. Secondly, we have noticed that magic is in part primitive science—a belief in the power of certain acts, words, or substances, albeit (we would now say) a mistaken belief. Similarly we feel, in regard to simpler minds, that the recourse to God arises partly from a quasi-scientific belief that God created and has supreme power over all, has worked

[1] Westermarck, *Moral Ideas*, vol. ii, p. 584.

miracles in the past, and can work them again. Magic and religion are concerned with supernatural powers, which are at the same time natural powers. Next it is important to notice the connecting links and stages that are plainly apparent or implied in the very definitions that we have chosen. The differences between them reflect the changes in the advancing human mind. As the mind develops, and its consciousness of its surroundings and of itself ever deepens, it appreciates more and more man's dependence on those around him— an appreciation created or enhanced by the increasing scale of social organization as we mount the economic grades—and this outlook man projects into the unknown world around him. The use of mechanical power to influence the outer world when other means fail becomes by degrees the appeal to an almighty being on whom he feels himself dependent. No longer does he presume to compel the intervention of spiritual beings by spells, by commands or threats: he appeals for help and seeks confidence. Finally the fetish he beats and cajoles becomes the all-powerful God, and as kingship and patrilineal and patrilocal society reach the climax of their development the appeal becomes an appeal to an anthropomorphic being, the supreme King and Father. In the last, and only in the last, resort he appeals to the King and Father less by rites and the food of sacrifice, and more by good conduct, taking his standards of good conduct from the familiar and traditional standards of conduct between man and man, for he has no others; and as those standards become increasingly ethical, the ethical element in religion grows, until in some of the most enlightened of modern minds and religions it survives almost alone.

But there is also, especially in simpler peoples, a doubtful border territory not mentioned or implied in either definition. Man's mental images have a continuity which is not limited to the continuity of the physical phenomena which they mirror. A man looks at the figure of his active, bustling friend, now motionless in sleep, and believes in the continuing activity and separate existence of a soul that wanders abroad while its possessor sleeps. His recollections of his own dreams may reinforce that belief. The figure of a dear departed lingers in the mind, and he softens the loss by believing in the continued existence of a tenuous and dwindling soul wandering in death. Affection, or a guilty recollection of past neglect, or a continuity of fear or respect, find outlet in pious acts of tending the grave of a parent, or supplying the soul with food and comforts for its after-life, or propitiating or fending off a dangerous spirit. Even the primitive Australians know a common mystical world of the ideal past, of the time when the physical world was being created, into which the events and figures of their recent life are reflected. Nearer to the border between magic or religion and law, we find among many peoples a belief in the uncleanness of persons who have committed certain acts, and therefore require purification—peoples as far apart as the Andaman Islander who has killed a man, and the Masai or Nandi who has slain a friend or an enemy of the tribe. These acts of tending the grave of the dead for a number of years, and later of sacrificing women and slaves at the obsequies of a Mangbetu noble to accompany him in the hereafter, of purification for unclean acts—do they belong to the domain of religion, or magic, or rather to a wider domain of which religion and magic form merely parts? The importance of these considerations in the present book is partly to emphasize how late and how little is the ethical content of magic or religion.

It is not to be expected that we should see the same regular and universal development in the progress of religion that we see in the evolution of law. The ideas embodied in a people's law must be the ideas of all if they are to be observed and obeyed. Religious ideas vary greatly from individual to individual in the same community, and especially the ethical part of those ideas. Observers of primitive peoples, though they may speak of the same practice of rites, have often obtained accounts of the most varied religious notions from different members of the same tribe. If Micah's fellow-countrymen had held the same religious views as he, we should not have known his name. In modern or mediæval Europe religious ritual observances may be common throughout a people, but he would be a rash man who would pretend to declare the religious conceptions of the man or woman in the street. Legal notions in a community

are part of a social organism that functions as one; and though
we notice that few, if any, tribes appear naturally to adopt
Islam who are of a lower or higher economic grade than that
of the Arabs in the time of Mohammed, there is no apparent
reason why a people of the lowest economic grades should not
be taught to absorb some elements of Christianity. Throughout known history peoples have adopted from foreign lands
the names and cults of gods, while their own system of law
has remained unchanged. Teshub was a god of the Babylonians and of the Hittites. The Romans and Greeks accepted
gods and religions from far and wide. The Gauls of the time
of Cæsar looked to backward Britain as the home and fountain-
head of their own faith, to which their priests were wont to
repair for spiritual refreshment, and in East Africa we find
several tribes who have taken a god and his name from a people
of a strange tongue.

No better example than the Andaman Islanders could be
chosen to exemplify the waywardness of the religious phenomena in a tribe, and the difficulty of assessing the accuracy of
the relevant data furnished by observers. The Andaman
Islanders are almost the lowest of all peoples, judged by
economic standards. Alone, perhaps, of all peoples they are
unable to make fire. Yet they have acquired some iron from
somewhere, and they have also a primitive religion.

The main part of their beliefs in this field, as can be said of
most other primitive peoples, is animism, the belief in
spirits—spirits of the land, the sea, and the sky. The soul,
or shadow, reflection or dream of every Andamanese leaves
him and wanders during sleep; and at death it leaves his body
and becomes a spirit, sometimes living in the sky, but usually
on land or sea. The spirits of land and sea are all spirits of
deceased persons. Spirits are the cause of all sickness. The
Andamanese personify to some extent the phenomena of
nature—for example, the sun, the moon, thunder, and lightning.
The sun is usually the wife of the moon, and the stars are their
children. Upon a lunar eclipse they frighten the moon into
showing himself again by lighting the end of a bamboo
arrow-shaft and shooting it from a bow in his direction.
But they also believe in two beings—one, Biliku, otherwise

called Puluga, and the other (the less important) Tarai. Biliku is in one aspect the north-east wind, which blows for half the year; and Tarai is the south-west wind, which blows for the other half. Biliku shows his anger by causing bad weather (as also do the spirits of the sea), and he shows it in no other way. In the opinion of all, he is angered by three things: the burning or melting of beeswax; the killing of an adult cicada, or the making of a noise when a cicada is singing, morning or evening; and the partaking of certain articles of food. Yet all Andamanese melt all their beeswax in the process of purifying it and making it usable; and the grub of the cicada is regularly eaten. Biliku is not angered by other things—for example, murder—and yet a killer is unclean, and must separate himself from the community and undergo purification for a matter of weeks, otherwise the spirit of the slain man will cause him to be ill.

According to E. H. Man, the distinguished observer to whom we are chiefly indebted for our knowledge of this people during the second half of the nineteenth century, Biliku, in their opinion, was never born, and is immortal and invisible. He created all, and is omniscient.[1] "He is the judge from whom each soul receives its sentence after death, and to some extent the hope of escape from the torments of Jereg-l'ar-mugu is said to affect their course of action in this life."[2] If anything in this field of knowledge is impossible, it is impossible that the Andamanese should conceive of Biliku as a judge—a functionary unknown on earth; the Andamanese who, in the Palæolithic time-scale, belong to an age tens of thousands of years before earthly judges are seen. When we are further told that they believe in a region below the earth to which the wicked are relegated, and which they know under the name of Chaitan (so like Shaitan, the Satan of Indian Mohammedans), it becomes even plainer that they have acquired these beliefs—if we can believe that they possess them—at some recent time from India or some other source. Never-

[1] And yet when they dig up yams—and yams belong to Biliku—they remove the tuber and replace in the ground the crown with attached stem, saying that Biliku will not notice that the yam has been taken.
[2] Man, p. 157.

theless it is plain that the Andamanese have a primitive religion.

There are similar difficulties in ascertaining the beliefs of certain others of the Food-Gatherers. The question whether the Tasmanians had a belief in a Supreme Being before the white man's coming, is impossible to answer in face of the conflict of authorities.[1] The Food-Gatherers of the southern tip of the American continent present almost equal difficulty. The general opinion appears to be that the Yahgan, Ona, and possibly the Alacaluf had a belief in a Supreme Being, but there is no evidence for such a belief among the Chono. It is unlikely that any other of the Food-Gatherers, except those we have mentioned, had any such conception.

But this difficulty in ascertaining the facts of religious belief or observance does not mean that religion has no general history; nor that its advance bears no relation to the advance in law; and if it has a general history, whose advance bears a relation to the advance in law, then the advance in religion must bear some relation to economic advance. In the history of religion the growth of its ethical content, and indeed the decay of magic, are aspects that leap to the eye. In the course of our description of the successive stages of economic progress, certain concomitant stages both of law and of religion thrust themselves upon our notice. It is the variety of religious belief that hides from us the uniformity of some changes. Different religions lay stress on the different needs or thoughts of man, to which they answer. A vast number of religions include a belief in spirits, especially spirits of dead ancestors, and a belief in a Supreme Being or God, or perhaps several gods. In some peoples the belief in spirits, especially spirits of the dead, develops into a religion of which the main component is a cult of ancestors; in others into a religion of which the strongest feature is a belief in one Supreme Spirit or Being associated with the sky, or more rarely with the earth; sometimes it may be that tribes coalescing into a nation bring with them each their own Supreme Being, and polytheism results;

---

[1] See Roth, pp. 53–7. He sums up at p. 57: " We may distrust all accounts of their ideas of a Supreme Being or of a future life. These were mere echoes of what they had been told by Catechists and Teachers."

in others, when chieftainship and patriarchy are well developed, the spirits of ancestor-chiefs or other heroes are raised to god-ship, and polytheism is reached by another route.

At the present stage at the end of the Second Agricultural Grade and the beginning of the Third, while all peoples continue to believe in varying degree in the existence of the soul after death and spirits of the dead, for the first time religion of a sort is to be found almost everywhere, in the sense that there is a belief in the existence of a Supreme Being. He is often the Creator. He is often all-powerful. He is not always invoked or prayed or sacrificed to, for the deceased ancestors, to whom the people pray, may be asked to intercede for them with him. Religion has, however, as yet practically no ethical content, except for the belief that the ancestors are angered and can be mischievous if the traditional ways are not followed on earth, just as they were angry in life when their sons departed from custom.

CHAPTER IV

CATTLE-KEEPERS

ECONOMICS

WE have so far, throughout this book, met with but two methods of gaining a livelihood—the first consisting of food-gathering and hunting (including fishing), and the second the cultivation of the soil. We now meet a third—namely, cattle-keeping, or the pastoral way of life; and its junction with horticulture and hunting brings about a major revolution in human economic systems and all that goes with them, and ushers in the first glimmerings of the modern world. We shall call this [1] the beginning of the age of barbarism, as distinct from the savagery that has preceded it. There have been a few pastoral peoples of a slightly lower stage of material culture than that which we have now reached,[2] and we shall continue to meet with them from time to time as they join the main stream at more advanced stages, but the respects in which they differ from the peoples whom we have considered are on the whole constant. The Pastoralists live mainly by keeping herds of cattle. They may also have flocks of sheep or goats, and in the north sometimes horses. They have little or no cultivation of the soil, and with them hunting is a subsidiary occupation. Their sustenance is mainly derived from milk. Generally the herding of the cattle is confined to the male sex (especially youths and boys), and therefore, since the women have no such independent economic function in the community as they had in the Second Agricultural Grade, their position has fallen *vis-à-vis* the men. Hence also descent and inheritance are patrilineal and marriage is patrilocal, and the father of the family owns the cattle and has a more or less absolute power over the members of the family. These

---

[1] Grade A3 (1).
[2] See, for the Hottentots (who combined pastoralism with hunting only), Schapera, *Khoisan*, Part III.

peoples are backward in the arts, and they do little trade indeed. They are avid of wealth—wealth in cattle. Cannibalism is gone; but there is some slight evidence of human sacrifice, a devotion to a simple religion, and a skilled practice of war created by the vulnerability of their own cattle-wealth to raids and the temptation to enrich themselves at the expense of neighbouring herds.

Such pastoral peoples have been found, and are still to be found, in many parts of the world, but one of their main spheres is and was at the junction between Asia and Africa, and a second in the plains of Eastern Europe, and Western and Central Asia. In North-East Africa, the Sinai Peninsula, Arabia, and the area between the Mediterranean and Persia there were always many pastoral peoples to be found. In North-East Africa we know them as the Hamites. In that area peoples spreading from Negro West Africa have mingled with the pastoral Hamites, and during the last millennium and a half have flooded with rapidity down the eastern side of Africa to the farthest south, ousting or mingling with the former Bushman inhabitants. These Negro-Hamites and Bantu peoples combine with horticulture the characteristics of the pastoral way of life.

Our first stage in the Third Agricultural Grade consists chiefly of East African tribes of the early part of the present century, and the bulk of the German tribes as we meet them in the pages of Julius Cæsar [1] and Tacitus.[2] Our East African peoples consist, in the north, of the naked Nilotes, of whom we may select as examples the Nuer and the Dinka, the Shilluk and the Anuak, all inhabiting the swampy region at the junction of the White Nile and the Bahr-el-Ghazal; and, farther to the south, the Acholi on the White Nile, and the Shilluk-speaking Lango of Uganda, immediately to the north of Lake Victoria. They also include, to the east of Lake Victoria, the so-called half-Hamites, of which we may instance the Masai, and the Nandi, Suk, and Kipsigis. All these peoples

---

[1] See especially *De Bello Gallico*, Bk. VI, *c.* 21 *et seq.* (published 51 B.C.). The Gauls of his time were considerably more advanced, and most belonged to the Central Codes.

[2] His *Germania* was published in A.D. 98.

are predominantly pastoral, especially the northern Nilotes and the pastoral Masai, whose cattle are not merely their wealth and their sustenance, but also their love and their life. To this same stage belong also a few Bantu-speaking tribes immediately to the east of Lake Victoria, of which we may take as examples the Bantu Kavirondo, the Akikuyu and the Akamba, of whom the first-named live a mixed pastoral and agricultural life, and the latter two tribes are predominantly agricultural rather than cattle-keepers, and their goats are of great importance to them and their cattle less significant than elsewhere.

"The Germans," according to Cæsar, "are not an agricultural people and live principally upon milk, cheese and meat." [1] In the pages of Tacitus,[2] only 150 years later, the tribes are described as also growing grain. There is no contradiction here : like our peoples of East Africa, though they grow some grain, their cattle " are indeed the most highly prized, nay the only riches of the people." "They are mostly, however, undersized ; it is chiefly their number that they value." [3]

The quantity possessed by each of these peoples (except the Masai) varies between half a head and two head per person on the average.[4] In addition, the Africans possess large numbers of sheep and goats. The Germans and other Northern peoples also had the horse, in which they took great pride. Agriculture (for it is no longer properly called horticulture) is still mainly the work of the women.[5] The general method of tilling the ground is the shifting system. The pastoral peoples

---

[1] *De Bello Gallico*, Bk. VI, *c.* 22.

[2] *Germania*, *cc.* 5 and 25.

[3] Ibid., *c.* 5.

[4] Among the Bantu Kavirondo, according to Dr. Günter Wagner, the Logoli own on the average two or three head of cattle per family, and the Vugusu nine per family. The Suk, according to Dr. Peristiany, two head per person. The Nuer and Shilluk appear to own a little more than one head per person, and the Lango (1932, official returns adjusted) about half a head per person. These had more cattle before the epidemics of rinderpest in 1890–1 and subsequently. The Masai are estimated to possess a million head of cattle, i.e., about twelve per person.

[5] According to Kipsigis tradition, indeed, agriculture was the discovery of the women. The tribe say they were originally pastoralists.

(that is to say, all the peoples mentioned above except the Bantu) move to new ground when the old is exhausted. The man cuts down the trees, if necessary, and makes a new clearing, burning the timber and bush; and the women and children level and till the ground, with rare assistance from the men. In some tribes, however, the men have also their own fields which they till.[1] In Germany the men do no tilling of the ground; the bulk is left for the slaves (serfs).[2] Only in recent years has the iron hoe begun to replace the digging-stick,[3] and except in Germany the plough has not yet made its appearance.[4] A few southern tribes have some notion of the rotation of crops [5] and some irrigation in the hills,[6] but generally speaking the continued practice of a shifting cultivation makes the rotation of crops unnecessary both in Germany and Africa. Markets have made some slight progress, and the most advanced tribes have cattle, grain, pots, skins, food, and various small manufactured articles to sell.[7] The bulk of the transactions in Germany [8] and Africa [9] are by barter, but cattle and often grain play a prominent part in the estimation of values and as a medium of exchange. There is no specialization of crafts except in the hereditary gilds of the smiths, and, among the Lango, also of the drum-makers. Pottery is generally the work of the women alone. They have as yet no wheel. The chief foods are milk, porridge, and beer.

[1] E.g., Kipsigis, Nuer.

[2] They occupy their own home on terms of supplying their master with a stated quantity of grain, cattle, or clothing (*Germania, c.* 25).

[3] Among the Akamba (1910) the iron hoe was still rare. The Nandi had the iron hoe, but used the digging-stick in rocky ground. The Akikuyu at the same date used a digging-pole and a spear-shaped iron tool. The Lango use an imported iron hoe, and previously a wooden hoe. This area had entered the iron age, not having known bronze.

[4] But among the Kipsigis in 1939 (Peristiany, p. 147) some were selling a few cows to buy a plough from the Europeans, and hiring it out to others at a large profit.

[5] Akamba, Akikuyu, Lango. Not the Nilotes.

[6] E.g., Akamba and Suk.

[7] See, e.g., a list of goods sold (1908) in a Kikuyu market, Routledge, p. 106.

[8] See *Germania, c.* 5.

[9] The Akikuyu also used beads till 1903.

There is no cannibalism and little of human sacrifice.[1] Religion shows a palpable advance,[2] for each of these African and German tribes believes in a single, all-pervading spirit,[3] creator and tribal God,[4] associated with the sun or sky, to whom they address occasional prayers for cattle, for children, and for other human needs,[5] and to whom most do sacrifice.[6] There are also human mouthpieces of the will of the God, prophets who have received a message in visions or other abnormal states of the mind; and there are oracles of the God (for example, at a grove or tree in Germany or among the Lango) who give answers on his behalf, and " priests " who officiate there and announce his will.[7] Even witch-doctors or wizards (as distinct from witches) may exercise powers derived from him. There is also a belief in the existence of spirits, mainly of deceased ancestors, who can be mischievous. With religion

---

[1] But among the Nilotes the rain-maker is a divine ruler of a sort who is often killed when he becomes old or sick. And in Germany the Semnones (*Germania, c.* 39), the Lombards (*c.* 40), and some other tribes (*c.* 9) indulge in human sacrifice in their sacred groves.

[2] Compare, e.g., *De Bello Gallico*, VI, 21, with the *Germania*.

[3] " They do not think fit to contain the magnitude of these celestial beings within four walls, nor to simulate them by any human likeness; they consecrate groves and call by the name of gods an abstraction which is only visible to the eye of reverence " (*Germania, c.* 9). Nor are there any graven images among the Nilotes. Among the Kipsigis, indeed, religious conceptions have so far advanced that whereas some say that Asis is the sun, or lives in the sun, most say that the sun is the form under which human beings perceive the divinity (Peristiany, p. 215).

[4] The names of the God are Asista (Nandi), Asis (Kipsigis), Asai (Bantu Kavirondo), eng-Aï or Ngai (Masai, Akamba, Akikuyu), Juok (Shilluk, Anuak, Acholi, Lango), Kwoth (Nuer), Nhialic (Dinka). Also among the Akamba, Mulungu. The name of a god spreads beyond the bounds of a language or a race. Eng-Aï is Masai for " the rain," and has no meaning in Bantu.

[5] The Kipsigis prays: " Asis, give us cattle. Asis give us strength, etc., etc. I have prayed." An Mkikuyu prays: " O Ngai my father, give me goats, give me sheep, give me children, that I may be rich, O Ngai my father."

[6] Not, however, the Akamba. The Bantu is a less religious man than the Nilote or half-Hamite (see Lindblom, p. 244).

[7] In some German tribes. They are highly revered in the community and can keep order at the public assemblies; but this is probably because these " priests " are also chiefs. See also on this topic *post*, p. 157.

(or religion and magic) comes the notion of the uncleanness of a number of acts, for example the killing of an enemy [1] or anyone else.[2] This is the sum total of the operation of religious belief. Both in Germany and Africa there is also a widespread practice of taking auspices as to the success of a journey, a raid, or a hunt, particularly by examining the entrails of sacrificial animals or observing the behaviour of birds or by casting lots.[3] Magic, on the other hand, has become less important, and the terror of witchcraft and the frequency of charges of witchcraft are reduced. Yet magic is not by any means absent, and indeed among some at least of the tribes the God can on occasion be outwitted, or some magical power may be used against him.

The average size of these populations has increased, but it is difficult to separate off a political community or distinguish a tribe from the larger amorphous conglomeration of which it often forms part. The loose confederacy of the Nuer tribes totals about 300,000 persons, and most of the individual tribes vary between 5,000 and 45,000 souls. The Bantu of North Kavirondo (consisting of some twenty tribes or tribal groups) number (1937) 312,000, and the total Kavirondo population just over 1 million; the Akikuyu (1931) are a tribe of 603,697, and the Akamba (of whom they are probably an offshoot) 235,000.[4] The tribe of the Kipsigis (1939) numbers 80,000, the Suk tribe (at present) 45,000, and the Nandi tribe about 48,000. The Masai number about 80,000.[5] On the other hand, the Shilluk form a nation and kingdom of about 100,000.[6] The figures of the German populations were in all probability of the same order.[7] The density of

---

[1] E.g., Masai, Nandi, Kipsigis, Lango, Nuer, Bantu Kavirondo.

[2] E.g., Masai, Nandi, Nuer, Bantu Kavirondo.

[3] E.g., Germania, c. 10, Kipsigis (Peristiany, p. 164), Lango, and elsewhere.

[4] About 1910. Akamba of Ulu and Kibwezi 115,000; of Kitui 95,000; and of Mumoni 25,000.

[5] Reduced from over 400,000 by the cattle plagues and famines of 1884 and 1890–1 and later. See for some further figures of East African peoples, R. R. Kuczynski, Demographic Survey of the British Colonial Empire, vol. ii (1949).

[6] Estimated by Schweinfurth in 1870 at over a million.

[7] As to the sizes of German tribes, see Krzywicki, pp. 79–83.

population varies from place to place according to its fertility and supply of water, but is on the whole considerable.[1]

The population of most tribes is now made up of isolated homesteads—or, as we should now call them, small mixed farms or small holdings—separated from the next by anything between 100 yards and a mile.[2] The homestead commonly consists of three or four huts, perhaps one for husband and wife, another for cooking or the occupation of slaves, another for a granary where much grain is grown; and if there is more than one wife, a hut for each wife and her children, and a hut or enclosure for cattle.[3] A brother may live with the owner: a son on marriage will commonly build his house near by, and a local clan or lineage tends to form. In some tribes a group of a few homesteads makes up a hamlet. Among most peoples there are, properly speaking, no villages, but where they exist they are small straggling affairs with a population between 50 and 700 souls,[4] and some are now walled [5] or fenced [6] for protection against attack.

As these local groups are self-sufficient, central tribal authority shows little advance in strength. In Africa it is only in the Shilluk nation (and to a less extent among the Shilluk-speaking Anuak) that there is a powerful kingship, and kings were apparently to be found only in a minority of German com-

---

[1] Among the Nuer (where the climate is an alternation of flood and drought) only 7 per square mile. The Bantu Kavirondo show an average density of 140 per square mile, varying between 54 and 1137. Kipsigis: 97. Akamba an average 19. Nandi 66. The soil of Kenya is amazingly fertile except in the semi-desert north. Nearly two-thirds is inhabited at an average of less than one to the square mile. Nearer to Lake Victoria, in the three Kikuyu and three Kavirondo districts, 4 per cent. of the total area of Kenya holds half its population. The whole of Kenya and Tanganyika is inhabited at an average density of 15 to the square mile (see Kuczynski, vol. ii, p. 102).

[2] E.g., Nandi, Suk, Kipsigis, Akikuyu, and the bulk of the Bantu Kavirondo. Tacitus dilates on this, *Germania, c.* 16.

[3] See, for some examples and figures among the Akikuyu, Routledge, p. 119.

[4] E.g., Nuer, Lango and Shilluk.

[5] E.g., Vugusu (Bantu Kavirondo) and Jaluo Nilotic Kavirondo.

[6] E.g., Acholi. Among the Akikuyu the homesteads were surrounded by a high green hedge or stockade.

munities. Among the congeries of tribes known as the Bantu Kavirondo there are political leaders of clans, but not even of tribes. Among the congeries of the Nuer there are chiefs and councils of tribes, but not of all the Nuer. Among the Akamba and Akikuyu strong councils of elders constitute a system of purely local government. Among the Nandi, Masai, Dinka, and Acholi the chief medicine man or rain-maker has a wider authority than anyone else. Religion has advanced enough to help to create something of a bond between independent groups, and the Shilluk king is both the temporal and spiritual ruler of the nation. As for the authority of the local chief, he has in most places, in the words of Tacitus, rather " influence to persuade than power to command." [1]

The scale and organization of war appear to have increased to some extent. The main object of a raid or war is the capture of cattle—that rich prize which is so easy to take. But in addition there is an increasing movement of populations, checked only so long as the British administration forbids war and invasion. In Europe 2,000 years ago the whole continent was moving, generally westwards, and few tribes in East Africa have been in their present habitat for more than three centuries. War is the more or less permanent relationship between the tribes, whether they speak the same language or not, provided they are not so far away—say more than 30 miles—as to be indifferent to one another's existence.[2] Even among the Bantu Kavirondo the tribes belonging to different tribal groups of that people were usually at war with a tribe of another grouping. The common type of offensive is still an attack at night after taking the auspices, and an approach to within striking distance; a halt from about 4 to 5 a.m., and an attack at sunrise. But there is a great improvement in tactical skill and military organization. In a battle of any size the Lango attack proceeds as a rule in three columns, the two wings in advance of the centre, which contains the best and most seasoned warriors. The latter await the advance of the enemy centre when his flanks have been crushed by the advancing wings. According to Tacitus the Germans commonly

[1] *Germania, c. 11.*
[2] But see Kuczynski, vol. ii, pp. 192-4.

attacked in wedge-shaped formation.[1] In a Kamba raid on
the Masai, one column, consisting of the best troops, attacked
the kraal of Masai warriors, and held them off while a second
column attacked the kraal of the married and captured the
cattle, and handed it over to a column of non-combatants,
whose retreat with the cattle, girls, and children was covered
by the first two columns.[2] The army is now commonly
organized upon some territorial or clan basis,[3] and whatever
the political organization or extent of central authority may
be, there are almost everywhere permanent war chiefs [4] or
elected generals [5] who are given great power in war. Among
the majority of these peoples the greatest of virtues is courage
and skill in war, and, according to Tacitus, when not at war
or hunting, the German male gave himself up to feasting and
sloth, leaving the work of the household to the women, the
weak, the aged, and the serfs. Young female prisoners of war
are generally taken as wives or slaves, and the children adopted,
but sometimes they are killed in the heat of battle. The men
are usually slain, but often taken captive. Slavery was very
mild and there was very little of it.[6]

One reason why the tribes are increasingly on the move
is the increase in population, resulting from the rising
standard of living, which produces a certain slight increase
in the birth rate and a drop in infant mortality (partly
owing to the availability of milk).[7] The woman is more

[1] *Germania*, c. 6.

[2] See Lindblom, pp. 189 *et seq.*

[3] Peristiany, *Kipsigis*, p. 164; *Germania*, c. 7.

[4] E.g., Nuer.

[5] *Germania*, c. 7.

[6] See Lugard, *The Rise of our East African Empire*, vol. i, pp. 173–4.
There was none, for example, among the Akikuyu (Routledge, p. 16) and
probably the position was the same in most of these peoples. See also
Kuczynski, vol. ii, pp. 190–2.

[7] We considered that among the Food-Gatherers 50 per cent. of the
children failed to reach maturity. See Driberg, *Lango*, pp. 146–7 for figures
relating to 521 children, of whom only 39 per cent. failed to reach maturity.
Lindblom, p. 87, gives figures showing that 27 per cent. of 231 Kamba
children failed to reach maturity. Hobley gives figures showing that 44·5
per cent. of 126 children of the Jaluo Nilotic Kavirondo failed to reach
maturity. See also Kuczynski, vol. ii.

prolific;[1] and partly because there is so much to do on a mixed farm, we have now reached the stage where children are considered one of the two great blessings, the other being the cattle. Gone are infanticide and (save in the case of unmarried mothers) abortion. Woman is the sole carrier of burdens, and, though treated with great respect in some tribes,[2] occupies from now on an inferior status to the man. Polygamy is in force everywhere in varying degree, but the number of wives taken is by no means increasing.[3] The women do not, as a rule, object

[1] See, for example, Driberg, *Lango*, pp. 146-7, where 100 wives (not necessarily all beyond the age of child-bearing) had 520 children. One wife had seventeen children; twelve had between ten and fourteen each, and twenty-seven had between six and nine children. Yet it is said to be customary among the Lango (as among these peoples generally) that there is no access to the wife from a few months after pregnancy begins until near the time of weaning—i.e., for about three years.

[2] E.g., Lango; *Germania, c.* 8.

[3] There are no reliable figures as to the number of wives that a man has. In Wagner, p. 50, taxation returns are exhibited showing that 88 per cent. of 11,039 men had only one wife each. Returns for taxation purposes are unreliable and probably underestimate the number of a man's wives, but these figures are probably not remote from the truth. (Compare some figures for Basutoland and Swaziland in Kuczynski, vol. ii, p. 31.) Lindblom, p. 87, exhibits figures showing that of twenty-six men all but nine had only one wife. But in both lists an insignificant number had more than two wives. In Germany we are told that the possession of more than one wife is limited to a small proportion of men, of the class of nobles (*Germania, c.* 18). There are more reliable figures of the proportion of the sexes among these African peoples, but not of the time when there was fighting. No doubt the proportion of the sexes varied from place to place (see also Driberg, p. 146). Certainly there is now everywhere a greater proportion of female than male adults, and the disproportion must formerly have been greater. It seems likely that among these tribes (as now) there was a substantial proportion of adult bachelors; that 70 to 85 per cent. of the married men had one wife; that about 15 per cent. of the married men had two wives; and the number of men with over two wives was insignificant, though a few had several and chiefs many wives. The man married at about twenty years of age and the woman at seventeen. Widows were mainly inherited, and are included in the above figures. If the man married a second wife it was not usually till he was about forty years of age and the woman seventeen. More males were born than females, but infant mortality (which was probably about 25 per cent. in the first year and 30 per cent. in the first two years and 40 per cent. by the time maturity was reached) was higher among the males than females, and the mortality among adult males was much higher than among adult females. If so, polygyny was a workable and convenient system,

to a husband taking a second wife. They frequently suggest it, especially when they are no longer young, in order to share the labours of the house. Moreover, the first (or great) wife has commonly a higher status than the rest, and an enlarged household means increased importance for her as well as for her husband.

---

and the fact that there was no access from pregnancy and during lactation (that is to say, for anything up to three years) underlined its convenience. The expectation of life at birth was probably about thirty-five years on the average. The woman gave birth to about five children on the average. A serious famine or cattle-pest would reduce the population by 30 per cent.

CHAPTER V

CATTLE-KEEPERS *(continued)*

MARRIAGE, INHERITANCE, AND PROPERTY

A T the close of the present stage and in the following two stages the institution of the bride-price (or bride-wealth) is universal and at its height. It is the greatest institution in the life of the barbarian, and this is perhaps a convenient point at which to describe it in the typical form which it has now reached. It began as a gift to the bride's father or next of kin to secure his consent to the marriage, and all the human instincts and emotions and human economic needs have gone to shape it and to fashion its rules. So highly do the father of the girl and the young man value her that the bride-wealth has grown and grown until now it is a great mass of property. For example, among the Bantu Kavirondo, the Logoli own on the average two or three head of cattle per family, or half a head per person, and the bride-wealth varies between one and four cows (apart from goats and hoes); the Vugusu own nine head per family, or about two head per person, and the bride-wealth varies between five and fifteen head. It seems unlikely that the Lango own more than half a head per person, yet the bride-wealth varies from four to ten head, and five is normal. Among the Nuer there are about one and a quarter head of cattle per person and the bride-wealth is about twenty head.[1] Accordingly, on the average the bride-wealth is at least as large or larger than the whole of the herd possessed by a boy's father, and as the father owns all the possessions of the family, it is out of the question for the average boy to obtain a wife unaided. The amount varies much, in each tribe, from family to family and season to season. Normally it comprises a heterogeneous collection of goods,

---

[1] Before the epidemics of rinderpest in the 1890's the tribes possessed a greater number of cattle, and the bride-wealth was correspondingly larger. When they were poorest in cattle the bride-wealth was paid in other things.

and custom now specifies the relatives of the bride on her father's and her mother's side who are entitled to a share in it, and defines their proportion; and lays a corresponding obligation on the relatives of the boy to take a share in the burden of providing it.[1] Among the Shilluk in a typical case the bride-wealth consists of seventeen (or some smaller number) of cows, a number of sheep (upwards of seven), and four hoes, two fish-spears, four other spears, a basketful of tobacco, and a bundle of firewood. The girl's father is likely to distribute ten of the cows to the girl's mother's family and four to the mother, and only three are retained by the father. The sheep will normally go to the bride's mother. Among the Germans the bride-wealth consisted in a typical case of a number of oxen, a caparisoned horse, a shield, lance, and sword.[2] The amount is so large that from now on cohabitation often begins when a reasonable proportion has been paid, and the rest is paid at intervals afterwards. In the next stage, in South Africa, it is not rare for a man to be still paying for his mother, and indeed the total sum may not be fixed before marriage.

The necessity of finding the bride-wealth is a great spur to a young man's industry, and postpones his marriage to maturer years. It helps to knit the family together, for he must rely on the aid of his father and relatives to provide the cattle; and it helps him to value more highly the wife it is so difficult to acquire. On the other hand, the fact that her marriage brings wealth to her family increases the self-respect of the bride. Moreover, the bride-wealth is a security to her against ill-treatment, for if she should leave her husband for good cause he would not be entitled to the return of it, and would therefore in all probability be unable to acquire another wife. The receipt by her relatives of shares of the bride-wealth places upon them a corresponding duty and interest to protect her against ill-treatment, if necessary by force, and in the event of calamity to support her and her children. The bride-price marriage has often been sternly put down at mission stations, and the result has often been sloth and increased immorality on the

[1] E.g., among the Nuer, mother's brother and sister and father's brother and sister.

[2] *Germania, c.* 18.

part of the man, and the desertion of a wife no longer valued.

It goes without saying, therefore, that it is a complete fallacy to regard the bride-price marriage as a sale of the woman. It is too fundamental and too much coloured by every aspect of life to be fairly described by analogy to any one other transaction—especially to a modern commercial transaction, the spirit of which is not even altogether that of a primitive exchange or sale. It is true that the words " buy " and " sell " may be used by an African to describe what occurs, and the Code of Æthelberht uses the word " buy " in the same connection, but it is a word that bears a different meaning from our own use of it because of the transactions which it embraces and with which it is associated in the minds of these peoples.[1]

As the communities become larger in size and the bride-wealth larger, disputes in relation to it arise more frequently, and custom defines also the circumstances in which it is recoverable by the husband. These vary somewhat from tribe to tribe, but the most familiar cases at the present stage are where he is entitled to divorce his wife for repeated (not isolated) infidelity; where she leaves him for another man (who will then pay her family a bride-price); and where she dies without leaving a child. In addition, before the marriage, cases are frequently arising where, after payment of part of the bride-wealth, the girl refuses to marry the man, and the father fails to return the goods (which, for example, he may have consumed).

Marriage among all these peoples is patrilocal and descent patrilineal. Yet the relationship with the mother's family is natural and real—we have seen something of it in regard to the bride-wealth—and especially the relationship between a man and his mother's brother.[2] So in Germany, as Tacitus tells us,[3] " a sister's son is held in as high regard by his uncle

[1] Among the Nguni peoples of South Africa, in the next stage, the words used for " buying " a bride and " buying " other things are often separate words.

[2] E.g., Lango, Shilluk, Kipsigis (Peristiany, p. 100), Germans,

[3] *Germania*, c. 20,

as by his father. Indeed some consider this relationship as the more sacred and the closer."

Of notions of property in goods, the main change to be recorded is that they are more firmly vested in the father of the family. To him belongs everything held by all the members of his household—his wife, and his sons and daughters who still reside with him—except that such things as the ornaments worn by the women are considered to be theirs in a practical but not a theoretical sense. The same applies, in a typical polygynous household, to the hut, cows, and goats which the husband assigns to each wife who has borne a child, for her upkeep and that of her family. These are all treated as being the property of her husband, though he allows his wife and her children their use.

There is also no great change in regard to property in land. As in the First and Second Agricultural Grades, notions of public or communal property in land continue to represent about 60 per cent. of all cases, as against 40 per cent. of private —that is to say, of individual or family property. But of the latter group, ideas of family property have continued to decrease and are now insignificant, for here, too, the father's proprietary capacity embraces all that the family holds. And in the more settled and less pastoral of these communities—namely, the Akamba and Akikuyu, where the local community does not move as a whole to new territory as the old is exhausted—there is complete private ownership of land, even of fallow land, including the right to sell it. Only the uncleared land, upon the outskirts of the community, which is used for general grazing or has never been marked out by an individual for his own cultivation, has no private owner.[1] As regards notions of communal property in land, ideas of tribal, clan, and village property will soon be giving way to the idea that the land is the chief's, but the progress is very slow. Land is plentiful, and among many peoples the whole of the local community moves yearly,[2] or at somewhat longer inter-

---

[1] Routledge, p. 39; Hobley, p. 82; Lindblom, p. 164.

[2] Tacitus describes this fully in *Germania*, c. 26, and Cæsar in *De Bello Gallico*, Bk. VI, c. 22. It appears from both accounts that the chiefs assign land to the head of the local or kinship groups, and the latter distribute among the householders.

vals,[1] to a new territory, which it clears and distributes among the fathers of the families in a customary way. The most advanced case is that of the Shilluk nation, which is governed by a strong kingship, ruling through high chiefs of provinces, and below them chiefs of districts, and, still lower, chiefs of village groups. Here the rules as to the holding of land are part of the incipient feudal system of the country. But this is the border of our next stage.

On the other hand, in regard to the inheritance of property there is great progress to be recorded; for now, for the first time, a man leaves behind him property of great value— namely, his cattle as well as sheep and goats (or horses)—and, in the mainly agricultural Bantu tribes, land also. Hence here, too, customs grow up, shaping detailed rules as to the devolution of property on death. It will be seen that the main origin of these rules is that the property is inherited where it is found, and accordingly goes to the member of the household, or other agnate,[2] who is most likely to take it; for that which customarily happens ought to happen.

At the present stage of development the main rules of succession are as follows:

First let us deal with the widows. Like everyone else, they must belong to some social group, and the group they belong to is their husband's group, which they joined by the bride-wealth marriage. On his death, therefore, as a general rule they go by quasi-inheritance to his brothers.[3] But among some tribes the elder widows (if there are more than one) go to a brother, and the younger or youngest to the deceased's eldest son by another wife;[4] and among other tribes all widows go to the eldest son by another wife,[5] and only if there is no

---

[1] E.g., Lango every three or four years.

[2] A man's *agnates* are his relatives counted in the male or female line as the case may be, but not in both. Cognates are blood relatives. For instance, where the patrilineal system of succession applies, a man's brother's son is an agnate: his sister's son is a cognate.

[3] Masai—half brothers by the same father; Nandi—next elder or next younger brother; Nuer—uterine brothers; Kipsigis—brothers, or, in default, cousins.

[4] Akamba of Kitui; Jaluo Nilotic Kavirondo.

[5] Akamba of Thaaka. He does not necessarily keep them all.

son old enough do they go to a brother of the deceased.[1] Among a few of the tribes a future son born to the widow is regarded as a son of the deceased, and even inherits a share of his property as such.[2]   Now the advancing religion begins to creep in and give a spiritual significance to this old rule of inheritance as it develops.

Next, as we have seen, it commonly happens in a polygynous household that, apart from the other possessions of the deceased, he has entrusted to each wife who has a child, a hut, cattle, and land[3] for their sustenance.   This property is not large, but the rule is that it is inherited by her sons.[4]

There remains the rest—that is, the bulk—of the possessions of the deceased (including any cattle there may be in the possession of childless wives).   In the first place, all passes to the eldest son by the deceased's chief (i.e., first) wife.   But he is not entitled to keep all for himself; he takes it as the new head of the family, subject to an obligation to provide for the rest.   Accordingly, in some tribes he is bound to distribute equally between himself and his brothers;[5] among others he is to distribute among them as needed (e.g., to provide a bride-price);[6] among others he gets a somewhat larger share than the rest.[7]   If any of his brothers are too young, he acts as trustee for them till they come of age.[8]   If the eldest son is incompetent, the brothers may in some tribes elect another son in his place;[9] and if there are no sons, a brother of the

---

[1] Bantu Kavirondo; Akikuyu.

[2] Masai, Akikuyu, Dinka, Akum, Kipsigis.   Not Shilluk or Lango.

[3] I.e., where there is private ownership of land—that is, among the Akikuyu and Akamba.

[4] Masai, Nandi, Kipsigis, Lango.   Among the Akikuyu and Akamba she generally succeeds *de facto*, and her eldest son generally succeeds her with an obligation to give a share to his uterine brothers.

[5] Bantu Kavirondo, Akikuyu, Jaluo Nilotic Kavirondo.

[6] Kipsigis, Lango, Akamba of Machakos.   Among the Akamba of Kitui the eldest son distributes under the supervision of his uncle.   Among the Akamba the family continues to cultivate the land together.

[7] He gets the lion's share among the Nandi.   Among the Akamba of Thaaka he gets one animal of each species more than do his brothers.

[8] E.g., Bantu Kavirondo.

[9] Masai, Lango.

deceased inherits instead.[1]   If the sons are young, the brother of the deceased acts as trustee till they come of age, and then distributes, accounting strictly for the young of cattle.[2]

The daughters of the deceased inherit none of his property. As marriage is patrilocal, they have already passed or will in due course pass on marriage into their husband's kinship group, and the property would be lost. But unmarried daughters must be looked after, and—and this is one of the benefits of the bride-price system to the woman—she will bring in bride-wealth to her guardian, and is therefore worth looking after. Among some tribes she is supported by the eldest son [3] or her eldest uncle; [4] but usually by the eldest son of her own mother.[5]   Her bride-price will usually go to him or be shared between her full brothers.[6]   Even the bride-price received for daughters during the lifetime of the deceased is often inherited by her full brothers.[7]   Though daughters do not inherit from their fathers, they commonly inherit their mother's ornaments and household utensils.[8]

No ascendants inherit.   Slaves often inherit as though they had been sons.[9]   Maternal relatives never inherit except that among the Lango (where the position of woman is exceptionally good) a sister's son inherits in default of a son or brother of the deceased.[10]   Among all these tribes headship or chieftainship generally descends in the same way as property.

So far we have been speaking of intestate succession, but we now hear of the beginnings of testamentary succession among

[1] Masai, Nandi, Akamba of Kitui, Lango.   In the absence of brothers the next of kin succeed.

[2] Masai, Lango.   Among the Akikuyu the brother must be younger than the deceased.

[3] Akamba of Machakos.

[4] Some Akamba, Jaluo Nilotic Kavirondo.

[5] Nandi, Akamba of Kitui.

[6] Nandi, Akamba of Kitui and of Machakos, Akikuyu, Bantu Kavirondo.

[7] Nandi, Kipsigis, Akikuyu, Lango.

[8] E.g., Nandi; and even share the plantations worked by the mother till they marry.

[9] E.g., Lango.

[10] But it may be made a condition that he shall come and live in or near the deceased's village.

the more advanced of these tribes—for example, the Kipsigis, Lango, Akamba, and Akikuyu—and we can be sure that there is a good deal more of it than observers tell us.[1] Feeling the approach of death, the head of the family will call its members together and announce his wishes regarding the disposal of his property both in goods and (among the Bantu) in land, partly to avoid disputes and partly to avoid injustice. Except in details his instructions are not likely to depart from the rules of customary—that is, intestate—succession, for these rules are right in his eyes, and if the departures were radical they would not be obeyed. But there are matters on which custom is silent, and matters of other kinds. For example, he might give his weapons to his eldest son. He might declare what debts he owed, and give instructions for their payment, and indeed his heirs would in any case be considered liable to pay them. He might declare what share was to be given by the eldest to the younger sons, saying, for example, that each of them was to have ten goats, and telling them " when they want meat or fat or dowries for wives to ask the eldest brother; but anyone not behaving himself is to take ten goats and go." [2] He might make vaying gifts to each of his wives, and, if the children were minors, say which brother or brothers were to take the property as trustees. Disputes as to inheritance do not normally come before a court but are settled in a family council.

These, then, are the general rules of inheritance, and already, it will be seen, they contain the bases of the modern law of inheritance, including, for example, in the person of the eldest son or brother, the modern executor, administrator, and trustee, and in these oral instructions the modern written will and testament.

---

[1] See Kipsigis (Peristiany, p. 212); Lango (Driberg, p. 173), Lindblom, p. 162, Routledge, p. 143. There are a few traces in the Second Agricultural Grade, see, e.g., Firth, *Economics of the New Zealand Maori* (1931), p. 350, and see Hobhouse, pp. 269, 271.

[2] Routledge, p. 144.

CHAPTER VI

CATTLE-KEEPERS (concluded)

CRIMINAL OFFENCES, CIVIL WRONGS, AND SUMMARY

WE now turn to the subject of offences against order. These are clearly divisible into criminal offences and civil wrongs, both in Germany[1] and Africa.[2] Criminal rules have made a little progress, but their enforcement still savours of lynch law. Death is the usual punishment for all crimes. Of incest the only change is perhaps that it is sometimes less gravely regarded, and the punishment is sometimes something less than death.[3] On the other hand, we hear everywhere for the first time, both in Africa[4] and Germany,[5] of a new addition to the list of crimes—namely, homosexuality and bestiality. Charges of witchcraft, as we have said, show a decrease from what we witnessed at the previous stage. We hear less of it in Africa, and Tacitus does not specifically mention it. A person caught practising witchcraft would commonly die by lynching—usually by being clubbed to death; and the same fate would be his if he showed up in a public place when the popular indignation was hot against him—for example, at the funeral of his alleged victim.[6] The person charged with the offence tends to be a poor and feeble specimen with no family to protect him or her, and the proportion of defenceless old women among the accused steadily grows.[7] There is a visible tendency to confuse brains with

---

[1] Tacitus, *Germania*, c. 12.

[2] See, e.g., *Lango* (Driberg, p. 209).

[3] E.g., Nandi (flogging by the women of the village, and destruction of the offender's house). Rape and adultery are also less severely punished than before (see *post*).

[4] E.g., *Bantu Kavirondo* (Wagner, p. 108).

[5] *Germania*, c. 12.

[6] E.g., *Lango* (Driberg, p. 241); *Bantu Kavirondo* (Wagner, pp. 275-6); *Nuer* (Evans-Pritchard, p. 167); *Akamba* (Lindblom, p. 279).

[7] E.g., *Akamba* (Lindblom, p. 178).

witchcraft. But there is here and there a certain tendency to take a somewhat milder view of the matter by punishing the offender as for a murder—that is to say, by sentencing him to the payment of blood-wealth, after trial and condemnation.[1] The offence of witchcraft is usually the causing of death by witchcraft, and there is now a pronounced element of poisoning in the conception of this offence. As we have seen, organized war is more practised and courage in war more highly prized than ever before, and cowardice in battle is now also a capital offence.[2] Cattle are so highly prized that the persistent theft of cattle from one's own people is also sometimes a heinous offence and capital.[3]

In regard to civil wrongs, an advance of the very greatest importance is to be recorded. It was noted, in our progress through the grades, how the increasing quantity of goods enabled a payment of valuables to be used more and more to buy peace from violent reprisals for a wrong. Now for the first time there are movables—namely, cattle (and to a much less extent sheep, goats, and horses) adequate in quantity and prized above all else—and the peoples of this stage are indeed avid of wealth. Now we reach the point where the rule is that the sanction for a civil wrong is the payment of cattle. Violent sanctions are not recognized; and if, for example, a murderer is killed in reprisal, there must be a payment of blood-wealth on both sides. The civil wrongs continue to be what they were before—homicide; wounding and assault; rape, adultery, and seduction; and theft. Let us begin with homicide, and register the steps by which the advance takes place from one tribe to another during the course of this stage. It will be seen how every factor of the economic and legal situation to which we have referred takes its part in moulding the content of the rule.

Upon a homicide being committed, the killer promptly takes steps to protect his life and property from reprisal on the part of the patrilineal clan—that is to say, the brothers, sons, and

[1] *Bantu Kavirondo* (Wagner, pp. 273–6); *Kipsigis* (Peristiany, p. 193).
[2] *Germania, c.* 12.
[3] Punished by Kingole (organized lynch-law) among the Akamba of Kitui and Mumoni. For the Kipsigis, see Peristiany, pp. 190–1.

cousins of the deceased. For the protection of his life he will (among the Nandi and Masai) hide himself for a time,[1] or (among the Nandi) take sanctuary under a tree [2] or by a river. No Nandi will kill a man who has taken refuge in this way.[3] If he is a Nuer he flees to the hut of a leopard-skin chief, because the chief is the subject of sufficient reverence to prevent anyone shedding blood in his presence; but the next of kin is watching for him, and, if he leaves the hut, will spear him. He has also come to cleanse himself from the blood of the slain.[4] Among the Kipsigis at this point the father (or son) of the killer brings a cow by way of ceremonial apology to the next of kin.[5]

This institution of the sanctuary we now meet for the first time, for it is unknown at previous stages, and we can easily understand why. The conditions required to create the institution of the sanctuary are briefly as follows. First, there must, of course, be a threat to life. Secondly, there must be a place where the refugee is temporarily safe, whether because the place is held in religious reverence or for some other reason. Thirdly, there must not be a general, recognized sanction of death for homicide, for, if there were, the sanctuary would not avail. Lastly, the communities must be so large that homicide is frequent enough to create a practice in this matter. These conditions now exist for the first time; the communities are large; the recognized sanction for homicide is now the payment of goods; and religion, though still in its infancy, is now available to serve a useful social purpose in preventing violent reprisals while blood is hot. But the part played by religion must not be exaggerated. The tribal God plays no part, and it is not by any means always religion that protects the refugee. Given that there are any places where a

---

[1] See Hollis, *The Nandi*, p. 73, and Hollis, *The Masai*, p. 311.

[2] Presumably a tree with sacred associations. As we have seen at this stage, trees or groves have often sacred associations—for example, in Germany and among the Akamba.

[3] The pursuer changes garments with him, and the latter is his prisoner or slave till ransomed by the subsequent payment.

[4] See, for the Nuer, Evans-Pritchard, p. 152.

[5] Peristiany, p. 193.

pursuer will hesitate to shed blood, or be prevented from shedding it, men who have slain will take refuge there.

So much for the steps taken by the murderer to protect his life. As for his property, the next of kin of the victim are fairly entitled to seize any cattle of the slayer on which they can lay hands,[1] or the cattle of any member of his patrilineal clan; and a Nandi who has slain commonly endeavours to forestall them by driving his herd into the cattle-enclosure of a friendly family or clan and mixing it with theirs.[2] But whether cattle have been taken in reprisal or not, the function at this point of the elders (or of the Nuer leopard-skin chief) is to make peace. They urge and entreat the avengers not to resort to violence.[3] On the one hand, self-respect and the pride of the clan urge the latter to vengeance; but the right to take vengeance is not approved by public opinion, and on the other hand an enormous sum of blood-money in the form of cattle is offered.[4] Sooner or later [5] they capitulate and agree to accept it, having lost no dignity in this process; but violent retaliation and feuds do occur.[6] Among the less advanced of these peoples (for example, the Bantu Kavirondo) the amount of the blood-wealth is fixed by the elders to meet the circumstances of each case; but it becomes fixed by custom in the course of the settlement of disputes—just as the market-price of an article is shaped by supply and demand—and most peoples of this stage have arrived at a definite figure of composition for homicide.[7]

The amount of blood-wealth is—as it needs to be—enormous. On the average it is something near double the amount of the bride-wealth in the same community, and would be

[1] For the Kipsigis, see Peristiany, p. 193; for the Masai, Hollis, *The Masai*, p. 311.

[2] Hollis, *The Nandi*, p. 73.

[3] E.g., the Kipsigis, Peristiany, p. 193.

[4] Tacitus describes the same situation in *Germania, c.* 21.

[5] To take an extreme case, among the Masai for two years the dead man's "head is still fresh," and they will not accept the cattle till then (Hollis, *The Masai*, p. 312).

[6] See, e.g., Lindblom, p. 156.

[7] The Germans had apparently arrived at the same point. *Germania, c.* 21: "luitur homicidium certo armentorum ac pecorum numero."

impossible for one man to pay without assistance. For example, among the Nuer, who possess about one and a quarter head of cattle per person, the bride-wealth is about twenty head, and the blood-wealth between twenty and forty head.[1] The Lango own about half a head of cattle per person, and the bride-wealth is about five head and the blood-wealth seven head.[2] Accordingly the killer seeks the assistance of his relatives, who, in the ordinary way, will contribute provided he pays what he reasonably can; and in the same way the blood-wealth received is shared among the agnates in a well-known proportion, so that, for example, among the Kipsigis every member of the clan-division of the victim gets some share of the cattle or its calves.[3] In this way the solidarity of the kinship group expresses itself in the rules that evolve. The killer's group—like its counterpart in Australia—has an interest in buying peace, for otherwise the persons and property of the members would be liable to violent attack. But if the same man committed the offence a second time they might decline to assist, saying, " Your blood be upon your own head "— that is to say, " Meet your blood-liability with your life," [4] and if the killer cannnot pay, the next of kin of the victim will kill him, or possibly a relative. Among the most advanced of these tribes a marriageable daughter or sister of the killer may be accepted in place of cattle,[5] or a person without means may work off the debt in slavery.

[1] For an East Jikany aristocrat twenty; among the Lou and Jagei tribes forty head (see Evans-Pritchard, p. 217).

[2] Among the Kavirondo generally (according to E.A.L., vol. 2, p. 141) the figure is relatively smaller. If the killer owned one or two cows, the elders would take all. If he owned five, they would take four; if ten, they would take seven. Of the following figures, taken from various tribes and sources, the first is the blood-wealth for a male adult; the figure in brackets is the bride-wealth :

Nandi, five cows, four bulls, fifteen goats (one cow, one bull). Shilluk, over ten head (over ten head): cattle owned by the nation about one head per person. Kipsigis, ten head, fifty goats (eight cows, twenty-three goats). Masai, 100 head. Akikuyu, 120 goats, one cow (forty goats, five sheep). Akamba of Kitui, fourteen cows, one bull (three cows, two bulls). Akamba of Thaaka, sixty goats (twenty-eight goats). Akamba of Mumoni, five cows (twenty-eight goats).

[3] Peristiany, pp. 193 et seq.   [4] E.g., Kipsigis (Peristiany, p. 199).
[5] E.g., Shilluk, Lango.

These rules are shaped not merely by the presence in the community of an adequate quantity of valuable possessions, but also by the relative absence of strong central authority. In its absence no other workable sanction could be envisaged except the lawless feud. It is also to be observed that these rules depend much on the relation of the two groups to one another. If the killer and his victim belong to the same kinship group, there will commonly be no payment whatsoever. There is not an avenging and a defending group; and there is no good purpose to be served in still further reducing the strength of the family or clan, or paying out cattle from one's left hand to one's right. If the killer and the victim belong to different tribes—or, in some communities, even different sections of tribes—there will be no common chief, headman, or other person who by his influence or authority over both groups may secure the payment and acceptance of a composition, and a feud or war or nothing may be the outcome. In a more advanced community, such as the Akamba, the strong local council enforces implicit obedience to its orders and punishes disobedience.[1] And the extreme case at this stage is represented by the strong Shilluk monarchy, where (by a new and important development of which we shall see more in the next stage) the greater part of the payments for homicide and other serious wrongs are collected by the king. Out of the ten or so head of cattle payable for homicide he is likely to keep for himself all except one or two head, which he allows the next of kin of the deceased to have.[2] The Germans are almost as advanced, for Tacitus tells us that " part of the fine is paid to the king or the State, and part to him who is being vindicated, or his relatives." [3]

These sanctions (except the fines payable to the king or the State) are clearly civil and not criminal in their nature. Such distinctions as are found in them are generally based on the extent of the loss to the clan of the slain, and not on the extent of the guilt of the offender—not, that is to say, on the

---

[1] Among the Akamba of Thaaka, for example, a man refusing to obey an order of the Nzama (or local council) is beaten and pays a bull to the elders.

[2] Seligman, *Pagan Tribes*, p. 46.   [3] *Germania, c.* 12.

presence or absence of an intention to kill. Nor has the community any interest—as it has in a criminal offence—to prevent a settlement between the parties. On the contrary, to secure such a settlement is the whole aim and purpose of such governmental authority as exists. Among some of the Akamba, whose law is more advanced than that of most of the rest, there is a distinction between intentional and unintentional killing,[1] and indeed the latter has the special name of Mbanga. But there is a payment for accidental killing of about half of the usual amount, and there are no tribes at this stage among whom accidental killing is free of blood-wealth. The main distinction among the peoples of this stage is between the killing of a man and the killing of a woman, for which again the composition is usually a half.[2] For a male the sanction is usually the same whether he be man or boy.[3]

The compositions for wounding and assault are lesser sums, and they do not begin to be fixed in amount till a later point—that is, till we reach the Akikuyu, Akamba,[4] and Lango. For example, among the Nuer there is no payment even for flesh wounds, and among the Nandi there is no composition even for loss of eye or limb, but the offender must slaughter cattle from time to time to provide the victim with food till he recovers. Among the Akamba there is a short table or code of payments for injuries, measured by the gravity of the loss to the body, and an example, taken from the Akamba of Kitui, is given below.

The sanctions for rape, adultery, and seduction are also pecuniary and strikingly small in amount—something near the amount of composition for loss of a toe. But in certain events they may be larger; for example, among the Akamba, if the woman should die in childbirth, a sum equivalent to her

[1] E.g., for unintentional killing, Akamba of Kitui (half composition); Akamba of Mumoni (bride-wealth for killing a woman); also Masai (elders settle the amount).

[2] All Akamba and Akikuyu.

[3] But among the Masai the composition is half for a boy, and among the Akamba of Kitui it was formerly so.

[4] But even among the Akamba they are not absolutely fixed, and are likely to vary with the defendant's means, see Lindblom, p. 156.

blood-wealth or bride-price may be payable, on the principle that the adulterer's act has caused her death. The sanction for rape is sometimes somewhat larger than for adultery or seduction. Among the Akamba a husband finding the adulterer *in flagranti delicto* could formerly kill him with impunity, but now no longer. Seduction of a young woman is often a mere prelude to marriage, and is cured by payment of a bride-price in the ordinary way, and among many or most of the peoples of this stage it is no wrong for a man of the husband's age-set,[1] or a brother, to have intercourse with his wife. Such a rule is widespread, and characteristic of the present stage of advance.

The sanction for theft, also, is usually pecuniary, and consists as a general rule of multiple restitution—that is to say, payment of an amount which is a multiple of the value of the thing stolen—but it also sometimes includes a beating; and for the repeated theft of the more valuable property, as has been said, there may be criminal and capital sanctions.[2] But the general rule is multiple restitution. This is a civil sanction. We must not feel surprise at the thought that for a civil wrong a man may receive more than the amount of his pecuniary loss. This is universal in civil law until modern times. Nothing less would be considered right; if the rule were simple restitution, the thief could never lose by his wrong, and moreover sanctions must be large if they are to be accepted as an alternative to violent reprisals. Like the modern damages for libel and slander, trespass, and breach of promise of marriage, they must afford compensation for wounded feelings as well as for pecuniary loss.

To sum up, as representing the most developed law of this

[1] E.g., Masai.

[2] Nandi (first offence, payment of four times the value of the thing stolen, plus a beating; second offence, confiscation of half his property, and destruction of his grain and a branded mark on the forehead; third offence, strangled and his cattle slaughtered). Masai (double value). Akamba of Kitui (single restitution plus one bull; for honey-barrel stealing, Kingole). Akikuyu (two to four-fold restitution; incorrigible thief killed). Lango (theft of cattle, three-fold restitution; if caught in the act of stealing, may be killed). Kipsigis (theft of cattle formerly capital; now double value).

stage, let us take the following code of civil sanctions of the Akamba of Kitui. It is, of course, unwritten; writing is unknown:

Homicide (except by accident)—
    Of a man . . . . . . 14 cows, 1 bull [1]
    Of a woman . . . . . . 7 cows, 1 bull
    Of a child (formerly; now according to sex) 6 cows, 1 bull
Homicide (accidental—Mbanga)—
    Of a man . . . . . . 7 cows, 1 bull
    Of a woman . . . . . . 4 cows, 1 bull
    Of a child . . . . . . According to sex
Injuries (intentional or not)—
    Loss of a finger . . . . 1 cow, 1 bull
    Loss of a toe . . . . . 1 bull, 1 goat
    Loss of a leg or arm . . . 7 cows, 1 bull
    Loss of both legs or arms . . 14 cows, 1 bull
    Loss of an ear . . . . 5 goats
    Loss of an ear (accidental) . . 2 goats
    Tearing an ear . . . . 1 goat
    Loss of an eye . . . . 1 cow, 1 bull
    Loss of both eyes . . . 14 cows, 1 bull
    Loss of a tooth . . . . 1 goat
    Loss of a tooth (accidental) . . Pot of tembo
    Loss of nose . . . . . 1 cow, 1 bull
    Loss of a testicle . . . . 4 cows, 2 bulls
    Loss of both testicles . . . 14 cows, 1 bull
    Loss of penis . . . . . 14 cows, 1 bull
Homicide or injury by a person of the same
    village or family . . . . Half composition
Adultery . . . . 1 bull, 1 goat
    If child born and dies before composition for
    adultery is paid . . . . 2 bulls, 2 goats
    If woman dies . . . . Blood-money
Rape . . . . 1 large bull equal to 1 cow
Bride-price . . . . . . 3 cows, 2 bulls
Theft—
    General . . . . . . Restitution plus 1 bull
    Honey-barrel stealing or habitual stealing . Kingole

[1] One bull goes to the tribunal as a court fee in the numerous cases where it is mentioned above.

We now turn to the means of trial. The holding of courts is a function of political authority. The hearing and just decision of disputes is a part of good government and the maintenance of order. Followers of the same leader naturally bring their disputes to him, for he alone has sufficient authority or influence to get his decisions carried out, and a reputation for good decisions increases his influence. If the complainant and the alleged wrongdoer belong to different tribes (or, among a people like the Bantu Kavirondo, who have only political leaders of clans, even if they belong to different clans) there will be no common chief whose authority may carry acceptance of his judgment. But within these limits all these peoples have courts. Among the less advanced, such as the Nuer, Dinka, Masai, Nandi, and Bantu Kavirondo, the courts are held by a few local elders; and this is also true of most courts among all these peoples. In the more advanced peoples, sometimes there is a chief who presides over the elders, and among the Kipsigis there is a personage whose special function it is to preside over the elders of a group of villages.[1] Their decisions are usually obeyed, for public opinion is behind them. A court of Kikuyu elders, before announcing its decision against a party, usually advises him to consult his friends, and he then retires with his supporters, and returns having admitted his guilt to them, and asks for lenience.[2] Among the Akamba so strong is local government that severe punishment is meted out for disobedience to the order of a court.

Claims are made before the court by the injured group, the head of the family or clan supported by its members. No woman has the right or need to appear in the role of a plaintiff, for her husband or father claims for her, but she may give evidence. In the developed court the tribunal receives a fee of a recognized amount for its services—for example, among the Akamba and the Kipsigis, in a case of homicide, a bull. Some disputes do not come before these local courts: for example, quarrels between members of the same family as to the right of inheritance, or upon any other topic, will normally be decided by a family council of elders, and even a homicide between members of the same family—at this stage as in the grades below—is usually settled within the family. Nevertheless the bulk of disputes are brought before the courts,

---

[1] Peristiany, pp. 178 f.   [2] Routledge, p. 204.

including a number of disputes in which no relief or remedy is asked for.

In its more developed form the hearing is taking much the same general form as in a modern English court. The chief (if there is a chief) and members of his council of elders sit in public. The proceedings are usually protracted, and the more curious among the population listen mainly in silence. But there is generally intense local interest in the proceedings of a primitive court, and the audibly expressed observations of the population necessarily have a certain effect on the mind and judgment of the court, which is always anxious that its decisions should meet with the approval of public opinion. The accused answers the complaint, and is cross-examined. The witnesses are heard, and there is considerable public confidence in the court. The chief (if a chief sits) listens in silence, and at the end passes judgment. The relation between him and the elders who sit with him is in the more developed court much the same as in other matters of government. They are his advisers, and their views influence him. If they are all of one mind he would not usually be thought entitled to decide against their opinion.

The trial is by evidence on both sides, and the evidence is, of course, unsworn. But sometimes the charge is upon a matter on which, in the nature of things, there will normally be no evidence except the defendant's—a charge of witchcraft, or a claim for compensation for adultery. How, then, is the court to decide the matter?

We have seen primitive man, in a number of instances, when he desires to bring about a particular result, and when normal, mundane methods fail him, adopting supra-natural means, whether they be called magic or religion or misconceived science. Similarly when he desires to ascertain facts upon which no evidence is forthcoming—for example, when he wishes to foretell how some future event will fall out—he betakes himself to the like means. All these peoples, as we have seen, employ to a large extent divination and the taking of auspices as to the success of a journey, a raid, or a hunt.

By a similar process of the mind, where there is no evidence (except the defendant's) on which a case can be decided—and only where there is no evidence [1]—methods of divination are in use to ascertain the guilt or innocence of the defendant. In practice this occurs almost always upon a charge of witchcraft [2] or a claim for adultery,[3] and occasionally upon a claim for theft where there was no witness of the act. In order to secure the added efficacy of a deterrent—for if the defendant does not undergo it he will be treated as confessing—or to extract an admission of guilt, the method of divination employed usually takes the form of an ordeal. These are of great number and variety, and one particular form tends to come into general use in each area. They are of three kinds—one a species of divination [4] (not strictly an ordeal at all), the second the act of undergoing a dangerous test, and the third a species of oath. The latter form of ordeal is later than the others. Typical examples are as follows : " May this (animal, spear, *kithito*, etc.) kill me if I do not tell the truth; or " May I die like this *sengi* " (beating a goat to death at the same time); [5] or " I swear by my sister's garment " (i.e., loin-covering); [6] or " by the dead," or " by my dead father." There are no ordeals by the name of the tribal god. The medicine-man commonly conducts the ordeal,[7] for its administration by an expert lends an impressiveness to its use, and this is of the highest importance to its efficacy. The ordeal is not applied to a witness.

Let us now attempt to define, in regard to the peoples of this stage, the position so far reached by the advancing law. Courts are to be seen everywhere, and in the more advanced tribes are strong and busy, and therefore laws can be said to be in force. They relate mainly to civil wrongs, and, in a much smaller degree, to crimes. The sanctions for most wrongs are,

---

[1] See, e.g., Lindblom, p. 165.

[2] In regard to witchcraft we saw, even among the Australians, detection of a witch by observing the direction in which the body of his victim pointed, or by mere declaration of the sorcerer.

[3] See, e.g., Seligman, *Pagan Tribes*, pp. 102, 129, 194, 334, 530.

[4] E.g., by watching the behaviour of an animal, Driberg, p. 240.

[5] Akikuyu.

[6] Masai (cf. *Lex Frisionum*, Tit. 12)—or, in the case of a woman, " by my father's garment."

[7] E.g., Lindblom, p. 173; Routledge, p. 213.

in the more advanced tribes, clearly defined—for homicide; for rape, seduction and adultery; for theft; and for wounding. There is also an occasional suit in relation to a new type of wrong—namely, trespass to land. There are well-defined rules as to marriage, inheritance, and property, and a few disputes upon these topics come before the courts—a rare case of a disputed claim to an inheritance of land; a few claims for the return of property (e.g., a cow) entrusted to a neighbour or friend, a few claims for the return of bride-wealth on the ground that the woman has defaulted, or for some other reason, and an occasional claim to a debt.[1] But the bulk of disputes relate to civil wrongs. Our code of Kamba sanctions, set out above, is to the same effect: it relates to nothing but sanctions for civil wrongs and the amount of the bride-wealth. Nowhere in these tribes is there to be found any technicality of procedure, though, of course, all courts have their regular way of getting through their business.

It seems obvious, therefore, that law is in full force. But we must not too hastily interpret the native mind. Very few of these peoples have a notion of law in the abstract. They are familiar with courts and actions in the courts, and find them fascinating, and they are familiar with judgments, but they have no word for " law." Even the Akamba, whose elaborate list of sanctions we have set out above, have no word for " law " in their language,[2] nor have the bulk of the other tribes whom we are considering. Where a word for " law " is found—as, for example, " *pitet* " among the Kipsigis—the main constituent in its meaning is the idea of " custom." The word, we are told, includes in its meaning " customs which carry with them definite material sanctions." [3] This is the farthest point, in this regard, reached by any of our tribes. The nearest that most of them approach to the idea is probably represented by " custom " and by " judgments."

[1] See for a selection of cases tried, Routledge, pp. 204–15.
[2] See, e.g., Lindblom, pp. 152–3. [3] Peristiany, p. 183.

CHAPTER VII

THE EARLY CODES

THE PEOPLES

WHEN we hear of the German peoples in the pages of classical writers after Tacitus, the names of tribes and groups of tribes are changing. This results no doubt from the movements of peoples and increases of population, but above all it results from the coalescence of new confederacies and nations. From about the year A.D. 200 we hear, for example, of the Alemanni (or All-men) on the upper Rhine;[1] and forty years later there appear on the lower Rhine[2] the Franks (or Freemen), who have taken the place of the tribes of that region whose names we read in Tacitus, and of whom nothing more is heard.[3] In A.D. 358 we first hear of the Salian or Salic Franks (Freemen of the Sea), who had now moved some little distance southward and dwelt in the area between the Meuse and the Scheldt. By this name they were distinguished from the Ripuarian Franks, who inhabited the bank of the Rhine. In that year the Salic Franks were defeated by Julian, but were left in possession of their lands as *foederati* or allies for protection against other barbarians. For a time they even served in the Roman forces, but by the year A.D. 400 Roman civilization and the Roman tongue had receded from the whole of this area, and with it had disappeared the Christian religion. The tribes of the Salic Franks ceased to recognize the authority of Rome and continued to press to the south.

When Clovis succeeded his father about A.D. 481 as king of the main body of the Salic Franks, they had advanced as far as the Somme through the crumbling ruins of the Roman

[1] Between the Main, the frontier of Upper Germania and Rhaetia.
[2] Between the Main and the North Sea.
[3] With the possible exception of the Chamavi of Tacitus, whom we meet as the Franci Chamavi in the Carolingian age and earlier.

frontiers. At his death in 511 he had become the founder of the French nation. He ruled over all the inhabitants of Gaul, Franks and Gallo-Romans alike, except for the kingdom of Burgundy, and Provence and Septimania in the south. The Ripuarian Franks had been induced by devious means to accept him as their king, and on Christmas Day in 496 he had astutely gained the support of the bishops by becoming converted to orthodox Christianity, instead of espousing the Arian heresy like the Burgundians and Visigoths. He had procured or connived at the assassination of the three or four independent kings of Salic tribes, and he had taken Alsace from the Alemanni. In the last few years of his reign, in a barbarous Latin, he had given written laws to the Salic Franks, now represented by the Salic Law, of which the oldest and best surviving text dates from the second half of the eighth century.

Nevertheless what had occurred was that a lightly knit nation of barbarian and mainly pastoral peoples had been let loose upon a civilization over half a millennium old. For a time the skill of determined rulers, the proceeds of plunder, old institutions and habits of government (even while they decayed and dissolved) maintained a French kingdom, but the kingdom was far too large to be held together by such organization and wealth as a culture of this stage can produce, and its break-up was inevitable.

Upon the death of Clovis, in accordance with Merovingian custom, the kingdom was divided equally between his four sons. There ensued between them and their successors a long struggle for the mastery, in which guile, war, and murder were frequent implements. Yet for a time the boundaries of the kingdom were widened, till they embraced all France except Septimania, and extended into Germany and Italy.

The seventh century was an era of sordid decadence. The fading light of Roman culture had been extinguished. The kings were puppets who married in childhood and died of debauchery. The country had broken up into the three kingdoms of Neustria, Burgundy, and Austrasia. The regal authority was wielded and usurped by the mayor of the palace of each kingdom, and in Austrasia the mayors formed a dynasty of their own. The struggles between the kingdoms were intense and war was almost continuous, till at length Pepin the Second, mayor of the palace of Austrasia, by his victory in 687 against the mayor of Neustria, became master of all Gaul except Aquitaine, and so remained until his death in 714. His successor, Charles Martel (716-41), by his great victory near Poitiers turned back the flood of Arabs who had emerged triumphant from the conquest of Spain. He extended Frankish rule wide into Germany, and before his death, though but mayor of the palace, was able to divide the kingdom between his two sons. When the elder, Carloman, entered a monastery which he had founded, the younger, Pepin, succeeded as mayor of the palace.

There followed a close relationship and a certain intermittent alliance between the growing powers of France and the Pope, a relationship which was fraught with important consequences for both. The position of Pepin and Pope Zacharias had certain common features. In France, though the power was in the hands of Pepin and his dynasty, he was not of the royal clan, and a succession of long-haired Merovingian puppets continued to reign, being displayed from time to time to the public so as to lend authority to the regime. The titular sovereign of Rome was the Emperor of the Romans, who still sent his edicts and messengers from Constantinople and was represented by his Exarch at Ravenna—though now that the Lombard monarchy controlled the bulk of Italy, the Exarch's road from Ravenna to Rome was a mere ribbon and the Bishop of Rome was its true ruler. In 751 the Lombards occupied Ravenna itself. With the encouragement of the Pope, Pepin had himself elected king by an assembly of the Franks, and the long-haired Merovingian of the day was thrust into a cloister with his son. When the Lombards continued to expand in Italy and to threaten Rome, Pope Stephen II betook himself to Pepin in an appeal for assistance and anointed him and his sons Kings of the Franks and Patricians of the Romans. To support the claims of the Pope there was produced to the Franks the "Donation of Constantine," a document forged about this time, by which that Roman emperor of four and a half centuries earlier is made to confer upon the Pope the rule over all bishops, to endow him with mighty estates in East and West and a rank and dignity above an emperor, and indeed to abandon to him Rome and all Italy while he removed his capital to the East. Pepin is said to have guaranteed to the Pope practically the whole of Italy including the Exarchate. In 754 and 756 he conducted expeditions which brought about the surrender of the Lombard King, and the deliverance of Rome from peril at his hands; and this connection with Rome brought a certain accession of culture to the Frankish domains. In the remaining years of his reign he forced the Saxons to heel, and effected the subjection of Aquitaine.

What Pepin had begun, his elder son Charles the Great continued and brought to achievement. He solemnly promised to the Pope to honour the undertakings that Pepin had given. He destroyed the Lombard kingdom and founded a lordship over Italy, including the papal dominions. By successful war he extended the boundaries of the Frankish Empire till it reached from Northern Spain to the Baltic and from the Atlantic beyond the Elbe.

To hold together this vast empire a great increase in the royal authority was needed, and this he had achieved by building a theocratic state, rearing himself, as it were, upon the structure of the growing Church. When Leo III succeeded as Pope he did homage to Charles as his overlord. Charles busied himself also with doctrine, called and presided over important synods, and passed ecclesiastical ordnances and measures for the regulation of the life of the Church. Finally on Christmas Day 800, to his apparent surprise and reluctance, he was crowned by the Pope in the name of God as Emperor of the Romans.

In more domestic matters a vast number of capitularies, or enactments, were issued to deal with a multitude of problems and details. Counts appointed by Charles governed their districts as representatives of the king, and tribal organizations slowly faded, at any rate in the West. The bishops in ecclesiastical matters were equally important officers of the state. Envoys of the king (*missi dominici*) toured the realm and inquired and reported on all things. There was a revival of letters, and at the king's behest, in the last few years of his reign, documents were prepared setting out or describing the legal rules of various outlying provinces of the Frankish Empire—the Lex Saxonum, the Lex Frisionum, the Lex Anglorum et Werinorum, and the Lex Francorum Chamavorum.

But this Empire rested upon the genius of Charlemagne. It was inevitable that upon his death it should be divided between his successors according to custom, and subdivided in every generation. It was inevitable that intestinal strife, together with the scourge of the Viking pirates and the attacks of Hungarians and Saracens, should break up the Empire, and that great nobles should strengthen their hold upon their districts and turn them into hereditary under-kingships, building up the complete feudal system that is later familiar to us.

We shall take the Franks of A.D. 500 to the death of Charlemagne in 814 as representative of the stage of advance which we have now reached—namely, that of the Early Codes. Across the Channel, beginning and ending a century later, we find representatives of the same stage in England.

The Angles, Saxons, and Jutes, who overcame what is now England from the middle of the fifth century, hailed mainly from the neighbourhood of Frisia in Northern Holland. They had never been Roman allies or directly influenced by Roman culture, and they were more backward than the Salic Franks. Moreover, they came not as organized armies but by sea and in small parties. In the course of the sixth century they formed ten small warring kingdoms, made up of innumerable smaller chieftainships, which covered the country. At the end of that century the leading kingdom was that of the people of Kent, ruled over by Æthelberht. In the year 597 he was converted by Augustine, who headed a mission dispatched by Pope Gregory the First. There survives in a twelfth-century manuscript the Code of the Laws of Æthelberht, traditionally legislation enacted by that king after his conversion. The same document contains additions to these Kentish laws, attributed to Hlothhere (who reigned from 673 to 685), and his successor Eadric, and Wihtred, who ruled at the end of that century. The supremacy then passed further north and west. Ine of Wessex, a contemporary of Wihtred, left a body of laws, and in the Midlands Penda had built a

Mercian kingdom out of a congeries of small tribes. The struggles between Mercia, Northumbria, Wessex, and the other English kingdoms were long and fluctuating. Mercia held the lead throughout the eighth century, and at the close of Offa's long reign at the end of that century he is said to have produced some legislation, but none of it survives. Soon Wessex under Egbert took the place of Mercia as the dominant power in England, extending so far to the north as Northumbria. But the ninth century was a period both in England and France of continuous attacks by Viking pirates, raiding, plundering, and burning on an increasing scale, and finally invading and settling. Letters and learning almost vanished. From about 875 the Danes were able to colonize Eastern England, mainly by imposing warriors upon the English cultivators. At the same time Wessex was attacked by land and sea. Alfred the Great, who succeeded as king in 871, conducted a desperate defence in the marshes of Somerset, and, biding his time, at length defeated the Dane Guthrum near Westbury. Thenceforth he was free for the most part to busy himself with domestic organization and reforms and the revival of religion and learning. A body of laws survives associated with his name. When he died in 899, his kingdom did not effectively extend north of the Thames, and the rest of England was broken up into a larger number of chieftainships than in the century before. It would then have seemed incredible that in the ensuing fifty years, under Alfred's son, Edward the Elder, and his three sons, the house of Wessex would so far extend its domain that the King of Wessex would be the only recognized king throughout all England.

We shall take the peoples of England of the period from A.D. 597 to 900 as representative of the stage of the Early Codes.

As examples of the same stage of progress among the peoples of the present day, we shall take the whole of the Nguni peoples of South Africa.[1] They are part of the Southern Bantu, tribes of mixed Bushman, Hamitic, and Negro race, who, beginning perhaps as long ago as A.D. 500, spread rapidly down the eastern side of Africa in much the same way that

[1] For authorities on the Nguni, see Schapera, *Select Bibliography of South African Native Life and Problems* (1941).

Teutonic tribes spread into Gaul, Spain, and Italy. By the fifteenth century they had reached South-East Africa, but they found no civilization awaiting them, either to absorb or destroy. The Nguni peoples consist of a few hundred tribes living in a long belt of South-East Africa stretching from Swaziland in the north through Natal and down to Port Elizabeth in the south, and from the escarpment of the Drakensberg to the sea. The Southern, or Cape Nguni, consist mainly of the Xhosa, Thembu and Mpondo, and the Fingo and other recent immigrants. The Northern Nguni are the Nguni of Natal, who number more than 200 independent tribes, including the Zulu, and are more advanced than the Southern Nguni.

Until the eighteenth century, wars between the tribes of South Africa arose usually out of disputes over boundaries or water-rights, the lifting of cattle, ill-treatment of a visiting subject, refusal to deliver up a refugee to a neighbouring chieftain, and the like. They were common enough, and took the shape—now so familiar to us—of raids upon an enemy village, which was reached by night and rushed at dawn. As many men as possible were killed, the cattle, young women, and children were taken and the huts burnt, and the raiders beat a hasty retreat. The chief kept as much of the booty as he desired, and distributed the rest among his warriors and council. Raid and counter-raid continued until the weaker chief sued for peace, and, if it were granted, paid a regular tribute of cattle or other property in token of submission and allegiance, commonly being permitted to retain a large measure of autonomy. Or then—or later if he discontinued the payment of tribute and was attacked and defeated once more—his whole territory might be absorbed, and he himself might be retained as district chief, unless the victor substituted a relative of his own.

But by the third quarter of the eighteenth century, partly because of increasing pressure of populations, the process had grown in scale and changed in character. An era of wars of conquest arose, tribes overcame and absorbed their neighbours, and kingdoms emerged. The familiar story of Shaka and the Zulu kingdom of the Northern Nguni shows what the peoples of this stage are capable of. The Zulu in 1750–75 were a tribe or clan of some 2,000 tribesmen. In the ensuing struggle for supremacy, Shaka, their king, by ruthless determination, military skill, and administrative foresight made himself in the ten years from about 1815 to 1825 master of a kingdom some 80,000 square miles in extent, covering the whole of what is now Zululand and Natal. The slaughter was on a scale unprecedented, and chaos reigned throughout native South Africa. Many of the smaller tribes were utterly destroyed. Many thousands of refugees, sometimes including entire tribes, fled in every direction. Fugitive tribes drove other tribes from their homes; even Zulu generals with the forces under their command themselves sometimes fled and established kingdoms elsewhere. Out of this chaos were founded the Rhodesian Ndebele, the Shangana, the Basuto, and other nations. The Zulu nation was built up from the remnants of over 100 tribes. The men of the same age-groups were organized into regiments and quartered in great barracks in various parts of the country, and trained for war while they herded the king's cattle and worked his fields. No man could marry till the king gave the word to the whole regiment to marry into a specified age-regiment of girls. War was perennial, and it was a relief to his people when the cruel despot was assassinated in 1828. Long before the British deposed Cetewayo in 1880, the whole of the Zulu nation had become so homogeneous that, although it has broken up into over 200 tribes, there is one uniform Zulu culture throughout Natal. During the same century, further north and west, the more advanced tribes of the Central and Late Codes (with whom at present we are not concerned), the Bamangwato under Khama, the South Sotho under Moshesh, and the Rhodesian Ndebele under Mzilikazi, similarly reduced their neighbours under their rule.

These brief historical sketches suffice to show that progress among these peoples of Western Europe and South Africa has in some respects continued in the same directions as before. The pressure and movement of populations are greater and the strength of central authority has grown, and with them the capacity for organized war and the degree of intelligence and foresight. There is a progressive advance from the beginning to the end of this period in England and France, and between the Southern and the Northern Nguni.

All these peoples in Europe and Africa are still mainly pastoral, and they attach the chief importance to their cattle, though their agriculture is on a somewhat larger scale than before. They still practise a shifting cultivation, tilling fields within a walking distance of their huts. These are worked for several successive seasons till they are exhausted, and new land is then cleared and cultivated. The pasture land is beyond. Their kinship unit and their local unit is still the homestead or household,[1] a group of, say, three or four thatched wooden huts occupied by a man and his wife or wives and dependent children, together with any other relatives or other dependents who may attach themselves to him. Accordingly, in the Teutonic settlement of England, such of the Roman-British towns as had not already been deserted in the economic decay of the third to the fifth centuries, dissolved into desolation and ruin, and plantations sometimes grew up in their midst. The same fate overtook to a large extent even the remaining cities of Gaul. Both in Britain and Gaul it was mainly the *villae* or *fundi*, the self-sufficient Celto-Roman estates, which survived. At this stage, though the amount of goods has increased, trade has made little progress as compared with the Akikuyu and the Akamba. Most families make for themselves what they require, and there are few regular markets. In France some workshops still survive for the manufacture of cloth, pottery, arms, and jewellery. Some valuables are imported from abroad, mainly through southern ports, but the commerce is chiefly in the hands of Byzantines and Jews. Barter is overwhelmingly the main commercial transaction, but in France and England there is a coinage,[2] in too small supply for common use.

---

[1] Zulu " *umuzi*," Xhosa " *umzi* "; and various names in Western Europe.

[2] At first copies of Roman coins of permanent types with the names of former emperors (reminiscent of the newly minted Maria Theresa dollars, dated 1780, now current in the Yemen) or sometimes with the names of contemporary emperors. In the second half of the eighth century Offa, King of Mercia, issued copies of Arab coins, complete with their Arabic inscription and the added words " Offa Rex." The Belgæ in South-East England, in 75 B.C. to A.D. 43, copied a coin of Philip of Macedon, which gradually deteriorated.

The populations remain variable and difficult to assess. At the beginning of our period the average size of the ten English kingdoms was about 70,000 souls, but the Mercian kingdom and the Zulu kingdom at their height numbered over 300,000 persons, and the Merovingian kingdoms were on a similar scale. The tribes themselves are everywhere small, and in South Africa some number no more than a few hundred persons, and most are only a few thousand strong. In England the figures must have been much the same. The density of population varies with local ecological conditions. South Africa has always been thinly occupied, mainly because of shortage of water and erosion of the soil[1]—in Zululand at a rate of only about 3.5 persons per square mile. England at this stage was comparatively densely populated—probably at a rate of some ten to twelve persons to the square mile.

In the household (which has grown somewhat in size among the more advanced of these peoples) the father is, as before, the head of the family, possessing complete power over the women and children. He is responsible to the outside world for their actions, and he represents them in litigation.

Above the household, the larger kinship unit is the patrilineal clan. The clan tends to prevail in a particular locality, for sons, as they marry, are prone to establish themselves near their father's household; but it may also be found in a number of scattered localities, and even in different tribes. The clans consider themselves to be derived from a common clan ancestor, and the clans of a tribe to be descended from a common tribal ancestor. Clans tend to branch off and separate into lineages, which are of especial importance among the Southern Nguni. The royal clan supplies the tribal chief.

But in addition to the patrilineal clan the other blood-relatives also play an important and an increasing social function. As in East Africa in the previous stage, they share, in a well-known proportion, the right to receive the bride-price and the blood-money (English *leodgeld* or *wergeld*) and the obligation to provide them. The Laws of Æthelberht, for example (§ 23), provide that if a homicide flees the country

[1] See the *Report of the Native Economic Commission*, 1930–32.

his relatives (*magas*) shall pay half the *leodgeld*;[1] and the Salic Law (cap. 62) provides that if a man is killed, half the blood-money (*compositio*) goes to the sons, and the other half is shared between the nearest relatives (*parentes*) both on the father's and mother's side. In Western Europe the terms for " clan " and " blood-relatives " (English *magas* or *maegth*, Frankish *parentela*, and numerous other names in Teutonic and Latin) commonly include both groups.[2] The maternal uncle continues to play an important part in Europe and South Africa.

The household is not only the basic kinship unit; it is also the basic local unit. Above it comes next the hamlet, the small or sub-district—not a village—consisting merely of the households situated on the same hillside or by the same stream. Among the Xhosa it is the *ibandla*; among the Northern Nguni it is the *isigodi* under its *unumzana*, or headman, with his council of notables; in France[3] it is the hundred under the *centenarius, thunginus,* or vicar, and his *rachineburgii* or notables. Above the sub-district there is the larger district (Xhosa, larger *ibandla*; North Nguni *isifunda*; Frankish *pagus* and English shire) under a district chief. He is a representative or subordinate of the king or (in Africa) of the tribal chief, and is assisted by his council of local notables and headmen of sub-districts. In France he is the *comes* (count) *graf* or *grafio*, assisted (especially in trials) by his *rachineburgii*. These district chiefs may be relatives of the king or tribal chief, or mere commoners. Among the less advanced of these peoples

[1] Compare the Kikuyu rule that if a homicide is not to be found, the brother is liable to pay half the blood-wealth. This rule, as will be understood from the account of the previous stage, is partly in favour of the brother, protecting him from unlimited vengeance or liability to pay the whole of the blood-money.

[2] In Norway the law of the north-west province of Trondjem, at the same stage of development but of a much later time, is represented in the interesting Frostathingslov. Here is specified the blood-money, and the members of the patrilineal clan (the *bauggildi*) who pay and receive it and the proportions in which they pay and receive. In addition, there are the *nefgildi* (the relatives on the mother's side), and they receive between them one-third of the total *wergeld*, against the two-thirds which go to the *bauggildi*.

[3] In England, too, it is the hundred.

one of these two stages above the household is often missing, and the organization is simpler.[1] Certainly among the Southern Nguni the districts tend to be occupied by the same clan and to coincide with membership of the same clan.

Central authority has continued to gain in strength, and every tribe (Nguni, *isizwe*; English, folk or *maegth*) has a tribal chief (Nguni *inkosi*, English *cyning*). The tribe slowly fades, giving way to the district, especially, for example, in Wessex and Western France, where there is a surviving Celto-Roman population possessing no tribes. Among the Southern Nguni the tribe is the basic political unit, and it is much in evidence at the same stage in early Eastern England. In France it is almost entirely swallowed up in the Gallo-Frankish kingdom of Clovis, and as that kingdom breaks, it breaks into districts. Among the Northern Nguni the tribe is for a time engulfed in the Zulu kingdom until the British conquest, when the kingdom breaks again into more than 200 parts which form tribes.[2] Among the Nguni a tribe can be defined as a body of people organized under the rule of an independent chief with a separate territory. The bulk of the tribe claims descent from the ancestors of the chief, but all tribes now contain aliens, for, as we have already seen, a successful chief gains adherents from other tribes, while an unpopular and unsuccessful chief loses followers. An increasing scale of war brings in aliens by conquest or drives refugees or shattered tribes into foreign groups. An intensifying struggle for the succession to chieftainship sends dissident or unsuccessful groups into other tribes.

Above the tribe and district is the nation, which is made up of a group of tribes or districts. In England ten small kingdoms had been formed; in France they were for the time being on a larger scale; but both in Africa and in Europe, and in this and the following stage, the kings are called kings of

[1] In Wessex the shire is governed by an alderman, and in Mercia (according to the land-books) by "dukes" or "princes," often relatives of the king.
[2] Among the more advanced peoples of Basutoland, Swaziland, and Bechuanaland the nations have continued to hold together.

their peoples, not of their territories,[1] for these populations are still mainly pastoral and not long settled, and their owner-ship of and identification with a territory not yet sufficiently definite.

The chieftainship of tribe and nation is now hereditary, but the rules of succession vary much from people to people. Among all the Nguni the successor is normally the eldest son of the chief's Great Wife (who is married as the Great Wife, and need not be the first wife). Among the Franks sons succeed in equal shares, but, in fact, frequent war leaves only one surviving. If a son is of tender years a regent rules for him till he reaches years of discretion (the age of twelve in France). Often the king's mother (like the redoubtable Brunhild, wife of Sigebert) is a powerful and able regent—and especially is she obeyed if, as is frequent in Africa, the old chief married her with bride-wealth (Nguni, *lobola*) contributed by the people generally.

The king of the nation, or tribal chief, is the ruler in peace and leader in war, the supreme judge, and (until the intro-duction of Christianity) the chief priest and magician. His person is sacred. Until the introduction of Christianity he has many wives.[2] He has the first choice of land, and as he receives much tribute[3] as well as fines (of which more anon), he is extremely wealthy. Let us examine his functions in a little more detail, remembering that there is considerable

---

[1] Clovis is " Rex Francorum "; and so is each of his successors, what-ever part of France he rules. Hlothhere and Eadric are " Kings of the Kentishmen." Alfred is at first " King of the West Saxons " and later calls himself " King of the Anglo-Saxons " (Angul-Saxonum Rex). Canute, as a foreigner, boasts himself " King of all England and King of the Danes " (I Canute). Even William I called himself on occasion " King of the English " (the Ten Articles of William I). The King or Paramount Chief of Basutoland is the " *morena e moholo oa Basotho*," " the Great Chief of the Sotho " (Schapera, *South Bantu*, p. 173), though he only rules over the Southern Sotho.

[2] In England the attitude of Christianity towards polygamy (a system not permitted in the Roman Empire) was a substantial cause of its repudiation by many a king in the seventh century.

[3] In France the Merovingians inherited a system of taxation which fell into desuetude, but tribute was paid in various forms and on various occasions.

development between the South and North Nguni, and between the beginning and end of our period in Western
Europe, and that our brief description must in the main
represent the conditions reached only towards the conclusion
of the present stage.

First, he is the ruler, or head executive authority, with
rights and obligations as such. He is generally assisted by a
number of advisers—a few elder relatives (such as uncles and
brothers) and a few of his district chiefs or headmen, and a
few other friends. At his accession they are commonly
advisers of his father, whom he retains until he finds his own
counsellors. He need not take their advice, but he would
rarely oppose their united opinion. They are to some extent
held responsible by the general community if he goes astray.
They should keep him informed of the state of public opinion
and of happenings within the tribe or nation and matters that
call for his attention. Included in this entourage are a number
of officials, who may be commoners, and the Merovingian
monarch of the sixth century and the Zulu chief will have a
few of such, dividing departments of the household between
them. One of them is his minister or chief adviser (among
the Northern Nguni the chief's *induna*; among the Xhosa
umphakathi omkhulu; and in Merovingian France the mayor
of the palace). He is usually not a member of the royal clan,
but a commoner of conspicuous ability and trustworthiness.
His office is not usually hereditary, but it often is so both in
Zululand and France, and it was so in Austrasia among the
descendants of Arnulf and Pepin I. He is the head of the
administration and head of the courts. The district chiefs tend
to fall under his authority. Any business which the king or
chief is required to attend to is sent to him first, and he sometimes commands the army. The court of the king or chief is
frequented by many people, some of whom take up permanent residence in the capital village where he resides.
Apart from his councillors, there are suitors and litigants,
and there are local headmen and district chiefs and their
induna or other officials, who come for instruction or to explain
away a matter which has come to the king's ears. There are
also those who have settled there in the hope of making an

official career or receiving some favour, and there is the king's bodyguard, which eats at his table. Its members are sent about his realm on commissions, and they are also stationed at his various estates about the country.

Tacitus told us, of the tribes of Germany of our previous stage, that "upon minor matters the chiefs [1] deliberate, and upon greater matters the whole tribe, except that even those matters that rest upon the decision of the whole people are first discussed by the chiefs." [2] It remains the general position throughout the present stage that the king or tribal chief rules subject to a tribal council (Nguni *ibandla*, or *inkundla*, English, *witan* or *witenagemot*). It consists of the district chiefs and headmen, the king's advisers and some of his relatives, and some commoners of influence and ability; but sometimes the whole tribe is specially assembled to hear, debate and publish a change in policy or a change in the law. Again, the king need not act upon their advice if they differ, but he would rarely if ever act contrary to their united counsel. When, however, the Franks first invaded Gaul, because of the great distances to be travelled, these national councils ceased to be held for a time, and it was only when a great military expedition assembled that they were in a position to express their opinions. They met, indeed, voluntarily from time to time in meetings of ecclesiastics and meetings of laymen to discuss matters of common interest, and the king perforce took notice of their views. At the end of the period, when order returns for a time under the Carolingians, the national council meets again, and becomes a significant part of the new constitution.

In brief, the power at this stage of an individual king or tribal chief depends to a large extent on his own ruthlessness and ability, but it has grown vastly. The typical Merovingian ruler was, like Shaka and some others in South Africa, a despot; and the system of government has been well described as a despotism tempered by assassination. Nevertheless, it is well understood in Europe and Africa that the king (or tribal chief in Africa) has no right to make changes in the law against or without advice. For example, Cetewayo, ex-King

[1] The tribal chief and a council of district chiefs or sub-chiefs.
[2] *Germania, c.* 11.

of Zululand, giving evidence before the Cape Native Laws Commission, stated that he had not, as king, the power to make a change in any law in Zululand unless the chiefs were consulted and agreed.[1] In fact he relies on them to publish it so that it may be obeyed.

In the most advanced of these nations—that is to say, in Zululand and Merovingian France—the king rules also through the prevailing system of local government. The chief of a conquered tribe or group might be retained as a district chief over his own people, but generally the king appoints his own count or *grafio* of the *pagus*, or *praefectus* of the shire, or chief of the *isifunda*, sometimes a relative, sometimes a mere commoner, or even one who was born a slave. The latter rules his district, hold his court or shiremoot, levies tribute, and pays over the surplus to the king; and he appoints a vicar, *centenarius*, *thunginus*, or headman to each division of his county or district. Sometimes the king appoints a *dux* or duke over the counts of an area.

As ruler of the nation or tribe, the king or chief controls the distribution and use of the land of the kingdom or tribe. He is often called the owner, but it is his land in a sense intermediate between a legal ownership and administrative management. He could not sell it, even if there were anyone to sell it to.[2] Especially when the community moves to a new territory, but indeed in all cases, he controls the division of the land among the chiefs, and as representing him they control the division between the heads of the households, and grazing is common to all. The district chief is responsible to the tribal chief for the administration of the land, as for all other matters,[3] and the local headman is responsible to him. In theory the king could deprive an occupier of his land for neglect of it, but in fact, in the words of Cetewayo, he merely " tells him he ought not to do such a thing, because his father did not." [4] Nevertheless in the chaos of the Frankish kingdom during the Dark Age of the seventh century the pyramid of the social structure has lost its summit, and often authority does not

---

[1] *Cape Commission*, p. 530.　　　[2] Ibid., p. 443.
[3] Ibid., p. 49.　　　[4] Ibid., p. 523.

extend above the *comes*. Below him, no doubt, the system is in general force.

The king is not merely the ruler in peace, but also the leader in war. As among the Germans in the pages of Tacitus, so among the less advanced tribes of the present stage—for example, the Cape Nguni—the army is organized by clans, and consists of all the able-bodied men of the tribe. But the system changes among the Zulus and the Franks. Finally, after the end of this period—namely, under Charlemagne—the obligation to do military service begins to be based upon the possession of land. Possession of a certain number of units of land brings with it the obligation to serve, and the number of men to be supplied each year varies with the total force required. At this point the feudal system, which has been developing during the previous two stages, is complete.

The king or tribal chief is also the chief judge among all these peoples. Small cases are heard by the local headman, and there is an appeal from him to the court of the district chief or shiremoot, and from district chief to the king's or great chief's court. If, on apprising himself of the circumstances, the local headman finds the case too important for him to try, he sends it to the district chief for trial, and similarly still more important cases are tried in the king's or great chief's court in the first instance. The latter are mainly the criminal cases, and disputes between district chiefs or great men of the realm. The headman sits with his local elders and notables, and the district chief similarly with his local counsellors or headmen. In France the notables and counsellors—the *rachineburgii*—are finally fixed in number at seven.

Lastly the king or tribal chief, before the introduction of Christianity, is the chief priest and magician of his people. What this means, and what effect the introduction of Christianity in Europe had upon the power of the king and the growth of law, we shall consider in some detail in a later chapter.[1]

[1] See *post*, Chapter IX.

CHAPTER VIII

THE EARLY CODES (*Continued*)

The Law

I N the laws of Æthelberht begins the great tradition of
English law and the great tradition of English literature.
The clauses are simply and tersely drafted and clearly
arranged. " This syndon tha domas, the Æthelbirht cyning
asette on Augustinus daege. (These are the judgments which
King Æthelberht set in Augustine's day.") So runs the superscription—words obviously written at a later time by an ecclesiastic of sorts: he seems at least as interested in Augustine as
in Æthelberht. He may even have taken the phrase from the
introductory words of the Hebrew Code: " These are the
judgments which thou (Moses) shalt set before them." [1]
The word " *dom* " (plural " *domas* ") meant a judgment—
what a man deems or judges—and a *deman* was a judge.

The Venerable Bede refers to this Code, and writing in Latin
in A.D. 731 he speaks of Æthelberht, among the other boons
which he conferred on his people, as having set forth for it,
with the counsel of wise men,[2] " decrees of judgments (*decreta
judiciorum*) which, written in the English tongue, are still
kept and observed." Plainly Bede was translating the word
" *domas* " into Latin.[3] Æthelberht, as he says, was " decree-
ing " what " judgments " should be given in the circumstances
set out in each of the laws.

The Code of Æthelberht, then, according to the tradition
expressed in its superscription and in the words of Bede,
consists of legislation—a conscious laying down of what we
would call " law." We now meet legislation for the first

---

[1] Exodus 21[1].

[2] I.e. *witenagemot* (council of wise men).

[3] The word " *judicia* " was, of course, used in the same way on the
Continent; cf. the *Liber Judiciorum* of Receswinth in Visigothic Spain,
about A.D. 654.

time. But is the tradition true? May not the Code have been merely a collection in writing of existing law? Can we believe that at this early stage of progress law was consciously and intentionally changed or created? By all means : legislation was not to be found in our previous stage in East Africa : it is universal in the present stage. The Salic Law is Frankish legislation—indeed the word " *lex* " in its title of Lex Salica is the ordinary Latin word for legislation—and there also survive separate, isolated Frankish statutes apart from the Lex Salica. Legislation is found everywhere among the Nguni peoples, quite distinct from the mere decisions of lawsuits. For example, among the Nguni, in cases which are tried in the court of the tribal chief, whether on appeal or by way of first instance, the chief himself does not usually sit. His *induna* and local councillors, hereditary or specially appointed for the purpose, try the case and report their view to him, and if he agrees they announce the decision. But quite apart from the decision of cases, changes in the law are made from time to time by the chief and his tribal council (who are mainly the district chiefs) after assembling and deliberating together at one of their meetings.[1] Indeed, Cetewayo, ex-King of the Zulus, giving evidence before the Cape Native Laws Commission of 1882, said (in the passage cited in the last chapter) that he had not, as king, the power to make a change in any law in Zululand unless the chiefs were consulted and agreed.[2] The same applied, we can be sure, in England.

We may go further, and say that legislation, at or about this stage, is inevitable. We saw the law grow, at our previous stage, to a sizable body of judgments. We even had occasion here and there to record changes in the law. We had seen, from the beginning of our story, society changing at a steadily increasing pace, and with it we watched an increase in the power of central authority. We saw at the same time a human intelligence slowly developing—at least in the matters which now concern us—and with it a growing intensity of consciousness of its environment. The present stage continues the process. Changes in society call for

---

[1] *Cape Commission*, pp. 4, 475.   [2] Ibid., p. 530.

changes in the law, and there is a central authority with sufficient influence to make them. Especially when such a revolution occurs as the conversion of a kingdom to Christianity, changes in the law are called for and consciously made by the central authority—that of the king or tribal chief with his council of state or tribal council. Similarly in South Africa it has been noted that the frequency of legislation has increased since the coming of the European. Change is not a new thing. On one occasion, even in the lowest of our grades, the most important of all changes was recently witnessed—namely, a change in the kinship system of an Australian community. The present changes are changes in the law.

Tradition does not say only of this Code, or only of the Salic Law, that it was legislation. Almost universally history and tradition relate that the Codes of which we read constituted legislation, and according to tradition in almost every nation law begins with the written legislation of a first, great national law-giver—Æthelberht in Kent, Clovis in France, Gundobald in Burgundy, David I in Scotland, Hywel Dda in Wales, Moses in Israel, and many others.[1] According to Greek tradition, each city-state in the colonies and the mother-country from 700 B.C. onwards had its own first great legislator, and the names of many survive.

The language of the Codes also shows them to consist of legislation. Substantially all the Codes of every age and every tongue are couched in the same style. " Gif frigman cyninge stele, IX gylde forgylde." (" If a freeman robs the king, he shall pay back nine-fold.") " Gif man mannan ofslaehth, medume leodgeld C scillinga gebete." (" If one man slays another, he shall pay as compensation the usual *wergeld* of 100 shillings.") From the Early to the Late Codes the language remains the same—namely, conditional sentences in the third

---

[1] There are certain exceptions. In Rome and the closely related Celtic tribes of Ireland and Wales the Codes (the Twelve Tables, Ancient Laws of Ireland and Ancient Laws of Wales) begin, according to tradition, with a collection of existing laws by a Commission, with legislation in the form of amendments, additions or exclusions. These traditions are of very doubtful reliability.

person. Less commonly a technical term is used instead of a condition—for example, " The King's mundbyrd shall be 50 shillings "—but never is a sentence of a Code of law in the second person. When, in modern times, we speak of legislation, we have in mind something immensely larger than this —often a change in the constitution of the State, or the creation of a new administrative service. But at the present stage law consists of little more than judgments on a few topics, and legislation prescribes new judgments. This reminds us that there is a further circumstance that creates the need for legislation—namely, the existence of a pyramid of courts. When there is but one chief or judge, legislation may not be necessary : the Code is instructing the judges what judgments they shall give in the circumstances set out in each of the clauses. The first part (the *protasis*) of each sentence sets out the circumstances : the second part (the *apodosis*) sets out the judgment they are to give. All the laws are " *decreta judiciorum* " (" decrees of judgments ").

But this does not mean that every Code consists solely of legislation, or of genuine legislation. We are here reminded that there is a further pre-requisite of Codes—though not of legislation—and that is the use of writing. The Zulus had legislation but no writing, and therefore no Codes. Codes are not only legislation, but also literature. They commence the literature of their country. They start by recording in writing the few changes that the first great legislator made in the law, and they are extended later by the addition of new laws. There is no reason at this stage why any person who possesses a document containing the decrees of the old legislator should hesitate to add to it any rule that is attributed to him in later times and is not to be found in the document. No one has a notion that there is something sacrosanct in the document which he has received. Indeed, the earliest literature of all countries proves upon examination to be the work of more than one hand, whether it is prose or poetry, sacred writings or profane—the books of the Old Testament, the Homeric poems, Burnt Njal, or the sacred literature of India. In the law there is special reason for this phenomenon. Law changes imperceptibly in the course of the giving of judgments.

In a sense every judgment creates new law, but law changes so imperceptibly that every rule tends to be regarded as existing from time immemorial. The modern lawyer vastly exaggerates the age of most of the laws he administers; small wonder, then, that later rules were attributed to the old law-giver, and added to his scanty written laws. Indeed, for a long time all important rules are attributed to him. In Northern Albania, for example, where less than forty years ago the law had not gone far beyond our present stage, all law and custom was attributed to Lek Dukagin. Whatever was done, was done " because Lek ordered it." [1] And so, in the early days of writing, when a written legal tradition has lasted sufficiently long, the laws of the old law-giver have often expanded into a collection of most of the important rules of law in existence at the date of the Code. Often also the early rules and additions have been altered from time to time to correspond with more modern usage, in the belief that the older parts were wrongly recorded because they differed from the current rules. The degrees of corruption are not the same in all Codes. The laws of Æthelberht—partly, perhaps, because Kent ceased early to exist as a separate kingdom—have suffered less. The Salic Law has undergone such amendment, addition, and corruption that it is not to be relied upon, or even understood, except in its superficial and general features. But all the Codes, except where they survive on the stone on which they were promulgated,[2] have suffered alteration and additions, and especially additions where we would expect to find them— namely, at the foot. The additions are naturally couched in the same language of legislation—namely, sentences in the third person. Even as late as 1291 Britton's serious treatise on the law of England, though largely based on the earlier work of Bracton, is put into the mouth of a king.

Hence the general nature of the Codes. They started with the written legislation of the old law-giver, and were altered and extended from time to time, in greater or less degree, to bring them up to date of the current law. The process only

[1] M. E. Durham, *Some Tribal Origins, Laws and Customs of the Balkans* (1928), p. 64.

[2] I refer to the Code of Hammurabi and the legislation of Gortyn.

stops when the country in question loses its independence and the laws cease to be in force—and not even always then. By now they have come to deal with a great multiplicity of subjects, and they are arranged more or less in accordance with the subject-matter with which they deal. Hence the name "Codes." For example, the Salic Law commences with two rules, which have been taken from a later capitulary (i.e., statute) and put at the head of the Code, together with a short commentary. Then follow groups of rules dealing with theft of animals, then damage done by trespassing animals, then theft of persons, theft by persons, rape, robbery, and so forth. But these documents remain legislation. They do not pretend to be Codes in the sense of containing the whole of the existing law : indeed, how could such a Code be written? They purport to be collections of legislation.[1]

One correction should be made in the above account. We have been considering the stages by which law has grown, looking at the past in the light of the present, and describing the ideas of the past by means of the language of the present, with all its modern implications and associations. It is not at all clear, for example, that the Kentishman of the time of Æthelberht had the modern notion of "law." He was familiar with "*domas*" (judgments of courts). He also had the word "*riht*" (right), which, however, is not found in the Laws of Æthelberht, though it occurs six times in the following Laws of Hlothhere and Eadric. It had much the same meanings as our present word, but the main implication of the word was that which is customary, and therefore right—not that which is moral, and therefore right. So the word signifies "custom," "customary"—and therefore also "right," because what customarily happens ought to happen—and also "justice," and "just conduct," and hence also the expression "to do a man right," meaning to do towards him what is customary, or to give him customary justice or satisfaction, as contrasted with doing a man wrong, or doing a man a wrong. These notions are simpler and less technical than those associated with our word "law." In brief, there has been little, if any,

---

[1] Some of the Late Codes are enacted as Codes—e.g., that of Hammurabi.

change from what we found in East Africa.[1]   Yet at the end of our present stage, or in the following stage, the notion of " law " with most of its modern senses does appear.

Before we consider the contents of these Early Codes we have still to see them in their true physical perspective.   The Frankish Code—the Lex Salica—begins with the legislation of Clovis in A.D. 500, and the Kentish Code of Æthelberht from A.D. 600, yet the latter is certainly no more advanced than the former, and even in A.D. 600 there is still no code from any of the nine other English kingdoms.   Further to the west, in Wessex, the first legislation—that of Ine—is a century later than Æthelberht.   In Central England the kingdom of Mercia produces no legislation till two centuries after Æthelberht, when Offa, who reigned from 757 to 796, is said to have given some laws, now lost.   The kingdom of Northumbria never produced written law of its own throughout the period of its survival.   This difference in date is not to be explained by a later conversion to Christianity.[2]   The explanation is economic. For centuries Kent had been some 150 years behind the greater part of Gaul in development, and more and more backward still was the rest of England further and further to the north-west.   As archæology shows us, for many thousands of years England stood at the edge of European culture.   Let us take an instance from the date of Julius Cæsar's invasion of the country in 55 B.C.   The main part of Gaul stood then at the stage of the Central Codes—a stage which we have not yet reached in this chapter—but in the north-east the Belgæ (thought to be partly of German origin) were behind the rest. Across the Channel the culture of Kent was hardly different, for in 75 B.C. or thereabouts the Belgæ had invaded England, and there were homesteads of tribes of the same name on both

[1] There is also the word " *aew*," which occurs only twice in the whole of the Anglo-Saxon laws, in later superscriptions to the laws of Hlothhere and Eadric, and of Ine.

[2] Southern and Central England were converted to Christianity by missionaries from the Continent, where written legislation was familiar. Northumbria and North Britain were during the same centuries converted mainly by missionaries from Ireland, where written legislation was as yet unknown.   These matters are mere details of the general economic picture.

sides of the straits. " By far the most civilized of the Britons,"
says Cæsar, " are those who inhabit Kent. This is a purely
maritime district whose culture does not differ much from that
of the Gauls," [1] and theirs must have been the degree of advance
of the peoples of the Early Codes. In the interior were populations of our previous stage—that of East Africa and Germany [2]
—for he tells us that " those of the interior do not for the most
part grow corn, but live on milk and meat and are clad in
skins." He records a familiar characteristic of that culture—
namely, the access of brothers to one another's wives.[3] Further
north and west were to be seen tribes representative of our
previous stage,[4] for in Gloucestershire, at Salmonsbury (and, we
can be sure, at other places), cannibalism was practised shortly
before Cæsar's time, and even more primitive cultures were to
be found still further to the north and west. In later Anglo-
Saxon times economic progress, better communications, and
more movement increased the size of the fields of culture and
of the kingdoms, but the differences remained. Until the
Norman Conquest and after, England remained at least a
century behind the Continent, and Wales and Scotland lagged
much further behind. The Ancient Laws of Wales [5] are
attributed to Hywel Dda, who reigned over part of it in the
first half of the tenth century, and the earliest extant version,
which dates from the close of the twelfth century, still betokens
the stage of the Early Codes; so that in that period of the
struggle of the small Welsh principalities against the English
invaders, the latter, among whom murder was now punishable by death, looked in horror at a barbarism under which the
sanction for homicide was the payment of so much cattle.
The ancient Scottish Code—the Leges inter Brettos et Scottos [6]
—is later by about a century than the Welsh Laws. It is
attributed to the traditional Scottish legislator, King David I
(1084–1153). It is very brief, and typical of the least advanced
of the Early Codes, and was still practised among the mixed
population of Galway in 1305, when it was prohibited by an

---

[1] *De Bello Gallico, c.* 5 (14).   [2] Grade A3 (1).
[3] See *ante*, p. 114.   [4] Grade A2.
[5] Edited in 1841 for the Record Commissioners by Aneurin Owen.
[6] Printed in the *Folio Scots Acts*, vol. i, App. III, pp. 663 ff.

Ordinance of Edward I.[1] In Iceland the traditional legislator was Ulfyot, who was believed to have given a code of law to the colonies about A.D. 930. It was not written, and nothing is known of its contents, but law of the stage of the Early Codes was in force in Iceland for a long time after. The Laws of Ireland (or Brehon Law Tracts) [2] purport to go back to the fifth century (for Ireland, though backward in comparison with Roman Britain, never received the setback of a Teutonic invasion), and they are hardly more advanced than the Welsh laws. To the north and east of France the peoples of Europe reached and passed the stage of the Early Codes in later and later centuries.

If we now look briefly at the law embodied in the Early Codes, we shall see very clearly their continuity from the previous stage of East Africa and Germany,[3] and also the progress that is being achieved.

In an earlier chapter we set out a " code of law " of one of the more advanced tribes of our previous stage [4]—the Akamba of Kitui. It is not the work of natives: it is not a code nor written; it merely represents a conspectus by European observers of decisions of their courts. It relates almost entirely to civil injuries—homicide, wounding, rape, adultery and seduction, and theft; and, of them, the bulk is taken up by homicide and wounding, which occupy over two-thirds of the whole. The sanctions are expressed in terms of cattle and goats. There is also a reference to the bride-price, and we might have added a few words relating to inheritance. There is nothing more. Similarly the most primitive of our Early Codes—the brief Leges inter Brettos et Scottos—also consists of practically nothing except rules of homicide and wounding, and the compensation is expressed in terms of cows. The longer Code of Æthelberht also consists in the main of rules relating to civil injuries (eighty-two clauses) and there remain six clauses relating to marriage. Indeed, as between the Akamba of Kitui and the people of Kent the proportion of

---

[1] Ordinacio facta per Dominum Regem Super Stabilitate Terre Scotie," vol i, *Folio Scots Acts*, p. 119.

[2] Published by the Record Commissioners, 6 vols., Dublin (1865–1901).

[3] Grade A3 (1). [4] Grade A3 (1).

rules devoted to each civil injury is still almost the same.[1] In the later Anglo-Saxon laws there is change, for much relates to procedure and much to theft. In the Salic Laws we see almost the same picture. The earlier part (Chapters 2–36) consists almost entirely of civil injuries, with a great increase, owing to economic advance, in the proportion which treats of theft, but of the later part of the Code (Chapters 1 and 37–69) about a half relates to procedure. Among the Nguni (where there are no written Codes) the law presents a similar appearance, except that there is no such interest in procedure, and we shall seek the explanation of this remarkable difference in the following chapter.

If now we look at the sanctions for civil injuries in these Codes and in South Africa, we see them rising out of a background of the law of our previous stage.

Generally speaking, the sanctions for homicide remain what they were. In the Leges inter Brettos et Scottos the compositions are still expressed in terms of cattle. In Æthelberht the sanctions are now pecuniary. The Latin word *pecunia* ("money") was derived from *pecus* (cattle), because in Rome, too, wealth and compensation originally took the form of cattle, and as they changed to currency, the word "*pecunia*" acquired its meaning accordingly. In England, too, the Anglo-Saxon *feo*, cattle (the same word as the Latin *pecus*) changed to "fee" and a number of other forms, while currency gradually took the place of cattle. In Kent, as in early Rome, the units of currency, in order to ensure stability, were based on the value of cows, or, as we should say, "tied" to cattle, as later currencies were "tied" to gold. The price of a cow was fixed by law at a shilling, and in Æthelberht's Laws, in the ordinary case of the slaying of a freeman, the blood-money (called *leodgeld* or *wergeld*) was fixed at 100 shillings. In fact, however, there was at this time little money in existence and most transactions took place in kind. A hundred cows was a vast amount of property (even though

---

[1] The first figure following in each case is the percentage in the Code of Æthelberht, and the figure in brackets is that of the Akamba of Kitui—Homicide 15 (25), wounding and assault 50 (51); rape, adultery, and seduction 15 (13), theft 9 (7), bride-price and marriage 7 (3).

cattle were comparatively numerous and undersized), and exceeded by far the fourteen cows and one bull of the Akamba of Kitui. Yet it was only the same amount as that of the usual blood-money among the pastoral Masai. A century later than Æthelberht, when a Wessex Code appears (the laws of Ine), it is the law of a sheep-rearing rather than cattle-keeping kingdom—as it remained for many centuries after—and a Wessex shilling was the value of a sheep. So, too, it was in Mercia.[1] As the Frankish kingdom was somewhat richer, the *wergeld* (*compositio*) was 200 *solidi* (i.e., 200 cows) for killing a Frank, and only 100 for slaying a mere Gallo-Roman. As in our previous stage, the body of relatives shared in the receipt of the money and (unless a man was in trouble too often) contributed towards the payment. If the homicide fled the country, his relatives were only liable to pay half.[2] If the slayer was a slave he was handed over to the relatives, and his master paid a lesser sum in addition. In the more advanced law of the later half of the Lex Salica, and a little later in England, homicide in aggravating circum-stances met with a far severer sanction, and if the slayer tried to hide his wrong, either by concealing or disposing of the body or runnning away after the deed was done, or failing to publish the fact, he was guilty of a wrong known as "murder," and the *wergeld* rose to much greater heights.[3] In certain circumstances the sanction for homicide in the late provisions of the Salic Law amounted to as much as 1,800 *solidi*.

The sanctions for wounding are of the same general nature as before. In the Scottish Code they are expressed in cattle,

---

[1] The Kentish shilling (a Roman ounce of silver) consisted of twenty *sceattas* (the *sceatta* being the predecessor of the penny). On the other hand, the Wessex shilling consisted of four and later five pence, so that (four or five sheep being of the value of a cow) the penny and *sceatta* were roughly equivalent. The Mercian shilling consisted of four pence.

[2] Aeth. *c.* 23.

[3] This distinction between "murder" and other homicide is arrived at in the eighth century in France (Lex Salica, *c.* 41 (2); Lex Rip. Tit. 15; Lex Fris. Tit. 22), but not in England till the tenth century (E. & G. 11; VI Æthelred, *c.* 36). Compare Deuteronomy 27²⁴. See also Burnt Njal, *passim*. Similarly in North Albania, the slayer always at once proclaimed his deed (Durham, p. 66).

and in Kent and France in money. There is the same ratio to
blood-money as in East Africa—for example, the loss of both
eyes or both legs is compensated by a full *wergeld*; and accordingly the sanctions for the various injuries are higher than
among the Akamba. The Code of Æthelberht contains an
absurdly elaborate and orderly tariff of forty clauses specifying
the sum payable for every kind of injury, beginning at the top
of the body with the wrong of seizing a man by the hair, and
ending with the loss of a toe nail. Some individuals in the
early Middle Ages enjoyed drafting such ideal systems, which
correspond to a code of legal principles with us. Sometimes
they assist us to detect later interpolations which spoil the order
of succession from head to foot.[1]

As we have seen, standards of chastity vary widely from
people to people in all grades, but generally at the present stage
the sanctions for adultery with a wife are growing in severity.
In Western Europe and in South Africa a husband is justified
in killing an adulterer caught in the act; and even when he is
not killed the sanction grows greatly in amount. In several
places in Western Europe the compensation payable is now the
full amount of her *wergeld* or a bride-price (the amounts of
which, as in East Africa, were approximately equal).[2] Among
the Nguni, while the sanction for adultery is usually a sum
payable to the husband, among some tribes (for example, the
Fingoes of the Cape) adultery was a serious crime punishable
by confiscation of all the offender's property, and among the
Fetiani the punishment was death.[3] Seduction was, no doubt, a
frequent prelude to marriage in Europe; but for carrying off a
girl by force and without payment of bride-wealth the compensation was heavy.[4] So it was for taking a widow who did
not belong to one by the right of inheritance.[5] Among the
Nguni, too, the sanction for rape is pecuniary. Polygyny,
though practised among the Nguni, is almost confined to

[1] Cf. the Laws of Alfred, *cc.* 65–77.
[2] Aeth. *c.* 31; Lex Baiuvariorum, *c.* viii, 1, 10; Lex Fris. Tit. IX De
Farlegani.
[3] *Cape Commission*, p. 43.
[4] Aeth. *cc.* 82, 83; Lex Salicá, *cc.* 13, 25 (1).
[5] Aeth. *c.* 76. Cf. Lex Salica, *c.* 44.

chiefs and notables and the wealthy; but Christianity brought monogamy from Rome to Kent and France, and sternly prohibited the polygyny of the chiefs and nobles.

The sanctions for theft are increasing in severity. In the Laws of Æthelberht the compensation for theft in the ordinary case of the stealing of a freeman's property is triple the value. The later Anglo-Saxon laws are full of provisions relating to theft, and in the Salic Law the subject takes up no less than a third part of the whole code, and very large sums are fixed for the theft of different species of animals. Among the Nguni the general rule is double value; but in all these nations, at the end of this period, a man is justified in killing a thief caught in the act.[1] In the laws of Hlothhere and Eadric we meet for the first time the problem that will exercise primitive law for a long time to come—namely, that set by the case where A recognizes his property in the possession of B, and alleges that B has stolen it and claims it from him, and B (as he does in a modern court if he has stolen it) says that he bought it from a third person.[2] In the Salic Law,[3] and everywhere among the Nguni and at the corresponding date in England,[4] we meet the celebrated " spoor law," which is characteristic of the present stage. This rule provides that if the fresh trail of missing cattle leads to a certain kraal or homestead, the occupant—that is to say, the head of the household—is liable for a theft unless he can disprove it (normally by showing that the trail continues further).

There are also a number of new civil wrongs (some of which we met with in the previous stage), and particularly the wrong of breaking through the fence surrounding a homestead, abuse and slander and false accusations, false imprisonment of freemen and the wrong of selling them abroad as slaves, and arson and damage to property.

This is the general background of the law, and shows a

---

[1] See, Wihtred, cc. 25, 28 ; Ine, cc. 16, 20, 35 ; *Cape Commission*, p. 86 (a thief found in the kraal at night).

[2] H. & E., c. 7.   [3] Lex Salica, c. 37.

[4] VI Æthelstan 4, 7, 8 (4). Cf. II Edward 4 ; V Æthelstan, 2. All these provisions are of the first half of the tenth century, but they are very detailed, and the spoor law was probably a little older than this in England.

certain progress as against the previous stage, but we have not
yet mentioned the most important or characteristic development.   The stage of the Early Codes is that stage at which the
important civil injuries, while their sanctions remain pecuniary,
take their first step towards becoming criminal.   The step
varies in nature somewhat from people to people, according
to local circumstances.   Let us first look at the Laws of
Æthelberht from this point of view.

It is often possible to obtain more insight into a code of
early law by observing the arrangement of the clauses in it than
in any other way.   The arrangement of the Code of Æthelberht is striking indeed.   It is not arranged (as would be usual)
in accordance with the nature of the wrong which is aimed at,
but in accordance with the status of the person wronged.
Clause 1 deals with wrongs against the Church and ecclesiastics,
clauses 2-12 with wrongs against the king, clauses 13 and 14
with wrongs against noblemen, clauses 15-72 with wrongs
against freemen (commoners), clauses 74-84 with wrongs
to women, and clauses 86 to the end of the Code with wrongs
against unfree persons.   It is only within these groups that the
rules are arranged according to the nature of the wrong.
Such an arrangement is also found in the equally primitive
Leges inter Brettos et Scottos, but is rarely, if ever, found elsewhere.   Eloquently the Code in this way paints for us the
picture of the quasi-feudal society that was described in the
previous chapter, and tells us that status was the outstanding
fact in the mind of the law.   Indeed, the number of social
classes in the community is astonishing.   The phenomenon is
not found to the same extent among the Nguni.   In the Laws
of Æthelberht only one class of nobles is as yet mentioned,
but there are several classes of half-free and unfree persons.

It is not merely the arrangement of clauses that tells us that
status was the outstanding fact.   So, too, do the sanctions:
for the compensation for every kind of wrong varies according
to the status of the person injured.   Clause 1 (for example)
reads : " God's property and the Church's (i.e., theft of it)
shall be paid for twelve fold; a bishop's property eleven fold;
a priest's property nine fold; a deacon's property six fold;
a clerk's property three fold."   A nobleman's *wergeld* is 300

shillings,[1] and a commoner's only 100 shillings. Not only this, but a wrong to any person may be a wrong to one in whose protection he was. As we have seen, if a man injures a member of a household, it is a wrong against the head of the household—a violation of his *mundbyrd*, i.e., protection or guardianship—and the head claims for it in the ensuing litigation. If a man seduces a commoner's serving-maid he pays the commoner the fee for a commoner's *mundbyrd*—namely, six shillings. If he seduces a noble's serving-maid he pays the nobleman's *mundbyrd* of twelve shillings, and if she belongs to the king, fifty shillings. The king's protection is beginning to extend itself far and wide. To molest any one of the king's lieges when he calls them together, or to slay a man on the king's premises, makes the offender liable to pay the *mundbyrd* of fifty shillings, and there seems also to be a rule that the killing of a freeman anywhere is a breach of the king's rights as the man's lord, for which the slayer pays fifty shillings to the king, in addition to the *wergeld* of 100 shillings which he pays to the man's relatives. In short, to kill a man—at any rate in certain circumstances, and possibly in all—has become an offence against the king, representing, as it were, the injured community. Homicide is no longer a matter that merely concerns the parties and their relatives. The social sense, the sense of national solidarity, is deepening, and the rights and interests of the nation are centred in the person of the king. The king is even taking the triple payment for a theft.[2] This notion of protection, with its complementary notion of allegiance, is highly characteristic of this stage of advance. For example, in France it was common, and often necessary, for a small Gallo-Roman landowner to surrender his land to a Frankish noble and take it back from him as his liege so as to obtain his protection in that troubled society. The same notions are to be found in the Salic Law, where we find the distinction between the *faidus* or compensation payable to a person for an injury done to him, and the *fretus* or *fritus*—fee for breach of the peace—payable to the king or lord in respect of the same act, if the person injured was in

[1] H. & E., *c.* 1. [2] Aeth., *c.* 9.

his *verbum* (*mund*, protection).[1] The Nguni have gone a step farther. It will be remembered that even among the Shilluk (the most advanced of our East African tribes of the previous stage), when a homicide takes place the bulk of the cattle collected by the king are kept by him; and among the Germans, according to Tacitus, part of the payment for civil wrongs went to the king or the State, and part to the person injured or his relatives. Among the Nguni every member of the tribe is under the protection of the tribal chief. The slaying of a tribesman or a serious wounding is a wrong against the tribal chief, and such a charge is tried only in his court.[2] Without prior formality, as a rule, he collects the cattle which constitute the fine,[3] and among many tribes the relatives have no claim of any kind,[4] though the chief may sometimes, in the case of a wounding, pay over part of the cattle to the injured man. In other words, though the sanctions for homicide and serious wounding still take the form of cattle, they are now fines, and not compensation, and the wrong is now in part a criminal offence, and not merely the concern of the parties. In some tribes, though the families concerned may compromise a case of homicide or assault, yet if it comes to the chief's ears it will be tried nevertheless and the fine collected.[5] The amount of the fine now varies not according to the status of the slain so much as the circumstances of the wrong and the means of the offender to pay. Among the majority of the Cape Nguni the fine for homicide is about ten head,[6] but among many of the more advanced of the Nguni where the offender slew the deceased " in anger "[7] the whole of the offender's cattle will be seized, though if the homicide was not in anger—i.e., not intentional—a smaller number (say, five to ten head) may be taken.

There are also other criminal offences at this stage, both among the Nguni and in Europe, of much the same character

---

[1] See Lex Salica, *cc.* 13 (6), 24 (5), 35 (7).
[2] *Cape Commission*, p. 85.   [3] Ibid., Evidence, p. 84.
[4] Ibid., p. 392.   [5] Ibid., p. 394.
[6] E.g., Fingoes, Gcalekas, Bhacas, Ngqikas (*Cape Commission*, p. 43).
[7] I.e., intentionally, see *Cape Commission*, p. 85. (The same distinction is applied in the opening clause of the Hittite Code.)

as in the previous stage—namely, treason, incest,[1] bestiality
and other sexual perversions, and above all witchcraft. Christianity does not by any means remove the belief in witches, or
lessen the seriousness of the offence. For these offences the
general punishment is death and confiscation of property, and
they are all tried in the court of the great chief.

All these are criminal offences in a very real sense. A civil
wrong may be compromised, but among the Nguni it is often
a crime to compromise a criminal offence [2] and even to fail to
report it.[3]

---

[1] Incest is often treated with surprising leniency in Europe and Africa.
Among the Nguni the sanction is a fine payable to the chief (*Cape
Commission*, p. 91).
[2] *Cape Commission*, p. 86.   [3] Ibid., p. 8.

CHAPTER IX

THE EARLY CODES AND RELIGION

HITHERO we have been concerned to point out similarities in the law of the peoples of the Early Codes. Now we have to speak of an abnormal but significant development in Western Europe. About the year 700 the Early Codes undergo a great change both in England and France.[1] Plainly economic development will not explain it, for it occurs at the same date in both countries, although economically England is still a century behind France, and nothing similar occurs among the other nations of the Early Codes. The change consists of the introduction into the written law of certain religious matter, and the explanation is highly instructive. The object of the present chapter is to contrast the religion of Western Europe with that of the Nguni peoples and to show the results that follow in the law.

The South African Bantu is a cheerful and extrovert person. Religion means less to him than to many other peoples, and he is far more interested in the mundane things of this world than in metaphysics and the after-life. Magic and witchcraft are nevertheless important conceptions. All the Nguni peoples distinguish between the witch (Zulu and Xhosa *zumthakathi*), who is more commonly a woman than man, and who endeavours to bring about the death of an enemy by magic, especially poison, and the wizard (Zulu *inyanga*) who practises the profession of magician and is at the disposal of any member of the public for a fee. The methods of the witch and wizard may often be the same : the difference consists in the purpose.

Various forms of ordeal and divination were occasionally resorted to by the Nguni for the ascertainment of the guilt or innocence of a defendant. But, as in our previous stage,[2] they

---

[1] The Early Codes of Western Europe after A.D. 700 are those termed the " Early Middle Codes " in the present author's *Primitive Law*.

[2] Grade A3 (1).

were used only in the absence of evidence. They were chiefly employed in charges of witchcraft [1] and adultery, but also in theft (which at this present stage becomes so important an offence). Apart from the poison ordeal for witchcraft, the main forms of ordeal were two: the ordeal by hot water and the ordeal by hot iron. The ordeal was not applied to witnesses, and the oath was unknown.

As for the religious beliefs of the Nguni,[2] they exemplify the views expressed in this book as to the main bases and origins of religion, and in particular the truth that man's mental images, and the emotions associated with them, have a continuity which is not limited to the continuity of the physical phenomena which they represent. The main difference between the religion of the Nguni and that of the peoples of our previous stage [3] is that among the Nguni (as among many other peoples) the ancestors figure more vividly than the God, and the religion is an ancestor-worship rather more than a worship of the God. They believe in a soul that wanders in sleep and survives as a spirit after death, continuing to live much as it did in this life. The most important spirits for them are the souls of the persons who were most important to them during life—namely, their parents and ancestors. These, on whom they relied so much in life, continue, as they believe, to interest themselves actively in the affairs of their descendants and their tribe, to resent breach of custom by their descendants, and to expect attention by gifts and sacrifice. They can send blessings if pleased, and disease, drought, and disaster if slighted. The more important and powerful they were on earth, the more important and powerful they remain, and above all in importance are the ancestors of the chief, the ancestors of the senior lineage of the tribe. They are pleased by sacrifice made by the senior living member of their family, and therefore it is for the chief, and for the chief alone, to perform the sacrifices to his ancestors. The ancestors declare their desires in various ways, and sometimes through prophets—persons who are

---

[1] Usually by divination or the ordeal by poison.

[2] See, for the religion of the Nguni, in particular Willoughby, *The Soul of the Bantu* (1928), and Schapera, *South Bantu*, Chapters X and XI.

[3] Grade A3 (1).

prone to see visions, and who become recognized as such (like the prophets in Israel and the *shamans* in so many parts of the world) by having once seen a vision or undergone a great spiritual experience. They prophesy good fortune for those who obey, and disaster for those who will not listen.

All these sacrifices are, for the most part, stereotyped, slight, ceremonious, and unemotional affairs. There is no question of the burden of sin and repentance, of self-abasement, or even of ethical conduct dictated by religion—except that it is right to adhere to the old ways, and that the ancestral spirits will be angered, and may do mischief, if customs are forsaken.

There is also a vague but universal belief among the Nguni in a Supreme Being connected with the sky. He is also the creator of all, and can deal out punishment, especially by sending disastrous weather. But he is never worshipped, and neither prayer nor sacrifice is offered to him. The ancestors can approach him as mediators on behalf of their descendants, like some important headman approaching a chief, or—as we might say—like a patron saint mediating with God.[1] In particular, they can appeal to him to send rain from the sky. It is the function of the chief—as it is in many another tribe— to obtain rain for his people by interceding with his ancestors by means of one of the many rain-making rites. He is also the custodian of various sacred objects and medicines, and magicians work at his command. He conducts other import- ant religious ceremonies for the whole tribe. In this sense only he is the chief priest, but there is no priestly caste or order.

These beliefs, and the belief in various mischievous local spirits of divers sorts, that beset the step of the traveller, are the bulk of the religious beliefs of the Nguni. Because their beliefs are such, there are no places, hallowed by religion, to which a man may flee to save his life. The sanctuary among the Nguni is the kraal of the chief counsellor, who also acts as a sort of Court of Appeal against any arbitrary action of the king.[2]

Something has been said in an earlier chapter of the religion

[1] Willoughby, *Race Problems in the New Africa* (1923), pp. 78 *et seq.*
[2] *Cape Commission*, Evidence, p. 83.

of the German tribes in the time of Tacitus, and though little is known of their religious beliefs between that date and the close of heathen times, there is no reason to infer any great change. As compared with the religion of the Nguni, the stress is rather upon the worship of gods than of ancestors, though the worship of the dead was general. As tribes coalesced into large communities each tended to bring their own Sky-god with them, and the numbers of gods and goddesses increased. It is plain that there was no room in their religion, any more than in the religion of the Nguni, for religious ethics or notions of the burden of sin or repentance. It is also plain that in most places there was no caste or order of priests. Perhaps in England there were more priests than elsewhere, but certainly in Iceland and Scandinavia the priest was but a chief or landowner who occupied land containing a shrine, and in this he officiated. The sacred trees and groves of Tacitus were turning into the pillared halls of temples and served as sanctuaries to fleeing offenders, but they were not by any means to be found everywhere. The king was in many places the high priest in the sense that it was for him to perform solemn sacrifices at the chief temples, and the health and prosperity of the community depended in part on his health and his sacrifices. Occasionally, like kings elsewhere, he was sacrificed for the community's welfare, and there is evidence of human sacrifice here and there, and the slaying of slaves to accompany their royal master in the next world. Apart from various methods of divination, all believed in the continuance of the spirit after death in a vague region of the underground near the place of burial.

Apart from various methods of divination, the guilt of defendants was ascertained, in the absence of evidence, mainly by the same two ordeals as among the Nguni—namely, the ordeal by hot iron and the ordeal by hot water—and these two ordeals remained in use in England and France for many centuries after the introduction of Christianity. Generally speaking, as among the Nguni, writing was not in use; for the so-called runic writing of Europe was appropriate only for inscriptions and was but rarely employed.

It is obvious, from what has been said, how complete a

transformation must have been wrought in the first century or two after Christianity was introduced.   No longer was there a tribal religion supporting the authority and prestige of the king, who was its necessary pinnacle or link with the great deceased ancestors.   Christianity was an international religion, and the priests derived their authority from outside the realm.   The appeal and power of religion would in any case have grown, but the Church grew to power partly at the expense of the strength of the kingship.   To the missionaries, indeed, who came to the little English kingdoms, these seemed trivial compared with the Merovingian monarchies, and it was their settled policy from the first to substitute a kingdom of England.   In the kingdoms both of France and England the authority of the king, at the time of the conversion of each kingdom to Christianity, enabled him to put forth legislation to meet the altered circumstances of the State, but the authority of kingship decreased, and everywhere the flow of legislation soon ceased as the king's power to enforce his laws diminished.   In the broken Merovingian monarchy of the seventh century there was no longer power to legislate and no longer legislation.   In the English kingdoms we find the same situation at the corresponding times.   Only when Charles climbed into the seat of an overlord of the growing Church could there again be a powerful, because it was a theocratic, monarchy.

In place of the dispassionate performance of the practices of heathendom, there grew a devotion to the new religion and a deep sense of sin.   The Frank and the Anglo-Saxon were as credulous and superstitious as they were ignorant.   They flocked to church at the ringing of the bells, and they dreaded the torments of hell.   In place of the perfunctory sacrifices to pagan gods came the lavish and constant gifts to the Church throughout life and at death's approach, and already at the close of the Merovingian age it is estimated that the Church held a third of the land of France.   By then the great men of the Church stood side by side with their kinsmen, the secular magnates, as landowners and administrators, sitting upon the councils of the kingdom and governing their estates, dispensing justice to the occupiers and leading them in battle.   By A.D.

700 they are in the position to claim, in the words of the opening clause of the Laws of Wihtred of Kent, that they are "immune from taxation," and while " the king shall be prayed for, they shall honour him freely and without compulsion."

The clergy had a monopoly of letters. All our codes and legislation were written by the hand of ecclesiastics. They were in sole custody of the texts, and hardly anyone else could read or write. Indeed, the words " clerk " and " clerical " still signify in our language both the writer and the priest. Though in the Dark Age of the seventh century learning of all kinds almost died away, the clergy were the sole inheritors of Latin letters, with all the prestige that this then involved. We must try to remember what this meant in the circumstances of the time. Scholarship was unknown. Even Cassiodorus, to whom more than anyone else we owe the survival of Latin texts in the sixth century, advises the monks of Vivarium, in his Institutiones Divinarum Lectionum, that emendations in the sacred texts should be as well written as the originals, " that they may rather be thought to have been written by the ancients." There was no knowledge of the past that would enable a cleric to distinguish a current tradition from historical truth, and no quality or motive that might deter him from altering or adding to the work of others.

In the early days after the conversion to Christianity, the Church took little or no active interest in the secular affairs of the State. It was concerned with an ideal State in the next world, not the present. But by the year A.D. 700 this attitude had become reversed. The new temporal responsibilities of the Church, as landowners, judges, and advisers of the Crown, could not fail to give them an interest in civil government.

The result of all these factors was that by the year A.D. 700 the Church had a standpoint and aims of its own in legislation. When Christianity was first introduced, the cleric acted as the royal amanuensis, faithfully recording what it was his duty to record—namely, the legislation of the king. By A.D. 700 he was often compiling, under the guise of legislation or a code of law of a people or the title-deeds of a religious foundation, that which was in the interests of the Church or expressed its aims. As for legislation, the Church had the power and influence to secure that the laws issued by the king were in the interests of the Church and religion as they conceived them. As to codes of law, they often compiled collections not so much of rules actually in force as of those which they desired to see in force; and all this in the unmistakable language of religion and holy writ. But, in addition, there were compilations of rules and title-deeds of property which were nothing more nor less than forgeries. Innumerable forged land-books were in the possession of English monasteries from A.D. 700 onwards purporting to confer upon them rights to land which they did not possess. Even the Canon Law of the Church was in large measure developed by means of forged decretals, being often additions to documents of authority, by which authority they sought to obtain credence. The Hispana of the seventh century was finally expanded by the middle of the ninth century into the fraudulent compilation of the Pseudo-Isidore, and, being accepted by the Popes, formed the foundation of a great legal structure. Forgeries were an important source of new law.

But for our present purpose it matters less to consider whether a document is genuine than to note the changes from the earlier documents which preceded. We begin, in the Code of Æthelberht, and chapters 2–36 of the Salic Law, with terse clauses of purely secular legislation with secular sanctions. From the year A.D. 700 onwards we find every gradation between collections of true secular law and forgeries. We find in the same documents a few scanty rules of secular law, rules of ecclesiastical law (that is to say, rules governing the conduct of ecclesiastics), rules of religious ethics, and even sermons—we find in the same documents rules with secular sanctions, rules with religious sanctions, and rules with no sanctions at all.

There were further reasons why the Church had come to take a practical interest in the secular law. One was the fact that in increasing numbers refugees whose life was in danger took sanctuary in churches, seeking the protection of a place where a pursuer would hesitate to shed blood. Very often they fled from the messengers of a king who sought to wreak revenge or inflict the capital sanction for a criminal offence.

The Church could not allow the sanctuary to be violated by the pursuers; and, on the other hand, it could not allow the privilege of sanctuary to be abused. Hence it was often compelled to hold some investigation into the circumstances, and the Codes from A.D. 700 have much to say on this subject. For example, the Lex Baiuvariorum (a bogus compilation of the middle of the eighth century) provides [1] that no refugee is to be dragged away until he has appealed to the presbyter or bishop; and in Wessex the Laws of Ine [2] (about A.D. 700) lay it down that if anyone is liable to the death penalty and he flees to a church, his life shall be spared, and he shall pay such compensation as he is ordered according to right.

Far more important was the change that was taking place in the ordeal. The ordeals by hot iron and hot water survived, but were undergone in church.[3]   In addition, the introduction of Christianity brought or spread the oath, and this, too, was taken in church—the holiest of places, whose sanctity was most likely to deter a guilty defendant from taking it, or to declare his guilt. At first it was used in the cases in which the ordeal had hitherto been used—that is to say, rarely and where there was no real evidence.   Accordingly its main use was in charges of witchcraft, theft—now becoming so common and so serious—and adultery. A man finds his property in the possession of the defendant, who says he has bought it outside the country or from a stranger who has disappeared, so that he cannot " vouch a warrantor." The defendant's story is tested by the oath.[4]   There are also various other types of circumstances, where the defendant is charged with a murder or other wrong, committed when no one was present. The trial before the secular court is adjourned for the defendant to swear his innocence in church with his hand on the altar.[5] The oath administered by the priest takes the place of the ordeal administered by the medicine-man.

These cases, all told, were uncommon, and in all other cases

[1] Tit. 1, Chapter 6.   [2] Chapter 5.
[3] See, for an account of their final form in England, and the circumstances in which they were administered, F. L. Attenborough, *The Laws of the Earliest English Kings* (1922), pp. 187-9.
[4] See H. & E., *c.* 16.   [5] See Wihtred, *cc.* 19, 20, 21.

evidence was unsworn; and so no mention of oath or ordeal is found in our earliest documents.[1] But the ecclesiastical mind takes great interest in ceremony and procedure,[2] and especially religious ceremony. A great many procedural rules for the taking of the oath arose in England and France, and this was largely because of the extent of the perjury committed, and the weakness of the kings and their courts. The oath continued to be used, in the words of the second half of the Lex Salica, only " where there is no sure (or definite) proof";[3] but now there are rules providing that the defendant must swear his innocence with a fixed number of " swearers," who take the oath with him   There are numerous references in the Anglo-Saxon[4] and Continental laws to " witnesses " giving " evidence " on oath, and it is plain that these " swearers " or oath-helpers, who swear with the accused, are supposed to be giving evidence of their own knowledge, though of course there is no rule excluding hearsay evidence. In France and England there are rules providing for a larger number of oath-helpers, or more responsible or substantial oath-helpers, the more serious the charge.   This is probably the furthest point reached in Anglo-Saxon England, and it is not likely that here a man was entitled to clear himself by oath where the evidence against him was plain—for example, where he was caught in the act.[5]

But this phrase in the Lex Salica, allowing the accused to clear himself by oath, with or without oath helpers, " where there is no sure proof," is a dangerous phrase. When the monarch is weak and his courts are weak—and in the Frankish kingdom in the dark age of A.D. 600–725 both were indeed weak—in a lawsuit between two great men of the realm before the king's court, the court may take refuge behind the phrase, whatever the evidence may be, and hold that there is " no sure proof."   The requisite number of oath-helpers is by degrees

[1] I.e., the Laws of Æthelberht, and the Salic Law, chaps. 2–36.
[2] The second half of the Lex Salica (from chap. 37) contains a great many accounts of customary procedure among the Franks, some of which are difficult to accept.
[3] See Lex Salica, cc. 39 (2), 42 (5); " Si probatio certa non fuit."
[4] See H. & E., cc. 2 and 4.
[5] See Ine, c. 37 (cf. c. 18), IV Æthelstan, c. 6.

increased, but perjury is rife, and the defendant can always find relatives or friends who will swear with him. The appropriate number of oath-helpers is fixed for more and more wrongs, and sometimes the plaintiff is given a right to nominate half of the defendant's swearers who will swear with him. By now it is plain that they are ceasing to be witnesses who depose to the facts. They are merely recording their belief in the innocence of the defendant.

The only result is that there is more perjury than ever, and plaintiffs begin to " take the law into their own hands " and resort to violence. This point was reached at the beginning of the eighth century, and a development of quite a different kind was taking place at the same time. There had recently been introduced into France from the Eastern Empire an improved breed of heavy war-horse, a saddle highly peaked in front and back, and the use of heavily armed and protected horsemen. Till now, like the Anglo-Saxon, the Frankish soldier had fought on foot, but the new method is spreading, and the training is becoming intensive and absorbing. In the succeeding centuries it is fundamental to the developed European type of feudalism. We are speaking of the king's courts in France, where a large proportion of the litigants were great men of the realm. In these circumstances, where the plaintiff refused to accept the oaths offered to him, the courts made the best of their unhappy position and allowed him to challenge the defendant to battle. He who has justice on his side will win, and the law contents itself with making rules for the conduct of the battle.

That this was the reason for the ordeal by battle is made clear by a clause of the Burgundian Code (Chapter 45) which does not pretend to be part of the original code, but to be a later enactment of Gundobald. It cannot be as early as Gundobald, but in other respects the passage speaks for itself: " Many, we find, are so depraved, that they do not hesitate to offer an oath upon things uncertain, and to commit perjury upon things unknown to them." In future, if the party to whom an oath has been offered refuses to accept it, and " believes, confident in the truth of his cause, that he can convict his adversary by force of arms, and the other party does not yield, licence to battle shall not be refused." And if a witness of the party offering the oath is defeated in the contest, every witness who offered to take the oath " shall be fined 300 solidi . . . so that they may delight in truth rather than perjury." No doubt the fact that the battle was an attractive and popular spectacle helped to heal the wounds in the prestige of the law.

In this way an abnormal spread of the use of the ordeal brought about what was, in a sense, a breakdown of the judicial system. To the Church the trial of lawsuits by the oath of God, based as it was on good biblical authority,[1] must have seemed entirely worthy of a truly theocratic State; but even the Frankish populace would not tolerate it—not, at any rate, the *jeunesse dorée* litigating in the King's Court. Ordeal by battle spread far and wide over the Continent, but it only reached England with the Norman conquest. But then it must be remembered that trial by oath had never spread so far in Anglo-Saxon England, nor did the Anglo-Saxon fight on horseback. His pony was adequate to take him to the scene of battle, but not to fight upon it.[2]

There is some evidence of a slight similar development in the law at a later stage in mediæval Christian Abyssinia. There are some Moslem peoples, of a like stage of development, where the impact of an advanced religion on a backward economy has produced a wide spread of the ordeal by oath, such as is found in Anglo-Saxon England or in France up to A.D. 700. For example, among the Sinai Bedouin, where the ordeal by oath is used only in the absence of sufficient evidence, among some of the tribes the defendant must be supported by the oaths of oath-helpers in the more serious cases, and the plaintiff has the right to dictate the oath and to choose the men of the defendant's family or tribe who will swear with him.[3] But, as we shall see, among the vast bulk of the peoples of the present and the past, the use of the ordeal spread but a little way even in the higher economic stages.[4]

---

[1] See, e.g., Exodus, 22[9].

[2] See Carl Stephenson, *Mediæval Feudalism* (1942).

[3] See A. Kennett, *Bedouin Justice* (1925), pp. 40, 41. They also use the ordeal by hot iron.

[4] See further as to the course of this development of the ordeal in the *leges barbarorum*, *Primitive Law*, Chap. 31.

BOOK III

EARLY CIVILIZATION

CHAPTER I

THE CENTRAL CODES

Economics

AT the stage of the Central Codes barbarism is at its close and civilization may be said to begin. In the sphere of religion the Central Codes mark the point at which religion everywhere—and not merely in Mediæval Europe—is well-developed and organized, and a powerful force. In the economic sphere they indicate a stage at which pastoralism and agriculture equally provide the sustenance of the people, and when villages and towns and organized markets are to be found. The pledging of persons for debt begins, and personal execution for debt. In the field of administration feudalism reaches its apex during this stage. In the law relating to personal injuries—the most precise of all tests of advance—the sanctions for homicide are on the verge of becoming capital, and the typical sanction for homicide is the handing over of a number of persons to the group of the slain. In the field of criminal sanctions there is a beginning of mutilations.

In Western Europe we shall take as nations representative of this stage the people of France between A.D. 800 and 1000.[1] and the English from 900 to 1100. Some centuries before this, and before the Frankish invasion, the Visigoths and Burgundians, who had been settled for some time in the Roman Empire before it ceased to be, had also advanced to this stage. The impressive fragments of the Code of Euric[2] (King of the Visigoths from A.D. 466 to 485) belong to the Central Codes; and so, too, does the excellent Burgundian Code of King Gundobald[3] (at any rate without its later additions) at the beginning of the sixth century. At last we reach back into the written records of the ancient world, and the Code of the

[1] The corresponding period in Germany and Eastern Europe is later in time,
[2] Zeumer, *Leges Visigothorum Antiquiores* (1894).
[3] *M.G.H.*, Legum Tom. 3.

Hittites [1] well exemplifies our present stage.   It dates from the period, round about the middle of the fourteenth century B.C., when the Hittite Empire, which stood on the outskirts of Mesopotamian civilization, was in its prime in Central and South-Eastern Asia Minor.

In Africa there is a great number of peoples from which to take our examples.   If we start from the area of East Africa from which we took instances of an earlier stage of advance [2]— namely, the homes of the Nandi, Kavirondo, and Lango— and move westwards round the north side of Lake Victoria, we reach a fertile and well-watered corridor bounded on the east by Lake Victoria and on the west by the chain of lakes Albert, Edward, and Kivu and the mountain mass of Ruwenzori.   Here are to be found the nations of the Baganda,[3] the Bakitara (or Banyoro),[4] and the Banyankole,[5] all of which belong to the stage of the Central Codes.   This corridor has been a strategic highway whereby Negro-Hamite pastoralists have migrated southwards from the Upper Nile to the plateaux of Ruanda and Tanganyika.   Still further to the south peoples of this stage are to be found in Northern Rhodesia. We may take as examples the Lamba people,[6] who dwell partly in North-West Rhodesia and partly inside the projecting south-east corner of the Belgian Congo;   and the Bemba tribe,[7] which inhabits the Tanganyika plateau in North-Eastern Rhodesia, between the four great lakes of Nyasa, Tanganyika, Mweru, and Bangweolu.[8]   If we start again from our East African tribes, and instead of travelling westwards move south-east towards the civilization of the coast of the Indian Ocean, we reach on the way, in an arid belt parallel with the

---

[1] See *ante*, p. 75.   [2] Grade A3 (1).

[3] See Roscoe, *Baganda* (1911); L. P. Mair, *An African People in the Twentieth Century* (1934).

[4] See Roscoe, *The Bakitara or Banyoro* (1923).

[5] See Oberg, " The Kingdom of Ankole in Uganda," in *A.P.S.* (1940).

[6] See Doke, *The Lambas of Northern Rhodesia* (1931).

[7] See Audrey I. Richards, *The Political System of the Bemba Tribe*, in *A.P.S.* (1940); *Land, Labour, and Diet in Northern Rhodesia* (1939).

[8] For the peoples to the south-west of the Lamba, see the *Ila-speaking Peoples of Northern Rhodesia*, by Smith and Dale (1920).   They belong to the same stage of advance.

coast and some 100 miles inland, the Wateita,[1] Waboni,[2] and Wanyika,[3] all of which tribes are of the same stage of advance. If, again, we start from the Nguni peoples of the east coast of South Africa, whom we took as instances of the peoples of the Early Codes, and move to the north and somewhat inland, from the less advanced Nguni of the Cape through the Northern Nguni of Natal, we reach the still more advanced South Sotho of Basutoland, the Northern Sotho, the Venda, and the Shangana-Tonga of the Northern Transvaal,[4] who are all of the stage of the Central Codes.

Some of the more backward tribes of West Africa also belong to the same stage, and there are a number of them in Nigeria and the Northern Territories of the Gold Coast, to whom we shall have occasion to refer.[5]

In detail these populations present a varying economic picture. In France and England, peoples that commenced in historical times, in their homes in Germany and elsewhere, as mainly pastoralists (as indeed the Celtic tribes of Wales and Scotland still were in A.D. 900 to 1100) have also become increasingly agricultural.[6] In places, even before this period, a shifting cultivation had already changed into a system under which land nearest to the homestead or cluster of homesteads formed more or less permanent fields (cultivated in a two-course rotation of cereals and fallow), while further away the grazing land was still held on the old shifting method—that is to say, parts were cleared and ploughed and cultivated till they were exhausted and allowed to revert to pasture, when other parts were cleared and ploughed.[7] But now we have, in addition, villages and groups of hamlets with large permanent arable

---

[1] See E.A.L., vol. i (1906), p. 102; vol. ii, pp. 143-4.

[2] See ibid., vol. i, p. 102.

[3] See ibid., vol. i, pp. 98 et seq.; vol. ii, p. 148; vol. iii, 121.

[4] See Schapera, Select Bibliography; and Schapera, South Bantu.

[5] For example, in the Northern Territories of the Gold Coast, the Tallensi (see Prof. M. Fortes' The Web of Kinship among the Tallensi, and in A.P.S., pp. 239-71). For examples from North-East Nigeria, see the Margi of Adamawa Province (Meek, Tribal Studies, vol. i, pp. 213 et seq.) and the Katab (op. cit., vol. ii, p. 78).

[6] This is also true of our peoples of South Africa.

[7] The same situation is found, e.g., among the Tallensi (see Fortes in A.P.S. at p. 248).

fields of well-known boundaries, and grazing land and wood and waste all within the known boundaries of the village. But the tilling of land is heavy work, and the men do not care for work. In England and France the lord abstains: the ploughing is done by the male slave, as it had been in Tacitus' time in Germany. As then, he is given a plot of land for his use, and allowed to put up his hut upon it, and his obligation is to give a return in kind for the land in his use, and labour-services as ploughman on his lord's demesne [1] in addition. The free churl or peasant works on his land and gives a rent in kind, and sometimes some labour services, especially at harvest. The women do the bulk of the hoeing. But at the end of our period, in Kent—still the most forward area of England—money-rents are becoming common.

Conditions among some of our other peoples are different in varying degree. In the kingdoms of Uganda the general picture is of a native negro agricultural people (the Bairu) ruled by a conquering, immigrant Hamitic or Negro-Hamitic pastoral people (the Bahima). In the result there is the same picture as in Western Europe of a non-tilling nobility and tilling serfs, and only the details differ, for in many areas of Western Europe, too, invading pastoralists had established themselves as a ruling class over native agriculturists. Among the Baganda the immigrant nomads were comparatively few in number, and a fusion of populations took place, so that only the royal family boasted of its pastoral descent. But in the more pastoral kingdoms of Bunyoro and Toro, and even more in Ankole, the cleavage remained strict. Intermarriage generally was unthinkable—the Bairu had, indeed, no cattle to pay a bride-price, nor were they allowed to possess or acquire any, or even to herd or milk their lord's cattle. The nobility of the kingdom continued to live almost entirely on milk, and eschewed vegetable food. Some favoured indivi-duals among the Bairu were rewarded by the king with freedom and land for conspicuous service and could inter-marry with a willing family of the nobility. The despised artisans were all of the Bairu.

---

[1] The demesne is the home farm, that part of the lord's land by which his family is supported.

The Bemba and Lamba peoples of Northern Rhodesia present a different picture again. Most of their land is, and has long been, infested with tsetse-fly, so that the Awalamba have few cattle and the Babemba none, and indeed the latter have no pastoral traditions. Accordingly, the Awalamba and Babemba are agricultural peoples with subsidiary hunting, and from these circumstances flow a number of results, differentiating them from the bulk of peoples of this stage—for example, matrilineal inheritance and matrilocal marriage. For the same reason, among the Babemba there is no means of storing wealth and no organized markets, and marriage is mainly by service instead of bride-price.

Again, some of these tribes in East and West Africa are portions of larger aggregates from which they have separated as colonizing groups, or are remnants of conquered peoples who have lost their independence and are subject-groups of native peoples of a higher material culture, or have been separated into groups by infiltrating tribes with whom they share a wide territory. Such situations in West Africa have been stabilized by British occupation, which has prevented the completion of processes of invasion and absorption, coalescence or massacre. All these factors produce important results in the field of government.

Again, there are wide differences between Europe and Africa. Africa south of the Sahara and Abyssinia—partly because it has been separated so long from most of the civilized world, and partly because of its unfavourable and enervating climate—is of a backward technology. Though the heavy plough was known to peoples of Western Europe of our present stage 2,000 years ago,[1] having been obtained from higher neighbouring civilizations, and though the ox-drawn plough was in general use in England and France long before A.D. 1100 and among the Hittites in 1350 B.C., it is only reaching Africa at the present time. The woman's hoe is, or was till the other day, the chief agricultural implement among the Baganda and all our other African peoples of this stage. There are no farm-carts and (except in Abyssinia and in

[1] It is thought to have been possessed by the Belgæ in England (75 B.C. and onwards). The soil of Africa is generally lighter.

West Africa north of the line of the Niger and the Benue) no horse or other riding-animal. Africa (south of Egypt and excluding Abyssinia) never achieved a system of writing of its own nor received one from foreign civilizations, or even from Abyssinia.

Again, where the soil of Africa is poor and where it is fertile, because of the unfavourable climatic and ecological conditions, the population is scanty in comparison with that which the fertility of the soil could support, and nowhere at this or previous stages is there a shortage of land. Consequently, except in parts of Southern Nigeria, there still persists the shifting cultivation in which the men clear the ground and the women work it till it is exhausted, and the results in the field of social organization are not unimportant.

Nevertheless, in spite of these and other differences that show themselves from place to place, agriculture has on the whole progressed, and its products have become considerably more varied. In England there is a greater proportion of wheat and less of rye and oats; and in Kent and among the Hittites there is a great interest in the planting of vines and fruit-trees.[1] There is no space here to list the varying products of agriculture in all these climates.

The average size of these populations has increased. The Baganda probably numbered between 2,000,000 and 3,000,000 in the third quarter of the last century, but as a result of civil war, famine, and the scourge of the tsetse-fly the number was reduced in the 1931 Census to 870,000. The population of Bunyoro was reduced by 1919 to 102,509, and of the neighbouring kingdom of Toro to 126,000.[2] The Bemba tribe number about 140,000. In South Africa the populations are

---

[1] H.C. ii, 1–9; Lex Burg., Tit. 31.

[2] The total population of the kingdoms of Buganda, Bunyoro, Ankole, and Toro is likely to have exceeded 6,000,000 in the middle of the nineteenth century. See, for some collected figures in regard to Uganda, Kuczynski, vol. ii, chap. IX. There is a separation of the sexes from pregnancy until weaning (which is when the child is about two years old) see Felkin, *Notes on the Wapanda Tribe* (1886); Roscoe, pp. 55–6; Lugard, *The Story of the Uganda Protectorate*, p. 30. For figures relating to the Wanyika and Wateita, see Kuczynski, vol. ii, p. 150; for figures relating to the Basuto and Swazis, ibid., p. 31; and for Northern Rhodesia, ibid., chap. XI.

again scanty. In England during this period the kingdom expanded, from a precarious hold over Wessex in Alfred's time, to a rule over a country-wide population of about 1,500,000 at the time of Domesday Book (A.D. 1086). The varying limits of the French monarchy preclude an estimate of its population. The King of the Hittites is likely to have ruled over a few hundred thousand souls.

The density of population has also increased, for an advance in agriculture enables the land to support a larger population. At one extreme, among the Babemba, where the soil is poor and dry and fly-infested, it is only 3.75 persons per square mile, and four per square mile over Northern Rhodesia generally; in England in A.D. 1086 approximately twenty per square mile; and the average density in the four provinces of Uganda is (like the population of the old kingdom of Buganda) about forty-four persons per square mile.[1]

The population no longer consists wholly or mainly of homesteads, but the bulk live in small villages or hamlets, usually climbing the slope of the same hill, like the Ganda village, or occupying the bank of the same stream. The Bemba village contains an average of thirty to fifty huts.[2] The Lamba villages consist of about twenty to thirty huts.[3] The South Sotho have numerous villages of from ten to fifty independent households, with a population of usually not more than a score of persons, and rarely more than 250.[4] In England even in the eleventh century, only a very substantial village had thirty households, though a few here and there were much bigger. Villages and hamlets of from two to six households were very common.[5] Water supply has much to do in determining the size of villages. In the north and west of England, where there are good springs of water everywhere, the hamlets were very small. In Eastern England larger

---

[1] Total population in 1931 3,500,000, and land area 80,000 square miles. The Bunyoro population is considerably thinner.

[2] Dr. A. I. Richards in *A.P.S.*, p. 89. The village is a kinship unit first and foremost. Under its shifting method of cultivation it moves every four or five years.

[3] Doke, p. 27.

[4] A. W. Hoernle in Schapera, *South Bantu*, at pp. 70 and 88.

[5] Clapham, p. 44.

villages tended to form on a suitable water-course. The same contrast is manifest in different areas of South Africa.

There are also towns of growing size. In 1086 London had perhaps a population of 12,000; York, Lincoln, and Norwich half that number; and Gloucester about 3,000; and there were several other important towns. The largest town everywhere is the capital of the king or paramount chief. Here the court is held, and the hereditary or other advisers and officers of the Government (including his relatives) reside, as well as the courtiers and young folk of both sexes who are being brought up at court for the king's service, and the messengers (Charlemagne's *missi dominici*) who go about the country on the king's business. In the towns, or moving about elsewhere to find custom, are some specialist craftsmen, still a somewhat despised class, and the travelling merchants, not quite so despised and mistrusted as they have been.

Towns mean markets. In Buganda King Mtesa had only recently introduced them when the British entered;[1] and similarly in England markets are not mentioned in the Anglo-Saxon Laws till the first half of the tenth century.[2] In England and Buganda they are regular and organized; a special official is in charge,[3] and there are market dues in proportion to the value of the goods sold.[4] In Europe and the Hittite Empire and elsewhere there are laws fixing the prices of a substantial number of commodities. The quantity of goods has increased, and the law is much troubled about the extent of theft, and a large proportion of the Anglo-Saxon and Hittite laws is devoted to this offence, which is now considered heinous. For the protection of the buyer against a claim by the seller or a third person that the goods are his and that the buyer has stolen them, it becomes a general practice to conduct all transactions of any importance before witnesses. Indeed, in order to lessen the traffic in stolen goods, some Anglo-Saxon

---

[1] Mair, p. 130. In South Africa and Rhodesia the soil is mainly poor and the populations scanty, and there is as yet very little of markets.

[2] See 1 Edward, *c.* 1.

[3] A special chief in Buganda; the " port-reeve " in England.

[4] In Buganda, according to Roscoe, 10%. For England (Billingsgate) see IV Æthelred, *c.* 2.

laws ordain that all transactions[1] or all transactions of any
value[2] shall take place before witnesses. The number of
witnesses is large—about five, on the average,[3] where the
goods are valuable; but then the transactions are oral, and false
evidence is rife. Even among the Hittites and in Western
Europe, though writing is in use for the purposes of government and administration, including the promulgation and
recording of laws, it is not employed in private business
transactions. Everywhere the bulk of transactions take the
form of what we will call " ready barter "—that is to say,
simultaneous exchange, leaving no obligations to be performed
on either side. We hear rarely, as we have rarely heard before,[4]
of a market rule that if a defect of a particular kind shows itself
within a certain number of days—e.g., the cow which was
purchased dies—the transaction is to be made good.[5] Otherwise there is nothing of a law of sale or exchange. Sale is in
any case uncommon, for money is hardly in use for the small
everyday transaction. Although there is a currency of some
kind among all these tribes who hold markets,[6] most payments,
whether for goods bought or rents or the services of an
artisan, are in kind. There is now a good deal of hiring, both
of goods and services, and the Hittite Code fixes charges for
both—some in silver and some in corn.

The hiring of goods is particularly important from the legal
point of view. For the first time, men are in possession of
other persons' goods under a commercial transaction, and
liable to return them. Evidence is still generally unsworn

---

[1] I Edward, 1 (no man shall buy except in a port—i.e., market town—in
the presence of the port-reeve or other unlying men, whom man can trust).
This, if it is a genuine law, was no doubt a pious hope.

[2] II Æthelstan, 12 (no one shall buy goods worth more than twenty
pence outside a " port," and he shall buy in the presence of the port-reeve
or other unlying man or before the reeves in folkmoot).

[3] II Canute, 24, fixes a minimum of four men, trustworthy witnesses, on a
purchase of livestock or other property over 4d. in value, whether in town
or country. The attitude and purpose of all these laws are shown by the
fact that they all refer to " buying," not selling. See also " Lex Burg.,"
Tit. 17 and 43; Code of Euric, c. 286.

[4] In regard to Kikuyu and Kamba markets.   [5] Ine, c. 56.

[6] Mainly silver coinage in Western Europe; among the Hittites silver
passing by weight; cowrie-shells in Buganda, etc.

(except in mediæval Europe), and there is a problem of a new kind where a man hires goods—for example, in Europe and among the Hittites, a working-ox for the plough or wagon—and, when the time comes to return it, says he cannot do so because it has been lost or destroyed. In modern English law the hirer is liable if the goods are lost or destroyed through his negligence, and the onus of proof is on him to show by his sworn evidence that they were lost or destroyed without his negligence; but he is not liable in the absence of negligence unless he has agreed that he shall be. At the stage of law represented by the Central Codes there is no notion yet of negligence. But, as in modern English law, it is not felt to be satisfactory that the hirer merely states his version of the facts, which no one can contest. The Codes apply the ordeal, which is now usually an ordeal by oath, and say that he must swear it. The Hittite Code provides : "If anyone hires an ox, horse, mule or ass, and it dies, or a wolf eats it, or it perishes in some other way, then he must give him (i.e., the owner) another : but if he says ' It died by the hand of God ' then he must swear it." The ordeal, that is to say, is being applied, as usual, to a case where there is not sufficient evidence to decide the matter—only a statement on the one side, and no knowledge on the part of anyone else. All genuine ancient Codes of this and the following stage have clauses, in growing numbers, applying the ordeal by oath to loss of goods, the subject-matter of a bailment.[1] There is also a good deal, in the Anglo-Saxon laws at this stage, of the use of the ordeal by oath where a man charged with theft says that he bought the goods from a third person whom he cannot produce. We have seen something of this before. The ordeal is again being used where there is no evidence to test the story of one of the parties. There is a good deal also of loan of goods for consumption, or loan on the terms that different goods are to be returned.[2] As

[1] E.g., Code of Euric, cc. 278–80; Edictum Theoderici, c. 119 (the only clause providing for the oath). A " bailment " is the term given in modern English law to a transaction in which goods of one man are entrusted to another to carry out a certain purpose and then return them to the owner. Hire and deposit are bailments, and so is a loan for use, but not a loan for consumption.

[2] Also some suretyship, see, e.g., Lex Burg., Tit. 17, 19.

money is not in common use, there are more of these transactions than there will be later. A man may, for example,
borrow a bull on the terms of returning a heifer later, the
greater value of the heifer affording the reward to the lender.
Such transactions are not legally important; if the borrower
loses the bull, there is no reason why he should not in due time
repay the heifer.

This great increase in trade and lending means an increase in
the extent of debt. In regard to debt, as in other matters, the
household functions as a group. A man who cannot pay what
he owes with goods or money can pay by the services of himself or a member of his household. Sometimes he will
himself go into what is in fact a voluntary slavery to work off
the debt. More commonly he hands over his unmarried
sister or unmarried child[1] who are living with him—not so
often his wife, for (apart from his affection for her) if he loses
the value of her labour he will indeed be in dire financial
straits. Sometimes he borrows goods or money, and pledges
his child or sister as security. Consequently, it is in accordance with current commercial practice and ideas of right,
when the courts begin—as they do here and there—to award to
the plaintiff in slavery a defendant who cannot pay a debt or
the pecuniary compensation for a wrong committed by him,
and who does not offer a child or sister. Consequently also
there is a vague beginning of the notion that the members of
the household (including slaves) are responsible for the debts
and wrongs of the head of the household, and (still more
vaguely) a notion that the head is responsible for their debts or
wrongs. The latter notion is more vaguely held because the
head of the household owns the goods of the household and
conducts transactions for the family, and the junior members
living with him are less likely to owe debts.

The notion of the responsibility of the household for the
debts of the head applies after the latter's death as well as in
his life-time. There is, for example, an idea that the household
that inherits a man's property should discharge the debts that

---

[1] E.g., Wagiriama (a Nyika tribe): debts may be paid by infant females
(*E.A.L.*, vol. i, p. 100). The Code of Euric, c. 299, prohibits parents from
selling, giving, or pledging children.

the deceased, or they, could have been made to pay during his life. This liability of the successors is not limited to a liability to pay out of the goods inherited. The deceased, in default of goods, could have been made to work off the debt by his labour or that of the members of the household, so there is no reason why this should not happen after his death.

But all these developments are arising slowly, and are as yet in their early stages. The rules of the law on these matters are not yet certain.[1]

Religion has continued to advance in power.[2] In most peoples there are now priests and shrines, and often temples of the gods. Amidst the endless variety of religions, those of the peoples whom we have chosen as examples may perhaps be divided into the following two groups. First, there are those, like the Babemba and the bulk of Bantu peoples, that lay the greater stress on the cult of ancestors, and see an unbroken succession between the dead and their living successors. The greatest of the dead are the dead chiefs, the guardian deities of the land; and the living chief is possessed during life of something akin to divinity, and becomes a god after his death. He is the proper or only person to approach his great ancestors. On his health depends the weal of the community. In many places about the kingdom shrines are erected to the great ancestors, and there are priests of cults and of shrines, and sometimes a priestly order with advisory and even judicial functions.[3] There are, on the other hand, religions, like that of the Baganda, which lay chief stress on the cults of gods (who may or may not be of the distinguished dead). The gods have their temples on the hill-tops, and the temples have their

[1] See, e.g., Doke, *Lambas*, pp. 80–3 and 64 *et seq.* A son is liable to work out his father's debt by slavery. A maternal nephew is responsible for his uncle's debt, and vice versa. A slave who commits adultery is killed and his master beaten. Where a slave steals, the master pays and beats the slave. The master is liable for the act of a slave who burns a grain-store, unless it was accidental. When children steal, the village headman usually orders a parent to make some payment: there is no punishment for the children.

[2] E.g., among the Wadigo all land is considered to belong to God (*E.A.L.*, vol. i, p. 100), and the land of the Tallensi belongs to the Earth Goddess.

[3] E.g., Babemba.

estates and priests, and even a hierarchy of priests, and often prophets who speak the will of the god when possessed. The king is of a semi-divine nature, and supervises the performance of their functions by the priests of the gods. Human sacrifice performs an important part in the rites of many of these peoples, and indeed the scale of murder is in some places enormous and appalling.[1]

In Western Europe the Church continues to advance in wealth, organization, and power. At the end of this period it owns about one-third of Kent, and probably as much of the rest of England and of France. The largest, best administered and most progressive estates are those of the monasteries and other religious foundations. In the realm of law the Church has attained a position of power and privilege that we shall later endeavour to describe.

---

[1] For the Baganda, see Roscoe. Dr. Mair (Chap. IX) points out that not all these occasions were of religious import.

CHAPTER II

THE CENTRAL CODES

FEUDALISM

THE king in Europe—and the king or paramount chief in Africa—is now at the head of a feudal nation or tribe,[1] and it is appropriate at this point to consider what we mean by this, and how it has come about. The basis of the system is supplied by economic needs. Government cannot be carried on without supplies, especially as largess is expected of the ruler, as it has been from the first, and always will be. His supplies cannot be provided by money, for there is not yet sufficient of it, and accordingly they must be provided in kind, by what we call tribute, and must take the form either of goods (mainly food) or services. In an agricultural or partly agricultural community (and all our peoples are such) tribute can only be got from the occupier of land, for on it he lives and finds his food; and this is commonly so even if he belongs to the small minority of the craftsmen.

One of the main functions of the chief is the administration of the land of the people and its fair division among the heads of households. Especially is this so when the people moves to a new territory; and indeed under a system of shifting cultivation villages may move every three or four years. The nation or tribe is at the present stage so large that at least two sub-administrators must be interposed between chief and householder. The land must be divided by the chief into districts, and allotted by him among district chiefs (many of whom are for reasons of safety and good government his relatives), and they in turn allot them to sub-chiefs of villages or (more often) groups of villages, who allot among village headmen and they among heads of households.

[1] He is now often called king of the country, not of the people, both in Western Europe and Africa, and the country has a name (e.g., Ilamba, Buganda, Bunyoro).

It depends on the personality and ability of the king or paramount chief, as well as upon the degree of coalescence of the tribes making up the nation, whether he rules the sub-chiefs and through them the householders,[1] or whether the sub-chief is almost independent;[2] but in all cases the householder necessarily pays his tribute to his immediate chief and the latter passes on part or the whole. Sometimes the householder performs services for the paramount chief, but (except in those territories where the latter is chief as well as paramount chief) the householder is carrying out his chief's duty to perform services for the paramount chief.

The householder who requires land in a particular district must go for it to the chief of that district, and the latter is the administrator-owner of the land of that district, as the king is of the land of the nation. To take three instances of strong central authority, among the Banyoro, Baganda, and Banyankole not only the land but all the cattle of the country was considered to belong to the king, and he could in theory take it away from anyone. At our previous stage of the Early Codes, and until the very end of our present stage, the householder has the freedom to leave an unpopular sub-chief and ask land from another to whom he comes under similar obligations; but as the density of population increases and the superfluity of land disappears that situation must ultimately end, for, if he gives up his land, none other may be available.

This relationship between subject and immediate chief, and between the latter and his head chief, extends not only to rights in land and obligation to pay tribute—both of which are aspects of government—but also to a third aspect—namely, the maintenance of order and the decision of legal disputes. Subject to rules providing for the reservation to the Court of the Great Chief of the most serious cases, the system is one of appeal from headman to district chief and upwards. In each court sits the local chief or his judicial officer with a group of local heads of households, nor could the system work unless they gave their services as members of the Court. It is as part of the system that they owe the duty of " suit of court." In

[1] As, e.g., in Buganda.
[2] As, e.g., among the Lamba people, or, at certain periods, in France.

the court of each chief are tried disputes between any two of his men—for their common chief can enforce his decision upon them—and disputes between two of his sub-chief's men, if they are especially difficult or specially affect the interests of the chief.

There is a fourth aspect of government. The king's functions include the duty of defending the land of the nation, and this necessarily involves the military service of the able-bodied men (who are not necessarily or solely the heads of households), and so every such man is under a duty of military service to his immediate chief, and he to his superior. This is part of his tribute in food and service. The armed men must feed themselves till they reach the frontier.

The new development at the present stage is, as we have seen, that the community becomes more settled in its territory, and its system of cultivation more settled. The economy is more agricultural; there is less superfluity of land, and the fields are more permanent. Accordingly a householder begins to hold (i.e., to be " tenant " of) a fixed, permanent share of the area occupied by the village. Out of this he pays his tribute, and by it he lives. As the chief does not dispossess a freeman (notwithstanding his theoretical right to do so), the freeman obtains a customary and heritable right to hold it. Similarly the sub-chief, originally appointed during pleasure, acquires by a normal legal process and mental process a hereditary post or fief, and so a rank in a developing hierarchy of nobles. The other new development is a specialization and elaboration of the military equipment which the citizen must provide for himself, and the prohibitive cost of the most elaborate.

Human beings erect their economic relationships into diverse philosophies. For example, in the kingdom of Ankole (one of the conquests of the Bahima) the State was, in the mind of the freeman, built upon a relation of *okutoizha* (clientship, homage, or dependency).[1] A Muhima cattle-owner would go before the *mugabe* (king) and swear to follow him in war, and undertake to give him periodically a number of cattle to keep this relationship alive. He was free (provided he did not

[1] K. Oberg in *A.P.S.* at pp. 128–9.

combine with others to do so) to put an end to this relationship by ceasing to pay homage; but till that occurred he was under a duty of military service, a duty to attend the king's kraal bringing periodic gifts of homage, and a duty to give cattle when the king was in temporary or special need.[1] When the client died, his heir reported to the *mugabe* and renewed the bond of clientship by giving a "cow of burial."[2] In return for military service and homage, the client was entitled to protection by the king's forces from cattle-raiders, and retaliation by the king against those who raided his cattle, and the king gave him the right to punish murder by blood revenge, and was also under a duty to maintain peace between his clients. The Bahima were cattle-keepers, not agriculturists. On the other hand, in the kingdom of Buganda, each person held his land from his superior on terms of service, and the king could give away anyone's land to another. These developed forms and relationships are characteristic of the more advanced and independent kingdoms of the present stage. They were to be found, for example, in some degree, in the Hittite Empire, for the Hittite Code contains a section of clauses relating to holdings of land on military and other services.

But in the view of most historians of mediæval Europe, the term "feudalism" is properly applicable only to that institution which grew in France from A.D. 700 onwards, and, adopted by those able administrators the Normans in Normandy and Sicily, was brought by them to England at the Conquest; and the term is not even properly applied to Anglo-Saxon England. They define the two characteristics of feudalism as being the personal relationship of vassalage and the grant of a benefice (or estate in land). There is nothing here that is confined to mediæval Europe. It might be convenient that a distinct expression should be reserved for that French and Norman institution, but its place in history is misunderstood unless it is appreciated that this is but an extreme form of an institution characteristic of a certain stage of economic progress irrespective of time and place. This form of feudalism seems to have arisen in the following circumstances.

In various peoples of this stage the rise of a specialized and

[1] Known in Europe as a feudal "aid."   In Europe a "relief."

costly type of military equipment has limited its use to a wealthy class. For example, among the Baganda, according to Roscoe, the warriors had spears and shields : the peasants joined them as bearers or followers with only clubs or heavy sticks. Among the Mangbetu of the Congo the freemen were armed with lance or throwing-spear and shield, the lower classes with bow and arrow.[1] Before A.D. 700 there was introduced into the eastern Roman Empire over its Asiatic border, and there developed, the use of heavily armed and protected soldiers mounted on an improved and heavy breed of horse with a highly peaked saddle. Till A.D. 700—as in England until 1066—the horse in Western Europe was a mere pony, suitable for transport to the battlefield or anywhere else, but not for battle. The Frank, like the Anglo-Saxon, fought on foot. About the year 700 began the introduction of the heavy cavalryman into France, and by the middle of the ninth century the process was complete. The required training was intensive; the cost of horse and equipment was enormous; [2] none but the wealthy—that is to say, the class enjoying the produce of wide lands and much cattle—could indulge in such a pursuit. There was no question of the king acquiring by taxes the money to provide himself with a mercenary force of this kind. The only method available, at this economic stage, of increasing the number of those able to turn out at need properly trained, with horse and equipment, as well as of providing the necessary complement of attendants, foot-soldiers, and food, was to give land to suitable, young, able-bodied men on terms of " knight's service"—that is to say, "boy's service." The produce from the lands in the knight's holding would enable him to acquire a horse and equipment, and he (or his lord) would be in a position to pass down to those holding land from him the obligation to provide the complementary supplies.[3] Or the king might grant a large fief or group of manors to a royal vassal on terms of providing a stated number of knights and

[1] *Les Mangbetu*, pp. 527 et seq.

[2] See Lex Rip., 36[11], according to which the total cost was forty-five shillings, equal to the cost of half that number of oxen.

[3] But warfare at this stage, both in Europe and Africa, still consists mainly of raids into enemy territory (for the Baganda, see Mair, p. 191).

the complement of equipment, foot-soldiers, and food. Upon the existing administration was engrafted the new practice, as William engrafted it in England after the Conquest— men holding on terms of knight's service, side by side with men holding on other terms of tribute. The new practice became a system gathering its own rules about it. The king was in theory entitled to remove the knight at his will, but subject to good behaviour he never did, and in most places the tenure soon became hereditary, and the king lost the power to interfere with the powerful landowner. While other tenants for the most part transmitted rights to land divisible among their sons, land held by knight's service came to descend by primogeniture, for to divide the land would frustrate the purpose of the holding. The essence of the matter was that an able-bodied male should be available to fill the office and perform the duties of the holding. New brooms sweep clean, and in England after the Conquest the status of the free sokeman (or free peasant) was depressed, and dwindled to a small class confined to a few districts, as William granted land to his Norman vassals. Finally, almost all the land in the country came to be held either on knight's service, or serjeanty (that is to say, on terms of providing foot soldiers, horses, arms, or other military needs), or by religious foundations in *frankalmoign* (that is to say, on a free tenure owing only the service of prayer). The system created a hierarchy of landed nobility, and it also created a new philosophy and a new set of ideals— those of chivalry—namely, prowess and fidelity.

That part of the ideals of chivalry which inculcates a respect for womenfolk dates from a later age, when little but the romance of feudalism remained.[1] The woman's position in the feudal age is still low, but there is a certain improvement. For example, there is evidence of a certain diminution in the practice of polygamy. Furthermore, we witness a certain return of matrilineal succession and matrilocal marriage. We see them both, for example, among the Babemba and Awa-

---

[1] In England it is the fourteenth and fifteenth centuries; in China the age of chivalry is the period after A.D. 220 (the feudal Chou dynasty having come to an end in 255 B.C.); in Japan it is the recent age of *bushido*, following the feudal period.

lamba, and in East Africa among the Wadigo [1] (one of the tribes of the Wanyika); and there is widespread evidence of them in West Africa. At first sight this return is surprising, but there are good reasons for it. As we have seen, society is becoming more agricultural and less pastoral; and pastoralism lowered the status of women and favoured patrilineal succession and patrilocal marriage. For example, the Babemba have no cattle, and the Awalamba hardly any. A second explanation is that the cognatic or blood-relationship is beginning to play a larger part, at the expense of the agnatic or clan relationship. We have seen it already in Europe and elsewhere. Among the Nyika tribes, though only the Wadigo have the matrilineal succession and matrilocal marriage, several tribes show combinations of the paternal and the maternal principle; and we see widespread at this stage a close and affectionate relation between a man and his mother's family, especially, of course, his mother's brother. The household is becoming the basic social group. Indeed, in town life there is little room for the clan.

A related change is a growing right of daughters to inherit. Till now it has been rare, and (in patriarchal societies) confined to unmarried women, who do not leave the clan. So far as we have any reliable evidence of inheritance in France and late Anglo-Saxon England, it indicates that daughters have been given a right to inherit in default of sons, and this even extends to the inheritance of knight's fees. It is this fact that makes necessary the lord's right of wardship and marriage. A daughter could not perform the duties of such a tenure, though a husband could. The lord's consent to the marriage of a prospective heiress was necessary during her father's lifetime: otherwise after the latter's death the lord, as guardian, was entitled to award the lady's hand to whatever suitor he wished —and he commonly awarded it to the highest bidder.

The bride-price marriage remains in full force, but there are signs at the end of the period that it is beginning to wane.

---

[1] Inheritance to strongest maternal nephews; failing them, to sons of deceased's mother; failing them, to sons or grandsons of maternal aunts. Daughters are disposed of in marriage by mother's brother (*E.A.L.*, vol. i, pp. 99-100).

The amount of the bride-price, although still substantial, bears a lower ratio to the wealth of the individual. Among the Awalamba, for example, it consists only of calico or a blanket of the value of a few shillings.[1] And in England at the end of our period it is provided that no bride-price is to be paid unless the suitor is willing to give something.[2]

[1] Among the Baganda it was usually one to ten goats, a few pots of beer, and several bark-cloths and cowrie-shells. It might, says Roscoe, take a year to collect.

[2] II Canute, 74 (after A.D. 1030).

CHAPTER III

THE CENTRAL CODES

The Law

THE Hittite Code, like the Central Codes of Europe, is the work of an ecclesiastic of sorts. It is a copy of an earlier Hittite Code, with notes attached to sundry clauses recording the changes in the law that have taken place. Unlike the Central Codes of Europe, it contains very little, if any, religious matter. That is what we might have expected. It belongs to the age of the Central Codes, but the priesthood is not likely to have attained as yet the power it achieved in Mediæval Europe. However, at the close of the Code is a separate group of added clauses of special interest to a priest.[1]

At our present stage the ecclesiastical orders in Europe (and, it would seem, the priesthood among the Hittites) had achieved considerable legal functions. Virtually the sole repositories of learning, with a monopoly of the practice of writing, they recorded the legal usages of the State, and advised the king on legal matters, and in England the bishops sat in the secular courts with the lay members. In addition, the Church in Europe (and probably the Hittite priests) were trying defendants for a number of criminal offences—namely, witchcraft, incest, bestiality, and adultery.

The origins of this jurisdiction were twofold. There is a certain relationship between criminal offences and religious offences. The former are considered by a people to be offences against the whole community; the latter to be conduct displeasing to God. The criminal law at all stages includes a small number of what we have called sacral offences. At the present stage religious notions have come to include conceptions according to which the practice of witchcraft, incest,

[1] H.C., ii, 73–86. They deal with bestiality, incest, adultery, and rape, the *levirate*, and possibly a *deodand*, or sacrifice.

188

bestiality, and adultery [1] are considered to be offences against God and to render a man unclean in a religious sense. Witchcraft, incest, and (from the time when it first appears in the law) bestiality have always been criminal offences, and almost always capital; [2] and adultery, by virtue of its close connection with marriage, has always stood at or near the boundary of the criminal law. We have seen adultery becoming a more serious wrong in our previous stage,[3] and it is now generally capital.[4] We must, however, clearly understand what we mean by saying that religious notions have come to include conceptions according to which these practices are offences against God. It would be contrary to all the facts that we have hitherto observed to surmise that the wrongfulness of witchcraft, incest, bestiality, and adultery have originated in a rule of religious ethics prohibiting or disapproving them. Man can only gauge what offends the mind of God by his notion of what offends the mind of man, and he must have a conception of an ethical God before he can attribute such ideas to God. Man must discover God from his own and the public conscience, and with the growth of that conscience rises his conception of godhead. Witchcraft, incest, bestiality, and adultery have been wrongful and criminal since the grade of the Food-Gatherers [5]—that is to say, for at least tens of thousands of years in the time-scale of evolution, among peoples who had no notion of God or religion. What has occurred is the growth of that which we may call (in the English idiom of 1950) the " social conscience." It shows itself in the standard of social conduct enshrined in the criminal law—that is to say, in man's standard of conduct between man and man; it shows itself also in the standard of social conduct enshrined in religion —that is to say, in man's standard of God's standard of conduct

[1] By adultery is meant wrongful intercourse with or by a married woman.

[2] E.g. Lamba: for incest with sister, driven out of the community by woman's brother; for incest with mother, daughter, or niece, man and woman both usually burnt. Lex Burg., Tit. 36: man pays a *wergeld* to the woman's nearest relative, and the woman becomes a royal slave.

[3] See *ante*, p. 148.   [4] See *post*, in this chapter.

[5] But adultery, from the first, was only sometimes criminal; and bestiality is not heard of as a crime till the beginning of Grade A3.

between man and man.   And at the same time the devotion
to religion, the organization of religion, and the power of
religion are growing.   These circumstances, therefore, form
one reason for the priestly jurisdiction in witchcraft, incest,
bestiality, and adultery.

But there is a second and equally important origin of this
jurisdiction of the priests.   Witchcraft and adultery have
almost always been tried by ordeal of some sort, for no evidence
is normally available of the commission of these offences, and
indeed charges of witchcraft and adultery have always furnished the bulk of the occasions for the use of the ordeal.   The
same applies in some measure to the less common offence of
incest, which is but a species of adultery.   At the present stage
the ordeal, whatever form it takes, is beginning to be undergone before the priest in the shrine, temple, or church, so as to
obtain the full advantage of the defendant's reverence for the
God who now abhors these offences, and the practice becomes
more pronounced in our following stage.[1]   If the defendant is
convicted in the ordeal, nothing remains except the power of
the king to impose the death sentence or to pardon.   As a
rule, in a feudal community, only the king can impose a capital
sentence.   These various considerations explain the clauses in
the Hittite Code which, dealing with certain sexual offences,
provide that if the defendant " is brought before the palace
door, the king can slay and the king can pardon, but he may
not appear before the king." [2]   The priestly Hittite and Anglo-
Saxon authors are anxious to maintain the priestly jurisdiction
to try the charge.

In Europe, ecclesiastics are also beginning to try the religious
offence of heresy, and questions of the validity of a marriage,
and disputes as to inheritance.   The reasons for this are easy to
understand.   For example, if they are to try charges of
adultery, they may have to decide in a particular case whether

[1] See Mair, pp. 189–90.   There is, for example, a case among the Margi
(Meek, *Tribal Studies*, vol. i, p. 218), and it is common among the Lamba
(Doke, p. 57) and many of the more backward tribes of Nigeria.

[2] H.C., ii, 74, 85.   Compare I Edmund, 3 (" If anyone sheds the blood
of a Christian man, he shall not come anywhere near the King until he
goes to do penance as the bishop or his confessor directs him "), V Æthelred,
29, and VI Æthelred, *c.* 36 (murderers, perjurers, or proved homicides).

the woman is married. As for inheritance, the Church has a vital interest in death-bed gifts of goods, and the dispute will normally be between the priest, who witnessed the oral gift to the Church, and the next of kin who contest it. In Europe the Church is also interesting itself in perjury, which is normally a breach of an oath taken in church.

Religious conceptions at this stage do not merely include witchcraft, incest, bestiality, and adultery among religious offences. As we shall presently see, homicide in some of its forms is now a criminal offence, and theft also is in some circumstances criminal, and there are several peoples of this stage among whom homicide (including killing by witchcraft) and theft are also religious offences. So, for example, the Awalamba believe that there is a " high god," generally called Lesa, and he is creator of all things and is feared, though there is no worship of him and hardly a prayer to him. It is said that he is angered when men sin deeply—when they commit murder, adultery, or theft; he punishes these acts by sending leprosy and smallpox.[1] Thou shalt do no murder. Thou shalt not commit adultery. Thou shalt not steal. We are approaching very near to our next stage of advance. But the ecclesiastical courts of Europe never achieved jurisdiction over homicide, because homicide is an offence which can normally be tried upon evidence, and so historically was not tried by ordeal as a matter of course, as were charges of witchcraft and adultery.

Until our present stage the sentence for a criminal offence has usually been either death or (latterly) a fine. A capital sentence now generally involves also the confiscation of all the offender's property. But even if an offence is capital, the offender does not always deserve the maximum sentence. In addition, there are now, for the first time, a good many sentences of mutilation passed by the king for criminal offences.[2] Mutilations are not altogether a new thing. In the Early

---

[1] Doke, p. 228. For homicide as a religious offence in England, requiring religious penance prescribed by the bishop, as well as compensation to the next of kin, see II Edmund, 4 (tenth century).

[2] E.g., Mair, p. 189 (cutting off lips, ears, a hand, or gouging out an eye. Reserved for offences against the chief, especially adultery with one of his wives, but could also be inflicted by a man on one of his own wives); Doke, p. 64; Anglo-Saxon Laws (see note 2, *post*, p. 192).

Codes corporal punishments of various kinds were a frequent sanction for civil wrongs by slaves who had not the means to pay a composition.[1] Now mutilations, the bastinado, even forced labour are imposed by a strong and angry king. A hand is cut off for persistent stealing, or ears for informing.[2] Mutilations ought to bear an appropriate relation to the offence, and, if they do, they afford a valuable deterrent to others and a convenient punishment intermediate between death and a fine. It must be remembered that there is no question, at this economic stage, of providing the luxury and expense of a prison[3] and a guard for malefactors. But in Europe and in Africa we see a widespread use of stocks to hold a prisoner pending his trial.[4]

The list of criminal offences is expanding with the growing strength of government, and the developing social conscience which supports its authority. It is more and more thought unsatisfactory that the individual should be left a prey to the strong, but we must not exaggerate the progress that has been made. In detail the list of criminal offences varies vastly from place to place. It develops in two ways. Partly it develops by making certain acts criminal wherever they are committed, and partly by making certain acts criminal only if committed in special circumstances. For example, in many places a breach of the peace on the king's highway, or disorderly conduct in the palace, or an offence against a member of the king's household—especially, of course, adultery with one of the king's wives—is criminal. It is an affront to the person of the

[1] See, e.g., Lex Salica, c. 35 (5) (if a slave kills a freeman he is handed over to the parents of the slain and his master pays half the composition); Alfred, c. 25 (fine for rape of a slave by a freeman; castration " as compensation " for rape of a slave by a slave).

[2] Doke, Lambas, p. 64. Mutilations are very frequent indeed among the Baganda. In the Anglo-Saxon Laws they grow steadily more frequent, see, E. & G., c. 10, III Edmund, c. 4 (of slave for theft); III Edgar, c. 4 (perjury: payment of *wergeld* or forfeiture of tongue); IV Æthelred, 5 (3) (penalty for coiners, loss of a hand, to be fastened up over the mint); II Canute, c. 36 (perjury), 53 (adultery).

[3] Indeed, practically all buildings everywhere are of wood and thatch, or mud. But see II Æthelstan, c. 1 (3) and (4).

[4] See, e.g., Baganda (Mair, p. 188, and Roscoe); Mangbetu, and England. A leg, or leg and arms, are put through a heavy log.

king, and punished by him accordingly, though if it had been committed elsewhere or against some other person it would be a mere civil matter dealt with by a local chief or headman. We have already seen instances in England. But, in addition, in most places, certain offences are criminal wherever or against whom they are committed. In England, towards the end of our period, they [1] include treason, murder (that is to say, secret killing), robbery, *forsteal* (ambush), *hamsocne* (armed attack on a man in his house), and *fyrdwite* (neglect of military service). The sanction for most of these offences is merely a fine, and the king often assigns to a local lord his right to receive it. It is an important source of revenue. But there are also crimes that are bootless—that is to say, not emendable by money—such as treason and murder and false coining, and some of these involve death and confiscation of property.[2]

Now let us turn to the civil wrongs, and we shall see that at the same time the more serious of them are slowly becoming criminal.

The first and most characteristic change is the change in the nature of the sanctions for the most serious civil wrong—namely, homicide. The relatives of the victim are no longer satisfied with pecuniary compensation. Homicide is heinous and abhorrent. The majority of men no longer consider it fitting to accept money or cattle for a life. There was always something of this feeling; but the threat of a blood feud was overcome by the enormous sum of the composition. Now it ceases to satisfy, and the threat of retaliation becomes more real and imminent. An equilibrium is reached in different ways by different nations, but in most cases the recognized sanction is now the handing over to the relatives of a specified number of persons in place of the slain. The precise form of the rule varies much from people to people. Usually the persons handed over are children or an unmarried sister of the

---

[1] Called in England " Pleas of the Crown "; in Normandy " Pleas of the sword "; and in Africa " Crimes of the Chief "; and various similar names.

[2] E.g., in the Burgundian Code housebreaking and robbery with violence are capital (Tit. 29); and theft of oxen or horses (Tit. 4, 47, 70). Certain thefts are criminal, and it is an offence to compound them (Tit. 71).

slayer, or slaves. If it is a sister, she is sometimes given to a brother of the slain, and when she has given birth to a child (who will take the place of the dead) is allowed to return to her people.[1] If they are children who are handed over, they often occupy a status intermediate between slave and free,[2] and sometimes the boys are allowed to return home on coming of age, but the girls remain.[3] There is a change, too, in the object of the sanction: it is to a less degree compensatory. For example, the pecuniary sanction usually varied according to the sex or rank of the slain: the new sanction usually varies according as the killing was intentional or not, and rarely, if ever, varies according to the sex of the slain. In the Hittite Code four persons are handed over when the killing is " in anger," two " when only his hand wrongs," and one when the killing is in the course of a fight, whether the deceased was male or female. But, as we have said, there is great variety in the rule. In some nations a number of persons are handed over if the killing is unintentional, but if it is intentional the court delivers up the slayer to the relatives to put to death; or the sanction is the handing over of a number of persons, and death of the slayer in default; or a pecuniary sanction, with death or the handing over of persons in default of payment. This sanction of the handing over of a number of persons is, as we have seen, in accordance with economic practices of the time.[4] There is nothing strange now in sisters and children being pledged or taken in execution for debt. Children are thought properly answerable for their father's wrong. And the practice rises naturally out of the blood feud, which is stayed on terms that a number of persons are handed over instead of the slayer. But in Western Europe these stages succeed one another so quickly that the new notion has not sufficient time fully to develop. In England at the end of this period, when a man is slain, intentionally or not, the slayer must still pay a *wergeld* to the relatives of the victim, a *manbot*

---

[1] E.g., Margi (Meek, *Tribal Studies*, vol. i, p. 217), Shangana–Tonga (Junod, *Life of a South African Tribe*, vol. i, pp. 441–2).

[2] E.g., Wanyika. In Southern Nigeria sometimes they are free, sometimes treated as slaves (Talbot, *Southern Nigeria*, vol. iii, p. 626).

[3] E.g., Wadigo (a Nyika tribe).　　　[4] See *ante*, pp. 177–8.

to his lord, and a payment for *mundbryce* to the king. But if it is a case of "murder" (i.e., secret killing) "he shall be given up to the kinsmen of the slain." [1]

These communities have arrived at certain notions upon the topic of homicide which it is perhaps convenient to mention here. Where no animate slayer is to be found, it is not uncommon that the human mind (as it is so prone to do) should do justice by analogy. If a man has been slain by an inanimate object—if, for example, a tree has fallen upon him [2]—it is sometimes dealt with as a human slayer would have been, and

---

[1] II Canute, *c.* 56. Among the *Baganda* the sanction for homicide seems to have been blood revenge by the feud, or the handing over of two women, or the payment of a composition, according to circumstances (Mair, p. 185). *Waboni*—murderer handed over to family of slain to be dealt with; if accidental killing, a person must be produced to fill the place of the dead man (*E.A.L.*, vol. i, p. 102). *Wateita*—for intentional killing much as before, but varies according to manner of death: the slayer or another man handed over, or payment in children or cattle. If killing by knife, ten times the penalty of killing by club. If killing by poison (cf. English "murder") he is made to take the same poison. If accidental homicide, one child handed over plus cattle. *Wanyika*—intentional killing, two to ten persons of slayer's family handed over to family of slain. In default, slayer handed over and killed. *Wadigo*—in cases of killing in cold blood four times the number of persons handed over compared with killing in the heat of passion (*E.A.L.*, vol. i, p. 98). *Wagiriama* —two persons handed over to family of slain (usually children). In case of killing of own brother or father, one person only handed over (because no blood feud). Killing of wife or child, no penalty. *Lamba*—court usually takes a number of persons (sisters and mother of the accused). Some of the women handed over to the heir of the deceased (or, in case of a child, to his maternal uncle) as slaves, others kept by the chief. But death sometimes imposed (Doke, pp. 62–3). *Babemba*—persons handed over. *Hittites* (see above). *Southern Nigeria*—widespread practice of handing persons over—see, e.g., Talbot, vol. iii, pp. 625–6. *Northern Nigeria*, see, e.g., Margi of Adamawa, feud and giving of garments, and handing over of a girl to deceased's brother to bear a child in place of him. If the deceased was killed by a member of a different local group, war. *Lex Burgundionum*, Tit. 2, apparently in cases of intentional killing, slayer handed over to be put to death. *South Africa: Northern Sotho*—death, and the slayer's relatives must also give to the relatives of the slain cattle to acquire a woman to bear a child to the deceased, or, if the deceased was a woman, to take her place. *Venda*—death or exile, and chief takes the property and whole family of the slayer. *Shangana-Tonga*—payment of a bride-price to obtain a woman to bear a child in place of the victim.

[2] E.g., Alfred, *c.* 13.

handed over to the next of kin to do with it as they will.[1] If a man is found dead among a strange community, but no slayer can be discovered, the community (by analogy with the spoor law for theft) is sometimes held liable to compensate the relatives of the slain.[2]   The institution of the sanctuary, because of the increase in the number of capital offences, and the changes that are taking place in the sanctions for homicide, grows in importance,[3] and the growth of villages and towns creates here and there a new feature, the village of refuge—a village where an important shrine or temple is to be found. For example, among the Lamba people a man who has committed murder, theft, or adultery may flee to such a village (of which there are seven in Ilamba), and is there seized and tried by the local chief. The pursuer remains outside. The defendant may be merely fined or, if the offence is sufficiently serious, he may be sentenced to death,[4] for there is now a beginning of the notion that the land is polluted by certain heinous offences, and the shrine-village must be freed from the miasma.[5] This conception sorts well with the sanction of outlawry. It is a characteristic feature of this stage, especially among peoples where the central authority is weak—for example, in Western Europe —that banishment or outlawry is imposed as a sanction for certain criminal offences. To some extent the law is making a virtue of necessity where it cannot reach the offender. But criminal offences which pollute the land justify and call for the exile of the offender. The effect of the sentence of outlawry is that the offender is outside the protection of the law, and may therefore be killed with impunity.

Sanctions for wounding are still pecuniary everywhere, and we still find short tariff-lists of payments varying according to the part of the body injured and the nature of the injury.[6]

---

[1] As in Athens as late as classical times.   [2] See H.C., i, 6.

[3] It is frequently referred to in the Anglo-Saxon Laws.

[4] Doke, p. 57. II Canute, c. 26, provides that there shall be no sanctuary for theft or treason.

[5] For example, Edward and Guthrum, c. 11, provides that " wizards, sorcerers, perjurers and those who secretly compass death shall be driven from the land, and the nation shall be purified."

[6] See, e.g., H.C., i, 7–16; Wateita (E.A.L., vol. i, p. 102): and in England the Leis Willelme, cc. 10, 11.

There is sometimes a liability to support a disabled victim and pay the medical attendance [1] until he recovers.   Where (as is usual) money is not in everyday use, this is the nearest equivalent.   In most places the sanction consists of a payment to the injured person and a payment to his lord [2] or king [3] or the elders representing the community.[4]

Adultery with a married woman varies much in heinousness from people to people.   As we have seen, it becomes criminal in this period.   In most places a husband who finds his wife and paramour *in flagranti delicto* is entitled to kill them both out of hand.[5]   But the king has an interest in the infliction of capital sentences.   A Lamba husband who has killed the pair must report to the chief.   Among the Hittites, if the husband does not kill the wife he cannot kill the paramour (a rule aimed at preventing conspiracy between husband and wife), though he may brand him on the forehead.   If he does not kill them, but accuses the pair before the king, the king can slay or pardon the pair.[6]   But among some of the less advanced Bantu tribes of this stage, if the husband sues for damages the sanction is still a modest one; [7] and the sanctions for adultery in the inept ecclesiastical courts of Western Europe consist of a whipping or other bodily penances, commonly remitted for money.

Rape (of a single woman) is becoming a capital offence at the end of this period.[8]   Seduction is still, and for long afterwards, a common prelude to marriage, and the sanction remains pecuniary.[9]

Theft remains generally a civil wrong for which the sanction is multiple restitution or a payment, but a person caught in the act of stealing anything of any value may be killed with im-

---

[1] I H.C., i, 10; Leis Willelme, *c.* 10.   [2] Western Europe.
[3] Western Europe ; South Africa ; H.C., i, 9.
[4] E.g., Wateita (half to person injured, half to elders).
[5] England at the end of our period. For the Baganda see Mair, p. 186, and Roscoe; Lambas, Doke, p. 67 ; H.C., ii, 83, 84.
[6] H.C., ii, 84.   [7] E.g., Wateita.
[8] Lex Burg., Tit. 12 : heavy fine, and death in default of payment. Lambas (Doke, p. 69) : death of the man and enslavement of his sister. England : death or castration. (In Alfred, *c.* 25, it was only a fine.) H.C., ii, 83 (death).
[9] Lambas (Doke, p. 69) ostracism.

punity.[1] This, as we have seen, has been the general rule for some time. The law continues to pay great attention to this offence, and the Hittite Code contains a long list of sanctions for theft of different types of property. Theft of animals continues everywhere to be a great scourge of society, and in the Hittite Code the sanction for stealing a Great Bull (that is, a bull more than two years old) is a payment of fifteen bulls; for a Great Horse, fifteen horses; and for a Great Ram, fifteen rams. In the Burgundian Code death is the sanction for stealing horse or ox,[2] and for housebreaking or robbery with violence.[3]

There are other civil wrongs contained in a lengthening list (especially trespass,[4] and slander or false charges), but there is no space here to speak of them.

Looking back upon the rules that have been referred to, we see that they are very much in a state of transition. This is not surprising: the tempo of change is for ever quickening. We also see that the conception of " law " has made considerable progress. From the early part of this stage (in England from the middle of the tenth century) it no longer denotes to the mind of the citizen a mere collection of judgments, an occasional statute, and anything that is just and customary. It embraces a more general and more technical meaning—a system of rules and principles which make up a distinct, independent and self-sufficient institution to which all men and all human actions are subject.[5]

[1] See, e.g., Baganda (Mair, p. 186): England, II Æthelstan, 1 (death for thief over twelve years old caught in the act), VI Æthelstan, 1.

[2] Lex Burg., Tit. 4, 47, 70.   [3] Ibid., Tit. 29.

[4] See, e.g., Lex Burg., Tit. 27; Lambas (Doke, p. 75).

[5] The word *lagu* (law) is taken over from the Danes about A.D. 930, and this is a tribute to the somewhat more advanced and technical conceptions which the Danes associated with the word. From the same source come such expressions as " by-law " (*by lagu* — town law). " *Riht* " continues in use with the various meanings of justice, claim, custom, deserts, and even law.

CHAPTER IV

A DIGRESSION

NON-PASTORAL PEOPLES

IN our previous three stages [1] we have been moving towards Central and West Africa. In our first two stages of the Third Agricultural Grade we were at the periphery of the Negro and Bantu world in North-East and East and South-East Africa. In our last stage we moved southward and inland from North-East Africa, and northward and inland from South-East Africa. Our next stage, of the Late Codes, is mainly to be found in West and West Central Africa. If we looked at the matter from the point of view not of the order of economic advance but of the diffusion of culture, we would see a process in the opposite direction, moving from the north into West Central Africa and thence spreading eastwards. That, for example, was the path taken when the use of iron came to this part of the world, only reaching the up-country tribes of East Africa some fifty years ago, when they had not yet achieved the use of bronze.

One of the peoples of Northern Rhodesia whom we chose as examples of the stage of the Central Codes—the Babemba—came, according to tradition, from the Congo, in Central Africa,[2] and has no cattle nor any pastoral tradition. Yet, making all allowances for this difference, we saw that its law was in essence indistinguishable from the partly pastoral peoples whose law we discussed. This serves to remind us that we have departed from the task which we set ourselves in regard to the Third Agricultural Grade. We defined that grade as consisting of peoples who practised a combination of pastoralism and agriculture, and we have traced advances in economics and law as pastoral peoples increased the extent of their tilling of the land. But there have still been tribes and

---

[1] Grade A3 (1), Early Codes (A3 (2)), and Central Codes (A3 (3)).
[2] From the Luba people, in the Kassai basin.

nations, of similar stages of advance, who possess no cattle, and especially is this so in Central Africa, mainly because the equatorial rain-forest is inimical to the spread of grassy plains, and the ravages of the tsetse-fly prevent cattle-keeping. Some of such peoples are mainly agriculturists, like the Babemba and Awalamba whom we have already discussed. Others are mainly hunters with a subsidiary agriculture. Their advances in the arts, including metal-working, prohibited us from including the former peoples in our Second Agricultural Grade, or the latter in our grade of the Hunters.

In Central America, too, we meet with many non-pastoral peoples. In North America we found tribes of the Second Agricultural Grade for the most part in the south-eastern area of what is now the United States—the Illinois confederacy in South Wisconsin, Illinois, Iowa, and Missouri; the Natchez in Missouri; the Powhatan confederacy in Virginia; the Pawnee confederacy in Nebraska; the Creek confederacy occupying the greater part of Alabama and Georgia, and the Seminole in Florida. Moving from thence towards the Late Code civilizations of Mexico and Yucatan, we meet with the Pueblos (especially the Hopi and Zuni) mainly living in New Mexico, Arizona and northern Mexican territory, and the Pima and Papago of South Arizona.

The advance of all these tribes of Central Africa and America is parallel to that of the pastoral-agriculturists, subject to certain differences arising from their hunting, or agricultural, and non-pastoral way of life. These differences are in the main concerned with property and inheritance: as always, the law relating to civil injuries remains more constant, for the differences in the method of subsistence have less effect here.

Let us then retrace our steps for a while, and choose a small number of these peoples, and briefly consider the progress that they make. It will serve to remind us of the advances that we have witnessed in reaching the end of the stage of the Central Codes, and it will serve also to remind us how little is the power of religion in some peoples and areas, even at the point which we have reached.

We shall take, selecting entirely at random, five African

peoples,[1] the Mandja,[2] Warega,[3] Mayombe,[4] Bangala,[5] and Mangbetu.[6] It will be seen that this is their order of development for all purposes, the Mandja being the least advanced of the five, and the Mangbetu the most.

The Mandja, Warega, and Mayombe stand at the level of the Early Codes, the rest at the Central Codes. All keep goats, as well as poultry and dogs, but no large cattle.[7] They all practise horticulture or agriculture, but (apart from the Mandja) their main occupation is the hunt. Their method of tilling the ground is much the same as that practised elsewhere in most parts of Africa. When a plot of land is exhausted, the man cuts down the trees to make a new clearing, and burns the timber and bush; and the woman (carrying her baby) and the children level and till the ground with little occasional assistance from the men. None possess the plough. The implement used by the women is the iron hoe,[8] which has generally taken the place of the digging-stick, and the only other implements in use are the axe and the knife. The favourite occupations of the men are (except among the Mandja) hunting and fishing, and (except among the Mandja and Warega) war, and for the last purpose they have the spear. Cereals (chiefly maize, millet, and sorghum) are grown, as well as other crops (mainly banana and manioc), but the plots are (except among the Mangbetu) generally small. All build good huts and possess the arts of

[1] These are all well described in volumes (mentioned below) of the *Collection de Monographies Ethnographiques*, publiée par Cyr. Van Overbergh (Brussels).

[2] In the Haut Chari of the French Congo between the Rivers Fafa and Kumi. See *Les Mandja*, by F. Gaud (1911).

[3] On the east side of the Belgian Congo between the Lualaba and Lake Kivu. See *Les Warega*, by Delhaise (1909).

[4] On the right bank of the Loango near the west coast of Africa. See *Les Mayombe* (Van Overbergh, 1907).

[5] On the borders of the Belgian and French Congo, on the banks of the middle Congo around New Antwerp. See *Les Bangala*, by Van Overbergh and De Jonge (1904).

[6] In the north of the Belgian Congo between the valleys of the Veli and Bomokandi. See *Les Mangbetu* (Van Overbergh and De Jonge (1909)).

[7] Among the Mangbetu, some chiefs had recently (1909) acquired some large cattle. The Warega, Mayombe and Bangala also keep sheep.

[8] About 6 to 7 inches long, on a wooden handle.

pottery (often, as in the grades below, reserved to the women), woodwork and ironwork, spinning, rope-making, dyeing, and a little weaving and tanning. Among the Mayombe, Bangala and Mangbetu there is also some painting and sculpture and the making of musical instruments.[1] Apart from the Mangbetu, there are substantially no specialized industries except for the ironworkers. There are no employees anywhere, and all work on their own account and are paid in money or produce. Trade is general and has increased sufficiently in some places to have given rise very recently to markets. The Mandja and Warega have no markets and hardly any trade between villages, but there are markets among the Mayombe, Bangala and Mangbetu, and the King of the Mangbetu takes a toll on sales.

Among the Mandja the trade is chiefly in food, when the successful hunter or fisherman rids himself of the excess of his bag or catch. For the most part each person can make enough of other things for the needs of himself and his family. But among the other tribes, with the increase in wealth and the growing specialization in manufacture, there is an increasing trade in goods—namely, skins, arms and other iron objects, ivory, and pottery. The extent of intertribal communication has increased to such an extent that a Bangala jargon (not to be confused with the Ngala tongue) has spread over the Congo, dropping much of its grammar in the process, including the characteristic Bantu alliterative concord.

The main transaction of trade is and remains barter—that is to say, the exchange of one article for another, with no obligations remaining on either side. But (in the absence of cattle) certain commodities which are imperishable, in universal use and therefore in constant demand, and of a common size or easily measured, begin to figure in the exchanges more frequently than other goods, because they are always worth taking in exchange. They can always be kept, and traded away without loss for something else when opportunity offers. Consequently they also begin to figure as measures of the value

[1] The Mangbetu are fine builders in wood, among the best ironworkers in the Congo, and skilled workers in ivory, and also in copper (of which most of their ornaments are made).

of other goods. Among the Mandja these articles are arrows : with the Warega salt, iron, and native cloths—and, since the coming of the Arabs, pearls, cowries, and copper—serve the same purpose to a large extent, and in addition they use circles of two sizes cut out of local snail-shells by the old men, and pierced and threaded to form necklaces. With the Mayombe, Bangala, and Mangbetu (apart from such things as spears, shields, arrows, knives, hoes, and squares of standard coarse cloth) small copper cylinders, rods, or ingots are in general use for this purpose (as they were in the earliest days of Rome). In short, certain suitable commodities are beginning to serve the function of money, and in that sense, in a small proportion of cases, the barter can be described as sale. The sale is, of course, like the barter, an instantaneous, " ready-money " transaction, with no notion of obligations remaining to be performed on either side. Only among the Mangbetu, earnest is sometimes heard of. Lending is not a transaction of which we hear anything among the Mandja or Warega, but with the Mayombe, Bangala, and Mangbetu there is a great deal of it. There is no such thing as lending at interest, but the return of a reasonable amount of other goods or produce is expected. If I lend a man a shield, I expect to get something out of the booty. There is no letting of land.

The increase in trade and lending brings an increase in debt. Among the Mayombe, persons may be given in payment of debt, and with the Bangala and Mangbetu there is a great deal of pledging and giving of oneself, wife, or children for debt.

Cannibalism [1] is at its height, and is so extensive that it is true to say that human flesh is one of the sources of food. With the possible exception of the Mayombe (and then perhaps only in recent times), all these tribes in the last quarter of the nineteenth century indulged in cannibalism to an extent probably not known in any other area. A human leg might be seen hanging in much the same circumstances as a leg of

[1] The word is derived from the practice of the non-pastoral Caribs of the Caribbean. In North America cannibalism was especially to be found among the more advanced peoples of the North Pacific Coast, Arizona and New Mexico, and Central America. None of them kept cattle.

mutton or pork elsewhere. Among several tribes it was customary to break a captive's limbs to prevent him running away, and leave him standing in water overnight so as to render the epidermis easily removable. The Mandja and Warega killed and ate all prisoners of war.[1] Among the Mangbetu all persons killed in battle were eaten, and captured children were a delicacy for the king's table. We found much cannibalism also among the most advanced of the Polynesians, at the close of the Second Agricultural Grade (for example, in Fiji). There and here no cattle are kept, but among pastoralists cannibalism is unknown.

The density of population has much increased in the localities favoured by nature. The Mandja in 1900 (though mainly agricultural) have poor soil and a density of only six persons per square mile. Among the Mayombe (who dwell on the bank of the Loango) the density is fifty per square mile, but varies much from district to district. In the fertile and well-watered country of the Mangbetu the density is 250 per square mile. The total population of all the Mandja tribes is only 25,000; of the Bangala tribe or tribes 110,000; and of the Mangbetu nation a little over a million.[2] In the absence of cattle-keeping there is at no stage a population living in homesteads. The smallest villages everywhere consist of only one or two families; and while among the Mandja and Mayombe the average size of a village is still only some 175 persons, the largest Mangbetu villages contain a population of about 1,500 persons, and the largest towns of the Bangala have populations of between 5,000 and 12,000 souls. A combination of hunting with a subsidiary horticulture often produces great concentrations of population.

No great change in vital statistics is to be observed in this stage, taken as a whole, as compared with what we have seen. Women continue to suckle their children for two to three years, and their husbands have no access from pregnancy to weaning. Polygamy is the general practice throughout these tribes; but polygamy does not mean larger families, for fewer

[1] Among the Mandja they were killed by the women.
[2] By "nation" I mean any group, containing more than one tribe, which is separately ruled.

children are born to a wife in a polygamous household: indeed, in some noble Mangbetu polygamous families many wives seem never to become impregnated.

For example, the population of the Mandja appears to have been stationary for a very long time. Thirteen Mandja men had between them twenty-nine wives, who had a total of sixty children, of which 62 per cent. were boys. Of these sixty children, twenty-four (that is, 40 per cent.) died before maturity. Three Mandja chiefs who completed their career had ten wives, and by them had nineteen sons (of whom twelve survived) and nine daughters (of whom four survived). Out of these eighty-eight children, therefore, only fifty-two (or 59 per cent.) survived to maturity.[1] Among the Warega the women seemed to give birth to an average number of about four children each, and the population was diminishing.[2] Of twenty-one married women of the Bangala under twenty-four years of age, four were under eighteen years and had no children; and the remaining seventeen were between eighteen and twenty-four years old, and nine of these had one child each, one had two, and the remaining seven had none.[3] The Mayombe had few children, and the population was diminishing. Old chiefs took many young wives. As an extreme case may be cited Djaber among the Mangbetu, with 250 wives, who gave birth to 100 children, of whom only ten survived.[4] Christians with one wife often had more children than the others.[5] Apart from infant mortality, the factors limiting the increase of population are chiefly warfare and cannibalism.

On the whole, the extent and frequency of war increase among these peoples. The Mandja are not so much aggressors as the victims of raids of the Arabs and invasions of the Banda, and the Warega are essentially peaceful; but the history of the Mayombe, Bangala, and Mangbetu, and especially of the last, is the history of wars. The general implement of war is the bow and arrow of the chase, but the Mayombe and Bangala

---

[1] *Les Mandja*, pp. 262 f.
[2] This was partly owing to the adoption of the Arab custom of marrying immature wives.
[3] *Les Bangala*, p. 201.   [4] *Les Mangbetu*, p. 297.
[5] *Les Mayombe*, p. 245.

also use spears and knives, and among the Mangbetu, while the lower classes are equipped only with bow and arrow, the freeman is armed with lance or throwing-spear and shield. Among the Bangala and Mangbetu, when peace is made, the conquered hands over part of his territory or submits to an indemnity. War in all these tribes is still a matter chiefly of sudden surprise raids, in which the men are for the most part eaten and the women and children captured; and often such raids are undertaken for the express purpose of getting supplies of human flesh.

The extent of slavery varies accordingly. The Mandja and Warega have no slaves, and kill and eat all their male prisoners, and take in marriage or adopt the women and children. Slavery is found in all the other tribes, but it is of a very mild sort. Among the Bangala a slave might have several wives and male slaves of his own, and among the Mayombe it was difficult, save by the dress, to tell apart slave and free. The slaves are those captured in war and not ransomed, or those born or bought in that condition.

Human sacrifice takes a parallel course of development. It is not found among the Mandja or Warega (though it is said that Mandja wives were formerly sacrificed on the tombs of their masters). But when any person of importance died among the Bangala, twenty or so of his slaves were killed to accompany him. Half of the body of each slave was buried by his side, and the remaining half eaten at the funeral feast. The Mangbetu similarly made sacrifices of women and slaves at the funerals of kings and nobles. Animals sufficed for the needs of commoners in the world after death. The situation among the Baganda and the Natchez was much the same.

The religious ideas of our tribes of Central Africa can be briefly stated as follows. They have all a belief in animism. They all (except the Mangbetu) use fetishes—so characteristic of this part of Africa—an assortment of the most diverse objects endowed by the native with supernatural virtues, holy and unholy. But in addition they all, with the exception of the most backward—namely, the Mandja—believe in the existence of a supreme being of a sort—Kalaga among the Warega, Ibanza among the Bangala, Zambi among the Mayombe, and

Kilima among the Mangbetu. He is sometimes the creator, and is often all-powerful, but they are very vague and contradictory about him. He is rarely invoked. They do not pray to him or sacrifice to him, and there is no cult of him. Sometimes there are one or two lesser gods also. There is certainly no belief in a god rewarding good and punishing evil, and indeed there is no ethical element in their religion. There is, indeed, practically no religion. As Coquilhat observed of the Bangala: " Leur esprit est ouvert, mais il est dévoyé par une éducation barbare, cinquante fois séculaire."

But we must add that among all these tribes, except the Mandja, methods of divination and the taking of auspices are in increasing use. The Mrega witch-doctor reads the future in a vessel of water or the entrails of an animal, or by one of a number of other methods. With the Mangbetu, divination and the taking of auguries have spread so far that no man would undertake a journey, and no ruler launch an attack upon an enemy, without first advising himself by such a means. Indeed, there is an official whose function it is to foretell the future on important matters of public interest.

From the least to the most advanced of these peoples governmental authority has much increased, and this increased authority enables them to hold together populations which are progressively larger and less simple and homogeneous. These communities have increased in size by various means—by a higher rate of natural increase; by a federating together of neighbouring tribes which, because of better intercommunication, are of closely similar culture; by an influx of aliens in similar circumstances; and (among the most advanced) because, through better-organized warfare, one community has absorbed another by conquest.

For example, the smallest and least advanced of the tribes which we have chosen—namely, the Mandja—are alone in having no organization above the clan organization—they have, that is to say, chiefs of villages and chiefs of clans, all with slight authority and not holding by hereditary right, but no chief of a tribe. Next, the Warega have chiefs of villages and chiefs of districts, with limited influence and always subject to the views of their council of elders, and always afraid to be too firm with their subjects or followers for fear that they will leave them for another chief. But they have also had at times a paramount chief—namely, a chief of a district who also exercised influence or authority as chief of a tribe. The rest of these tribes all have paramount chiefs of tribes as well as village and district chiefs. The Bangala, for example, some 110,000 in number, are variously called by observers a tribe, a number of tribes, or a nation, and there is a paramount chief of all the Bangala who possesses authority subject to the opinion of the assembly, every member of which has a right to the expression of his views. The paramount chief does not interfere in the affairs of a district (other than a district of which he is the district chief) unless invited to do so, and then only to give his good offices as a mediator in settling the local dispute. At the other extreme the Mangbetu (the most advanced of these tribes, and numbering over a million souls) consist of a group of tribes who now feel themselves to be one, but who at some time past were conquered by Mangbetu, who now form an aristocractic ruling class; and here the paramount chief or king of the nation has great (we are indeed told, unlimited) power. As a rule all these chiefs of village, district, tribe, or nation exercise authority only with the assistance and approval of their councils of notables.

Here is a development of feudalism, for in all these tribes notions of authority have also their aspect as notions of property in land—in other words, to the extent that the chiefs govern the communities, they govern the lands. Often a village chief refers to the land of his village as " my land," [1] but it is his rather in an administrative than proprietary sense. In all these tribes or nations land is plentiful, for the density of population is still modest, and the plantations are mostly small. In most of these tribes, when a man requires land for himself and his family, he will commonly betake himself to the chief of the village or territory in which he desires to live, and land will be assigned to him. There he can build his house and till the land, and while he occupies it it is his—indeed, any previously unoccupied land is his while he occupies it—and when

---

[1] But among the Mayombe the land of a village is considered to belong to the clan which occupies that and the other villages in that district.

he relinquishes it, the house and land return to the community represented by the chief. In return he must recognize the chief's authority, and he owes him duties. For example, he may be required to pay a pre-arranged part of the harvest of his land; or, if he desires the sole right of fishing in a reach of river, pays his duty in fish. Ideas of family right have dwindled to small proportions.

All these communities, except the Mandja, have produced distinct social ranks. For the most part these are based on the possession of wealth, for growing wealth produces a tendency to value a man according to his means. Among the Warega, for example, to climb from one social class to another requires merely sufficient wealth to pay for the ceremony, and the highest class consists mainly of old men. Similarly with the Bangala, every owner of a few wives and slaves calls himself a *mukunzi* or notable. But the Mangbetu also recognize the aristocracy of certain families, and below the chiefs and above the ordinary freeman and the slave is a class of freemen who do not engage in labour and are largely relatives of the chief.

The bride-price marriage is found among all these peoples, but is least developed among the Mandja and Warega. As there are no cattle and no one currency, the bride-wealth is paid in a variety of commodities—among the Mandja usually about 360 arrows, five copper bracelets, and two knives of jet; among the Bangala two or three slaves, two or three necklaces, and two or three empty bottles. The Mangbetu give slaves, animals, iron, spears, knives, and dogs. As the bulk of these five peoples are hunters, it is not surprising that marriage is everywhere patrilocal and inheritance and descent patrilineal.

Since land is vested in the clan or chief, is there for the asking, and reverts to the chief or clan on being abandoned, there is no inheritance of land at this stage. There is also little inheritance of goods, for there are no cattle, and new huts can quickly be built. The available goods consist mainly of articles of adornment and domestic use and weapons of the chase and war. A good deal of this goes with its owner to the grave. Consequently the rules of inheritance have received but little development as compared with the Second Agricultural Grade. In all these communities the succession (as was usual in that grade) goes to one person: among the Mandja (who are closest to that grade) to the eldest child, male or female, except that if she is married a younger child succeeds. Elsewhere the succession is usually to the eldest son, but among the Warega usually to the eldest brother. Everywhere the widows are taken by a brother of the deceased or a son (not being a son of the widow). There are no wills. In all these peoples the wife occupies her own hut; and the goods which her husband allowed her and her children to hold and use during his life, together with such goods as she brought from her father's house or acquired by barter—hoes, jewels, ornaments, domestic animals, and utensils—all pass to her eldest son on her husband's death.

As for movable goods, the male head of the family is considered throughout these peoples to own the goods of the family. With the increase in wealth, and the diminishing cohesion of the larger kinship groups, he gains supreme authority over the members of the family, and among the Mangbetu has rights over them of life and death. The children own nothing of their own: even the sons own nothing till they leave him to set up a separate home.[1] If he ill-treats them, the chief may intervene with persuasive words, but that is all. Nevertheless, the wife is considered to hold as a quasi-owner the things she uses or acquires.[2]

The criminal offences are, as before, mainly witchcraft, incest and treason, and the like offences. Incest is comparatively rare. Treason, which is found as early as the Mandja,[3] consists of treacherously associating with the enemy or plotting against the chief, and (among the more advanced tribes) offences against his household—for example, adultery with a wife of his.[4] Charges of witchcraft are everywhere. There

[1] *Les Bangala*, pp. 227–35; *Les Mangbetu*, pp. 333, 339.
[2] But among the Warega, household utensils brought from home by the women, or later acquired by them, are considered to belong to the husband's mother or his first wife.
[3] *Les Mandja*, p. 421.
[4] This is a common crime in Africa, for an elderly chief usually has a young wife or two.

is hardly such a thing as natural death—only death by violence and death by witchcraft, and even a man who has been eaten by a wild beast may have met his end owing to the witchcraft of another person, in bringing the animal upon the scene.[1] The proportion of defenceless women charged steadily grows, and even among the Warega the accused are more often than not of the female sex. Many of the accused are merely unpopular members of society. The punishment for criminal offences is generally death by poison. But among the Bangala and Mangbetu mutilations are frequent, the bastinado, forced labour, and even imprisonment in chains.

The civil wrongs are the same as elsewhere, mainly homicide, wounding, rape, adultery, seduction, and theft. Among the Mandja, Warega, and Mayombe, the sanctions are generally pecuniary. Unlike the peoples of the Early Codes, they have no one currency to take the place of cattle, and that is why we find among them no table of fixed compositions. The amount of the sanction is assessed by the elders in each case. But, as in the Early Codes, there are corporal punishments for slaves, and adulterers caught in the act may be put to death. Theft is heinous. In the nations who have reached the level of the Central Codes—that is to say, the Bangala and Mangbetu —the same changes show themselves as in the peoples of that stage. For homicide without extenuating circumstances the accused is usually handed over to the next of kin of the slain, who may, at their choice, kill, eat, or sell him. If there are alleviating circumstances and the accused or his relatives are wealthy, he may be ransomed. A homicide caught in the act may be put to death. As we have seen, religion has little power in the Congo and among none of these peoples are there sanctuaries in which a man might take asylum. The sanction imposed by a court for wounding is pecuniary. Adultery is capital. The injured husband may kill the adulterous pair caught in the act, but he often allows the man to ransom himself by a heavy sum, and contents himself with mutilating his wife in the ear or leg. A girl or a ransom may be accepted from the adulterer in place of his life. The sanction for seduc-

[1] See, for example, *Les Bangala*, p. 265.

tion is pecuniary. Theft is heinous through these peoples, and often criminal. If the owner sues in a court he may recover a multiple of the value of the goods, or the thief may be awarded to him as a slave, but he may slay or eat the thief caught in the act, or cut off his hands. Among the Mangbetu, however, violent self-help is not permitted, and the king often punishes the thief with amputation of the ears.

Courts develop in the way we have seen elsewhere. There are developed courts throughout these peoples. Even among the Mandja the chief may punish a man severely for refusal to pay a sum which has been awarded, and among the Bangala and Mangbetu if the defendant does not obey a judgment his wife or child (or, if he has none, he himself) may be seized and awarded to the creditor, who may use their services or sell them. There is great public interest and confidence in the courts, and all kinds of disputes are brought before them. The court of the king or paramount chief alone tries the more serious cases. The defendant is brought before the chief, or chief and elders, and is cross-examined. No witch-doctor plays any part here. The trials are by unsworn evidence, and among the Mandja the use of the ordeal as ascertaining guilt is unknown. Among the Warega and Mayombe we hear of it only in regard to charges of witchcraft, where (as generally throughout the Congo) the ordeal by poison is applied. This is a criminal case, and there is not much formality about it: a mounting public agitation, an outcry, the accused (if he is not speared) hauled off to the witch-doctor, sometimes terrified but more often confident in the result; the poison given by the witch-doctor; and the result usually death, and a howl of triumph from the mob.[1] No doubt the ordeal has a simple origin. Poison is the normal method of execution for a crime; and when it is given to a man and he vomits and survives, then on the principle that what happens ought to happen he is deemed to be innocent. When we reach the Bangala and the Mangbetu the ordeal has a much wider use. One of a large assortment of ordeals (including the oath) and methods

---

[1] See a terrible account of the application of the ordeal in *Les Mayombe*, pp. 402–3.

of divination is used for the trial of both crimes and wrongs,[1] but only where there is not evidence on both sides; and mainly in charges of witchcraft.

So much for our digression into the non-pastoral peoples of the Congo. Their ways are not attractive to us. Our own civilization originates with pastoral peoples, Semites, Germans, and others. Let us return and continue our story as we left it at the close of the stage of the Central Codes.

[1] See *Les Bangala*, pp. 383–7, and *Les Mangbetu*, pp. 487–90. Among the Bangala, when the assembly comes to an important decision each chief may solemnly swear an oath to carry it out (p. 403).

CHAPTER V

THE LATE CODES

General View

THE fascinating period that follows the age of the Central Codes is pregnant with the civilizations of the world. It gives birth to all the great religious faiths of man, whatever the time and whatever the place. Never again does religion hold such power over the mind of man. Yet at the end of this period comes the parting of the ways, and some peoples advance to a theocratic and others to a secular government. The jurisdiction of ecclesiastical courts is at its height, but the same crisis affects them at the close of this age, and in one nation they disappear, in another their authority is limited and defined, and in others they advance to oust all other jurisdictions. Feudalism is at its height, but begins to wane before the end of the period. There is a far-reaching economic advance, and money is now in wide use, and the banking or deposit of money is first seen. Towns show a great spread in number and size, and there is a notable increase in the extent of specialization in trades and occupations. The same age gives birth to the world's great legal systems in Babylon and Rome and England. The law of crimes and the law of civil wrongs continue to grow closer together, and now they are at their nearest, but are about to grow apart again. The blood feud is at its height. Intentional homicide is punishable with death, and in regard to serious wounding the doctrine of an eye for an eye and a tooth for a tooth makes its brief appearance. The tempo of change continues to quicken, and the movement of change is continuous.

In England this age is represented by the period from A.D. 1100 to 1300, and in France and Italy from about 1000 to 1250. In Palestine the age is that of the Old Testament, and in Rome it is the period of the so-called Twelve Tables, at the beginning of the known Roman history. In Athens it is the eighth and seventh centuries B.C., the age of Draco and his Code, and the rest of Greece is represented at a similar date.[1] The Middle Assyrian Code of about 1400 B.C. belongs to the same stage of advance.[2] Much of India stood at this stage from about the ninth century B.C. to the seventeenth century A.D., and much of China during at least the last 3,000 years; and finally at the dawn of the world's known history of law, and yet almost at the close of our story, we reach in Sumer and Babylon, about the end of the third millennium B.C., the Code of Eshnunna and that of Hammurabi, the latter one of the most advanced of the codes of this age. Vividly it is borne in upon us how much time and how much of the genius of individuals and of peoples was needed to build up our civilization. From the Sumer and Accad of over 4,000 years ago to Western Europe in A.D. 1300 is one great story and one field of culture, and behind the written records of Mesopotamia lie hundreds of millennia during which mankind has progressed, by the steps which we have tried to describe, to the efflorescence of the civilization contained in its documents of clay and stone. It is not a story of uniform advance. In the Indus valley, civilization was destroyed 3,500 years ago at the coming of the Aryans. Once, 2,000 years ago, it was everywhere destroyed save in the East, and this may well be repeated, for though at that time it covered but a narrow field, and now its spread is infinitely enlarged, so, too, is the means to destroy it. From the time when we first know it well—in Mesopotamia from the third dynasty of Ur, the dynasties of Isin and Eshnunna and the first Semitic dynasty of Babylon— the progress of civilization is slow in that region, and it is not till the Neo-Babylonian period of the sixth century B.C. that we can say that the law has passed beyond this stage and into what we may call the modern era. In China the progress has been far slower. Yet there has been advance, and the field of civilized culture is wider, and communication far easier, than ever they have been before.

[1] In the Homeric poems the earlier Iliad belongs to the period of the Early Codes and the later Odyssey to the end of that age; see *Primitive Law*, p. 149.

[2] See *The Assyrian Laws*, translated and edited by G. R. Driver and Sir John Miles (1935).

The miracle of that century, the sixth century B.C. and the few years before and after, has been noticed more than once. In Greece it gave birth to the Orphic and the bulk of its other religions. The same period in Palestine witnessed the reformation under Josiah[1]—an event whose religious import cannot be exaggerated—and the lives of Isaiah, Jeremiah, and Ezekiel. In Persia the religion of Zoroaster swept the country. In North-West India at that time Brahmanism reached its full development, and a new religious birth formed Buddhism, named after Gautama the Buddha,[2] whose devotees now number a third of the population of the world, and Jainism, whose origin is chiefly attributed to Vardhamana Mahavira during the same years.[3] Nor were these the only religious sects of the age: an old text speaks of sixty-three different philosophical schools of the non-Brahmans of the time of Buddha,[4] and the Jain writings are full of accounts of heresies. In China that same century was the great age of Confucius [5] and Lao-Tse.[6] This phenomenon is not to be explained by ease of communications over that vast area; and what could these religions have taken from one another? The explanation is afforded by all the facts that we have surveyed: all these peoples in that century stood at the stage of the Late Codes. In the centre of that field Babylon had reached and passed it, and the countries on the periphery had reached it.[7] The same stage of the Late Codes produced similar miracles in later times and other places. Western Arabia had just attained this stage in the days of Mahomet, when it gave birth to another of the world's great faiths, and only a century after his death the faithful ruled from the Indus to the Pyrenees. It was the same age in Europe, between A.D. 1100 and 1300, that witnessed the incredible episode of the Crusades, when at the bidding of a

[1] 621 B.C., the year when a " book of the law " was discovered during repairs of the Temple.
[2] Born a Brahman prince and lived about 560 to 480 B.C.
[3] Lived about 540–468 B.C.
[4] *Sacred Books of the East*, vol. x, 2, p. 93.
[5] About 551 to 478 B.C.
[6] Born 604 B.C.
[7] Those nearer to the centre—namely, Palestine and Persia—earlier than the rest. In the Far East, China stands apart.

hermit and a pope armies from almost every part of Western Europe and a hundred thousand common folk toiling on foot, that had never strayed from their native villages, and did not know Europe from Palestine, set out to win the Holy Land from an infidel of a higher culture, and after countless hordes had died on the way established for a brief spell a model feudal monarchy in Jerusalem. It was in the same age in Western Europe, and not least in England, that the scanty resources of mere villages in men and material raised up vast architectural wonders to the glory of God.

From some of these countries little survives of their law in the times that have been mentioned; from others much remains; but from all there is far more evidence than the mere creation of a national religion or moral philosophy, to show that they stood at the stage of the Late Codes. Of the law and economics of Western Europe, Babylon, and Assyria in this era much is now known. In Palestine a fine Code of law, of the centuries around the sixth century B.C., survives in its religious literature.[1] The year 621 B.C., the year of the commencement of Josiah's reforms in Judah, produced in Athens the Code of Draco, of which enough survives in tradition to show the characteristics of a Late Code. In India remain legal writings typical of the Late Codes. In China the sixth century was not only the age of Confucius and Lao-Tse; it was also part of the later period of the Chou dynasty,[2] when the country was being welded into a unity under a feudal monarchy, and the law contained the severe corporal sanctions and other institutions characteristic of the Late Codes. So, too, did the law of feudal Tibet before the conversion to Buddhism.

We have not, in previous chapters, made reference to China or India, for it is not till the peoples of those countries reach the stage of the Late Codes that their literature provides reliable contemporary evidence of their law and life.

The Chinese civilization may be as ancient as that of Egypt and Babylonia, but at all times it was almost wholly isolated from other civilizations, and it has progressed more slowly

---

[1] Exodus 21[2] to 22[17].   [2] About 1122 to 256 B.C.

than any other.   In all probability it originated in and around the great eastward bend of the Yellow River. .Tradition speaks of rulers of the third millennium B.C., but the stories of their achievements are wholly unreliable.   The Hsia dynasty that followed,[1] still ruled over a small territory, little more extensive than the valley of the Yellow River, and the country was feudal, ruled by chiefs or nobles holding under the king. The Shang (or Yin) dynasty [2] saw little change in the government of the kingdom, but considerable advance in culture, especially in pottery and writing.   The Chou dynasty endured from 1122 to 256 B.C., and from the tenth century B.C. true history is thought to begin.   Throughout this period China was still feudal.   King Wu, when he succeeded to the throne and founded that dynasty, partitioned the realm among the barons who had followed his arms, and in the ensuring centuries, as an individual ruler was weak or strong, so the barons were more or less independent.   But the territory of the kingdom steadily widened, although the absorption of smaller into larger feudal States reduced their number (according to tradition) from 124 in the early days of the dynasty to 72 in the time of Confucius.   The last centuries of the period are the classical age of China.   They created the pattern of the culture and the law that survived till the present century. The Chou dynasty and the feudal age of China ended in 249 B.C., when one aggressive state—that of Ch'in—swallowed up the rest.   Shih Huang Ti, the First Emperor, ascended the throne in 246 B.C. and welded the now wide domains of the empire into a unified State of thirty-six provinces.

Through Chinese history we hear of successive penal codes, the first, indeed, being attributed, in the unreliable Shu Ching, or Canon of History, to an Emperor Shun of 2317-2208 B.C. But dynasty after dynasty issued a code of laws—a group of legislative clauses—which was usually adapted from the code of a predecessor.   That of Li K'uei in the fourth century B.C. was something of a model for those that followed, and the code of the Emperor Yung Lo of the Ming dynasty (about A.D. 1430) had something of the completeness of a code in

[1] 2205 to 1766 B.C.   [2] 1766 to 1122 B.C.

modern sense.   Upon it were based the Ta Ch'ing Lü Li, the
the Statutes of the Ch'ing (or Manchu) dynasty, which
remained in force till 1912.   All these codes, from the time
when history dawns in China, belong to the stage of the
Late Codes.[1]

Substantially these codes are codes of criminal law, and have
given to some the impression that there is no Chinese law but
criminal law.   Nothing could be further from the truth: all
our codes, even up to this stage, have consisted mainly of
offences against person and property, and at the close of this
stage, as we shall see, the more serious offences become criminal.   There remains, in China as elsewhere, the whole of the
civil law, of marriage, inheritance, property and commercial
transactions; and (as is characteristic of this and the previous
age) there is, except in regard to commercial transactions, a
vast variety in its rules from district to district, and especially
in the rules of inheritance.   There is also in China a pronounced system of local government—a father is responsible
for the wrongful acts of his family, a local official for
those in his charge, and the national law of wrongs is brutal
and severe: hence the villagers—and the Chinaman is a
villager—are loth to call in the forces of law, and prefer to
settle their disputes among themselves.   The law, therefore,
of marriage, inheritance, and property shows as much variety
as with other peoples of the Late Codes, and we shall say
something of it in its place.[2]

But the Chinese economy has been static for so long, the
pattern of its civilization and law so permanent, and its population so large, that the penal law is of supreme value to us,
exemplifying in its wealth of illustration and distinctions, as
no other system does, the spirit of the law of the Late Codes.
It throws more light on the meaning of the Babylonian and
Hebrew codes and the Twelve Tables than can easily be got
from any other source.   We shall take the people and law of

[1] For a useful English summary of these Codes, see title " Law " in S.
Couling's *Encyclopædia Sinica* (Oxford University Press, 1917).

[2] Of the various descriptions in English of life in the Chinese village
perhaps the best is *Peasant Life in China*, by Hsiao-Tung Fei (Routledge,
1939).

China during the three millennia from the tenth century B.C. to A.D. 1900 as representative of the Late Codes.[1]

The written legal tradition of India is very different. It is the tradition of Aryan-speaking peoples that invaded India from the north-west in the second millennium B.C. and later, destroying the Indus valley civilization that lay in its path. This was part of that great movement of Aryan peoples from Northern Europe or Asia, that spread southwards into Persia, Greece, Italy, and the West in the second and first millennia B.C.

The earliest documents of the Hindu literary tradition are the 1,017 hymns of the Rigveda, mainly consisting of invocations to their many gods. They are generally regarded as dating from the period 1200 to 800 B.C., but contain matter of many ages and are not to be taken as contemporary accounts of the civilization that produced them. They hold little that pertains to the subject-matter of this book, but there are many indications in them that (like the peoples of the Homeric poems) the communities to whom they refer stood at the close of the age of the Early Codes. The authors of this collection were the Brahmans (priests, and probably hereditary priests for the most part) whose concern was to record these ancient hymns and the religious tradition that they embodied. These communities in North-West India were small: they were ruled by kings, but the kingly authority was weak. We hear nothing of cities: the people lived in villages, perhaps surrounded by hedge or earth-bank. Their economy was mainly pastoral, and the cow was their dearest possession, but they also lived by agriculture, and knew the ox-drawn plough and cart and something of irrigation. The horse was ridden, but not in war: kings and nobles fought from chariots, and the well-armed warrior wore a helmet and coat of mail. The common people fought on foot, and the weapons of the time were bows, spears, lances, swords, axes, and stones. There were markets, but goods passed by barter, not sale. The cow was the chief standard of value, and money was not in use.

---

[1] Although there has of recent times been a little advance beyond that stage. For the best treatise in English on this law, see Alabaster, *Notes and Commentaries on Chinese Criminal Law and Cognate Topics* (London, Luzac & Co., 1899).

The only contract of which we hear is the loan. A man might be enslaved for debt. Society was not yet dependent on slave labour, and there was a beginning of specialization of occupations. There is little of law and trials in the hymns, and it is unlikely that the Brahmans had yet become judges or had yet taken an active interest in the law. There is no mention of ordeals. Marriage was monogamous except among the princely class, and was with bride-price. The levirate was observed where a man left a widow but no children. The system of *wergelds* was in full force, and the sanction for killing a man was the payment of 100 cows. Theft, housebreaking, and highway robbery were the most frequent offences. Theft was still a civil offence: there were stocks for the offender, but no capital punishment. Incest was a crime.

In short, there is nothing here that differentiates these small kingdoms from any of the others that we have examined, standing at the close of the period of the Early Codes and the beginning of the Central Codes. The literature that follows, that of the later Samhitas, the Brahmanas, Aranyakas, and Upanishads, is usually attributed to the period of 800 to 500 B.C. The scene has shifted further to the east and south. There has been a great development of religion and philosophy. The ritual has grown to great proportions, and animal sacrifice is much in evidence. The Brahman is " a receiver of gifts, a seeker of food and liable to removal at will." Some are humble priests of the village, officiating for a local noble, but some are spiritual advisers of the king and members of his entourage. The king's authority is stronger, and he rules over large territories. Feudalism has developed. The king is wont to grant to nobles the right to receive food from the common people, and in place of peasant proprietors we hear rather of landlords cultivating their estates by serfs, or merchants trading by means of slaves. In short, as we see in Norman England in the period of the Central and Late Codes, the free peasant holding on a feudal tenure is slipping down to the status of a serf, and the slave is being lifted to the same status. The castes are not yet completely formed. We hear of an increasing use of heavy ploughs, and even of the use of manure, and there is an increasing variety of cereals. Meat is still being

eaten, and an ox is slaughtered to feed a guest. We hear of
towns, a great development of industrial life, and a greater
specialization of occupations. There is a familiarity with a
large number of metals. Of legal matters there is very little,
so that we may be sure that the Brahmans are merely priests,
and not yet judges. There is only one mention of an ordeal.
The sanction for homicide is still private vengeance tempered
by the *wergeld*, with its varying number of cows (ten to 1,000)
for the different ranks of the population, and, over and above,
a bull for the king. The status of women is falling : polygamy
spreads among the wealthy, and the woman owns no property
and has no right of inheritance. The desire for male offspring
is more and more marked.

From this point India enters the age of the Late Codes,
evidenced by all that we can glean of political and economic
conditions in the early Buddhist and contemporary literature,
and the Dharma Sutras and Dharma Sastras of 500 B.C. and
onwards. The various religious and philosophical schools
had each their own Sutras (or rules of conduct), and the
Dharma Sutras (of, say, 600 to 200 B.C.) were prose rules of
law and practical life, and the Dharma Sastras were later collections of such rules in verse. Of these, one of the most
celebrated and authoritative is the Code of Manu (or Manava
Dharma Sastra) of perhaps 200 B.C. By this date, as happened
in other lands, the priests had assumed an active participation
and interest in the administration of the law. They were, above
all, the scholars and the clerks, they were advisers of the king
on legal as well as other matters, they advised the judges
upon disputed questions of law, and the king's assistant judges
were themselves Brahmans. The Code of Manu contains all
the practical rules whereby a Brahman should govern his life
in all its aspects, his food and dress, his daily rites, his relations
with his fellow-man and the king, and his legal activities ; and
the central core of the book is a treatise upon the law—what
the law is, and what it ought to be. A little earlier, and to us
more valuable, is the Arthasastra of Kautilya, only discovered
in the present century. In this we obtain most valuable and
detailed information of the law and administration of the period
of the Maurya Empire in India, which flourished from about

320 to 280 B.C.; and Megasthenes and other Greeks bring further light. The law of India remained law of the Late Codes for some 2,000 years longer, and among the less advanced of the native States a century or two longer still, but we shall take in particular the law of the period of Manu and the Arthasastra as illustrating the age of the Late Codes.[1]

In Africa, too, are to be found a great number of peoples of this era. In South Africa, continuing to move north and west, we reach Bechuanaland, where several of the less advanced peoples of the stage are to be found.[2] These are the Tswana cluster of the Sotho group of Bantu peoples, of whom the largest nation are the Bamangwato. In East Africa the level of the more advanced peoples of the Late Codes is well represented in the feudal kingdom and Empire of Abyssinia as it stood in the year A.D. 1935;[3] and the Gallas of Southern Abyssinia and Kenya[4] lag but a little way behind. But the bulk of African peoples of the Late Codes are to be found in West Africa, where they include the great majority of the nations of Nigeria,[5] the Gold Coast, and

[1] For an introduction to the law of India, see *Cambridge History of India*, and especially vol. i, chaps. IV, V, VIII, IX, XII, and XIX; the *Arthasastra of Kautilya*, trans. R. Shama Sastri, Mysore (1908–10); the *Manava Dharma Sastra*, trans. Bühler (*S.B.E.*, vol. xxv); the *Narada Smriti and Brihaspati*, trans. Jolly (*S.B.E.,* vol. xxxiii); the *Dharma Sutras of Apastamba and Gautama*, trans. Bühler (*S.B.E.*, vols. ii and xiv). For the developed Hindu Law, see J. D. Mayne, *Hindu Law and Usage* (ed. 1950). See also *Ancient India and Indian Civilization*, by Masson-Dursel, De Willman-Grabowska, and Stern (trans. M. R. Dobie, 1934). For an example of a backward native state (Nepal, which in A.D. 1830 represents the close of the Late Codes), see " Criminal Law and Procedure in Nepal a Century Ago," by L. Adams (*Far Eastern Quarterly*, vol. ix, No. 2, 1950). This refers to memoranda and articles left by Brian Houghton Hodgson in 1820–40.

[2] See Prof. Schapera's *Handbook of Tswana Law and Custom* (1938).

[3] See Miss Margery Perham's *The Government of Ethiopia* (1948) and bibliography therein, and also C. Conti Rossini, *Principi di diritto consuetudinario dell' Eritrea*, 1916, and C. H. Walker's *The Abyssinian at Home* (1933).

[4] See, e.g., *E.A.L.* vol. i, p. 101.

[5] For Northern Nigeria see *The Northern Tribes of Nigeria*, by C. K. Meek, 2 vols. (1925); and for some of the more backward peoples of that region, the same author's *Tribal Studies in Northern Nigeria*, 2 vols., 1931. For a detailed economic and political study of a Northern Nigerian feudal State (Nupe), see S. F. Nadel, *A Black Byzantium* (1942). For Southern

Ashanti.[1] It is not surprising, therefore, that in Northern Nigeria, where cattle and horses can be bred, Islam, which also originated among the less forward peoples of this age, has spread, and still spreads far and wide.

In Central and South America, too, we find notable civilizations of the Late Codes. Here, before the Spanish conquest of the sixteenth century, empires extended, at the time of their greatest development, over the largest part of a region covering North America, south of the middle of Mexico, and reaching through Southern America along the lofty plateaux of the Andes, and across the area between them and the Pacific coast, as far south as the River Maule in Chile—in total, that is to say, from about the eighteenth degree of latitude north to the thirty-fifth degree south. In this great area were two main homes and centres of ancient civilization, not so ancient as those of Babylonia and Egypt, but possessing certain similar natural advantages. They were by inland lakes and rivers, and though much nearer to the equator, enjoyed the same mild climate because of their greater height, for they were all situated upon plateaux of the cordillera of the Andes, which in North America spreads out into a great tableland covering inland Mexico and Guatemala and Yucatan. One of these homes of civilization was in the valley of Mexico, which includes five lakes within its area and is situated at a height of some 7,500 feet above the sea. Here at the time of the Conquest the dominant people were the Aztecs of Tenochtitlan [2] (now Mexico City), immigrant hunters from the north into a civilization many centuries earlier, inhabiting a town built on an island in the lake of Mexico (then Tezcoco). Of the other

---

Nigeria, see P. A. Talbot's *The Peoples of Southern Nigeria*, 4 vols. (1931); and for a detailed study of a Southern Nigerian people (the Ibo) see C. K. Meek, *Law and Authority in a Nigerian Tribe* (1937).

[1] See Rattray, *Ashanti* (1923); and *Ashanti Law and Constitution* (1929); Sarbah, *Fanti Customary Laws*, and Danquah, *Akan Laws and Customs* (1928). See also the Report of the Gold Coast Commission on Native Courts (*Government Gazette*, Jan. 31, 1895, pp. 27-34).

[2] For the peoples of Mexico, see W. H. Prescott, *History of the Conquest of Mexico*, 1843 (new edition published by Swan, Sonnenschein & Co., 1890); T. A. Joyce, *Mexican Archæology* (1914); G. C. Vaillant, *Aztecs of Mexico* (1941).

peoples in that region, mention must be made of their allies, the Tezcucans, who had reached a still higher level in science and the arts. A second home of civilization, closely connected with Southern Mexico in culture, and forming with it one cultural field, was in the well-watered tableland between Yucatan, Guatemala, British Honduras, and the northern portion of Honduras. This area was occupied by the civilization of the Maya, which had flourished at a date some centuries earlier than the Spanish conquest.[1]

In South America the home and centre of the highest civilization was in the Central Andes, around the valley of Cuzco and Lake Titicaca and the river-basins of that region, all at an average height of some 11,500 feet, and in a latitude of about 13° south. In the four centuries preceding the arrival of the Spaniards, the tribe of the Incas, coming from Lake Titicaca, had built by conquest over innumerable small Indian States an empire extending from the Andes to the Pacific coast, and reaching from southern Colombia through Ecuador, Peru, and Western Bolivia down to the River Maule in Chile—that is, from the equator to a latitude of 35° south.[2] In Peru, in Mexico, and in Guatemala these empires were able to support themselves by the diverse products of the hot, the temperate, and the cold regions of the plains, the slopes, and the highlands, and lived in the main by an intensive agriculture.

Of all these peoples of the present and past, the least advanced are the nations of West Africa and Bechuanaland, and the Gallas, and the English of the early twelfth century. Eshnunna, the Hebrews of the Old Testament, the Romans of the Twelve Tables,[3] and the Peruvians, Mexicans, and Maya continue the line of progress, and the most forward of all are the Assyrians of the Middle Period, the Babylonians of the close of the third millennium B.C., the Abyssinians in modern Africa

---

[1] For the Maya, see Joyce, *Mexican Archæology*.

[2] For the Andean civilizations see W. H. Prescott, *History of the Conquest of Peru* (1847, Everyman's Library ed., 1924); *H.S.A.*, vol. ii (*Bureau of American Ethnology, Bulletin* 143, vol. ii) (1946); Garcilasso de la Vega, *The Royal Commentaries of Peru*, trans. by Rycaut (1688), and Markham.

[3] The nations up to this point are referred to in the author's *Primitive Law* as of the Late Middle Codes.

and the peoples of China and India.[1]   The corresponding stage in Western Europe is the later thirteenth century in England. The canvas upon which we must endeavour to paint is a vast one, and it will no longer be possible to do justice to the details.

But though in this era the power of religion is at its height, it would be a false surmise that even now there is confusion at the boundary between religion and the law.   Indeed, how could there be confusion between rules of conduct enforceable in the courts and rules of religious ethics or ritual observance? Nevertheless, as we have often seen, there is a close relation in all ages between the criminal law and religious or magico-religious thought, and since, among the nations of the Late Codes, the laws of criminal and of civil wrongs are at their closest to one another, it is not to be wondered at if religion and law, though distinct, are at their closest.   Let us illustrate by one or two examples the relation between them.

The notion of the confusion of law and religion among the Hebrews of the Old Testament is partly derived from mis-translation.   The rules of conduct or belief which are sanc-tioned by religion are not called " law," except in a figurative sense, in the Hebrew original.   The word there used, and translated as " law " in the English Bible, is " torah " which signifies " instruction " or " direction," and is never used in reference to the secular law.   But the Hebrews had a separate word for the secular law—namely, the word " mishpat " (plural " mishpatim "), of which the literal significance is " judgment."   They had the same notions that we hold of the nature of the secular law, and, like the Anglo-Saxons, Baby-lonians, Sumerians, and so many other peoples, marked by the use of a word meaning " judgment " the simpler and basic ideas which they had reached in earlier times upon this topic, and also their appreciation of the essential difference between legal and religious rules—namely, that breaches of legal rules are enforceable in the courts.

A historical introduction to the giving of the *Torah* and the

[1] The reader will observe, in the text and footnotes of the following six chapters, with what precision this order is maintained in the details of law and economics.

law is contained in the book of Genesis and the book of Exodus to the nineteenth chapter. Chapter 20 contains the Ten Commandments, or, to translate the Hebrew more accurately, the Ten Words (or maxims). They are set in a language never used in legal codes—they are couched in the second person, and in general terms, and do not condescend to detail the facts to which they refer, nor to specify the punishment that will attend upon a breach. Then follows the sentence: " Now these are the laws (*mishpatim*) that thou (Moses) shalt set before them," and these words introduce nothing less than a fine example of an ancient code of laws,[1] in the form with which we are now so familiar, the clauses succinctly drafted and in proper order with reference to the subject-matter, couched in the third person, and specifying their secular sanctions. This document we will call the Hebrew Code. Those who hold the belief that the whole Pentateuch was issued by God to Moses will observe the great contrast, in the respects just mentioned, between this code and the rest of the Pentateuch, and will perhaps conclude that this was the body of secular laws issued to Moses. Those who hold more modern beliefs know that this code (which forms part of a document commonly termed the Book of the Covenant) is generally regarded as the oldest part of the Pentateuch. In its later days the Code has been slightly expanded under the hands of priestly rulers, but it remains a code of civil law. Indeed, this process of addition by priestly hands is but part of the process by which, on a wider scale, the Code was brought into the Pentateuch, a priestly compilation of the fourth century B.C.

The surviving fragments of the Roman Twelve Tables do not evidence any confusion between law and religion. The legal fragments are rules of normal form and content couched in the third person; the religious, which chiefly prescribe the method of interment of the dead, are for the most part commands in the second person without sanctions. According to tradition the Twelve Tables were a code of law compiled about 450 B.C., but this is a period long before the birth of history at Rome, and all our surviving fragments are quota-

---

[1] Exodus 21^2 to 22^{17}. For a translation and commentary see *Primitive Law*, chaps. xi, xii.

tions direct or indirect from an edition of laws from various
sources by one Sextus Ælius in about 193 B.C., and the view
taken in this book is that they represent law of about that date,
though they probably include some rules dating from earlier
times. Nevertheless the law in force in these early days of
Rome gave birth to the main principles of the classical Roman
law, and from these well-known principles the early law can
be fairly reconstructed and is shown to be law typical of the
Late Codes.[1]

Nor does the Hindu law of this age evince any confusion
between law and religion. For example, in regard to the Code
of Manu, it is generally agreed by the best authorities (to use
the words of Sir Henry Maine) " that the codified law—Manu
and his glossators—embraced originally a much smaller body
of usage than had been imagined, and, next, that the customary
rules, reduced to writing, have been very greatly altered by
Brahmanical expositors, constantly in spirit, sometimes in
tenor. Indian law may be in fact affirmed to consist of a
very great number of local bodies of usage, and of one set of
customs reduced to writing, pretending to a diviner authority
than the rest, exercising consequently a great influence upon
them, and tending, if not checked, to absorb them." [2] There
are many parts of India where Hindus do not acknowledge
the authority of the Smritis, and yet, apart from local variation
in detail, their rules of law are much the same, except that the
Brahman authors have in their compilations given a religious
purpose to a law, or have stated it in a form amended to sort
with their religious ambitions, or have added rules with the
like purpose. Elsewhere Maine observes of what he terms the
" religious oligarchies of Asia " that " their complete monopoly
of legal knowledge [3] appears to have enabled them to put off
on the world collections not so much of the rules actually
observed as of the rules which the priestly order considered

---

[1] See *Primitive Law*, chap. xiv.   [2] *Village Communities*, p. 52.

[3] These words, however, exaggerate the power of the priesthood. It
was not a " religious oligarchy " in India. The kings were always the
rulers. The Brahmans had the monopoly, not of legal knowledge, but of
writing. But, as such, they kept the records of the courts, in so far as they
were kept, and they wrote the only text-books.

proper to be observed. The Hindoo Code, called the Laws of Manu, which is certainly a Brahmin compilation, undoubtedly enshrines many genuine observances of the Hindoo race, but the opinion of the best contemporary Orientalists is that it does not, as a whole, represent a set of rules ever actually administered in Hindostan." [1]

As for the law of China, we need not stay long to inquire whether there is confusion here between law and religion. Indeed, in the Hebrew and Christian sense of the word there is little of religion in China. There is, or was, a vague belief in the existence of a Supreme Being, to whom no worship was addressed (except by the emperor). Some animism still exists. Confucianism and Taoism are systems of philosophical and ethical belief, and much the same may be said even of Buddhism. Indeed, the original doctrine of Taoism had its birth in the great interest in law that we see everywhere in this age. It taught that there is a Tao (Law) working in all things, infinite and eternal, and that it is the part of man to allow this law to work. The so-called ancestor-worship of China is what we have seen among so many peoples: the word " worship " is singularly inappropriate: it is little more than an expression of gratification at the excellence of one's ancestors. Separate and apart is the law—mainly, as ever, a law of sanctions for wrongs—applied in the courts, brutal, pitiless, and bloody.

There is no confusion between law and religion among any of these peoples, and when indeed we reach the Codes of the rest of the forward nations of this age—all the Sumerian, Babylonian, and Assyrian legislation—we find no religious matter in them; and this though they date from the beginnings of recorded human history. In regard to the African and American peoples of the Late Codes we are in a happier position, for we can observe with our eyes the relations between their law and religion, and there is no confusion to be seen. In Bechuanaland, for example, where law is often spoken of as having been instituted by God or the ancestor spirits, there is no confusion to be seen between *molao*, which is law, or a

---

[1] *Ancient Law*, p. 15.

law, and a breach of which may be punished in the courts, and a mere *mokgwa*, or custom, breach of which is not so punished.[1]

Yet religion is growing apace, and religion and law are closer together than ever before. In South Africa, as in China, the power of religion is slight, and the closeness of the relation between the two can be better exemplified in pagan West Africa, among the less advanced of the peoples of this stage.

Among one of the most advanced of the nations of the Central Codes—namely, the Lamba—we noticed [2] the emergence of a belief in a " high god," commonly called Lesa, who is angered when men sin deeply, when they commit murder, theft, or adultery. He punishes those acts by sending leprosy and smallpox. These offences are not merely religious, but also partly criminal. If we look at some of the mingled remnants of peoples dislodged and broken by invasion and migration in West Africa—for example, the Tallensi of the Northern Territories of the Gold Coast [3]—we find that they have no distinct tribes and no well-marked social unit above the clan. Between members of different clans who were traditional enemies, homicide could only lead to blood-feud or war, whichever it should properly be called. But within the same clan there appears to have been no sanction for homicide except the displeasure of the Earth Goddess.[4] Homicide was a grave sin against the Earth and the ancestors. The elders of the segment to which the murderer belonged sent to beg the forgiveness of the chief or Earth Custodian, and the family of both the slayer and the slain offered, as expiatory sacrifices to the Earth Goddess and the ancestors, a number of animals fixed by the chief and elders. The sanctions for adultery or wife-stealing were of a similar religious character. Not so theft. A thief caught in the act was severely beaten and disgraced if he were a fellow-clansman, but, if not, his eyes

---

[1] Schapera, *Tswana*, pp. 35–6 and 39.   [2] *Ante*, p. 191.

[3] See Prof. M. Fortes, *The Dynamics of Clanship among the Tallensi* (1945), pp. 177, 250, and in *A.P.S.*, p. 269. See also the same author's *The Web of Kinship among the Tallensi* (1949).

[4] We have often noticed that within a kinship group there are no legal sanctions for homicide because there is no benefit to be got by the group from taking another life within it or transferring property from one member to another.

were put out, or he suffered other mutilation. Among these peoples, then, murder and adultery were religious offences, but theft had hardly become so. A similar situation is found among the bulk of the Ibo of Southern Nigeria,[1] but among some of them for theft, too, sacrifice must be made to Ala the Earth Goddess.[2] We may take another example from the Jukun of Central Nigeria. They know of Ama (" mother " or " creatrix "), who, like a number of deities of this stage in West Africa, Greece, and elsewhere,[3] is an Earth Goddess and Creatrix. She is the patroness of childbirth and queen of the underworld: she causes the grain to ripen. What men consider evil in this world, she, too, considers evil. She is a retributive deity. The doers of evil in this world suffer punishment in the next, in the underworld over which she presides, and especially the doers of murder and witchcraft. She demands chastity, too, from men and women, and those who commit adultery must atone for their sin at her shrine. They confess and offer a sacrifice of beer before the shrine of Adama, and suffer the penance of thrashing and washing.[4]

Lastly we may take an example from a more forward nation, the Hebrews. Here the religious ethics of the people are summarized in the Ten Words, or Ten Commandments. Of these the first to the fourth are purely religious, but the fifth to the ninth—the core and probably the earliest of these maxims [5]—impose religious duties which, as we shall see, correspond to criminal or partly criminal offences. They are set out in order of heinousness, and include the same criminal-religious offences which we have met with in West Africa. 6. Thou shalt do no murder. 7. Thou shalt not commit adultery. 8. Thou shalt not steal. 9. Thou shalt not bear false witness against thy neighbour. The last is new.

---

[1] See Talbot, vol. iii, chap. 25; and Meek, *Ibo*, p. 210.

[2] See, e.g., Talbot, vol. iii, p. 647.

[3] For Southern Nigeria see table in Talbot, vol. ii, pp. 55 *et seq.*, and 71 *et seq.* There is, however, a belief in a (male) Supreme Deity almost everywhere in Nigeria (see, e.g., Talbot, vol. ii, p. 17), and a belief in an Earth Goddess, as well as a hierarchy of lesser deities and spirits.

[4] C. K. Meek, *A Sudanese Kingdom* (1931), pp. 197-8.

[5] Certainly they are the earliest in form, for they alone are couched in a brevity deserving the appellations of the Ten " Words."

As the peoples advance, even within the age of the Late Codes, there are changes in religious ethics as well as in law. In every people at and above the stage of economic advance of the Old Testament appears the fifth great ethical and religious principle—perhaps now become the highest of all—" Honour thy father and thy mother." It is the first moral and legal principle of the Hebrew Decalogue. It is the fundamental ethic of China, ancient and modern. We shall see how it comes about.

Bound up with the relations between law and religion, are those existing between the priesthood and the civil government, and between ecclesiastical and civil courts, and something will be said of them in later chapters.

CHAPTER VI

THE LATE CODES (*continued*)

ECONOMICS

THE vast majority of these peoples live by agriculture and cattle-keeping with subsidiary hunting and fishing. There have been, and still are, among them a number of purely pastoral tribes, such as Fulani in Northern Nigeria, some of the Gallas in Southern Abyssinia and Northern Kenya, and Semites in the Near East ; and on the other hand the peoples of the well-forested lands of the Guinea coast, including practically the whole of Southern Nigeria, the Gold Coast and Ashanti, cannot rear cattle because of the prevalence of the tsetse fly; and cattle were unknown in America. These are extreme examples : in most nations a combination of agriculture and cattle-keeping provides the main sustenance of the people.

Both in Northern and Southern Nigeria in 1921 approximately 76 per cent. of the occupied adult males were farmers,[1] and this proportion is roughly characteristic of all the less

---

[1] Northern Nigeria, 1921 Census, agriculture was the occupation of 77 per cent. of the occupied adult males, and hunting the occupation of an insignificant number (Meek, *N. Nig.* vol. ii, p. 214). In Southern Nigeria the corresponding figure was 75·8 per cent. (Talbot, vol. iv, p. 162). In Northern Nigeria the total area of cultivated land was about 7·7 per cent. and the average acreage per cultivator 3·5. Even in Northern Nigeria the livestock was scanty. The total livestock was 2¼ million cattle, 1¾ million sheep, 4¼ million goats. Total human population 9,998,314. Percentage of pastoralists 1 per cent., being 2·3 per cent. of the occupied men, and 1·5 per cent. of the occupied women. In Abyssinia as against an estimated human population of 5 million there are 7 million head of cattle and 18 million sheep and goats and 1,600,000 horses, see *Guida dell' Africa Orientale Italiana*, Milan, 1938, p. 96. But the population of Abyssinia might then be anything between 5 and 10 millions. In Bechuanaland, as in Northern Nigeria, the average holding is of about 3½ acres (see Schapera, *Tswana*, p. 201).

advanced peoples of the stage.[1]   The products of agriculture are now many and varied, but less in England, where root-crops are not grown.   In Africa and America the heavier work of clearing the land is done by the man, and the work of hoeing and planting is still mainly the task of women and children.   The hoe is still the implement of agriculture in America [2] and Africa, except in Abyssinia [3] and some districts of Africa (such as Bechuanaland), where the plough has recently been introduced; and ploughing is man's work, as it is in Europe and elsewhere.   Yet the heavy ox-drawn plough was in use in Babylonia and Egypt in the third millennium B.C. and in India in 1000 B.C., and a light hand-plough was in use in China in 500 B.C.[4]   The farm wagon (equally old in the ancient world) has been recently introduced into Abyssinia and Bechuanaland : until then the wheel was unknown in Africa south of the latitude of Egypt, and it was unknown in America.   Irrigation canals, terrace-cultivation, the use of manures,[5] and some rotation of crops are generally familiar, but in England the absence of root-cultivation restricts the scope of rotation to an alternation between cropping and fallow.[6]

The specialization of occupations has made great strides, and the list of distinct callings in West Africa, England, Babylon, Abyssinia, China, India, and elsewhere is very large.[7] There is a considerable increase in the number of craftsmen and artisans of various kinds, who now number some 5 per cent. of the working population.   These crafts are hereditary in the

[1] In India in 1911 the percentage of persons actively engaged in farming was still 65, a figure which suggests that during the time when the Code of Manu was being compiled the percentage was much the same as in Nigeria or little smaller.   In England the figure cannot have been very different at the same stages.   In China it is still about 70 per cent.

[2] The Peruvians also wielded a heavy hoe which may be termed a foot-plough.

[3] Where it is an ox-drawn plough pointed with iron.

[4] Sheh Ching (trans. Couvreur) p. 439.

[5] Especially in Peru, with its rich supplies of *guano*.

[6] Beginning to change during the period from a two-course to a three-course rotation (two-thirds cropped and one-third fallow).

[7] For a list of occupations in Northern Nigeria, see Meek, *N. Nig.*, vol. ii, pp. 224 f.; for S. Nigeria see Talbot, vol. iv, pp. 162 f.

vast majority of cases,[1] and among them the priestly calling is generally hereditary;[2] and a child who is to be taught a craft which is not that of its father is sometimes given in adoption to a craftsman. Early in our period, however, apprenticeship (where the child lives with the master for a fixed number of years) makes its appearance in twelfth-century England[3] and elsewhere.[4] Traders are more difficult to number: they are said to account for 3·6 per cent. of the occupied population in Northern and 8·6 per cent. in Southern Nigeria. Everywhere the women are active in petty trading in the markets.[5] Pottery, now often of great beauty in America and China, is still their province in most places,[6] and they have a virtual monopoly of spinning[7] and are very active in weaving.[8] They have also a virtual monopoly of brewing, and the ale-wife, or brewster, is a prominent figure in thirteenth-century England, and the female wine-seller in Babylon.

There is a great extension in the number and size of markets, and in England and almost everywhere else the kings and the towns receive tolls on the value of goods sold, or rent for stalls, or taxes on the value of goods imported or exported. In the larger markets sections are set apart for the sale of specified commodities.[9] So important have the markets become that there are market courts to deal with disputes that arise or crimes that are committed there.[10] Foreign trade from the

[1] Nadel, p. 47: Prescott, *Peru*, p. 33; China, India, England, and elsewhere.

[2] For Nupe, see Nadel, p. 47; for Abyssinia, Perham, p. 110; for the Hebrews see the Old Testament (priests and Levites). In India the calling of Brahman, or priest, was hereditary from earliest times.

[3] See Clapham, p. 133; P. & M., vol. i, p. 672.

[4] For Nupe, see Nadel, pp. 257, 266. Apprenticeship was and is common in China and India throughout our period.

[5] Meek, *Ibo*, p. 19; Talbot, vol. iii, p. 904; Nadel, Nupe, p. 332; see also *A.P.S.*, p. 248 (Tallensi); and Fortes, *The Web of Kinship*, p. 103.

[6] Meek, *N. Nig.*, vol. ii, p. 224 (13,214 women and 3,443 men engaged in pottery).

[7] For Peru see Rowe, p. 241. Cf. English "spinster."

[8] Meek, ibid., 36 per cent. of the weavers are women. Cf. English "webster" and "wife."

[9] E.g., in Bida (Nupe), and Mexico (Joyce, p. 129), and London.

[10] E.g., Abyssinia, England, Nupe, Mexico (Joyce, ibid.), India and China.

river ports near the coast is now quite considerable, and, for example, the Code of Hammurabi has much to say of the relations between merchants and the mercantile agents with whom they have invested money in a venture. Money is in general use in the towns.[1] In the ancient world the main currency everywhere was of metal passing by weight—silver in Babylonia, Assyria, and Palestine; copper in Egypt and Rome.[2] Such is the growing nicety of commercial transactions. In England a coinage continues in use as before—namely, the silver penny, with a subsidiary gold coinage; and a coinage appears in China and India early in our period. We now hear of a beginning of banking—the deposit of silver—in Palestine [3] and Abyssinia,[4] in Babylon [5] and Assyria. But everywhere money is only in general use in the towns. In Hammurabi's Code, for example, while the hire of artisans[6] is fixed in silver, that of shepherd, herdsman, or harvester, of ox or ass for threshing, or of wagon, driver, and oxen for transport, is defined in barley.[7] There continue to be a goodly number of ordinances fixing prices and hiring charges, and especially wages.[8] Such things are not confined to the twentieth century A.D. In the eighteenth century B.C. Hammurabi's object was partly to maintain the level of wages, but to judge from the contemporary tablets lesser amounts were paid in fact. There are doctors everywhere among these peoples both in Africa and the ancient world—and in many places they are barber-doctors and barber-surgeons [9]—and Hammurabi fixes their fees, too, and their punishments for unsuccessful operations.[10]

The development of trade and crafts brings into existence

---

[1] In Peru we are asked to believe that no money was yet employed.

[2] But in an earlier period in Rome the unit had been a copper rod a foot long. Copper rods are in use among many peoples in West Africa. See for the various currencies of South Nigeria, Talbot, vol. iii, pp. 187 *et seq.*

[3] Exodus 22[7].   [4] Perham, p. 215.   [5] *C.H.*, 122–6.

[6] Tailors, brickmakers, stone-cutters, carpenters, builders, etc., *C.H.*, 274.

[7] *C.H.*, 257–8, 268–72. The position is much the same in Eshnunna (see clauses 3–9), in China, and India (see, e.g., *C.H.I.*, vol. i, p. 287).

[8] See Eshnunna, 1–9.

[9] E.g., in Nupe (Nadel, pp. 298–301) and Western Europe.

[10] *C.H.*, 215–25.

gilds of merchants,[1] and then gilds of craftsmen in various callings, and they become more and more common from the beginning to the end of the period of the Late Codes. Some of the early gilds, as in Bida, the capital of Nupe,[2] and in the early Buddhist literature of India,[3] partake to some extent of the nature of other feudal institutions, for the head of a gild is entitled to dues and respect from the members. In India from the fourth century B.C., in China at a similar date, and in many places elsewhere, they make regulations for the conduct of their members and hold courts for the trial of wrongs committed by them,[4] and even enrol defence levies from among them.[5] It is by the combined effect of the gild mentality, a growing specialization in industry, a deepening religious feeling and a static economy that the caste system is created in India. In England, where gilds appear at the beginning of our era, we hear a great deal of them, not merely in London but even in the smaller towns. They are treated to some extent with the suspicion that trade unions arouse in later days, and again and again we are told of craftsmen who are fined by the town for forming an association without charter or permission. Whether they pay the fine is not so clear.

The arts burst into maturity, especially the building of royal or sacred edifices among the Peruvians, Mexicans, and Maya, and in Egypt, Babylon, Assyria, Western Europe, and India. Even Nigeria has at times during the last thousand years produced works of art of the highest excellence,[6] and the peoples of West Africa have exerted a large influence on the music of the modern world.

These and other advances enable the land to maintain an

---

[1] Mexico, see Joyce, pp. 126 f.   [2] See Nadel, *passim*.

[3] *C.H.I.*, vol. i, pp. 206–7.

[4] Similarly in Mexico the gild of travelling merchants held its own courts for criminal and civil matters (Prescott, p. 71).

[5] Western Europe, and India (Maurya Empire, fourth century, B.C.) Arth., pp. 341, 346, Manu, viii, p. 41. For the gilds of China see Morse, *The Gilds of China*; and *Journal of the North China Branch*, Royal Asiatic Society, vols. xii and xxi.

[6] For example, the terra-cotta and bronze heads from Ife of the twelfth to fourteenth centuries A.D., reproduced in *Man*, 1949, vol. xlix, pp. 1 and 61.

increasing population; the size of tribes and nations and the density of population wax, and the rate of fertility rises. The English kingdom doubles its numbers during the period to some 3½ or 4 million inhabitants, and nations of similar proportions are to be found in several places. The Ibo tribe in Southern Nigeria and the Hausa of Northern Nigeria are of much the same size.[1] According to Dapper, the King of Benin in Central Nigeria could muster in 1668 an army of 20,000, which could easily be increased to 100,000 men, and his capital was five or six Dutch miles in circumference. The various empires that ruled in West Africa in recent centuries have often been very large. The subjects of the Inca numbered about 7 millions or even more. The population of the Abyssinian Empire—a matter of guesswork—is of similar dimensions, something between the limits of 5½ and 12 millions.[2] The population of the Chinese Empire is said to have reached 50 millions in 156 A.D. At the other extreme, in South Africa, the thirsty earth can only sustain a tenuous population, and in Bechuanaland the largest nation—that of the Bamangwato, including its subsidiary peoples—hardly exceeds 100,000, and the smallest is but little more than 1,000.[3]

The density of population continues to increase accordingly. Over the whole extent of West Africa and of the highlands of Abyssinia the density exceeds that of any other large area of Africa south of the latitude of Egypt.[4] The density of the Central Andes exceeded that of any part of the rest of South America.[5] In England of the period, and in Northern Nigeria, the density is about forty persons per square mile. In Southern Nigeria it is much higher,[6] and it was much higher

[1] Ibo, in 1921, approximately 4 millions (since, much increased). Hausa (in Nigeria alone) 3,629,562 in the 1931 Census.

[2] See recent references in Perham, pp. 264–6.

[3] 1936 Census, see Schapera, *Tswana*, pp. 1–5.

[4] See Fitzgerald, *Africa* (7th edition), p. 108. I exclude the incredibly fertile shore of Lake Victoria Nyanza.

[5] See Steward, *H.S.A.*, vol. v, pp. 663, 676.

[6] For the density of Nupe, see Nadel, p. 11. The density of Southern Nigeria in 1921 was 91 per square mile, and of Iboland 297. Over all Nigeria in 1921, 54 per square mile. Gold Coast Colony (1931 Census), 66 per square mile, and (including Ashanti and the Northern Territories) 36. On the plateau of Abyssinia the density is over 20, as it was in the Central Andes.

in parts of ancient Egypt, Mesopotamia, China, and India. Again, at the other extreme, the density of the Bechuanaland reserves is less than 2·2 persons per square mile.

The towns have much increased in number and size. Northern Nigeria, with 10 million inhabitants in 1921, contains five towns with populations between 20,000 and 50,000 each, forty-four towns with populations over 5,000 each, and 1,087 with populations over 1,000. Southern Nigeria with a population of 8,371,459 has one town (Ibadan) with a population (including its farming suburbs) of 238,094,[1] and twenty-three towns of over 20,000 souls each. The presence of pastoralism, as we have often seen, breaks up the population into small units, and whereas in Northern Nigeria the population of the towns is only 0·2 per cent. of the total, and the population of the urban areas 5·2 per cent.,[2] in Southern Nigeria, where there are no cattle and no breeding of horses, 69 per cent of the population lives in the towns,[3] although 75 per cent. of the population earn their livelihood by farming. For the same reasons—namely, the absence of cattle and horses —the proportion of Mohammedans in Southern Nigeria is only 4·6 per cent. (as against 86 per cent. pagans), whereas in Northern Nigeria the figures are 67 per cent. and 32·8 per cent. respectively. The population of Cuzco, the capital of the Incas, was estimated by the Spanish at 200,000, including its suburbs. In England the average village now probably contains about 300 persons, and the Peruvian villages were of a similar size.[4] In modern India and China, too, the average village numbers 300 inhabitants.

The populations held together in these growing States continue to be less homogeneous in character. Many of them— perhaps we may say the bulk of the independent States of this stage of advance—are appropriately termed " empires "—that

---

[1] Talbot, vol. iv, p. 13. [2] Meek, N. Nig., pp. 173-4.

[3] On the other hand, in the Bechuanaland Reserves the villages or towns are few and large, but during the agricultural season from November to June the bulk of the population scatters in small family settlements among its fields, and, moreover, the cattle, instead of being kept at hand, as in most Bantu peoples, is maintained in the veld at grazing-posts, often twenty to forty and more miles away, Schapera, Tswana, p. 11.

[4] Rowe, p. 228.

is to say, States which include within their boundaries separate racial groups. There have been many such in Nigeria in recent centuries containing Sudanese and Negro populations.[1] Abyssinia—a name that by one derivation means " mixed population "—combines Semite, Hamite, and Negro nations. Hammurabi legislated for an empire including Semite and Sumerian populations, and so did Bilalama and Lipit Ishtar. Even Palestine held, within its boundaries, not only the twelve Hebrew tribes, but also Hittite, Philistine, and other racial groups; and before the end of this period Rome ruled over Greek and other subject States. The ruler of Abyssinia is the Negus Negusti, the King of kings. Such, too, was the ruler in Assyria and Babylonia.

This development has been brought about by continued change in the character and purposes of warfare. Its scale is larger, it is better organized, and conducted with greater art; its weapons are specialized and efficient, its objects are envisaged from the commencement, and they are commonly the gain of territory for economic ends. It was mainly to increase his receipts of tribute, to extend his private possessions, and to gain land on which to settle his followers and soldiers that Menelik II, Emperor of Abyssinia, conducted the conquest of the Galla south during the two decades beginning 1875. But wars are also undertaken for the sake of religion. The followers of Mahomet wage it to spread the true faith of Allah; the Inca to extend the worship of the god of his house, the Sun; the Aztecs to maintain the supply of human captives for sacrifice ; and the West European to free the holy land from the infidel. Of religion we need say nothing here except to note the progress of certain customs and institutions of which we saw the rise at the close of the Central Codes. We can watch the steady increase of human sacrifice in Mexico [2] and Peru and among the Maya,[3] and the growth in Peru, Mexico, Guatemala, Sumer, Egypt, China, India, and elsewhere of the slaying of wives and slaves to accompany their royal or noble master in

---

[1] For the kingdom of Nupe see Nadel, pp. 69 f.; and for Nigeria generally, A. C. Burns, *History of Nigeria* (1929); A. W. Bovill, *Caravans of the Old Sahara* (1933); C. K. Meek, *N. Nig.*, vol. i, pp. 98 f.
[2] Prescott, pp. 38 f.   [3] Joyce, pp. 261 f.

the hereafter.[1] The embalming and preservation of the bodies of the dead is widespread in Egypt, America, and West Africa.

Feudalism is at its height, but is beginning to wane. The emperor, king, or chief, whose power has continued to strengthen, controls all the land of the State, and in theory it is held at his will and pleasure.[2] According to the strength of the central authority, the personality of the king, or the difficulty of communications, the ruler below him may be a semi-independent prince or (as in Peru) a mere administrator who rules at the will of his absolute master, or something between the two extremes. In either case he is a great land-holder while he holds his office.[3] The tenures of land vary vastly in the same nation, and this is characteristic of the present stage. The duties of the holding are imposed on the land, whoever holds it. There is land held on terms of military service:[4] sometimes it is inalienable,[5] and sometimes it is tenable by women on condition that they find an able-bodied male to perform the service.[6] There is often land held by other public officials on terms of service to the throne or stool —for example, the Babylonian and Abyssinian tribute-gatherer.[7] Sometimes the king grants to the knight[8] or official land held by a number of free peasant cultivators, so that he may be supported and enabled to perform his public duties by means of the fixed proportion of produce and the labour services which the latter are bound to give him, as well as by the domain in his own possession.[9] Individual churches, monasteries, and temples hold land by gift of the king free of duties or in *frankalmoign*, and thereby also become lords of the

---

[1] In China till the seventeenth century A.D. Sutteeism is now at an end in China and India, but in many country districts of China it is still scandalous (though legal) for a widow to remarry.

[2] For example, in England, China and India throughout our period.

[3] For Peru, see Prescott, pp. 22–3; for Mexico, Prescott, pp. 12 f.

[4] *C.H.*, 26–39, and England, Nupe, Abyssinia, Egypt (till the New Kingdom at least).

[5] *C.H.*, 36–8.

[6] E.g., Abyssinia (Perham, p. 161), England, and Nupe (Nadel, pp. 117, 181).

[7] In Abyssinia the *gultenya*; for Babylon, see *C.H.*, 36–9.

[8] Abyssinian *farasenya*.   [9] England, Abyssinia, etc.

free peasant cultivator. The latter (now a member of an increasingly depressed class in England and elsewhere) bears the brunt of the maintenance of the State and its public services and its growing body of officials, and commonly pays to the Government a fixed proportion of his produce (in Palestine and Abyssinia a tithe in grain), as well as labour dues, and now taxes.[1] Except on those lands that are the king's domain, they pay them, as a rule, to intermediate chiefs or officers of one kind or another. But in the same nation entirely different types of tenures are found in different localities. There is also every variety of systems of cultivation. In some places the village or kinship group shifts to new land every few years; in another there is the fixed village with fixed common fields allocated in strips. In many of these communities it is necessary for the appropriate authority, either because the village moves to another locality or because one family increases and another does not, to allocate land afresh from time to time: so that the right of a freeman may be not so much a right to hold a particular field or group of fields, but rather a right to be allocated land according to his needs, or a combination of both rights.[2] So, for example, at this stage we find in parts of India,[3] and on the Eritrean plateau [4] and elsewhere different forms of what may be called joint village communities. And so, too, for example, we find in Peru, Mexico, ancient Palestine, modern Eritrea, and Bechuanaland [5] systems under which any member of the tribe or clan or other local kinship group [6] is entitled to be allotted land by the local village headman, district chief, or king when he marries and sets up a household.

[1] In Peru the tribute is mainly in the form of labour, Prescott, p. 36, Rowe, pp. 265 f. In China the land tax is the main source of revenue till our day.

[2] As in Bechuanaland (Schapera, *Tswana*, p. 197) and among the Hebrews.

[3] See B. H. Baden-Powell, *The Indian Village Community* (1896), and *The Origin and Growth of Village Communities in India* (1899).

[4] See S. F. Nadel, "Land Tenure on the Eritrean Plateau," in *Africa*, vol. xvi, pp. 21–2, 99–109.

[5] Schapera, *Tswana*, p. 197.

[6] In Mexico, the *calpulli* (Joyce, pp. 116–17). In the Central Andean civilization the local chief or *curaca* redistributes the land annually or as necessary between the members of the *ayllu*, a local group of a more or less endogamous nature (Rowe, pp. 253 f.; Pozo, p. 483).

Lastly, among the most forward of our peoples—for example, in Babylon—we may find the fixed village with separate, permanent, heritable fields, and a man may let or lend the use of his land for reward. In Babylon this is usually on the *metayer* system—namely, that he provides the use of oxen, plough, seed, or other required equipment, and receives a fixed quantity or proportion of produce.[1] In England, at the end of the period, the land is usually let at a rent.

But feudalism is not concerned merely with rights to land, but also with personal relationships—the European vassalage or homage. We saw a system of *okutoizha* (clientship, homage, or dependency) between king and patrician subject already in force in the advanced Central Code kingdom of Ankole. We see the same system of "clientship" in force in Nupe, Peru,[2] Mexico, and other lands in the earlier stages of the Late Codes. A commoner of Nupe desiring land or more land could give himself into the service or "patronage" of a land-owning overlord, and thus secure land as well as political protection by an initial gift in kind, occasional presents, expressions of homage, and a tithe from his crop.[3] In Rome something of the same relationship of *patronus* and client existed in our period,[4] and survived long after.

There is infinite variation of this general picture. We cannot expect to see feudalism so clearly developed where, as in Bechuanaland, there is no limit of available land, but only of rain, and a field may perhaps be cropped only once every few years. We cannot expect to see a feudal system in full operation among a people that has lost its independence to a European Power. Land tenure, military defence, government, the collection of revenue, and administration of justice are all facets of the same economic system. If the chief is subjected to a foreign governor and a foreign system of law, his authority is necessarily diminished and the whole system weakens or breaks. Yet both in the great empires and among the smaller tribes of the present stage we can see it at work in varying

---

[1] *C.H.,* 42–52, 60–4.   [2] Prescott, p. 12.

[3] Nadel, pp. 195 f., 122 f., and *passim*.

[4] The so-called Twelve Tables include a passage: "Cursed be the lord who defrauds his dependant."

degree, and it is everywhere in some degree among the independent nations of the past of whom we have adequate knowledge. It is these circumstances that in West Africa gave origin and scope to Lord Lugard's system of administration by indirect rule, for, indeed, feudalism is itself a system of indirect rule, and the same scheme has been more recently applied also to the Babemba and some other of the more forward peoples of the Central Codes.

Feudalism, as we have seen, is part of an economic system under which payments are in kind, and not in money. But the advance in trade, in markets, and in wealth is sounding its death-knell.[1] There is an increasing quantity and use of money, and it is already in general use in the towns. In England from the middle of the twelfth century[2] tenants holding on knight's service avail themselves on an increasing scale of the opportunity to pay scutage (or shield money) instead of military service, just as the villeins are paying tallage. This development affords the king the means of providing himself with a mercenary, professional and mobile army. At this stage there are already in early Egypt,[3] Nupe,[4] England, Abyssinia,[5] and elsewhere small but growing professional forces of the nature of bodyguards. In the end the king will find it less convenient, and indeed unnecessary, to rely on his vassals to call out their untrained tenants to war, and in the English wars of the fourteenth century his strength will consist of mercenaries. Meanwhile in modern Abyssinia apart from his bodyguard the king's forces are still for the most part men holding on knights' service and the general able-bodied male population. The knight proceeds to his rendezvous, followed commonly by one or two baggage-animals loaded with food, two or three tenants who owe him labour services, and slaves carrying equipment. So far as possible, they live on the native

---

[1] Eshnunna and its Code contained more of feudalism than Hammurabi's Babylon 200 years later.

[2] Beginning with the campaign of Henry II against Toulouse.

[3] Under the New Kingdom—that is to say, from about 1600 B.C.—mercenaries become predominant in the army. Indeed, till this date there is hardly anything that can be called an army.

[4] See Nadel, pp. 108 f.

[5] See, e.g., Perham, chap. ix.

peasants so as to conserve their supplies, but woe upon the scattered and defeated forces if they attempt to repeat this on their way home from the battle through the peasants' fields. The general male population can only be called to war, and not to training, and for the most part they are useless for the purpose. Little by little, rents and taxes will take the place of tribute, small professional armies will supersede enormous feudal levies that leave their holdings and devastate the native fields, the growing power of the central authority will exercise one uniform jurisdiction over the country, and feudalism will end.

CHAPTER VII

THE LATE CODES (*continued*)

MARRIAGE, INHERITANCE, AND PROPERTY

IN place of the varieties of social classes which we have hitherto observed, the more advanced peoples of the Late Codes are generally divided into three great ranks—namely, the lords, the commoners, and the unfree. For example, in Domesday Book, below the lords, there were sokemen and freemen, then came the villeins, then bordars and cottars, and lastly slaves. These various classes were slowly depressed, and in the thirteenth century the villeins are unfree [1] and the slaves (*servi*) and the bordars and cottars are no longer heard of. There are now, below the lords, the freemen (*liberi homines*) and the villeins (*villani*), people who hold by the custom of the manor as understood in their lord's court. In England, then, of the thirteenth century, the freemen now consist of the two great classes of the lords and the commoners, and indeed Parliament, which took its shape in that century, perpetuates the division. In Rome we know these classes as the patricians and the plebeians, in Babylon and Eshnunna as the *amelu* and the *mushkenu*, and in other places by other names.[2] In some lands the division is largely identical with that into members of the ruling race and members of the subject race or races. In Rome and Babylon, for example, the patrician and *amelu* was as a rule, in all probability, a member of an old Roman or Semite family; the plebeian or *mushkenu* of an immigrant conquered, or Sumerian stock. The former may have been a person of means and a land-

---

[1] Compare Eshnunna, 30.

[2] In Bechuanaland, among the Kgatla, as the *bakgosing* and *badintlha* (Schapera, *Tswana*, p. 31). In Palestine the "princes" and the rest. In Peru the nobility consists of the Incas and *curacas*, and the rest are commoners. In some places foreign groups, absorbed into the expanding nation, are treated separately by the law—for example the *peregrini* in Rome after the conquest of Italy, and the *bafaladi* among the Bamangwato and Tawana.

owner and cattle-keeper, and the latter a person of little means, a tenant's dependant or client, a cultivator, tradesman, craftsman, or artisan. But with the development of trade, plebeians and commoners gained entry into the ranks of the patricians and gentry, became land-owners and held on knights' service or other military tenure.

Above them was royalty; below them everywhere were the slaves in large numbers, limited to foreigners, and gained by capture or purchase; or serfs, bound to the soil and often representing a conquered population.[1] In the modern world slaves only survive on a large scale in Abyssinia.

Intermediate in status between free and slave were the home-born debt-slaves, or pawns. We have already seen them in the age of the Central Codes. They consisted of children or unmarried sisters, and less commonly of wives,[2] who were given by the male head of the family as security for the repayment of loans, or were sold in a time of famine or calamity to raise food, or were taken or awarded by judgment of a Court for the father's civil wrong or debt. Less commonly a man sold himself because of inability to find food.[3] The right of a father to sell his child for debt is clear in India and China throughout our period. But in all the more advanced of these peoples the hiring of free workmen begins to be common. As we have seen, the status of the free peasant is falling, for he is an easy victim of oppression where the amount of his tribute, taxes, and labour duties is uncertain and every day increasing. Equally pitiable is the lot of the unsuccessful town-dweller. Men, women, and children might go into this semi-slavery and never come out. Accordingly almost everywhere in the Late Codes is legislation limiting the period of debt-slavery— in West Africa,[4] in Palestine [5] (six years), and in Babylon [6]

---

[1] In Mexico, therefore, much as in England, there is the landed nobility holding on military or other feudal tenures; below them the plebeians (*macehual*), freemen holding as members of a *calpulli* or tenants at a rent; and below them the serfs bound to the soil (Joyce, p. 117; Prescott, p. 14).

[2] See Exodus 21[3], *C.H.*, 117.   [3] For Mexico, see Joyce, p. 133.

[4] See, e.g., Talbot, vol. iii, pp. 633, 635. For the Mexican restrictions, see Prescott, pp. 18 f.; Joyce, p. 133.

[5] Exodus 21[2] f, Deut. 25[12] f. See also the many provisions for the proper treatment of the debt-slave, Exod. 21[20-21, 26-27].   [6] *C.H.*, 115-17.

(three years); and in Rome there was probably a similar law, for there survives a rule of the Twelve Tables which provides that if a father sells (i.e., pawns) his son three times he shall be free of the paternal power. In Abyssinia creditors can still be seen walking along the streets, with their debtors shackled to them. The situation arises from the economic inability of the community to provide sufficient prisons. These laws, limiting the period of debt-slavery to a specified number of years, whatever the amount of the debt, might be difficult to understand, except that we can watch the institution at work in West Africa and can see that both in pawning and execution for debt the debtor is taken as security; he is not considered to work off the debt, but his labour represents only the interest upon it; and the law imposes a cancellation of the debt after a fixed period.[1]

The power of the head of the family is now at its height, and where the marriage is regular extends over all the members of the household. Let us first consider the marriage.

The institution of the bride-price is still seen among all these peoples, but is waning. It is normal everywhere in Africa,[2] and among the Hebrews,[3] Romans,[4] Peruvians, Mexicans, Maya, Egyptians, Assyrians, Sumerians, and Babylonians, and in China, India, and Western Europe. But at the end of the period the amount bears a decreasing ratio to the wealth of the people, and in some places is not paid. For example, it was not always paid in Babylon;[5] and in some areas of Abyssinia and in some Indian writings it is even regarded as shameful to accept it,[6] and in England it begins to disappear at the end of the twelfth century. There is a further new development. Among many peoples of earlier stages of advance we have seen some small marriage gifts from the wife's father. From the beginning of the Late Codes these gifts

---

[1] See, e.g., Nadel, p. 312, and *passim*; Rattray, *Ashanti Law and Constitution*, p. 54; Talbot, vol. iii, p. 633.

[2] See, e.g., Meek, *N. Nig.*, vol. i, pp. 201–3; Meek, *Ibo*, chap. XI; Talbot, vol. iii, pp. 425 *et seq.*; Rattray, *Ashanti Law and Constitution*, pp. 22 *et seq*; Schapera, *Tswana*, pp. 14, 138–47.

[3] Exodus 22[16–17]

[4] The *coemptio* obviously originates with the weighing of the copper bride-price.   [5] *C.H.*, 139.

[6] C. H. Walker, pp. 25, 26; and contrast Manu iii ("this would be a sale") with viii 204, and ix 98 with ix 97 and viii 366.

become more common and bear a greater proportion to the size of the bride-price. Often the gift is merely the bride-price itself, released by the girls' father as a present to the young couple.[1] Such a gift is not mentioned in the Hebrew Code, but among the Romans,[2] Assyrians, and Babylonians, and in China and India, this marriage-portion is general and important. In Babylon it was given by the wife's father and was usually larger in amount than the bride-price.[3] It was inherited by the children on their mother's death. In Abyssinia we can see the same changes in operation in Mr. Walker's valuable and entertaining little book.[4] If the bride's father is a man of great means he may perhaps not only release the bride-price to the young couple, but add thereto an amount equal to half or even the whole, and the total will be common " partnership " property of husband and wife, as it is in modern France.

But in the Late Codes the main problem set to the developing law is somewhat different—namely, how to treat the looser marriages. Monogamy is spreading, and is universal by the time we reach the Romans,[5] Assyrians, Sumerians, Babylonians, and Abyssinians. But it is characteristic of these heterogeneous populations of the Late Codes that there are also looser marriages. Looking generally at the nations of West Africa [6] and Bechuanaland [7] and indeed the Romans, Sumerians, Egyptians, Assyrians, and Babylonians, we see in each nation at least two forms of marital association. There is, first, the strict, regular

---

[1] See, e.g., Meek, *N. Nig.*, vol. i, pp. 96–7; Nupe, Nadel, p. 351. This is common in many country districts of twentieth-century China. For S. Nigeria, see Talbot, vol. iii, p. 459, Table 15. For Bechuanaland, see Schapera, *Tswana*, p. 203. In Bechuanaland the results are strange. Among the Bamangwato, Khama forbade the payment of bride-price. Among the Kgatla, however, a man is not considered properly married unless *bogadi* (bride-price) is paid; and accordingly, unless it has been paid, no church will marry him.—Schapera, *Tswana*, pp. 146–7.

[2] At any rate in later times.　　　　　　[3] C.H., 164.

[4] *The Abyssinian at Home*, pp. 25–6.

[5] Not before—not in West or South Africa or America and not among the Hebrews. But few men among all these peoples, except the chiefs, have more than two wives, and the vast bulk have only one. In Mexico the Chichimec were monogamous, and see Prescott, *Mexico*, p. 72.

[6] See, e.g., Talbot, vol. iii, p. 427; Rattray, *Ashanti Law and Constitution*, chap. IV.

[7] Schapera, *Tswana*, pp. 138–42.

marriage in which the wife cohabits permanently with the husband in his house, a bride-price has been paid, the children are considered to belong to the husband, and they and the wife are under his hand or power. In early law religious ceremonies of marriage are most unusual, but where they are found (as sometimes in the more advanced peoples of England,[1] Rome [2] and Abyssinia[3]) they also mark the regular marriage : elsewhere there is usually nothing more than a social ceremony, such as the leading or escorting of the wife to her husband's house.[4] The second type of marriage is a looser union; no bride-price is paid, but only gifts and maintenance; the woman continues to reside in her father's house, or does so for a period; and the children are considered to belong to her or her brother or family. The latest Codes have a good deal to say of the wife " living in the house of her father," [5] and the rights of the various interested parties in respect of children, property, and inheritance. The Roman law arrives at the result that the wife is under the hand of her husband, and the children are in his power, if there has been payment of bride-price, or a religious ceremony or permanent cohabitation.[6] Otherwise they are not, but it is still a marriage. Concubinage, of which there are various forms in Africa,[7] is important in Palestine and Mesopotamia, China, and India. Its object in Babylon and elsewhere was to enable a man whose wife was childless to take another freewoman for the purpose of begetting children, without thereby impairing the status of the true wife and without binding himself towards the second woman by all the duties of a husband if she should also be childless. Her status

---

[1] A large part of the population in the thirteenth century did not marry in church.

[2] *Confarreatio.*

[3] But, apart from deacons, Abyssinians rarely marry in church : partly because there is no divorce in such a case, and no second marriage even after the death of a spouse.

[4] The Roman *deductio in domum.*

[5] See especially Assyrian Women's Code, 25-38.

[6] The fragments of the Twelve Tables included a provision to the effect that if a woman stayed away from her husband's house for three nights or more in a year, that was not permanent cohabitation for this purpose. There was probably the same rule in Eshnunna, see clause 27.

[7] E.g., Schapera, *Tswana*, pp. 155-6; and commonly in West Africa.

is carefully provided for in the Code of Hammurabi.[1] In all these matters the law endeavours to arrive at a consistent system. The Babylonians were truly a remarkable people, with their practice of embodying in writing every important transaction, but Hammurabi takes our breath away when he provides that unless there has been a written marriage-deed "that woman is no wife." [2] Yet the rule is the same in modern China.

Among, then, the more advanced peoples of the Late Codes, in every case of a regular marriage—that is to say, a marriage evidenced by payment of bride-price, permanent cohabitation in the husband's house, or religious ceremony, as the case might be—the husband and father is lord and master of the household and of every person and thing in it. The wife is under his power,[3] and in Mesopotamia, if she goes abroad, goes veiled.[4] Subject to the contents of a marriage deed in civilized Babylon, everything she brings into the house is his property,[5] and this was the rule in England from about 1250 to 1870.[6] The sons, too, so long as they live unmarried in their father's house, are not generally considered to hold property of their own, legally free from his control,[7] any more than the other members of the *familia*, *chia*,[8] or household—namely, the slaves. "Three persons," says Manu, "a wife, a son and a slave are declared by law to have in general no wealth exclusively their own : the wealth which they may earn is regularly acquired for the man to whom they belong." [9]

The father has a general power of life and death over the members of the household, subject (among some peoples) to

[1] *C.H.*, 144-7. Among the Hebrews the woman was often a female debt-slave (see Exod. 21[2] f.) or a slave.

[2] *C.H.*, 128. Compare Eshnunna, 27.   [3] Latin " *manus*."

[4] See especially the Assyrian Women's Code. Even in classical Latin " to marry a man " is " *nubere viro* "—" to put on a veil for a man." The Chinese wife is generally married in a veil.

[5] See A.C. 35, 3, 4, and 6.

[6] The rule is not generally reached till after the stage of the Twelve Tables. In Africa it is rarely true that the wife has no proprietary capacity or that what she acquires belongs to the husband. See, e.g., Schapera, *Tswana*, pp. 151-4, 220; Meek, *N. Nig.*, vol. i, p. 281. Indeed she is the chief trader, Nupe, Nadel, p. 332.

[7] Rome, China, and Babylon (see *C.H.*, 7) and in many places in Africa (see, e.g., Schapera, *Tswana*, pp. 220-1).

[8] Chinese household.   [9] Manu viii, 416 ; Narada v, 39.

the views of a family council.[1] He cannot (except for a criminal offence) be proceeded against for ill-treatment of them. Indeed, it is he who takes all proceedings for wrongs to its members : they are wrongs to him whether in his own person or as representing them. This is well brought out by a verbatim account given by Professor Schapera[2] of a trial before the paramount chief of the Bamangwato, in which the father of a boy who had seduced a girl belonging to the defendant's group says, "I had spoiled (i.e. seduced) their child, and we agreed to marry her," and so forth. It is the complement of this aspect that among the most advanced peoples of the Late Codes the father is liable for the wrongs of the members of the household. But we must make a distinction here between the liability for the wife and the liability for the sons. By the end of our period—namely, in the Code of Hammurabi[3] and in England of the thirteenth century[4] and not before—the husband is liable for all the wrongs and debts of his wife. But in many places sons leave home almost as soon as they are old enough to incur liabilities in trade or for wrongs, and in regard to sons there is not, in the less advanced peoples of this stage, any general rule of liability of a father for his son's debts or wrongs. The rule varies from place to place, though he usually pays.[5] But at the end of the stage of the Late Codes, when corporal sanctions are general for serious wrongs, the rule in Babylonia and in thirteenth-century England is that the father must hand over to the injured plaintiff any subordinate member of his household (or mainpast) who has committed a serious offence (or felony), or, if he does not comply, the father must pay a fine.[6]

[1] See, e.g., Schapera, *Tswana*, p. 183.
[2] *Tswana*, pp. 298 f.   [3] *C.H.*, 151, 152.
[4] P. & M., vol. ii, p. 132. The rule is not reached among the Hebrews, or in the Twelve Tables, but probably represented the law soon after the latter Code.
[5] See Schapera, *Tswana*, p. 50 (father responsible, except in regard to an offence punishable corporally); *Gold Coast Native Courts Commission*, pp. 31 f. In modern India a man is not liable for debts contracted by wife or son unless the money was spent for the benefit of the family.
[6] P. & M., vol. ii, p. 530. For Rome see *Gaius*, vol. iv, pp. 75 f. This liability originated in the Twelve Tables for theft (i.e., about 200 B.C.), the

As for the liability of the wife and children for the husband's and father's wrongs and debts, we have seen this rule making its appearance at the end of the period of the Central Codes, and it is general in the Late Codes.[1] Even after the father's death, the children are liable for his debts, and can be taken in execution in respect of them.[2] It is not till after the end of our period (that is to say, in modern England and India and the mature Roman law) that the liability of sons to discharge their father's debts is limited to the assets that they inherit from him.

It is significant of the power and status of the *paterfamilias* that at the end of the period of the Late Codes wrongs committed by his children against him are punishable with the greatest severity. It is a capital offence in the Hebrew Code or in modern Chinese law for a son to strike or curse his father.[3] In the Code of Hammurabi the man striking his father loses his hands.[4] In China a man is well entitled to kill his wife who strikes or abuses his parent. And a woman caught committing adultery may be mutilated by her husband or put to death as he pleases.[5] This is the law among all the more advanced of the peoples of the Late Codes.

We saw among the peoples of the Central Codes a certain return of matrilocal marriage and matrilineal descent and inheritance where no cattle are kept, and this is widespread also in West Africa in the same circumstances—for example, in Ashanti.[6] But all the nations of Europe and Asia of which

---

Lex Aquilia (about 169 B.C.) for damage to property, and the praetor's edict (of similar date or a little later) for robbery and personal injuries.

[1] See, e.g., Eshnunna, 24.

[2] See, for the Hebrews, 2 Kings 4 (children); for Babylonia C.H., 117 (wife); and the rule survived into the mature Roman Law.

[3] Exod. 21[15, 17]. It is also a religious offence, see Lev. 20[9].

[4] C.H., 195.

[5] A.C. 3, 4, 15, 16. See C.H., 129; and thirteenth-century England. Eshnunna 28 goes farther: " She shall not get away alive." For China, see Alabaster, pp. 251 *et seq.*

[6] Similarly cannibalism survived on a large scale till very recently among the peoples of Southern Nigeria except the Edo and Yoruba (Talbot, vol. iii, p. 831, map). No cattle can be reared in this region. It was conspicuous also among the Aztecs, where prisoners of war were eaten by their captors after sacrifice. The Peruvians reared the llama as well as

we have spoken were cattle-keepers as well as tillers of the soil, and descent is generally patrilineal among them. In Northern Nigeria the Mohammedan pastoralists, invading from the North, have all brought the patrilineal system with them. At the same time we saw among the peoples of the Central Codes that the clan was beginning to wane, especially in the towns, and this process continues (as it has continued until today). In twelfth-century England and in Bechuanaland and else-where the larger social unit in the towns is not the clan, but the ward, though the ward may sometimes be in large part a kinship group. As the clan wanes, the household stands out the more. This process has not, however, proceeded very far during our period. Accordingly, in default of children, in-heritance is to members of the patrilineal clan, and not to the nearest cognatic relation.[1]

In West and South Africa generally the eldest son still retains a certain prior right of inheritance, and among the Hebrews he receives a double portion.[2] But as feudalism wanes the priority of the eldest son wanes with it. At the end of our period, among the Assyrians, Sumerians, Babylonians, Abys-sinians, Chinese and Indians, and elsewhere, apart from land held on military tenure, sons inherit equally land and goods, and unmarried daughters have a right of support and a limited right of succession in default of sons. In the absence of other heirs, it is not uncommon to find among the earlier peoples of the Late Codes that a slave inherits.[3] But there is an infinite variety in detail in the rules of succession in force among various peoples and in different districts of the same

innumerable guinea-pigs, and there is no evidence here of cannibalism. In Peru descent is patrilineal (Rowe, p. 254).

[1] For an example of a system of matrilineal succession, see Rattray, *Ashanti*, p. 41. The succession is to (1) mother's brother; (2) in default, to brothers in order of age; (3) mother's sister's son; (4) sister's son; (5) sister's brother's son; (6) mother's sister's daughter's son, etc.

[2] Deut. 21[15-17]. In modern China, though all sons inherit, there is a certain limited priority of the eldest: but the rule varies from place to place (see, e.g., H. T. Fei, p. 66).

[3] See for Ashanti, Rattray, *Ashanti*, p. 43 (inheritance to a female slave, the descendant of the deceased or his ancestor and a female slave). For the Hebrews, see Gen. 15[2]. Among the Romans, too, slaves probably inherited in default of clansmen.

people. Among the more forward peoples of this stage it is very common for brothers, on the death of their father, to live together and manage the estate as a whole—for example among the Hebrews,[1] Romans, Assyrians,[2] Babylonians, Sumerians,[3] Chinese, and Hindus.[4] There is no longer that superfluity of land that we find in most places in Africa. Indeed, the superfluity is gone even in Southern Nigeria and Abyssinia.

We have no more space to discuss intestate succession. Succession by will begins to make great strides in this age. In South and West Africa [5] and among the Hebrews [6] the will is oral and informal. A man at the approach of death may call his family together and announce his wishes regarding his property, departing as a rule only in details from the customary mode of succession, or merely supplementing it. Indeed Deuteronomy 21[15-17], fulfilling the conservative role of religion, forbids the father to give the double portion of the eldest to another son. In the more advanced peoples of Rome, Assyria, Babylon, Abyssinia,[7] India, and England wills are common. In Babylon written wills are general, and we see signs in Rome and Babylon and Abyssinia that it begins to be considered the duty of a man to make a will of his property. But there are necessarily restrictions on the right of a man or woman to leave property by will, and especially land held upon certain tenures; and it is rare for a man to depart, save in detail, from the customary rules of intestate succession.[8]

[1] See, e.g., Deut. 25[5].   [2] See Vat. 10001, Text No. 2.

[3] C.H., 165, 166, 178 : Eshnunna, 38.

[4] Manu. IX, 104 f. Then later, when they decide on partition, they take their share, in Mesopotamia, China, and India.

[5] See, e.g., Rattray, Ashanti, p. 238; Schapera, Tswana, p. 230.

[6] See, e.g., Gen. 24[36]; 2 Sam. 17[23]; 2 Kings 20[1]; Deut. 21[15-17].

[7] See C. H. Walker, pp. 17, 52, 198.

[8] For example, in Bechuanaland, if a man's will departs to any considerable extent from the ordinary rules of inheritance, an aggrieved person will appeal to the chief to adjust the matter.—Schapera, Tswana, loc. cit.

CHAPTER VIII

THE LATE CODES (*continued*)

CONTRACTS

THE development of social organization accompanies and requires a growing precision in conduct and in mind. In Nigeria, for example, there is a far greater propensity to count and measure. The means used are various parts of the human body—for example, the fingers and hands are used for counting, and the span, the cubit, the thumb-width, the foot, and other bodily measurements for length.[1] Markets bring or accompany many important and unexpected results. They must, for example, be periodic and held at times well known over an area, and it is largely the market which gives rise, in many of the less advanced peoples of the Late Codes, to the conception of the "week." In Nigeria, North and South, it may be a four-day week, or a five- or seven- or eight-day week: it bears usually some relation to the easily recognized period of a month, and usually some reference to the market.[2] In most places in Southern Nigeria the days of the week are named by reference to the market—" the day before market," "market day," "the day after market," and so forth. Among the Ibo we find the reverse—the markets are named after the days of the week on which they are held, but the relation is no less close. More rarely the week depends not on the market, but on some other economic event, such as the beer-brewing system among the Jukun of Northern Nigeria. The week commonly has a day of rest and festivity; usually this is one of the other days of the week, but sometimes it is market day.[3] As religion gains in power, the stage is set

[1] See also Meek, *N. Nig.*, vol. ii, p. 153. The facts were much the same among the Hebrews and Romans and others, and many of these measurements remain with us.

[2] The Aztec markets were usually held on the last day of the five-day week (Prescott, *Mexico*, p. 53).

[3] See Meek, *N. Nig.*, vol. ii, p. 154; Talbot, vol. iii, pp. 869 f; and for modern Peru, Valcarcel, p. 479.

for the evolution of the Hebrew Rest-day and the spiritual conceptions that surround it. The most forward peoples of this age, especially the Mexicans, Maya, Babylonians, and Chinese, make great advances in astronomy.

In the days before currency and markets, and at their early beginnings, we noticed barter of cattle, grain and small articles; and enough of barter to create a familiar scale of values. So, for example, in a mainly pastoral people a heifer fetched such and such a quantity of grain, a bull bore a certain constant relation in value to a heifer, and a goat to a bull. Among mainly pastoral tribes the chief measure of value is cattle. In a later age, when one or more types of imperishable articles, which can be counted or easily measured, such as arrows, standard-size squares of native cloth, blocks of salt, or ingots or rods of copper [1] are in general demand in a community, these things upon exchange bear a familiar relation in value to one another and to more perishable articles. These relations do not fluctuate from day to day: except in famine or other calamity they are traditional and familiar. But the increase in populations, the improvement in communications, trade, and markets, and the expanding use of currency, create market-prices which fluctuate from time to time and even from day to day, so great is the temporary demand for one article or the supply of another; and this is manifest in England when we reach the thirteenth century. Among the more backward peoples of the Late Codes we may see the two prices side by side—in Bechuanaland, for example, with its tenuous population, pots, milk-pails, and similar utensils are still exchanged for their content in grain, two goats for a sheep or a bag of corn, ten goats or five bags of corn for a heifer. Even in face of the recent introduction of European currency, a heifer is generally sold among the Bamangwato and Kgatla for five

---

[1] Copper rods are the characteristic currency of the early Late Codes—they were the chief currency of Nigeria till the advent of the Europeans, and in West and West Central Africa generally; they were the chief currency of Rome before our period, and the Greek *obol* was a rod. The change from rods of a specific length to weighed metal is an advance in precision. Weighed gold dust passed as currency in some parts of West Africa and in Mexico. For Mexican currencies, see Joyce, p. 129; for the Maya, ibid., p. 287.

pounds, a sheep for one pound, a goat for ten shillings, corn at one pound per bag, goatskins and sheepskins at one shilling each, irrespective of the prevailing market-prices.[1]

In the end, there is no commodity that is more apt than metal to serve as a currency. It is imperishable and can be worked, and is needed for a vast variety of purposes. One metal tends to prevail in an area as the main form of currency. At the same time the result of increased trade and markets and increased use of currency is a debasement of currency in mass and quality, for there is a great temptation to get more goods for the same apparent quantity of metal. For example, in Rome during our period—namely, during the wars of 350 to 250 B.C.—the bronze " as " deteriorates from about 12 oz. to 2 oz. Accordingly, the metal currency passes by weight—raw copper or bronze in Rome and Egypt, silver in Palestine, Sumer, Babylonia, Assyria, and elsewhere. In England from the beginning of the thirteenth century the silver content of the penny begins to drop at an increasing rate.[2]

Even at the end of our period the metal currency, as we have seen, is in use in the towns (including the markets), but not in the countryside. Here is employed a relation of values in other commodities (in Babylonia, barley). We must always bear in mind, right up to the twentieth century A.D., the economic backwardness of the countryside in relation to the town—the lesser mobility of the population, the greater prominence and solidarity of local kinship groups, the more hereditary occupations, the lower standard of living, and the greater extent of barter. Even in thirteenth-century England, Lancashire and the North-West are still mainly pastoral.

But where money comes into use it turns barter into sale. This change is of vast importance in commerce and law, but it is equally important to observe that the only change is the substitution of the currency-commodity for some other commodity on one side of the transaction. Barter, as a commercial transaction, was almost invariably an instantaneous

[1] Schapera, *Tswana*, p. 242.

[2] From A.D. 1100 to 1300 the average silver content of a new penny fell only from 22½ to 22 grains, but in the next century it fell to about 15, and in the following century to about 11.

transaction.[1] Both commodities changed hands at the same time, and nothing remained to be done on either side. The same observations apply to sale. It is everywhere a ready-money transaction. Even at the end of this age, in the Old Babylonian period, a transaction was not considered a sale unless it was a cash transaction. Otherwise it was never recorded in a sale-tablet alone. Even our modern English tongue records the same state of things, for the word "sell" originally meant "deliver," and the word "sale" still primarily denotes an instantaneous and completed transaction.[2] Indeed, even in a modern market, a retail transaction which is not for cash is a rare event.

All important transactions are conducted before a number of witnesses. We have seen something of this before, but throughout our period it is universal in England, Africa, Rome, India,[3] and everywhere else. We have seen the reason for this—to meet a possible charge of theft by a third person (or the seller) claiming to be the owner. If we had any doubts that this was still the reason, the Codes of Eshnunna [4] and Hammurabi, the Assyrian Laws, and the tablets tell us so in the plainest terms. As in modern times, even writing (where writing is in use) is not thought to obviate the necessity for witnesses (especially as neither party can write), but the number of witnesses is larger than with us because fraud and conspiracy are more rife, and perhaps life more uncertain. In Babylonia there may be anything between one witness and twenty, and five or six is an average number. In West Africa today we have the further advantage of being able to observe that witnesses receive a customary gift or payment for their pains, normally a fixed proportion of the amount of the price.[5]

This, then, is the universal type of the most important

---

[1] Sometimes, especially at a boundary market, it is "silent barter": the parties put side by side the articles they propose to exchange, and the matter ends when the goods change hands, or the parties retire, in silence—see, e.g., Valcarcel, p. 478.

[2] The Roman "*vendo*" originally indicated a cash sale, and *emere* a "taking."

[3] Manu viii, 201, 202.   [4] Eshnunna, 41.

[5] See, e.g., Rattray, *Ashanti*, pp. 232, 234; *Ashanti Law and Constitution*, p. 368.

commercial transaction at this stage—namely, a ready-money sale (in the most advanced peoples, metal currency weighed out at the time) before a number of about five or six witnesses. The witnesses (and the writing, if any) are for the benefit of the buyer, not the seller (as of course they must be in a cash transaction). So in the Mesopotamian contract at this, the Old Babylonian period, the transaction is always expressed from the point of view of the buyer, " So-and-so has taken for so much silver such and such an object," not " So-and-so has given," and the seal is always the seal which will be of use to the buyer—namely, the seal of the seller. The early Romans call the transaction " *mancipium*," a " taking," not a " giving."

Everywhere, too, the important sales are of the same subject-matter—in Rome, Mesopotamia, Egypt, and elsewhere, land, cattle, and slaves, and among a people who engage largely in a water-borne trade, like the Babylonians and Egyptians, ships also.[1] But we must make one very important qualification. Sale of land is rare in the early part of the present stage, and the change arrives only with the Hebrews and Romans. We need not repeat the reasons that have already been given in this book. In part the change comes with the pressure on the land. In Bechuanaland it is plentiful and necessary, and no one will or need pay for it.[2] So, too, in parts of Northern Nigeria. In the area of Nupe west of the Kaduna, land-tenure on the traditional tribal or village basis still remains: there is no pressure on the land and no sale. In Cis-Kaduna there is a complex system of land ownership, great pressure on the land, and much transferring of land, amounting in extreme cases to outright sale. Generally in Nupe there is much borrowing or leasing at rents, but no sales.[3] Nor is there selling of land in most of Southern Nigeria, though there is some leasing, borrowing, and pledging.[4] In Bechuanaland, parts of West Africa, Palestine, Eritrea, India, and many other places at this

---

[1] The surviving Babylonian and Egyptian sale-tablets record mainly sales of land, cattle, slaves, and ships; and also sacred offices and the income therefrom, for the temples retained their records for a longer period.

[2] Schapera, *Tswana*, p. 203.

[3] Nadel, pp. 181 *et seq.*, 190 *et seq.*

[4] Talbot, vol. iii, pp. 682 *et seq.*

stage, a man's right is or includes a right to have land allotted to him from time to time as a member of a village or kinship group, and consequently he cannot sell the land allotted without the consent of the other members; and they have a preemptive right to purchase before a stranger. Consequently, if there is a sale it is usually to the next of kin, but the bulk of transactions in relation to land are pledges, and "once a mortgage always a mortgage." In Palestine a man who sells his land may still redeem it within a certain period,[1] and if he does not do so the right to redeem goes to the next of kin; but sales are frequent.[2] By the time we reach the Romans, Babylonians, Chinese and Hindus, though some land is inalienable, out-and-out sales of land are common; and in thirteenth-century England, too, there is now for the first time a ready market in land, which is sold, leased, and exchanged.[3]

These sales are all sales of specific items of property—such and such a field (naming it), a particular bull or cow, a particular slave, "Nasir Ninip, a weaver of embroidered cloth, slave of So-and-so," and so on. Thus it is that in Rome by the year 270 B.C. a rule is evolved by the conservative Roman mind that land in Italy, cattle, and slaves are only properly transferred in the presence of Roman citizens and a man holding a copper balance, and the buyer ("taker") declares, "I say this (slave, etc.) is mine by Roman law, and he be taken by me with this copper and this copper balance"—and he strikes the balance with the copper and gives it to the transferor. The Romans were then still generally illiterate, but this transaction in later days remained an oral transaction long after writing was in general use. The Sumerians, Babylonians, and Assyrians, and to a less extent the Hebrews and Egyptians, used writing to evidence all their important transactions, the Egyptians and Hebrews papyrus, and the Mesopotamians clay tablets. In twelfth- and thirteenth-century England, and among all these

[1] E.g., Lev. 25[29] and *passim*.
[2] See, e.g., Ruth, 4; Jeremiah, 32, an account of the conveyancing methods of the time.
[3] N. Neilson, in *The Cambridge Economic History of Europe*, vol. i (1941), pp. 440, 446. Eshnunna is an intermediate case; clause 39 suggests that a man only sells his house when in financial straits.

peoples who used writing, the Hebrews, Romans, Egyptians, Assyrians, Sumerians, and Babylonians, the general form of the document was the same. The parties could not write, and the document was written by a scribe, witnessed and sealed by a party.[1] This is still the form of the modern English deed. The Romans used no writing, and theirs (the *mancipium*) was an oral deed. Both finally became conveyances, the form of which gave them their validity. In England slavery takes the form of serfdom, and therefore there is no separate selling of slaves. Consequently, the important dealings are in land and cattle, and the deed is mainly used for sales of land.

There is no barter of specific [2] valuables, either in Rome or Babylon; these are normally disposed of in the towns and by way of sale, in the way we have seen. There is no sale of a large quantity of non-specific goods—that is to say, of a quantity of produce: such transactions usually take place in the country and by barter. When a large estate disposed of its produce—say its present produce of oil—to another estate which would deliver so much of its produce of corn after next harvest, this credit-barter was recorded in a loan-tablet. It was not a sale, but a credit-barter. In Rome, indeed, the transaction retained the name of *mutuum* (" exchange " or " barter ") in classical times.

So much for the cash sale, but exceptionally there are sales on credit, where the purchaser is to pay in the future. These were so exceptional that the Babylonians did not regard them as mere sales: they drew up two tablets, one a sale-tablet recording a cash sale, and the second a tablet recording that the seller has lent the buyer such-and-such a sum (the amount of the price), which the buyer will repay on such-and-such a date; or recording a deposit by the seller with the buyer of the amount of the price, or an account declaring the buyer to be in debit to the seller in that amount, and recording that he will repay on a certain date. Similarly, if the transaction were one

---

[1] It was not till the thirteenth century that the ordinary freeman in England had his own seal (P. & M., vol. ii, p. 224).

[2] A sale of " specific " goods is in English law opposed to a sale by description. In the former case there is a sale of a certain article or articles; in the other case an agreement to sell goods of a certain class.

under which the buyer paid in advance and the seller agreed to deliver in the future, a sale-tablet was drawn up recording a cash sale, and a second tablet recording the seller's debt in respect of goods. In Rome by 200 B.C. they arrived at the practice-book rule (which survives in the fragments of the Twelve Tables) that any of these extra terms, if stated at the time of the oral *mancipium*, would be binding.

There were no mere agreements to sell in which payment and delivery were both to take place in the future—what the English law calls an executory agreement of sale—the peoples of this stage do not do business in that way. But there is quite a little here and there of the giving of " earnest." X may want to consider whether he will buy a certain article from Y. Y lets him consider the matter till, say, the following day, on conditions that he pays him a small sum which he will forfeit if he decides not to buy. We see this practice in West Africa, but it is not sufficiently important to find its way into the Babylonian tablets or the Roman forms of transaction.

In Bechuanaland and West Africa loan of money at interest was not known. Among the Hebrews it was just creeping in —a loan of money remunerated by money—that is to say, interest. Hence, in the Old Testament, religion exercising its normal function of resisting innovation (in this case a salutary function) prohibited " usury," [1] and the rule survived in England with wide exceptions till 1865. But in all the more advanced peoples of the Late Codes, thirteenth-century England, Rome, Babylon, Assyria, Abyssinia, China, and India, the loan of money at interest is common. In England, kings, monasteries, and land-owners are widely borrowing at interest, and loans upon a rent-charge of 10 per cent. per annum are normal.[2] In Babylon the rate was as high or higher— 20 per cent. and more could be got. Loans by a money-lender on the security of the crop of a field (a form of security corresponding to the letting of land on the *metayer* system) were very common, and Hammurabi was concerned to check its abuses.[3] In Rome and elsewhere the money lent was weighed out, as before, at the time of the transaction.

---

[1] Lev. 25[36-37].   [2] Clapham, p. 181.   [3] *C.H.*, 49-52.

Then there are the bailments of goods, which will be returned in the future, loans of goods for use, deposit (especially of silver), and hire of ploughs, wagons, and oxen (with or without drivers). The process that we saw in the Central Codes continues. The ordeal by oath is brought into use to meet the case where the borrower or hirer says that the ox died, or was eaten, or the property destroyed without his fault.[1] These clauses are more numerous and more detailed in the Late Codes, the more advanced is the people.

Then there is the hiring of servants. It is hardly found till now, but is becoming common. In the Code of Hammurabi the agricultural servants are hired by the year, and they are paid in the rural subsidiary currency of barley. The town workers are paid by the day in silver. So they are among the Hebrews (" The wages of a hired servant shall not abide with thee all night until the morning ")[2] and elsewhere. In England in the thirteenth century the unskilled workman in the town (the "journeyman" or "day-worker") is paid generally a silver penny a day (like Jenny in the nursery rhyme); the agricultural worker is hired by the year and paid mainly in kind; but there are extra harvesters engaged in England, Eshnunna, Babylon and elsewhere who are remunerated for the work or the day.

The letting of land grows increasingly common. Pledges of land and persons are common, and so is suretyship, and partnership is spreading; but we have no space to speak of these things. We have, however, seen enough to realize that there has been a large-scale development in this branch of the law and that there is now a good deal, not of the law of contract, but of the law of contracts, or rather of types of commercial transactions. There is not yet nearly enough of this to give rise to a general theory of contract—that, for example, a contract is made by an offer and acceptance in the same terms —or to give rise to a law that an agreement must be carried out or a breach of contract compensated for. It is not that these peoples do not think that an agreement should be carried

---

[1] See, e.g., Eshnunna, 36, 37.

[2] Lev. 19[13]; Deut. 24[15]. But the agricultural worker was probably hired, as a rule, by the year (cf. Isa. 21[16]), or for three years (Isa. 16[14], Deut. 15[18]).

out.   At this stage commerce does not proceed on the basis
that agreements must be carried out: no one relies on a
mere agreement on both sides to do something in the future,
and consequently no one can be damaged by a failure to carry
it out.   Law does not pretend to compensate where there is
no loss; and men do not trust one another—or need to trust
one another—in trade to that extent.

CHAPTER IX

THE LATE CODES (*continued*)

The Priests, the Scribes, and the Schools

ALL these written records of transactions, wherever writing is used, in Palestine, Egypt, Assyria, Sumer, Babylon, Abyssinia, China, India and England, are drawn up by " scribes." The rise of the profession of scribe is an important development in our history, and we must find out who they were.

With the increasing wealth and advancing organization of society and the growing power of religion, the ecclesiastical orders have reached impressive numbers, wealth, and strength. We can only guess at the precise figures. In England in the thirteenth century the various religious orders number perhaps a quarter of the adult male population, and own at least a third of the land. In modern Abyssinia the best conjecture is about the same.[1] In modern Tibet the figures are at least as large, and in Mexico and Peru they were much the same.[2] In Egypt, Assyria, and Babylonia, and in Palestine in the fourth century B.C., the figures must have been very large. In the Old Testament writings we can watch the growth of the priesthood to numbers, power, and wealth. The hereditary priestly caste of the Levites began, in all probability, as attendants at local shrines (like so many in Nigeria), depending for their support on voluntary offerings, and they held no land. Levi's task was to minister before the Lord : " Levi hath no share nor allotment with his brethren : the Lord is his allotment." [3] Therefore is preached the duty of charity towards him : " The Levite that is within thy gates, thou shalt not forsake him; for

[1] See Perham, p. 109.
[2] In Peru the priesthood received the produce of one-third of the land. In Mexico we are told 5,000 priests were attached to the principal temple in the capital, and there were several hundred smaller temples in each of the principal cities (Prescott, pp. 32–4).
[3] Deut. 10[9], 12[12], 18[1].

266

he hath no share nor allotment with thee."[1] But the story changes, and in the end not only does the Levite receive his share of inherited property,[2] but he sells it and takes the proceeds,[3] and he also receives the tithe;[4] and forty-eight cities and their suburbs are to be taken from their owners and allotted to the Levites to dwell in.[5] No land in the cities of the Levites may be sold,[6] and if pledged it is perpetually redeemable.[7]

In Sumer, Babylon, and Assyria, in Egypt, England, and Abyssinia, the finest and most developed estates are those of the great temples and churches. Their power in the State is enormous. Pharaoh needs give them great offerings to secure their friendship and support. We need not recapitulate the various aspects of their strength. They are great landowners, and as such have large secular jurisdiction over their tenants, as well as absolute disciplinary control over the members of their own orders. The princes of the churches are among the most prominent of the great men of the realm, who sit in the king's privy council of advisers and in the great representative council of the landowners and governors of the State. The priests at their numerous shrines in West Africa apply the local ordeals to test a charge of witchcraft, adultery, or theft, and manipulate the local oracles. The priesthoods, as we saw, have come to exercise a jurisdiction among their worshippers in matters of witchcraft and heresy, in adultery, incest, and bestiality, and in disputes as to marriage, divorce, and succession. In the middle of the period of the Late Codes the growing organization of society creates in some places a dividing line between the jurisdiction of the ecclesiastical and the secular courts, and the former obtain for their exclusive province the matters that have been mentioned. In England this division is only partly enacted by William the Conqueror, and is the effect of the Constitutions of Clarendon in 1164. In Palestine it appears at the corresponding date—namely, in

[1] Deut. 14²⁷, 12¹⁹. The allotment is of land.
[2] Ezek. 44²⁸, 45⁵; Deut. 18⁸.
[3] Deut. 18⁸.   [4] Deut. 26¹²; Num. 18²¹.
[5] Num. 35¹⁻⁸; Josh. 21⁸. These cities include the cities of refuge (Num. 35⁶, ¹³).
[6] Lev. 25³⁴.   [7] Lev. 25²⁹. See also *Primitive Law*, chaps. XI, XII.

the exilic period—though it is attributed to an earlier king.[1] In Rome it must have occurred before our story begins.

This is the period of an intense struggle between the two orders for the control of the State. The ecclesiastical writings of the age are full of reproaches and abuse of the kings. There is much of it in the historical books of the Old Testament. In Rome we hear little to the credit of the kings. In the fourth chapter of Manu [2] it is declared that a king is equal in wickedness to a butcher who keeps 100,000 slaughterers. To accept presents from him is a terrible crime. In this conflict in England, Thomas Becket is murdered in 1170, and the boundary of the province of the English ecclesiastical courts remains fixed much where it was before, and so continues for many centuries. In Rome the laity gained control about the year 194 B.C., but the " Chief Priest " (the Pontifex Maximus) who was usually a lawyer, continued throughout the life of the Republic to exercise much the same jurisdiction as the ecclesiastical courts in England. In Egypt the issue was in the balance. About 3000 B.C. at Heliopolis the priesthood of Ra had gained control and founded the fifth dynasty. Two thousand years later the High Priest of Amen usurped the throne at Thebes and founded a short line of priest-kings. In Judah, as in later days in Tibet after the conversion to Buddhism, the priesthood conquered and the government became a theocracy. In Abyssinia, by a law of A.D. 1942, at one blow the whole of the ecclesiastical jurisdiction was removed except for the disciplinary authority of the Church over its own officers, and the infliction of purely spiritual penalties.[3] In Sumer, Babylon, and Assyria something of the kind had already occurred before our knowledge begins, and there is no sufficient

---

[1] 2 Chron. 19. See Ezra 7[25] f., and also Deut. 17[8]. The same situation is widespread in the world today. Among the Mohammedan Emirates of Northern Nigeria the secular law governs secular matters, and the Mohammedan ecclesiastical law governs much the same matters as in the English ecclesiastical courts (mainly marriage, divorce, and inheritance). In several British possessions these questions are either reserved to the decision of the religious courts of each community (as in Palestine under the former British Administration) or are decided in accordance with the law administered in those religious courts (as in Aden).

[2] Verses 86, 87.   [3] Law of November 30, 1942, article 10.

evidence of any surviving jurisdiction of the priests except that ordeals are still taken " before the God " in the circumstances and cases with which we are familiar.

These changes accompany changes in the written law which survives. The Hebrew Code, though secular, comes to us in a collection of legal and religious writings. The surviving Roman fragments of the " Twelve Tables " include some religious matter; but the Codes of Eshnunna, Assyria, Isin, and Babylon are all purely secular. The same change occurs at the corresponding date in England. From the close of the twelfth century the surviving legislation is unmixed with religious matter, and the first lawyer's treatise of the Laws of England, attributed to Glanville, dates from about 1187. In India the first codes unmixed with religious matter appear at a corresponding date—namely, those of Yajnavalkyo of the fourth century A.D. and Narada of the fifth.

The age of the Late Codes is the first in which the use of writing is widespread. In earlier stages of advance, writing is unknown in Africa, and hardly in use in Rome or Peru. Moslem civilization brings it to Northern Nigeria, and its use is common among the Chinese,[1] Hindus, and other peoples of the second half of the age of the Late Codes. Schools first make their appearance in this age, and they are important in our story. There has been, a little while before this, the teaching of writing to students of the priesthoods in the temples, monasteries, and churches. It was little enough. Even in modern Abyssinia, though the priest can read Ge'ez—the dead language in which the psalter and the liturgy are written—he cannot as a rule understand it; and in modern China the Buddhist priest does not understand Pali. The knowledge of letters increases, and the profession of letters—the profession of the scribe—is now a separate calling on the fringe of the ecclesiastical orders.[2] The scribe is not a priest, but his calling is a specialization that has crystallized out from the priesthood, so that in Babylon the same ideogram signifies both priest and scribe, just as in modern English the words " clerk " and " clerical " still signify both the priest and the writer.[3]

---

[1] From the Shang dynasty onwards.   [2] For Mexico, see Prescott, p. 47 f.
[3] But in Egypt "priest" and "scribe" are denoted by different hieroglyphs.

In the Old Testament the scribes had close connections with the priests, and are often mentioned with them, but they were not priests. They copied the sacred texts, but they also drew up the secular legal contracts and other important private documents, as did Baruch the scribe when Jeremiah bought the field that was in Anathoth of his uncle's son, and weighed him the money, even seventeen shekels of silver, and subscribed the deed and sealed it, and called witnesses and weighed him the money in the balances, and took the deed of the purchase, both the sealed and the open according to the law and custom, and in the presence of the witnesses that had subscribed the deed, before all the Jews that sat in the court of the guard, charged Baruch to keep them safely in an earthen vessel, according to custom, that they might continue many days.[1]

The scribes were held in great awe by the populace as the learned men of their age. There is an amusing account of the modern dabtara (scribe) by an Abyssinian chatting in Mr. Walker's *The Abyssinian at Home* :[2] " The dabtara ... will have studied from his boyhood in the house of some Alaqa (Head of the Church) having learnt the Ge'ez tongue; for all the Mass and holy books are written in Ge'ez and also the hymns. Nor does every priest know Ge'ez. But a dabtara is not a priest, and will remain outside the Choir, striking the drum and sistrum and clapping his hands and singing the Qiniei (hymn). . . . A great church may have fifty dabtaras who receive their food from the Head, and these may wander from one tabot (church) to another. . . . Some, wandering here and there in the towns will write cunning spells for the profane. . . . Also one may cajole a woman, and if the husband strikes his wife, saying, ' Thou hast been to the house of the dabtara,' he may give her a medicine, and if the husband takes his rifle to kill the dabtara, it will not fire, or the bullet will miss. . . . Also if the husband goes to the assembly to accuse him, it is not possible for him to utter words, for the dabtara will gaze at him and cause his eye to remain fixed and his mouth to be silent. One dabtara there was who, being imprisoned in chains, did but blow upon them ' uf! uf! ' and

---

[1] Jer. 32[6-14].   [2] Pp. 115 f.

they were loosened." There is an amusing account of the profession of the Egyptian scribe in the instruction of one Tuauf to his son.[1] In Egypt the priests taught the scribes from boyhood in considerable numbers to copy religious texts and keep the temple accounts, and they were also employed by kings and nobles to keep accounts and manage their estates. They were also sent on missions by the kings. In Babylon, too, they are a separate profession, and in a substantial Sumerian or Babylonian town they will live in a separate quarter. They finally become the letter-writers and petition-writers of the illiterate East—for example, in China, India, Aden, and elsewhere.

In short, the possession of writing is in process of being transferred to the layman. It ceases to be possible for an unscrupulous or credulous cleric to lead the laity astray by a false document. The first schools for the laity are opened in England in the twelfth century, and in Rome, according to tradition, in 250 B.C.[2] In Rome the revolt against the priesthood is, according to tradition, a revolt against their monopoly of letters (which, as in Mexico, involved a control of the calendar [3]) as well as against their authority.

This process of transfer of writing to the layman is an incident in the transfer of influence from the priesthoods. Another incident is the beginning of the rise of a new class in the State—that of the successful traders, who may buy land and become members of the equestrian order in Rome, or of the landed gentry elsewhere, and wielders of power and influence in the State. It is too early as yet to say much of this. It is only in the towns that the influence of the new class is marked, but by the end of our period the towns are indeed becoming a power in the State. In England numerous charters are granted to them from the beginning of our period. They issue by-laws for the regulation of wages and prices and the establishment

[1] British Museum Nos. 10182, 10222, cited by Wallis Budge in *The Dwellers on the Nile* (1928), p. 40.

[2] Plutarch, Quaest. Rom. 59. For the schools of Peru, see *Garcilasso de la Vega*, pp. 244, 266 f.; Prescott, *Peru*, pp. 11 f, 70 f. For the schools of Mexico, see Joyce, pp. 122 f., Prescott, *Mexico*, pp. 33 f.

[3] Prescott, *Mexico*, p. 57.

of courts, and for their governance in other respects,[1] and representatives of the towns already sit in the Parliament of 1265.

The appearance of schools is part of a much wider movement. The human intellect is astir and searching for knowledge. In Palestine there are also schools of the prophets, and schools for the study of religious ethics, where men sit at the feet of the sages. The nucleus of the book of Deuteronomy is generally considered to be the product of one of them. Our surviving version of the Twelve Tables is also a school book, and was so used for a century afterwards,[2] and so is the Code of Manu.[3] In India and China the schools and sects are legion. As we have seen, there is no confusion, in the minds of the people, between law and the rest of the teaching of the schools, but the development is sometimes by the same methods—a principle is extracted from a set of facts and applied to new sets of facts, and thereby developed. Let us take an example from the old Hebrew Book of the Covenant. Exodus xxiii, verse 4, reads as follows: "If thou meet thine enemy's ox or his ass going astray, thou shalt surely bring it back to him again. If thou see the ass of him that hateth thee lying under his burden and wouldest forbear to help him, thou shalt surely help with him." The more advanced and detailed form of the Deuteronomy school book (Deut. 22[1]) runs thus:—

" Thou shalt not see thy brother's ox or his sheep go astray, and hide thyself from them; thou shalt surely bring them again unto thy brother. And if thy brother be not nigh unto thee, or if thou know him not, then thou shalt bring it home to thine house, and it shall be with thee until thy brother seek after it, and thou shalt restore it to him again. And so shalt thou do with his ass; and so shalt thou do with his garment; and so shalt thou do with every lost thing of thy brother's, which he has lost, and thou hast found, and thou mayest not hide thyself. Thou shalt not see thy brother's ass or his ox fallen down by the way and hide thyself from them; thou shalt surely help him to lift them up again."

---

[1] For Mexico, see Joyce, p. 131.   [2] Cicero, De Leg. II, 4, 9; 23, 59.
[3] A metrical version of pre-existing Dharma Sutras (i.e., prose collections of rules of conduct for everyday life) of the school of the Manavas.

No less is the interest in law and litigation, indeed it is such an interest as is probably never equalled again. One has only to look at the codes of the more advanced peoples of this age —the Hebrew Code, the surviving fragments of the Twelve Tables, and the Assyrian, Sumerian, and Babylonian Codes, with their precise language and their wealth of legal experience, to know that they were the products of men who had made a special study of law. In China the notion of law gives rise to the original Taoist system of ethics—the doctrine that there is a Tao, or law, eternal, infinite, undefinable, working through all things.

At the close of this period, in thirteenth-century England and in modern Abyssinia, the professional advocate is much in evidence,[1] and even in the middle of the period important schools of law are to be found in Western Europe and else-where. At that point the economics and law of Western Europe had reached to the stage represented in the Twelve Tables. The principles derived from the law of those tables had formed the foundation and framework of the classical Roman law as represented in the compilations of Justinian. Students in Western Europe read these compilations with a new understanding, for they had now practical meaning for them, and such was the passion of the study to which they gave rise that in 1219 Pope Honorius III forbade the study of Roman Law in the University of Paris, and in 1234 Henry III forbade its use in London. But in the newly founded Universities of Oxford and Cambridge its study proceeded unchecked, while in London, in the Temple, a new school studied the common law of England. Soon, in the King's Courts at Westminster, the cleric, as advocate and judge, administered the common law of England, concealing his tonsure beneath the coif.

What, then, does "law" now signify to these peoples of the Late Codes? We can best arrive at this by examining their language. Let us take as an example the Hebrew Old Testament word for "law"—namely, "*mishpat*"—and see what are its various meanings. If the same word is used with

[1] Not everywhere among the peoples of the Late Codes, e.g., not in China and probably not in Babylonia.

a number of meanings, they must be associated together in the mind of the people. "*Mishpat*," as we have seen, means primarily and above all else a "judgment." So do most other words used with the meaning of "law"—for example, the Babylonian and Sumerian equivalents, just as did the Anglo-Saxon "dom." That is because the essential factor that distinguishes law from anything else is that law is enunciated in the courts, and is enforceable in the courts. It is true that, in the view of many individuals among the Tswana peoples, Hebrews, and Babylonians, the Law was given by God, but that is a belief or theory as to its origin, not its nature. Secondly, the verbal root of the word ("*shaphat*") means not only to judge, but also to govern. In early Hebrew history the "*shophetim*" ("Judges," singular "*shophet*") were both judges and chiefs, and the magistrates of the kindred Phœnician peoples were *shophetim*. It is evident, therefore, that these peoples realized that not only was law enunciated in the courts by judges, but it was also laid down in statutory form by rulers, and "*mishpat*" signifies not only a judgment but a statute or ordinance. This is its only connection with religion, for to the religious mind "*mishpat*" (law) originated from God, and so occasionally the ethical or religious laws laid down by God are referred to figuratively by the religious writers of the Old Testament, as the "*mishpatim*" of God—the judgments or ordinances of God. Thirdly, law exists not merely in judgments and statutes, but also in the form of custom and customary conduct—the conduct of the citizen according to right custom; the conduct of the judge according to right custom. *Mishpat*, therefore, also means "custom" and "justice." Lastly it signifies a man's legal "right." [1] In short, "*mishpat*" means "law," with all our uses of that word except the modern use in natural philosophy, such as to signify the laws of motion, the law of nature. These are derived senses which must await the time when science has made further progress.

---

[1] *Mishpat* also occasionally seems to be used to signify a law-suit, the place of hearing, the act of giving judgment, and the execution of it.

CHAPTER X

THE LATE CODES (*continued*)

LEGAL PROCEDURE—HOMICIDE

THESE peoples evince a deep interest in law and a love of litigation, a keen sense of right and wrong—and especially of their own right and the wrong of others—and a devotion to their religion. They are full of confidence in their opinions, and extremely boastful. These things produce some curious results in the procedure of their courts, and perhaps the most curious and the most interesting are what the Romans called the " *legis actio per sacramentum* " or " procedure by oath " or curse (for oath and curse are much the same), and the " *sponsio* " or forensic " wager." The first is never found except at our present stage : the forensic wager appears for the first time at this point, and as part of the procedure by oath, but outlives it, and survives for some time longer. The two institutions are not by any means universal.

To complete our picture of the legal background, we must remember that in this feudal age, and especially in the first half of the present period, it is a necessary part of the constitution that feudal lords of various degree have in most matters jurisdiction over their tenants, though some disputes (called Crimes of the King [1] or Pleas of the Crown [2]) are so serious, and some questions are so difficult that, after a preliminary inquiry sufficient to ascertain its nature, the case must be sent up to the court of a superior lord or of the king. In the result, there remains a welter of different jurisdictions, some being, indeed, coterminous with the boundaries of vassal kingdoms, and (at any rate in detail) there are different rules of law and different procedures in force in different areas of the State.[3] Further, we must remember that the body of rules

---

[1] E.g., in Nupe (Nadel, pp. 166, 172).
[2] England. For the same system in Mexico, see Prescott, pp. 16 f.
[3] See many examples in Rattray, *A.L. & C.*

of law has grown vastly in extent, and the administration and practice of the law have already begun to be something of an art, and consequently here and there detailed and technical rules of procedure and of law have evolved.

In civil disputes—with which alone we are at present concerned—the supply of litigation outstrips, as it were, the demand. This was perhaps always so, but it is more obvious now. There are always disputants asking for their disputes to be heard. In Abyssinia, indeed, it is a generally recognized duty on the part of any disinterested person to accept the role of a reconciler when asked so to do by utter strangers as he travels along the road. If he is unsuccessful in solving their differences, at their request he will take them to the lowest-ranking judge in the vicinity, reporting the dispute.

This pressure of litigants is such as to increase the importance of the institution of suretyship, which is already much in evidence in a variety of circumstances. Litigants must often find a surety to pay the judgment fee or the amount of the judgment before their cases will be heard. Even this is, of course, insufficient to gain a hearing for a trumpery dispute in the court of a Great Chief, king, or emperor. But a man often desires that his trivial quarrel should be heard in the Great Chief's court—either because of a sense of its vast importance, or his desire for the pomp and publicity of that court, or his mistrust of the efficiency or impartiality of the local court. He achieves this result by swearing the Great Chief's oath, or, in other words, by conditionally cursing him.

For example, in Ashanti a man may have a quarrel with his neighbour as to whether a particular tree is within his boundary, or whether the other has trespassed upon his land, or has struck him, and may desire that the dispute shall be tried in the court of a particular *Omanhene* (or Tribal Chief). He says, for example, "I say this tree is on my land." The other says, "I say it is on mine." The first swears, "May fetish So-and-so kill *Omanhene* X if it is not on my land." [1] The other

[1] Or, e.g., "I swear the forbidden name," or "I swear *Omanhene* X *Wukuda.*" *Wukuda* (Wednesday) is the day when a certain calamitous defeat was sustained by the Akwapim and others. For instances of the working of this procedure by oath, see Gold Coast Commission, pp. 30 f.; Rattray, *A.L. & C.*, pp. 379 *et seq.*; Danquah, pp. 69 f.

swears, "May fetish So-and-so kill *Omanhene* X if it is not on *my* land." This puts quite a different complexion on the case. *Omanhene* X has a very definite interest in the matter, and, moreover, a criminal offence, a crime of the chief, has been committed by one or the other. It is now the duty of anyone who hears the words spoken immediately to arrest both parties, and he is entitled to be paid a specific fee for so doing. The two parties are reported to the chief whose oath has been sworn; in some places they are put in the stocks meanwhile, for both are prima facie guilty of cursing the *Omanhene*, or they may be released on giving sureties for their attendance and the payment of court fees. The question at issue—namely, which party was in the right (for example, whose tree it was or whether there was a trespass or assault)—is then tried in the Court of the *Omanhene*, and whoever is found to be in the wrong is guilty of a criminal offence and punished accordingly, either by fine payable to the State,[1] or even (in former times) capitally. The successful party pays to the court "*aseda*" (content money) by way of thanksgiving.

This procedure is applicable to every kind of civil dispute, and is found throughout the Akan peoples of the Gold Coast and Ashanti, in Rome in the period of the Twelve Tables and for some time after, and in modern Abyssinia. There are variations in the procedure from place to place, but the essential incidents are the same everywhere: the curse or oath, the surety, and the fine. Yet the procedure arises in each place quite independently out of similar circumstances. Though general in the Gold Coast colony and Ashanti, it is not (so far as I know) to be found in Nigeria. There was no cultural contact between ancient Rome, the modern Gold Coast, and the Abyssinian highlands. Nor does its existence depend on the tenets of the national religion. Few religions could differ more than those of ancient Rome, the Gold Coast, and Christian Abyssinia. The procedure by oath spreads, and threatens to oust the simple procedure by summons in all these areas, and this is because its extension is the measure and means of the extension of the power and jurisdiction of the

[1] Often partly used to pay the expenses of a sacrifice to propitiate the fetish.

king or paramount chief over the whole kingdom or empire, as feudalism dissolves. But as his jurisdiction spreads and widens, the oath loses its meaning. In modern Abyssinia, where the incidents of the procedure are the same, the form is "*Menelik Yimut*" (Let Menelik [1] die!). It is used in joining every sort of issue in litigation in all courts, and even in concluding legal transactions. When an agreement has been made (for example, an agreement of marriage), or an allegation has been made in court and denied, the one will commonly say to the other, "*Man Yimut*" (Who is to die?) and the reply is made "*Menelik Yimut*" [2] (Let Menelik die). In other words, the old oath has become a mere method of indicating the binding character of what has preceded. So in Rome, when we hear of it, the oath is disappearing from the procedure, though its name remains.

In all litigation in ancient Rome, as in ancient India and modern Abyssinia, the wager, too, plays a prominent part, whatever the nature of the issue to be tried. It is a result of that characteristic boastfulness to which we have referred. Any stake may be made, but in modern Abyssinia it is usually either a " mule," " a horse," or " honey." If, for example, a man stakes a mule on the result and loses, he pays a judgment fee of twenty Maria Theresa dollars, and if he wins he receives ten dollars from the other side. No doubt a high stake impresses the court with the sincerity of the wagerer.

But some people love technicalities in the law, and to other peoples they have less appeal. The Nigerians, the Tswana peoples, the Babylonians, Sumerians, Assyrians were more interested in justice than law; the English, the Akan peoples, the Romans, and the Abyssinians appreciated technicalities. The history of the ordeal illustrates the difference, as it also illustrates the difference between countries where the power of the priesthood and religion was great, and those where it was small. Among the Tswana peoples the ordeal has disappeared: we saw little of it among the Nguni of South

---

[1] Emperor of Abyssinia from 1889 to 1913.

[2] Question and answer corresponding, as in the Roman stipulation, so as to impress on the parties, and on the mind of bystanders who may have to bear witness to it in the future, that an oral agreement has been arrived at.

Africa, but among the Tswana it has gone. In China it was of no importance at any time. In Abyssinia, as in England and among the Akan peoples, the oath was extended to witnesses, and therefore, since the taking of an oath was a serious and dangerous thing, and the parties could not fairly be expected to tell the truth contrary to their interest, they were not allowed to give evidence, a rule which lasted in England in civil cases till 1851 and in criminal cases till 1898. In Palestine, Babylonia, and Assyria the ordeal by oath was not commonly used except in the type of case with which we have become so familiar—namely, disputes in relation to bailments, and other disputes where evidence on one side only was available. Otherwise evidence was generally unsworn.[1] In India the position was much the same, though the use of the ordeal steadily increased from the Central to the Late Codes.[2]

In this age, too, the old trial before chief and elders becomes a trial before jurors—neighbours sworn to decide the truth— in England in the thirteenth century and in Abyssinia today. In Abyssinia the difference between this oath and that in the procedure by curse can be easily seen. Instead of the oath "Let Menelik die," the juror swears, for example, "May God judge against my soul! May he disperse the foes of Menelik from afar with the cannon, from near with the sword!"[3]

Now let us turn to the substance of the law applied in the courts, and first to the civil injuries, commencing with the most serious of injuries, homicide.

We noticed at our previous stage of the Central Codes that pecuniary compensation was ceasing to satisfy the relatives

---

[1] The great Prescott (*Mexico*, p. 17), after quoting from Clavigero the statement that in Mexico the accused might free himself by oath (" *il reo poteva purgarsi col giuramento* "), innocently enquires : " What rogue, then, could ever have been convicted? " The matter is not so simple as that.

[2] In the Sutra literature (say 600 to 200 B.C.) there is nothing of ordeals except a reference in Apastamba. The ordeals increase in Manu (two ordeals), viii, 114 and the succeeding authors. See, e.g., Brihaspati xix, 4 (nine ordeals.) In the later authors the oath is extended also to the plaintiff.

[3] C. H. Walker, p. 149.

of a slain man. There was a growing sentiment against the acceptance of money for the life of a relative. Homicide was becoming heinous and abhorrent, and the blood-feud was no longer to be stayed by a payment of cattle or currency. The general sanction for homicide was the handing over of a person or number of persons to take the place of the slain—or, in other words, the sanction was now midway between a pecuniary and a capital sanction, and at the same time midway between a compensatory and a punitive sanction. Keeping pace with this change there was a change in the distinctions to be found in the amount of the sanction. When it was pecuniary and compensatory, the distinctions chiefly followed the status of the slain—if he was a man, the sanction was commonly double that for a woman, and in such areas as Western Europe, where there were several pronounced distinctions of rank, each rank had its own *wergeld* or blood-money. But in the Central Codes the distinctions were now chiefly according to the extent of the guilt. If he killed in anger, the number of persons to be handed over was larger; in England, if he killed by ambush, the offence was altogether more serious and was criminal, and not emendable by money. In most of these peoples an allegation of homicide was triable only in the court of the king or paramount chief.

This many-sided process of change continues.[1] There is now a vivid consciousness of the sanctity and uniqueness of life. It is the first and most fundamental of those rules of the Decalogue which impose duties between man and man, and (except for treason) intentional homicide is the most serious of wrongs everywhere. Among all the peoples of the Late Codes, the normal sanction for intentional homicide is death, and it is by the appearance of this rule that we mark the commencement of the age of the Late Codes. So, while in Central Nigeria there are a few peoples among whom the sanction for homicide is not capital [2]—and similarly in England it is not capital before the middle of the twelfth century—and

---

[1] In Eshnunna we are told in clauses 48 and 55 that capital offences are only triable in the King's Court.

[2] See Talbot, vol. iii, pp. 625 *et seq.*, map on p. 627, and Table 19; and Meek, *Tribal Studies*.

therefore we do not assign these peoples to the Late Codes, from this point onwards intentional homicide is everywhere a capital offence.[1]

But the feud between the kinship groups continues to be the effective factor in securing satisfaction or retribution, as it has been from the beginning of our Third Agricultural Grade, with the one difference that it is no longer to be stayed by payment of a vast sum of compensation. Accordingly, this, more than any other age, is the age of the blood-feud, and it is mainly upon the blood-feud that the execution of justice against a homicide depends. In the result the process that we have long watched, by which the wrong of homicide becomes a purely criminal offence, continues to drag slowly along.

The typical circumstances of an act of homicide are much the same as they have been since at least the beginning of the Third Agricultural Grade. The slayer flees, if he can, either abroad, if he is near a frontier, or to some other place that will give him protection for a while. So, for example, in the border counties of England in the twelfth and thirteenth centuries the number of fleeing homicides is very large, and on the Abyssinian border the Italians in Eritrea in 1935 were complaining bitterly of the depredations of outlaws. Where religion has little power—for example, in Bechuanaland—the slayer flees to the homestead of a senior adviser of the king— for example, among the Bamangwato, the homestead of the chief's mother. Elsewhere (as among the Hebrews, English and Athenians) he flees to a church or shrine. But intentional homicide is now so heinous an offence that if, on the trial that follows, the slayer is found guilty of intentional homicide, the sanctuary does not avail him. He is handed over to the next of kin to exercise his privilege of exacting retribution. If it be a non-religious sanctuary—for example, the homestead of the

---

[1] See Talbot, *loc. cit.*, Schapera, *Tswana*, pp. 260–1, Meek, *N. Nig.*, vol. i, pp. 271 *et seq.*, Rattray, *Ashanti Law and Constitution*, pp. 294 *et seq.* For England, see P. & M., vol. ii, p. 458 *et seq.* Hebrew Code, Exod. 21^{14}, and Num. 35. For Mexico, see Joyce, p. 131; Prescott, p. 17. For Peru, see Rowe, p. 271. For the Maya, Joyce, p. 283. The Codes after the Hebrew do not set out the punishment for intentional homicide (but see Eshnunna, 24). For a full account of the Chinese law of homicide at the end of the nineteenth century A.D., see Alabaster.

queen-mother—it does not avail him, for intentional homicide now partakes of a criminal as well as civil nature; if it be a religious sanctuary, it avails him not, for intentional homicide has now become a religious as well as a legal offence. With the growth of towns, these recognized shrines have often become "cities of refugees"—well-known towns where a famous shrine exists—among the Hebrews they are cities of the Levites. We saw this situation reached among some of the most advanced peoples of the Central Codes—for example, the Lamba. Apart from trials at sanctuaries, there are trials in the court of the king or paramount chief, and among many peoples the sentence is that the accused be handed over to the next of kin to put to death.

What, then, is there to prevent the next of kin from accepting a money sum or a number of persons in lieu of the life of the slayer? In fact, among some of the least advanced of the peoples of this stage it is a well-recognized rule that the next of kin may accept compensation in lieu of a life, and there is a frequent practice to do so. Among the nations that we have chosen to exemplify the law of the Late Codes, this practice is most common among some of the peoples of Northern and Southern Nigeria,[1] but it is also found in a lessening degree among the more advanced peoples of the Late Codes.

But there are a number of factors that militate against the acceptance by the relatives of compensation. There is pride,

[1] In the Moslem States of Northern Nigeria the general rule is death unless the relatives agree to accept blood money in lieu (Meek, *N. Nig.*, vol. i, p. 271). Among the pagans of Northern Nigeria families often accept compensation or another person. As to Southern Nigeria, see Talbot, vol. iii, Table 19. Summarizing his data in regard to seventy-one sub-tribes of the Ibo, we are told that in thirty-seven sub-tribes the rule is hanging for intentional homicide, in three sub-tribes the slayer is handed over to the next of kin to treat as they wish, in seventeen sub-tribes the rule is that either the slayer is hanged or compensation in money or the handing over of persons is accepted if the family of the deceased agrees, in eleven cases the rule is that a number of persons (usually wife or children) are handed over. Among a few of the thirty-seven tribes referred to above, where the sanction is hanging, we are told the practice is that if the slayer flees and cannot be reached, a brother or other relative may be put to death in his place.

solidarity of kinship, and public opinion that thinks lightly of families who accept it. For example, even in modern Abyssinia it is recognized to be the right of the family to accept compensation, but such a family is held in low esteem.

There is another aspect of the same ethical rule—namely, the religious aspect—which serves to prevent the acceptance of compensation. In many lands, in England and West Africa, among the ancient Hebrews, and in Greece up to classical times, it takes the form of a doctrine that the spirit of a slain man cries to his kindred for vengeance and may not be appeased save by the death of the offender, and his presence pollutes the land and destroys its fertility. " Thine eye shall not pity him," says holy writ to the next of kin, " but thou shalt put away the (guilt for) innocent blood from Israel, that it may go well with thee."[1] "Ye shall take no ransom for the life of a manslayer liable to death for he shall surely die. . . . So ye shall not pollute the land wherein ye are, for blood it polluteth the land and no expiation can be made for the land for the blood which is shed therein, but by the blood of him that shed it. And thou shalt not defile the land which ye inhabit, in the midst of which I dwell: for I the Lord dwell in the midst of the children of Israel."[2] The same doctrine survived in Athens throughout the classical age, where the law was attributed to the legislation of Draco, of the period of the Late Codes.[3]

In most of the peoples of the Late Codes death is imposed either by hanging,[4] stoning,[5] or by throwing down the culprit from a high rock,[6] in each case so as not to draw more blood than is necessary. In some cases the execution is by the next of kin slaying the culprit with the same weapon and in the same way as he slew his victim.[7] Sometimes this is

---

[1] Deut. 19[13].   [2] Num. 35[31] f.

[3] See *Primitive Law*, c. 15; G. M. Calhoun, *The Growth of Criminal Law in Ancient Greece* (1927).

[4] England, most places in West Africa, and Peru.

[5] England, Palestine, Peru, Mexico.

[6] Rome, Abyssinia, England, Peru, Bechuanaland (Schapera, *Tswana*, p. 261).

[7] Bechuanaland (Schapera, *loc. cit.*). See the incident related in Talbot, vol. iii, p. 626.

done before the culprit is thrown from the rock. In most cases the next of kin takes the initiative. In Abyssinia the present Emperor in 1925 devised an ingenious method of suiting the requirements of the law and obviating its apparent barbarity, by a device by which the co-ordinated sights of four rifles are directed upon the man condemned for murder, who is strapped to a plank, and the next of kin can fire the rifles at once by a simple mechanism.[1]

There is another factor which militates against the acceptance of compensation for murder—namely, that in many lands—and especially among the more advanced peoples,[2] the king may still prosecute, and the death sentence still awaits the murderer.

The distinctions in the gravity of the sanctions for homicide continue to be increasingly based on the intention of the slayer. In England at the date of the Norman Conquest we saw that killing by ambush was already unemendable by money. This is a test based upon the circumstances of the act, but before the end of the twelfth century the rule gives birth to the wider, generalized rule, based purely upon intention, that any killing with malice aforethought is capital. The law has become more technical, and therefore more static, and both rules survive for a while side by side. The position is precisely the same among the Hebrews. " A man smiting a man, who dies," says the Hebrew Code, " shall surely be put to death. But if he lay not in wait, but God brought it (or him) to his hand, then I shall appoint thee a place whither he shall flee. But when a man uses violence to another to slay him with malice, thou shalt take him from my altar to die." [3] The precision of the language is to be noted; the second verse is an exception from the first, and the third from the second.

Accordingly, in the Late Codes intentional homicide is everywhere capital. But it does not by any means follow that unintentional homicide goes free. There has been a loss to the family, and homicide is still partly a civil wrong. There is as yet no clear or universal doctrine on the matter. There is, for example, nowhere as yet so general a conception as

[1] Mérab, *Impressions d'Ethiopie* (1929), vol. iii, p. 218.
[2] See *post*, p. 286.　　　[3] Exod. 21$^{12-14}$; cf. Deut. 19^{13}.

"killing by negligence"—or, indeed, as "negligence."
There is merely intentional and other killing. The latter is
dealt with differently among different nations. Among the
more backward—for example, in Northern Nigeria—the
question whether the killing was intentional or not is commonly
a suitable matter for the ordeal, as being directly within the
knowledge of the accused alone.[1] Among more advanced
peoples—for example among the Hebrews at the very close
of the Old Testament period—the question what was intended
is chiefly to be answered, just as in a modern English court, by
considering the type of weapon used.[2]

But even if the killing is unintentional, there is no question
of the slayer going scot-free. Such a rule could not satisfy
the next of kin or obviate a feud. In countries, such as England,
Palestine or classical Greece, where the slayer normally takes
sanctuary, if he is found at his trial not to have killed intentionally, he is not delivered up to the next of kin; but if he
sallies forth before a defined period has passed by—in Palestine
before the death of the High Priest, or in some countries
before the lapse of three years[3]—he may be killed with
impunity. Where sanctuaries are less in use, there is a variety
of other sanctions. In Southern Nigeria (but not elsewhere
to any extent) in the majority of cases the slayer pays the
expenses of the burial of the deceased; in many cases in
Nigeria, Ashanti, and elsewhere, he pays compensation to the
relatives of the slain; in many cases he pays a fine to the
king.[4] In the most advanced peoples legislation fixes the

[1] Meek, N. Nig., vol. i, pp. 272-3.   [2] Numbers, c. 36.
[3] E.g., at some periods in ancient Egypt, and in some parts of S. Nigeria.
In England, under the Assize of Clarendon (1166), he can abjure the
realm and be escorted abroad.
[4] For S. Nigeria, see Talbot, vol. iii, Table 19. Out of 115 sub-tribes
or districts, in forty-eight cases the sanction is the payment of burial
expenses; in seven cases burial expenses plus a fine; seven cases, burial
expenses or the handing over of a person; five cases, burial expenses plus
the handing over of a person; ten cases, a person handed over; ten cases,
a fine alone; one case fine plus compensation; nineteen cases compensation
alone; three cases, the same sanction as for intentional killing (see also
Meek, Ibo, p. 210); two cases, the same if the killing was negligent; four
cases, no sanction at all. In N. Nigeria and Ashanti the sanction is generally
compensation (Meek, N. Nig., vol. i, p. 273; Rattray, Ashanti Law and

sanctions for killing in a variety of defined circumstances, which we might regard as instances of negligence, as, for example, where a man is gored to death by an ox known by its owner to have gored in the past,[1] or where a man is killed by the collapse of a house which the defendant built for him.[2]

The third type of killing is killing in self-defence. This last is an offence which deserves a pardon, but needs a pardon.[3]

The wrong of homicide has not therefore, even intentional homicide, and even at the close of the Late Codes, become everywhere and in all respects a criminal offence. Even among the Hebrews it is the next of kin who takes the initiative, and the accused is not stoned by the community, as for a crime. Even in classical Athens the proceedings are civil, or in part civil, and only the next of kin can sue. Looking generally, however, at the matter, it is now partly a criminal and partly a civil offence. In England, for example, neither the king nor the relative can pardon the accused so as to save him from proceedings by the other.[4]

There is one rule or institution, bearing a special relation to homicide, that may appropriately be mentioned here—namely, what in England is called the " benefit of clergy." This applied not merely to charges of homicide, but to any felony—that is to say, any offence (except treason) so serious as to be punishable by death and confiscation of property; but of these the most frequent was intentional homicide. In England the clergy are a separate estate of the realm, and an ordained clerk can be convicted only in an ecclesiastical court, and punished only by such sentence as that court can inflict. Certainly he can be arrested by the sheriff, and charged with murder, and a jury can decide whether he is innocent; but

---

Constitution, p. 296). In Bechuanaland, among the Ngwato and Kgatla nations, there is apparently no sanction, except a fine if the killing was negligent (Schapera, *Tswana*, p. 261). These few references to negligence, if accurate, may show European influence, or may merely be a compendious way of recording the substance of the decisions.

[1] Exod. 21^{29}; Eshnunna, 53–6.   [2] *C.H.*, 229.

[3] See for England (thirteenth century), P. & M., vol. ii, p. 479. For Northern Nigeria, see Meek, vol. i, p. 273.

[4] For the effect of the developing law upon the deodand, see *Primitive Law*, pp. 157 f. See also P. & M., vol. ii, p. 473.

if they find against him he can only be convicted in the bishop's court after a trial under the canon law. The canon law tries him by the process of compurgation by oath, and the bishop's court is inept, and no doubt he usually manages to find oath-helpers and clears himself. But if he is convicted, he is never put to death, for the ecclesiastical courts never pronounce a death sentence—he may be whipped, even branded, banished, or immured, but not killed. In those days—early in the thirteenth century and thereabouts—almost everyone who could read and write was still a cleric, and there must have been in the public mind, to justify this exemption from the death sentence for felonious " clerks," a notion that the life of a man who could read and write should not be lightly lost, and that he deserved a privilege. But, a little later, at the end of the century, when the knowledge of writing is spreading fast, benefit of clergy becomes the privilege of everyone who can read, or pretend to read, a verse of the Bible. He is merely burnt in the hand. In India we see the earlier stage. The Brahman is not put to death for homicide or any other capital offence except treason; he can be branded or even blinded, but more commonly he is banished; and the same rule is still found in backward Nepal in the 1830's. We see the late English stage in modern China. The privilege is not that of the priest—it does not avail the Buddhist priest—and indeed priests are treated by the law with exceptional severity, as those who should know better—it is the privilege of the literate. No graduate—even if he has bought his degree —suffers the capital punishment, unless at least the offence be rape or robbery or something of a disgraceful character.[1]

[1] Alabaster, pp. 114-15.

CHAPTER XI

THE LATE CODES (*continued*)

"An Eye for an Eye and a Tooth for a Tooth"

TURNING from homicide to lesser personal injuries, we
meet the most famous rule of primitive law, and the
one more misunderstood than any other. This is the
rule of " an eye for an eye, and a tooth for a tooth," as the
ancient Hebrews called it,[1] or the "*talio*" of the Roman
Twelve Tables. It only emerges in the age of the Late Codes,
and is characteristic of the second half of that period.

We are sometimes told by travellers and observers of
retaliation for injuries, practised among early tribes who
possess no courts. It is not with this kind of phenomenon
that we are here concerned. Among peoples who have no
courts, a man who considers himself wronged, or his friends
or kindred, totemic or local group, commonly vent their
irritation according to circumstances upon the offender, or
some member of his group, or some innocent bystander; or
they may be appeased by a gift, or take no action at all. This
is neither law nor retaliation. There is as yet no law of
personal injuries among them. On the other hand, it is
probably true both of modern and early England that a man
struck upon the face commonly strikes back or attempts to
do so. This, too, is no law of retaliation. In modern England
both are guilty of assault. In Anglo-Saxon England each is
liable by law to pay pecuniary compensation to the other
according to the nature of the injuries done. In this chapter
we are concerned with a law—that is to say, a rule enforceable
in the courts—providing for retaliation—that is to say, the
infliction on the offender of the like injury to that inflicted by
him.

At the commencement of the Late Codes intentional homicide had ceased to be a wrong calling for compensation,

---

[1] Lev. 24[20].

and had everywhere become a capital offence. The law was now death for death. When we reach the second half of the period of the Late Codes we see that the more serious personal injuries are also thought to call for corporal sanctions. It is no longer tolerable that, in this age of growing disparity of wealth, a man of means should be permitted to wound or break a limb of his neighbour and be immune from any but a pecuniary sanction, whether it be compensation payable to the injured person or a fine to the king or chief. The pride and solidarity of the family will not endure the affront, and vengeance is no longer to be stayed by money. Nor does the growing social conscience of the people tolerate it. As yet there is no means of achieving progress except by corporal sanctions, for there are, for example, hardly any prisons. They appear now for the first time and in very small numbers, but there is no question of the State providing nourishment in idleness for every malefactor in this violent age. The prisons are mere dungeons; [1] in modern Addis Ababa there are only one or two; they are dens of disease, and prisoners must be fed by their relatives here and in thirteenth-century England, in India and in China, if they are to be fed at all. Nor is there any question of a system of State-initiated prosecutions: the law exists for the head of the family to vindicate the injuries of its members.

We have already seen in the Central Codes a good deal of corporal sanctions, including horrible mutilations, for criminal offences; another aspect of the present development is that severe intentional personal injuries are undergoing a process of transformation into criminal offences—wrongs thought to be offences against the king or community, and not merely against an individual.

So we find that the sanctions for serious wounding and broken limbs are turning from pecuniary to corporal sanctions recognized by law. In some of the more advanced countries, where central government is strong, the law will not recognize self-help in these matters. In others it will recognize self-help within the limits of strict retaliation. In many countries, in a proper case, a court of trial will order the infliction of the

[1] For Peru, see Rowe, p. 271.

like injury upon the guilty defendant, by the injured plaintiff
or even by some officer of the court.

But there is one difficulty in this part of the law that is not
to be found in the law of homicide. A killing is a precise
and distinct type of offence : a personal injury less than a
killing is anything between the most serious and permanent
maiming and a mere graze or blow. Nature knows no dividing line. Even in a modern court pecuniary compensation
is the appropriate sanction for most negligent injuries, and
even at the close of the Late Codes it is always the most
fitting sanction for a minor injury, whether intentional or
not.

In truth, there is never at any stage of law, and not even
in the Late Codes, a rule of " an eye for an eye and a tooth for
a tooth." There is only a maxim or principle or aspiration
which appeals to some writers more than others, but which
is in practice limited in application to a vaguely defined class
of the more serious injuries. Let us trace its history, first in
England in these two centuries in order of time, and then in
the other countries from which our examples are taken, in
order of economic development.

We noticed that at the end of the period of the Central
Codes in England—namely, about the year 1100—there were
still some obsolescent tariff-lists of compensation for wounds
according to the part of the body injured and the nature of the
injury, as well as a payment to the lord or king of the injured
person; but we also now heard of a rule of law that the
offender is liable to support the latter and pay the medical
attendance until he recovers. The twelfth century is a period
of transition of which we know too little in detail. The
tariff-lists of wounds disappear. As in regard to homicide,
the feud is in greater evidence. Wounding and *mayhem* (the
latter being defined as the loss of use of a member serviceable
in a fight) are becoming partly criminal, and at the same time
the sanctions are becoming corporal, and sometimes they
involve the loss of life or limb. But this is nothing more than
the change that is taking place in the sanctions for crime. At
the commencement of the thirteenth century every kind of
mutilation is being imposed upon the convicted criminal—

death by throwing down from a rock,[1] hanging,[2] stoning,[3] beheading, burning, drowning, castration, loss of hands, feet, eyes, ears, nose, and lips—and, as always, especially upon the unfree. Then from the same date—namely, 1200—we begin to hear advocates of sentences of an eye for an eye and a tooth for a tooth for those guilty of wounding or *mayhem*.

The so-called " Ten Articles of William I "[4]—typical in several respects of the whole series of early English laws, of which they are almost the latest—illustrate well what is occurring. They form one of a number of collections of legislation attributed to the Conqueror, some part of which is probably genuine. This particular collection dates from about A.D. 1120, and the last chapter reads : " I also forbid that any-one should be slain or hanged for any offence, but let his eyes be gouged out and his testicles cut off." This is an edifying sentiment. The clause, no doubt, includes all offences in its scope, and is characteristic of this period when, as we have seen, a sense of the sanctity of life is beginning to loom large in the public mind, and at the same time the number of mutilations is greatly increasing. There is also a later version of the same collection, sometimes called the Willelmi Articuli Retractati,[5] dating from about A.D. 1210. Like many or most later versions of early laws, the scribe has included additions which bring the law up to his date. The corresponding chapter (c. 17) now reads : " We also forbid that anyone should be slain or hanged for any offence, but let his eyes be gouged out or his feet or testicles or hands cut off, so that the living trunk may remain for a sign of his treachery and ill-doing, for according to the size of the wrong should punishment be inflicted on evil-doers."[6] The last sentence is perhaps the first expression of

---

[1] The Roman method of execution.

[2] The usual West African method.

[3] The capital punishment for crime among the Hebrews.

[4] Beginning " Hic Intimatur " ; see in A. J. Robertson's *The Laws of England from Edmund to Henry I* (1925), p. 238. Liebermann assigns them to a date between 1110 and 1135.

[5] Robertson, pp. 244 f.

[6] In regard to feudal Japan W. S. Gilbert describes it as the sublime object of making the punishment fit the crime.

the rule of the *talio* in England. It increases in popularity, and at the end of our period Britton (1291)[1] advocates an out-and-out *talio* of member for member, wound for wound, imprisonment for imprisonment. And yet it was never true in England or anywhere else that wounding was always punished in accordance with the principle of an eye for an eye.

The history of the matter in other lands is the same. In Nigeria the tariff-lists of compensation for personal injuries seem only to be found in the north, where a compensatory sum in proportion to the amount of blood lost is common among the Moslem States.[2] In Southern Nigeria the sanction of a compensatory sum is found only in about 11 per cent. of the cases, and the tariff-list has gone. Here in 34 per cent. of the cases the sanction is a fine, and in about 35 per cent. the rule is that the offender is liable to pay the doctor's fees for curing the patient, and often to care for him in the meantime. The rule of retaliation is as yet comparatively rare in Nigeria. In Northern Nigeria retaliation for loss of eye or limb is found in one or two Moslem States such as Hadeija, and among one or two pagan peoples such as the Igara. In Southern Nigeria retaliation is only found in about 6 per cent. of the cases. There is, however, a new development in Southern Nigeria. The feud provides the only sanction for wounding in a number of cases, for we are told that in about 12½ per cent. of the cases there is no trial for wounding.[3] In Bechuanaland there is usually a fine or a thrashing for a serious wounding, but

---

[1] Britton, I, 123-4, and see also Fleta, p. 59.

[2] Meek, *N. Nig.*, vol. i, p. 274.

[3] For sanctions for wounding in S. Nigeria, see Talbot, vol. iii, Table 19. In regard to 143 sub-tribes and districts, his data may be fairly summarized as follows: In sixty-two cases the offender is bound to get his victim cured and pay the doctor's fees, often also feeding and caring for him in the meantime or doing his work on his farm. (These sixty-two cases include thirteen cases where the sanction is the payment of doctor's fees plus a fine; and nine cases of the payment of doctor's fees plus a small compensatory payment.) In fifty-nine cases the sanction is a fine (in thirteen cases of which the accused is liable to pay the doctor's fees in addition). In twenty-one cases the sanction is the payment of compensation (half of these cases include payment of doctor's fees). In eleven cases there is retaliation. In twenty-two cases there is no trial for wounding.

sometimes the victim is ordered by the court to inflict upon the defendant the same injury as he suffered.[1]

In the Hebrew Code, if we understand it aright, as in Southern Nigeria and in England at the corresponding period, the general sanction for wounding seems to be that " he shall provide for his time of inactivity and shall surely cause him to be healed " [2]—that is to say, that he is liable to see that his victim is thoroughly cured, and must pay the doctor's fees and support him while he is disabled. But a few verses later, in a quite inappropriate place, the rule is stated: " If there is mischief then thou shalt give life for life, eye for eye, tooth for tooth, hand for hand, foot for foot, burn for burn, wound for wound, bruise for bruise." This appears to be a late development and interpolation, and the same rule is stated in what appears to be an addition at the end of Chapter xix of Deuteronomy: " And thine eye shalt not pity: life shall go for life, eye for eye, tooth for tooth, hand for hand, foot for foot." The doctrine is also fully stated in the later book of Leviticus.[3] These statements have the merit of making clear what is apparent elsewhere [4]—that the rule of *talio* is conceived of as applying to homicide as well as wounding. As homicide has become capital, some think that wounding should be punished by *talio*. The passage in Deuteronomy, however, only refers to our *mayhem*—loss of a member.

The position is much the same in the only two surviving clauses of the Roman Twelve Tables, that are concerned with personal injuries. One provides that " If (a man) has broken by hand or club a bone of a freeman, he shall pay 300 (asses)." [5] The second clause contains the rule of " *talio* " for *mayhem* : " If (a man) has broken a member, unless he makes his peace with him [6] there shall be like for like " (" *talio esto* "). Much ink has been used in endeavouring to define the distinction

[1] Schapera, *Tswana*, pp. 258–9. [2] Exod. 21$^{18-19}$.
[3] Chap. xxiv, e.g., " And if a man cause a blemish to his neighbour, as he hath done, so shall it be done to him, breach for breach, eye for eye, tooth for tooth; as he hath caused a blemish in a man shall it be rendered unto him. And he that killeth a man shall surely be put to death."
[4] See, e.g., the incident related in Talbot, vol. iii, pp. 626–7.
[5] The " as " was a monetary unit.
[6] I.e., by payment of compensation.

between " bone " and " limb " : but that is to pursue a mirage. The limits of the rule of the *talio* are always of the vaguest, and, as in the Hebrew Code, the second rule may be of later date than the first. Among the Gallas of Kenya, too, the general rule for serious wounding is said to be the *talio*.[1]

In Eshnunna there is no trace of *talio*; the sanction for wounds is pecuniary.[2] But when we reach the Code of Hammurabi, 200 years later, and that of Assyria, we find, as in England in the thirteenth century, the rule of retaliation at its height. Not that the rule is so expressed in so many words : these are true codes—that is to say, collections of legislation, not school books. Summarizing them we may say that, between persons of the same class, for minor injuries the sanction is generally pecuniary; for wrongs committed by a commoner upon a noble the sanctions are corporal, re-taliatory, and savage [3]—we must not forget that Babylonian society was still partly feudal—and the same applies to wrongs against a parent; and for serious wrongs sentences of retalia-tion are prescribed. " If," says the Code, " a man has caused the loss of a nobleman's eye, his eye one shall cause to be lost." [4] " If he has broken a nobleman's limb, one shall break his limb." [5] " If he has caused a commoner to lose his eye or broken a commoner's limb, he shall pay one mina of silver." [6] " If a man has made the tooth of a man that is his equal to fall out, one shall make his tooth fall out." [7] But the retaliation—whether of life or limb—is ordered as between the protagonists to the lawsuit, who are the heads of families, and that is so whether the injury is caused to them or to their household. So " if a man has struck a nobleman's daughter and caused her to drop what was in her womb, he shall pay 10 shekels of silver for what was in her womb." [8] " If that woman has died, one shall put to death his daughter." [9] " If a builder has built a house for a man and has not made strong his work, and the house he built has fallen, and he has caused the death

---

[1] *E.A.L.* (1906), vol. i, p. 101.   [2] Eshnunna, 42–7.

[3] Cf. Manu viii, 279. Assault by a man of a low caste on one of the three highest castes, foot cut off for a kick, lips cut off for spitting, etc. Compare the crime of petty treason in England late in the thirteenth century.

[4] *C.H.*, 196.   [5] *C.H.*, 197.   [6] *C.H.*, 198.

[7] *C.H.*, 200.   [8] *C.H.*, 209.   [9] *C.H.*, 210.

of the owner of the house, that builder shall be put to death." [1]
" If he has caused the son of the owner of the house to die,
one shall put to death the son of that builder." [2] In Abyssinia,
China, and India [3] in our period the sanctions for wounding
are of the same general character.

Well might a Hebrew looking round upon the familiar
scene—the pawning of children for their father's debt, their
seizure on account of his debt after his demise, the retaliation
visited upon the children for his wrongs—well might he
conceive of God as a "jealous God; visiting the iniquity of
the fathers upon the children unto the third and fourth generation of them that hate me." The prophets Jeremiah [4] and
Ezekiel [5] and the authors of Deuteronomy [6] might rail against
such doctrine as impious and immoral, but the common man
might well continue to think that what occurs must be right
and just, and God must so have willed it.

Adultery and seduction and rape we have spoken of so
often, that we need give them little more space. There are,
as ever, differences in the standards of sexual morality from
place to place, but there is little change from the previous age.
In the majority of cases, adultery with a married woman is
criminal, and often it is a religious offence. In England, as
mutilations tend to take the place of capital sentences in this
period, the right of the husband, who takes his wife in adultery,
to put them both to death seems to give place to the right to
emasculate the adulterer. But the inept ecclesiastical courts
are gaining exclusive jurisdiction over sexual offences, and
the sanctions imposed by them are mere penances, often
redeemed by money payments to the Church. [7]

In Nigeria adultery is often a religious offence, but in many
areas sexual morality is lax. In Northern Nigeria among the
Moslem States the sanction for adultery is in theory stoning to
death, but in practice a public flogging often takes its place.
In other places the sanction may be compensation, a fine,
imprisonment, public whipping, or slavery. [8] In Southern

---

[1] C.H., 229.   [2] C.H., 230.   [3] See ante, p. 294, note 3.
[4] Jer. 31[29].   [5] Ez. 18.   [6] Deut. 24[16].
[7] P. & M., vol. ii, pp. 484, 544.
[8] Meek, N. Nig., vol. i, pp. 275 f.

Nigeria the sanction is usually a fine.[1]   In Bechuanaland, too, sexual morality is lax, and the husband beats his wife and claims damages.   Among the Hebrews, where adultery was probably triable in the ecclesiastical courts, the guilty man and woman were both liable to be put to death.[2]   So, too, among the Mexicans,[3] Peruvians,[4] Maya,[5] Assyrians [6] Sumerians, Babylonians,[7] Chinese,[8] and Hindus; [9] but, since the offence is now criminal, the man is not liable unless he knew she was a married woman.[10]   As always, adultery is an offence of which direct evidence is not usually available, and probably among all these peoples the ordeal is in use to test a charge of adultery.[11]   But, as in earlier stages of progress, while the husband is well entitled to put both his wife and the adulterer to death (though not, perhaps, to slay the adulterer alone, for that might savour of conspiracy between husband and wife),[12] if he brings proceedings instead, the offence is criminal, and the king can be merciful, and the sentence is commonly less in China,[13] India, and elsewhere.   In Abyssinia, under the new Penal Code of 1930, the sanction for adultery is reduced to three years' imprisonment.   Among the peoples of the Late Codes the " talio " for adultery is occasionally found,[14] but it is uncommon.   Where it is found, the rule is usually that the wronged husband may similarly treat the wife of the

[1] See Talbot, vol. iii, Table 19.   Summing up his data of 162 sub-tribes or districts, in fifty-seven cases the sanction is a fine, in eighteen cases a fine plus compensation, in thirteen cases a fine plus sacrifice to the offended earth goddess Ala or the ancestors, in twenty-five cases we are told that the sanction is damages, and in four cases the talio.

[2] E.g., Lev. 20^{10}; Deut. 22^{23} (the latter case is that of a betrothed virgin).

[3] Joyce, pp. 131 f.; Prescott, p. 17.   [4] Prescott, p. 261; Rowe, p. 271.

[5] Joyce, p. 284.   [6] A.C. 12–16.

[7] C.H., 132; Eshnunna, 26, 28.   [8] Alabaster, pp. 253 f.

[9] E.g., Manu viii, 371 f.—the woman to be devoured by dogs and the man burnt alive.

[10] A.C., 14.

[11] C.H., 132 (the river ordeal).   For the Hebrews see Num. 5^{11} f.

[12] See A.C. 13–16, C.H. 129.

[13] Alabaster, p. 369 (military servitude for the adulterer, and imprisonment and flogging for the woman).

[14] See above as to S. Nigeria.   It is also found occasionally in the Gold Coast, and see A.C. 55, 56 (rape of a virgin).

adulterer, or (if he is single) his future wife or his brother's wife.

Rape of a married woman is treated in much the same way as adultery with a married woman. Rape of a maiden, on the other hand, is generally a lesser offence, but almost invariably criminal. In England it is punishable by castration and blinding.[1] In Southern Nigeria the sanction is almost invariably a fine,[2] and it is also apparently pecuniary among the Hebrews.[3] Among the Assyrians one of the sanctions is the *talio*,[4] and among the Babylonians it was probably capital. In China the normal sentence is strangulation; but if the girl is under twelve years of age, decapitation (a more serious punishment from the point of view of the state of the mutilated criminal among the shades). In India the normal sentence is castration. Seduction of a virgin is a common prelude to marriage. If her father or the offender objects to the marriage, the latter pays the bride-price [5] or a multiple of it.[6]

Theft continues to meet with varied treatment but growing severity among the various peoples of this age. In England theft is semi-criminal: it is slowly becoming a plea of the Crown. In the twelfth century it is commonly punished by payment of the double value.[7] In the thirteenth century the new semi-criminal action of trespass is brought for it, and the unsuccessful defendant is imprisoned until he makes fine with the king. Robbery has been a plea of the Crown for some time; and burglary is a crime—the offence of breaking into houses or churches. Now theft becomes criminal. Among the many peoples of the Late Codes there are a number of distinctions in theft that we meet again and again. There is the difference between the thief caught in the act (what the Romans called " manifest theft," and the English " open theft " [8]), and other thieves, and death is the punishment for the thief taken in the act. Then there are differences in the place of the theft—for

---

[1] Bracton, f. 147–8 b.   [2] See Talbot, vol. iii, Table 19.
[3] Deut. 22²⁸.   [4] A.C. 55, 56.
[5] Heb. Code Ex. 22.   [6] A.C. 55.
[7] Glanville, I, 2; XIV, 48.
[8] Or they referred to the thief as " hand-having."

instance, theft in a market or on a highway is capital in some places in Southern Nigeria and elsewhere. Then there is the difference between theft of things of little value—in England "petty larceny," which is theft of something under twelve pence in value—and other theft ("grand larceny"). In England the latter is capital in the thirteenth century. And then there is the thief who has been convicted before, and he is usually sold or killed.

The various peoples whom we have chosen as representatives of the stage of the Late Codes show much the same changes. In Bechuanaland the ordinary rule is still payment of the double value, but the thief with stolen cattle in his possession was liable to be killed or mutilated in the hands.[1] Among the numerous peoples of Southern Nigeria the law is much as it was in England in the twelfth century.[2] Among the Hebrews there is a larger multiple of restitution for sheep and cattle. The thief is sold if unable to pay, and the burglar caught breaking in at night can be killed with impunity.[3] Among the Peruvians, Mexicans, and Maya, according to the gravity of the offence, the thief makes restitution or is enslaved or killed.[4] In Assyria and Babylonia, Abyssinia, China, and India the general rule, as in England in the thirteenth century, was death for the thief who stole property of a substantial

---

[1] Schapera, *Tswana*, p. 271.

[2] The data in Talbot, vol. iii, Table 19, can be summarized as follows: Refund, nine cases; fine, twenty cases; fine and refund, thirty-two cases; public humiliation (exhibited round town, or exposed naked or publicly rubbed with ashes, or flogged, or all these, and sometimes fined in addition, or fined in addition and also ordered to refund), thirty-two cases; killed or sold for first offence, sixteen; mutilation or torture for first offence, five; death for thief caught in the act, especially housebreaker, four; death for theft in certain places (market, highway robbery, burglary) six; death for theft of specially valuable property, four; thief tied up till he pays the owner's demand, eight; thief sold if unable to pay, nineteen; killed if unable to pay, three; left alone if unable to pay, two; thief sold for second or later offence, twenty-five. Death for second or later offence, six.

[3] Exod. 22$^{1-3}$. So, too, in Eshnunna, 12, 13. The similarities between this and the Hebrew Code, which is of the same economic stage, are often striking.

[4] For Peru, Rowe, p. 271, Prescott, p. 26; for Mexico, Joyce, p. 131, Prescott, p. 17; for the Maya, Joyce, p. 283.

value, whether caught in the act or not.[1]   If the value was less, the sentence might only be the cutting off of hand or nose, or transportation, or fine, or multiple restitution.

These continue to be the main wrongs in an expanding list, and it is plain from what has been said that at the close of the period of the Late Codes they have become criminal. It is also plain that at this point the boundary between the civil and the criminal law has become more vague and shadowy. But even as late as the close of the twelfth century Glanville begins our first treatise upon the law of England with the words: " There are two kinds of pleas: one criminal and the other civil." In the thirteenth century the main wrongs of the old civil law stand at the boundary. Nevertheless we must not forget that there are wrongs of a lesser kind which are certainly civil; and the distinction between the civil and the criminal law still stands.

There are also purely criminal offences, some tried in the ecclesiastical and some in the king's court. There is, as ever, witchcraft, commonly tried by ordeal, and in Babylon and Western Europe by the ordeal of water.[2] There is, above all, treason [3] and there is the new and serious crime of suicide; [4] and incest, too, another branch of law of which the ecclesiastical courts are making a sorry mess; and there is blasphemy [5] and other crimes.

The penalty for criminal offences,[6] other than those triable in the ecclesiastical courts, is now commonly the loss of life or limb and the confiscation of all property.[7] In thirteenth-century England these offences (now known as felonies, that is to say, heinous deeds) bring to the Crown the important

[1] Assize of Clarendon (1166), cc. 1, 12, P. & M., vol. ii, p. 494 f. A.C., 3 ff.; C.H., 6, 7, 10, 14, 15, 19, 21, 22, and 25. See the phrase in § 10: " the buyer shall be put to death as a thief." For China, see Alabaster, p. 394; for India, see Brihaspati, xxii, 2; Manu, viii, 320.

[2] See A.C., 47; C.H., 2.

[3] For Mexico, see Joyce, p. 131; for Peru, Bennett, p. 26.

[4] For Ashanti (where the corpse was solemnly tried and beheaded) see Rattray, A. L. &. C, pp. 299 f. For China, see Alabaster, pp. 303 f.

[5] Prescott, Peru, pp. 26-7.

[6] Including the civil-criminal offences which have been discussed.

[7] See, e.g., Schapera, Tswana, p. 48. This is general in England, China, India, and the other more advanced peoples of this stage.

profit of confiscated land. But mere death and forfeited property are not thought in England a sufficient punishment for treason. The convicted traitor—after a poor trial, for the king was the accuser, the victim, and the judge—was liable to be dragged by a horse to the scaffold, hanged, disembowelled, burnt, beheaded, and quartered. The Assyrian sanctions for serious offences were of like brutality, and often profited the king by including a period of forced labour. The Abyssinian sanctions were till recent years of a similar severity. In China the sanctions for crime have evinced an unspeakable refinement of brutality throughout at least the last three millennia, from " lingering death " (or slicing to death) downwards. In cases of treason, in order to destroy the family and future happiness of the offender, a sentence of death upon all his sons and grandsons could be imposed, and this remained the law in 1900. If the sons had not reached puberty, the sentence upon them was commonly reduced to emasculation. In India the sanctions were little less severe. In all these peoples are to be found, among the sanctions for serious offences, the so-called " sympathetic " punishments, of which we have seen several examples. For rape, for example, the offender's wife is not raped (as in the *talio*) but he himself is castrated. For a kick administered by the offender to one of higher rank, the offender is not kicked but his foot is cut off; for abuse his tongue is torn out; for theft his hand is removed. It would be too great a refinement, and would not be true of the facts, to distinguish these sanctions too nicely from the *talio*. To the mind of the time the sentence imposes fair and equal retaliations.

In these ways the criminal law is expanding as the social conscience develops and the royal authority increases. In Ashanti, England, Babylonia, Abyssinia, and elsewhere the court of the emperor, king, or paramount chief, formerly limited to the trial of treason, a few other crimes of the king, and disputes between his direct tenants, is extending its power over the whole country, ousting a maze of local jurisdictions and slowly spreading one coherent system of law throughout the land.

BOOK IV

THE MODERN AGE

CHAPTER I

BEFORE THE INDUSTRIAL REVOLUTION

Civilization is a quality of the material culture of a people. Law is its distilled essence. The law of a people is the instrument by which its orderly activity is maintained and protected. It is also a measure of its civilization. But it is more than these things; for they are but facets and functions of a human institution that is universal from the first appearance of barbarism. Every part of the law, as we have seen, is not an equally precise measure. At the heart of it lie the laws relating to personal injuries, for they are mainly independent of local conditions of soil or climate or the local method of subsistence or aptitude for technological advance. At the other extreme, in such matters as tenures of land and inheritance of property, there is much wider variation, both from people to people and, in the Central and Late Codes, in the same people. Yet the law remains the distilled essence of the civilization of a people, and this is why we have found it undergoing a common process of change as civilization advances.

To measure the law against the progress of civilization is to light on historical truths that might otherwise be difficult to reach. Is progress won by absorbing the ideas achieved by other civilizations, or by independent acquisition at the same stage of material advance? It is idle to pretend that one answer is true of all humanity in every age. Had there been no independent advance there could never have been any advance. And again it is not every available idea that is absorbed. The question is not merely as to the origin of an idea, but why it was adopted. We can at least see that ideas achieved by one people will not be adopted by another people (though they may be adopted by individuals) until it has reached an economic level at which they have practical significance for it—that is to say, until it has reached a similar level. We have illustrated this in considering the revived study of Roman law in Western

Europe, when it reached the stage of economic advance of ancient Rome, out of which were born the principles of the classical Roman law. Yet the compilations of Justinian had been at all times available to the student and were in part familiar. The same truth is illustrated by the Renaissance in Europe. It was conceived by many till lately that this arose out of the fall of Constantinople to the Turks in 1453, when refugee scholars fleeing from the infidel first brought Greek letters to the West. Such a view omits to take account of the work of Arab and Jewish scholars during several centuries, and the rebirth of learning that had already occurred, and it would be far nearer to the truth of things to make the following crude arithmetical calculation. In Athens the period of the Late Codes ended with Draco in 620 B.C. or somewhat later, and this was the age reached by Western Europe in the thirteenth century. The literature of Classical Athens was two centuries later than Draco, and Western Europe was not ready to understand or absorb it till the fifteenth century. Such thoughts are a corrective to the doctrines of the extreme diffusionist school of anthropologists, represented by the late Dr. W. J. Perry. He saw, in civilizations as remote as that of the Incas, features found in the culture of ancient Egypt, and explained the presence of almost every cultural element everywhere by assuming a diffusion from ancient Egypt. If this were credible, it would still be material to observe that the diffusion is only to peoples of a like stage of progress. We have, however, seen many other facts incompatible with such a theory. Immediately south of Egypt are innumerable more backward peoples between whose culture and the ancient civilization of Egypt there is nothing in common. It is only further off, in West Africa—among peoples of a comparable economic level—that many resemblances can be detected, and to the extent that they betoken diffusion from without, it is diffusion from the north, a millennium or two after these same cultural elements had ceased to be found in Egypt.

These considerations suggest that it is not progress in law alone that goes with economic advance: that there is an accompanying progress in the development of the intellect, and even in religion, and even in the arts. There are obviously respects in which this is true and respects in which it is not true. When food-gatherers take to agriculture they lose one faculty of mind, but gain another; and if civilization is to develop from stage to stage there must be men capable of imagining its growing complexities. Yet this is not to say that any modern mathematician is greater than Newton. Poets have not grown greater since Shakespeare, nor Nigerian sculpture since the schools of Ife: yet the types of art of a people are closely connected with its economic level. Cave drawings may be all that a palæolithic age can produce: in beauty they may yet be unsurpassed. In religion we have seen in various lands how certain new ethical conceptions grow into it at a certain stage of economic advance, yet nothing can be more dissimilar than the quality of religion among different peoples of the same economic level. For example, in the dominions of the Aztecs, apart from exceptional festivities such as the dedication of the great temple of Uitzilopochtli in 1486, when 70,000 captives are said to have been sacrificed, by the time of the Spanish conquest some 30,000 human beings are estimated to have been immolated in each year.[1] In Atlcaualco, the first month of the year, which marked the cessation of the rains, large numbers of children were sacrificed to the rain-god, and it was considered of good omen if they wept upon their way to the place of sacrifice, for their tears portended plentiful showers. In the course of the second month, Tlacaxipeualiztli, prisoners of war were brought to the temple of Uitzilopochtli, their hearts were cut out in life with a knife of stone, their bodies were thrown down the temple steps and flayed, and their skins assumed by their captors. Commonly the flesh was offered as a choice dish at a banquet given by the latter to their friends. The third month was a month of first fruits, and in the course of it children were sacrificed to Tlaloc.[2] We need not continue the like recital for the rest of the year. The ancient Hebrews were of a similar level of economic advance. "Will the Lord be pleased with thousands of rams," says the minor prophet Micah, " or with ten thousands of rivers of oil? Shall I give my firstborn for my transgression, the fruit of my body for

[1] Prescott, *Mexico*, pp. 38-9.   [2] Joyce, pp. 65 f.

the sin of my soul? He hath shown thee, O man, what is good: and what doth the Lord require of thee but to do justly,[1] and to love kindness, and to walk humbly with thy God?"[2]   "Thou shalt love thy neighbour as thyself," says the ritualist book of Leviticus, "I am the Lord."[3]   "Is this the fast that I have chosen," says an unnamed prophet in the book of Isaiah, "the day for a man to afflict his soul? Is it to bow down his head as a bulrush and spread sackcloth and ashes under him? Is not *this* the fast that I have chosen, to loose the bonds of wickedness, to undoe the bands of the yoke, and to let the oppressed go free? Is it not to deal thy bread to the hungry and that thou bring the poor that are cast out to thy house; and when thou seest the naked that thou cover him?"[4]   So premature a passion for social justice, so precocious a growth of the social conscience, betoken, like some Magdalenian drawing of a running deer, the genius that cannot be paralleled. But we have noted that murder and theft do not appear as religious offences till a certain economic stage is reached, and that a set practice of human sacrifice is characteristic only of the same stage of advance.

This suggests that we shall be nearer the truth if we regard the relation between institution and economic advance as one of probability. It is very doubtful if it can be said of any religious conception or practice that it is universally found among the peoples of a certain economic level. It can sometimes be said that it is only found, if at all, among people of a certain level; it can often be said that it is more frequently found at one level than at any other. Law is more closely entwined with the rest of material culture. It was not the law of Israel that a man should deal out his bread to the hungry or clothe the naked when he met him. We have seen in regard to the procedure by curse or oath, that it is widespread in circumstances that belie imitation, that it is never found except at a certain point of material advance, but that it is hardly found in half the peoples of that stage. On the other hand, some fundamental rules of law—for example, the rule that intentional homicide is capital—are reached everywhere at a certain economic level. In short, it is generally true to

---

[1] *Mishpat*.   [2] Micah 6[8].   [3] Lev. 19[18].   [4] Isa. 58[5] f.

say that in any department of law the peoples of a given stage of material culture may produce rules of any one of a limited number of species—others they do not produce. To a lesser extent the same applies to other institutions.

Why, then, is there this specially close relation between legal and economic progress? We have noticed many reasons. A rule of law must accord with the notions of a people, not merely of individuals. A rule of law is formed mainly by the impact upon economic circumstances of general human emotions or physical reactions—for example, the combined effect of resentment at the slaying of a member of one's group, a fear of reprisals, a desire for peace, and an offer of cattle. There is, therefore, even a difference between the sanctions for homicide in an early pastoral (that is to say, capitalist) society, where the sanction is a fixed number of cattle, and those at a similar level in a non-pastoral people, where, owing to the paucity of valuable goods, with which to stay the blood-feud, the sanction is less defined. In a vast number of cases the origin of a rule of law or a judgment is but economic expediency, and this is no less true of modern law, with its vast bulk of rules that pertain only to the organization of the State, its departments, and its functions.

Let us very briefly—for the bulk of law grows enormous—continue our story from the Late Codes onwards, and notice some salient features of development that illustrate this theme. We have little material for comparison except the English and the Roman Law. They are different in certain ways. It is curious how long some features of a national culture survive. In England there is no confidence in ideas; institutions are mainly shaped by time, circumstances, and compromise, common sense, and practical wisdom. In Anglo-Saxon England the ideas of the Continent, that guided men's actions in the matter of law and government—an extreme feudalism, and trial by oath and battle—were never allowed to develop to their ideological conclusions. It needed a Norman Conquest to foist them upon the country. Out of the circumstances of the age of the Late Codes, Rome extracted legal principles that formed the foundation of her law, and continued to solve her legal problems in the light of principle. England tended rather to decide each of her problems on its merits, and alone of the countries of Western Europe never adopted the principles of the Roman law. This has remained true of the life of England in all its departments, and this independence of Roman ideas makes a brief comparison of the greater interest. Rome never reached an industrial age, and we shall first look very briefly at the period from A.D. 1300 to 1700 in England, and 200 B.C. to A.D. 200 in Rome, for the year A.D. 200 represented the zenith of Roman economic and legal eminence.

We need not take time to notice developments that we have watched so long. The tempo of change continues to quicken. Populations grow larger—in England and Wales from 3½ to 6 millions. The density increases accordingly to about sixty persons per square mile; the towns advance in number and size. Greater London in A.D. 1700 holds about 674,000 persons (of which the City and Southwark number only 250,000). The population of Rome in A.D. 200 is perhaps 1¼ to 1½ millions.[1] But both countries are still overwhelmingly rural. In England Norwich and Bristol, the two greatest provincial towns, each contain no more than some 30,000 inhabitants. The wealth of both countries increases. The power of the central authority continues to grow. It is easier to see this in Rome, where the republic was succeeded by an absolute monarchy, than in England, where for a time a Tudor monarch may wield the appearance of absolute power. The test of the strength of the central authority is the activity of the governmental function and the extent of its power to enforce its decrees. Government must in the last resort depend on the acquiescence of public opinion, and the question is, How much control over the life of the people does popular opinion support?

Feudalism departs, leaving only its shadow behind. In 1660 the Restoration Parliament (repeating in part an Ordinance of the two houses during the Civil War) abolished military

---

[1] Carcopino, *Daily Life in Ancient Rome* (English translation, 1941). Beloch, *Die Bevölkerung der griechisch-römischen Welt*, estimates the population of the Roman Empire at the death of Augustus (A.D. 14) as already totalling 54 millions.

tenures and the distinctively feudal incidents of the tenures in
free and common socage, but in theory until 1925 the Crown
remained the owner of all land in England. In Rome feudal
tenures had disappeared. The English king had long become
the direct ruler of his kingdom, and his courts administered
throughout the land one system of justice—the common
law—save in so far as local courts or other systems operated
by his franchise, permission or authority. The populations
of the English and the Roman dominions had become less
homogeneous in race, for the former now included possessions
in the West Indies and elsewhere, and the Roman Empire grew
to its widest extent.

But though, with the decay of feudalism, the nobility had
ceased to be the rulers and judges of their tenants and serfs,
they remained their landlords, and continued to exercise almost
a monopoly of public offices and a vast social influence. In
England at the beginning of this period they were the barons
who composed the House of Lords. Below them was the
advancing class of the knights of the shire, not great landowners, but mainly tenants-in-chief of the Crown, forming
the bulk of the Commons. The ranks of nobility were
thereafter continuously reinforced from families successful in
trade, and the advisers and lieutenants of the Crown were
drawn almost entirely from them. In Rome, throughout
the days of the republic, similar social distinctions were
conspicuous. For the Lords substitute the Senate. The
older patrician aristocracy, as it died out, was supplemented
from plebeian families who had attained to curule office.
From these ranks alone it was the practice to fill the Senate,
and they formed a ruling caste. A second ruling class grew
up below it, that of the knights—the equestrian order—formed
by those who possessed a property qualification of 400,000
sesterces (some £10,000 in the money of A.D. 1950), having
as a rule obtained their wealth in trade. Under the Empire
these orders became sub-divided and their constitution more
rigid, and admission was controlled by the Emperors. There
was, in addition, a property qualification of a million *sesterces*
(about £25,000) for entry to the senatorial order; and in the
towns of Italy society was organized mainly on a basis of

wealth. But, in addition to this practical monopoly of office in the State there remained a vast social influence. In Rome the relationship of homage between patron and client continued. Almost everyone paid this respect to someone else above him. In return, the patron was obliged to assist his client, and advise him upon his legal difficulties. The client paid a daily call on his patron, and if in need collected a gift of food or money, and by the end of the first century A.D. this " *sportula* " was fairly fixed at a rate of 6¼ *sesterces* (three and sixpence) per day. In Rome, below the senatorial and equestrian orders and above the freedmen and slaves was the *plebs urbana*, the common people of the city. At the end of the period, between one-third and one-half of the population is estimated to have been supported out of public charity, and fewer than 150,000 heads of Roman families to have been self-maintained. It continued to be considered one of the main functions of government to provide largess to its subjects, and the emperors appreciated the necessity of keeping the populace contented with bread and distracted by exciting entertainment. There were a few thousand millionaires, and the bulk of what we would now call the middle class vegetated in semi-starvation.[1]

The proportion of the population which finds its sustenance on the land slowly diminishes, and the proportion of traders and craftsmen gradually expands. Trades and crafts in England and Rome are organized in their gilds and corporations, each with their patron saints or gods, making rules for the control of their members and the furtherance of their professional interests.

By the end of our period the clan or *gens* has ceased to be of practical or functional significance. Throughout the period the system of inheritance is moving towards the succession of the nearest relatives by blood, whether the relationship is traced through males or females, and of wife or husband. The family has become, as it were, ambidextrous, the right hand being the paternal. The bride-price has disappeared, and only the marriage-portion or marriage-settlement remains. In England the *patria potestas*, the father's power over

---

[1] Carcopino, pp. 65–6.

the persons and property of his children, had never been carried to the extremes of Roman principle. At the close of our period they had largely disappeared in Roman law or practice. Gone was the power of life and death over the children, and in A.D. 200 the father could not even lawfully expose his new-born infant on one of the public refuse-dumps of the city. The wife, too, had ceased in practice to be under the " *manus* " or " power " of the husband. In England he continued to become owner on marriage of his wife's chattels, though means could now be taken to avoid this result.

Yet in spite of all these changes it is worth noticing to what extent in England the law of A.D. 1300 is still in force.

In A.D. 1300 the father of the family was the person to sue in the courts in respect of a wrong to any member of his mainpast or household (Roman " *familia* "). In 1950 he can still sue for any tort committed against himself or his wife or servant, or his daughter who is living with him. He cannot sue for a wrong to his son, for in 1300 a son early left his father's household. Anything the father recovers in any such action belongs to him. He cannot sue for a breach of contract committed against his wife, servant, or daughter, for in 1300 no action for a mere breach of contract could yet be brought in the king's court. Before 1846[1] he could not sue for damages for an act causing the death of a wife or daughter, because by 1300 the sanction for homicide had ceased to be pecuniary and become capital.[2] For the same reason, he is still unable to sue for damages in respect of the death of a servant, though he can still sue for injury to him. In 1300, if a man's daughter, living in his household, was seduced, even with her consent, and became pregnant, he had a claim for compensation against her seducer, and still has, and the amount of the compensation does not now, any more than it did then, depend on what he has lost. If, on the other hand, someone committed adultery with his wife, this was in 1300 a criminal offence, and the ecclesiastical court was the appropriate tribunal, and the position so remained until after the middle of the nineteenth century. The husband still brought

---

[1] The Fatal Accidents Act, 1846.
[2] See Admiralty Commissioners *v.* S.S. *Amerika* [1917] A.C. 38.

an action in the ecclesiastical court claiming damages for
" criminal conversation," and does so now in the Divorce
Court, whether he also petitions for a divorce or not.   But
if in 1300 he came upon his wife and the adulterer *in flagranti
delicto* and killed them both out of hand, it would not have
been murder then, nor was it till the other day.   On the other
hand, if his daughter was raped, that was in 1300 a crime
cognizable in the king's court, not the ecclesiastical court.   It
was a heinous deed, a " felony," punishable with castration
or blindness and confiscation of his property to the king, after
which it would be idle to sue him for damages.   At the present
day an action for damages would be equally rare, and though
the accused is no longer castrated or blinded, but placed for a
while in a public building and maintained at the public
expense, and since 1870 there has been no confiscation of
property for felony, yet if an action for damages were brought
before the accused were prosecuted, it could be stayed by the
court.   What applies to rape applies to theft.   Theft was
already capital in 1300 if the goods were over twelve pence
in value.   And if a man intentionally killed a burglar in
the act in 1300—or till the other day—he would commit no
offence.

The general structure of the criminal law has also remained
much the same.   There are still three types of criminal offences
triable before a jury in England.   First there is treason—
the offence that had become criminal long before the days of
the Late Codes—and this continued to be tried under a procedure containing archaic features of its own; and it was only
by section 31 of the Forfeiture Act, 1870, that it was provided
that the sentence need no longer include the drawing of the
condemned man on a hurdle to the place of execution, and
after execution the severing of the head from the body, and
the dividing of the body into four quarters.   Secondly, there
are the " felonies "—the heinous wrongs, formerly civil, that
became criminal and triable by the King's Court in or about
the thirteenth century—chiefly murder, felonious wounding,
rape and theft, burglary and housebreaking.   These are still
tried under a separate criminal procedure of their own.   The
list has been much swollen by numerous Acts of Parliament

creating new " felonies," but their nature remained the same.
Lastly, there are all the other crimes, mere " misdemeanours "
or " bad behaviour," mainly civil wrongs that became crimes
after 1300, and they are tried under a procedure much the
same as the trial of a civil action with a jury.

Then, in regard to the law of property, until 1870 a married
woman had no capacity to own property (though to some
extent by certain technical means this result could be avoided),
and until 1935 her husband was liable for all her debts and for
all civil wrongs committed by her.   Questions of the inheritance of goods were until the middle of the nineteenth century
still tried by ecclesiastical courts, and they had still exclusive
jurisdiction on all questions relating to marriage.

Why, then, do old rules of law of the age of the Late Codes
survive in England and Rome?

The law has by the time of the Late Codes become so large
a body of rules that, like other bodies, it has begun to possess a
life of its own.   It is administered by professional judges and
a profession of lawyers.   Its practice has become something
of an art.   It has its technicalities like other arts—aspects that
a layman cannot always expect to appreciate.   Moreover,
there are so many rules of law that they have no reason, and
cannot be understood or remembered by judge or practitioner,
unless a principle can be drawn from a group of rules, which
gives sense to the whole.   The developed human mind is
for ever looking for explanations, and seeking principles that
explain and relate facts.   So, too, with law.   By a process of
analysis and synthesis, principles are continually derived from
a growing mass of facts.   These principles connect with one
another, and it becomes difficult to change the law on any
topic without affecting the rest.   It is not thought wise or just
or practicable to alter it, and it is for the most part left to
develop of itself.   But as the tempo of social change quickens,
law for the first time seems to lag behind.   As it becomes more
technical, a law of procedure also forms, and becomes similarly
unyielding to change, but not as early as the substantive law.
Procedure has a history of its own, and its changes reflect
developments in the structure of society.   As we look back
we obtain an impression—partly illusory—that it is by pro-

cedure that the law has been altered. Let us take one or two illustrations from England and Rome.

We saw among several nations of the Late Codes (including early Rome) that the jurisdiction of the king or paramount chief was extended by means of the action by curse, till it bade fair to become the chief method of bringing an action, and mere civil disputes were turned into a criminal offence— the offence of cursing the king—which he could try. In England, before the close of the period of the Late Codes, a similar process begins. We noted in England as early as the end of the age of the Central Codes that *hamsocne* or hamfare (the armed attack on a man's house and land) was a criminal offence, a plea of the Crown. Then in the middle of the thirteenth century the king is issuing a writ of trespass " *quod vi et armis clausum fregit* "—"for breaking into a man's close with force and arms " against the king's peace. It is, as before, a criminal offence, and the convicted defendant is outlawed or imprisoned until he makes fine with the king. But he is also condemned to pay to the complainant damages, including the value of any goods of the complainant which he carried away. The law has not altered : it is merely an improvement in the machinery or procedure by which justice will be done, and the relief which will be granted. Damages—the payment of whatever a man has lost, as distinct from payment of a fixed tariff-sum for all cases—are a recent innovation, found in the Late Codes in various places.[1] There was a further improvement in that the claim was heard under the new procedure of trial with a jury, and the defendant was not to be allowed to challenge to battle, any more than he was to be allowed to invade an Englishman's home by force of arms. Along with the growth in the authority of the Crown and the spread of its jurisdiction, spread the scope of the writ. After all, any use of force may be called " force and arms." That is a matter for the king's judges, and they were not taking a narrow view of the jurisdiction of their court. Little by little it ceased to matter whether the writ contained the words " *vi et armis* " or not, and you could issue the writ in a case where

[1] See, for example, Eshnunna, 5; and, in Rome, *Institutes*, Bk. IV, Tit. IV, 7.

your goods were carried away or you were assaulted, whether you alleged that your land was broken into or not. It would not be correct to say merely that the widening use of the writ extended the authority of the king or his court. It would be right to add that an advancing public opinion or public conscience made a mere violent assault or a violent removal of the complainant's goods a criminal offence, and at the same time supported an extension of the civil jurisdiction of the king's court at the expense of local courts. We have seen that in the Late Codes the civil and the criminal law came close to one another. Hence arose the civil wrong of trespass to land, goods, or person, triable by the Crown.[1] Meanwhile in 1285, as procedure in its turn tended to become fixed and unchangeable, the Statute of Westminster the Second provided that writs were to be issued by the clerks of the chancery— that is to say, of the State secretariat—in " similar cases," i.e., analogous cases, to the old when occasion arose. What this was intended to mean is not so clear, but the result was that there were added to " trespass," during the succeeding centuries, such wrongs as we would now call nuisance and deceit and malicious prosecution and detention. The action of " case " (i.e., " similar case ") was even extended to circumstances where no positive wrongful act had been done by the defendant but he had merely failed to do something that he had undertaken (" *assumpsit super se* "), and in this way by the middle of the sixteenth century the king's courts came to be trying breaches of simple contracts. Looking back, it almost seems that the law was growing, in Maine's famous phrase, " in the interstices of procedure." But the substantive law had changed because the economic circumstances had altered. In the period of the Late Codes, as we saw, no one was considered commercially bound by a sale unless he had received some share of the bargain. Sale was still a cash sale, and in Rome and England, at the end of the period of the Late Codes, it gave rise to the idea of a con-

[1] In Rome, too, the same period is that of the development of the action of trespass (the Actio Legis Aquiliæ). This, too, was probably criminal, as well as civil, in origin, and the development was in many respects alike in Rome and England.

veyance, a formal act which transfers the property in a thing; and the procedure of a cash sale [1] came to be used as the form of a conveyance. By the sixteenth century the commercial and legal notion had grown up that an oral agreement to buy and sell, to hire or to do other things was binding, even if there had as yet been no fulfilment on either side, and in Rome it is likely that the same position was reached at about the end of the republic. Probably accelerating rises in prices brought about that result. If a man broke his contract to sell you goods, you might have to pay more elsewhere in a rising market, and thereby suffer damage. In England in the course of the sixteenth century the price of most staple commodities and foods increased six-fold. But neither in England nor in Rome did the law ever reach the stage at which every plain, formless, oral agreement was binding. In England there had to be " consideration."

However, it is true to say that in the period with which we are dealing there is a concentration upon procedure both in Rome and England. The way a question of law presents itself is, whether such and such a writ or action is competent to you in such and such circumstances. The syntheses are not yet large. In England we are dealing with " forms of action," and so, too, we are in Rome under the " formulary procedure."

In this period there never arose an action for negligence, either in Rome or England. If a man did damage to the property or person of another, he was liable, unless he did so by inevitable accident, and so he was liable if he did so negligently. But no one could be sued merely because he failed to take some action which he would have taken if he had been a careful person.

Arising out of the same circumstances was a curiously similar and fundamental development at the same relative point of time in England and Rome. After the Late Codes no one could alter the law in Rome or England except by statute, but within a few years afterwards the Praetor (the Roman Minister of Justice) from about the middle of the

---

[1] In Rome the oral *mancipium* or weighing out of the bronze price before witnesses; in England the sealed deed.

second century B.C., and the Chancellor (the head of the chancery and the King's chief legal adviser) during the fourteenth century A.D., began to grant new remedies in certain defined circumstances. They could not alter the law, but they received a great many petitions asking for justice, and often in cases for which the law made no provision. At first the Chancellor and the Praetor made some procedural improvements by which relief could be given to meet the particular case and assist the working of the law, but little by little they were building up a body of rules which supplemented the law, and even in fact superseded it, for they could by the remedies which they granted make the law useless to the litigant. In this way grew up a separate system of rules, Equity in England and the Praetorian Law in Rome. They dealt largely with different problems: in England the chief doctrine of Equity was the trust, which played a smaller part in the Praetorian rules. But there was this in common between them, that they constituted systems which, while they in effect supplemented and widened and modernized the law and removed many of its shortcomings, remained separate from it. By the middle of the sixteenth century in England and the middle of the corresponding first century A.D. in Rome, these systems, too, became rigid and stereotyped.

The prevalent conceptions of the nature of law differed little in Rome and England in these centuries. At their close there is another curious, parallel development in both countries. The Greeks of earlier days had devoted thought to a philosophy of law, and had long before achieved a notion of "natural law," that idea of law which is the abstract and perfect original to which its mundane embodiment corresponds. They saw in legal systems features common to the laws of the peoples of the world, and these, being universal, seemed of a greater truth, and mirrored the law of nature: the others, characteristic of each several system, were but fortuitous and arbitrary. Cicero, who played no little part in bringing Greek philosophy to Rome, wrote, too, of natural law, but it is doubtful if the conception made much impression on the Roman mind till the end of these centuries, the years about A.D. 200. It is strange then to see such doctrine set out in the works of great lawyers of that date, such as Ulpian and Gaius, and even stranger to see it in the forefront of students' text-books. Gaius, in more sober language, begins by observing that " the law that each people has laid down for itself is peculiar to it and is called its civil law . . . whereas whatever natural reason has laid down among all men is observed by all peoples alike, and is called the law of the nations, as being used by all nations." Ulpian goes further : natural law is what nature has taught all animals; hence, for example, the union of male and female, which we call marriage. This is before the days of science : but he is speaking of the " laws " of nature, in much the sense of Newton's " laws " of motion, as well as of the law of nature as the Greeks spoke of it. By the law of nature, he says, all men were born free; and slavery was only introduced by the law of the nations.[1]

. This notion of the law of nature, or of the nations, was familiar also to many scholars in the Middle Ages, but it is only in the period corresponding to the age of Ulpian and Gaius,—namely, about the year 1700—that it became common and meaningful. It played a large part in forming Grotius' conception of a new " law of nations," and in the phrases of Locke and Rousseau and others, helped to set alight and to terrify the Western world. " All men are by nature equally free and independent, and have certain inherent rights of which, when they enter into a state of society, they cannot by any compact deprive or divest their posterity." [2] " We hold these truths to be self-evident, that all men are created equal, that they are endowed by their Creator with certain unalienable Rights, and that among these are Life, Liberty, and the pursuit of Happiness." [3] " Men are born, and continue to be, free and equal as of right. Social distinctions can only be founded on the public benefit. The aim of all political association is the preservation of the natural and imprescriptible rights of man." [4]

[1] See Aristotle, Politics I ii, 3.

[2] Virginian Declaration of Rights, June 12, 1776.

[3] From the Declaration of Independence of the United States of America, July 4, 1776.

[4] From the Déclaration des Droits de L'Homme et du Citoyen (1789), and the French Constitution of 1791.

CHAPTER II

SINCE 1700

HUMANITY does not progress at an even, or evenly increasing pace. It seems to us, looking back with the scattered information at our disposal, that it has always progressed by fits and starts. There have been times and places when men seemed to be imbued with a power and freshness of mind and an enthusiasm more than human, and a capacity to do greatly whatever they put their hand to. We think of Athens in the fifth century B.C., when so large a company of the men of genius of all time lived within those narrow walls; or of Florence in and about the fifteenth century A.D., when it was taken to be natural that a man who had enjoyed the education of a gentleman was a painter and a sculptor as good as men can be, and possibly a goldsmith to boot, and perhaps a writer, with a few scientific inventions to his credit—when Michelangelo painted the ceiling of the Sistine Chapel reluctantly, protesting that he was a sculptor. We think perhaps of the majesty of Rome at the close of the republic, in the days of Julius and Augustus Cæsar and Virgil and Horace and Cicero; and even of little England in the age of Elizabeth, holding her own against the empire of the Spaniard and putting forth great poetry and drama on every hand. It is hard to see any relevance in the fact that these were (by the measures of this book) identical dates in the economic time scale.[1] It is idle to seek for explanations of such things. With our present knowledge, these are the miracles that distinguish man from his surroundings.

In England we compare this blaze of life with the dull, slow centuries that preceded and followed. How little the centuries from 1300 to 1700 had to show! The population of the country had nearly doubled between 1100 and 1300, and, making all allowance for plague in the fourteenth century, it is strange that it did not even double again in the four centuries that

---

[1] Two hundred years after the close of the age of the Late Codes.

followed.   Those two centuries from 1100 to 1300 had shown
so impressive a political advance in England under its able
royal administrators, when the common law was being built!
In Rome, too, how great had been the progress in the years
from 350 to 200 B.C., when she was transformed from a small
city-state, fighting desperately for existence against the Gauls,
to a great world-Power, and the Roman law was created.
And how great had been the advance among all the other
peoples whom we mentioned, in that same stage of the Late
Codes.   Yet, with the exception of that flowering of the
intellect in the Elizabethan age, those four centuries in England
were slow and disappointing, as they were indeed in Rome.

In Rome from A.D. 200 there set in an unbroken economic
recession and final disintegration, and an equal retrogression
in the world of the mind.   A city in which almost a third of
the population were slaves, and almost another half of the
population partially dependent on public largess, and where
the bounds of the ruling class were narrow and finite except
for freed slaves of emperors and nobles, and its members
became ever richer by their monopoly of public offices and
appointments, while the bulk of the middle class lived on the
verge of starvation—such a city could flourish only while
free slave labour and booty continued to come in vast quantity
from victory in foreign war, or at least a new economic system
extorted a vastly increased income from the soil or foreign
trade.   None of these things occurred, and inevitably in the
succeeding centuries, attempting to maintain her predominance
in face of a falling income, Rome tightly controlled the bodies
and minds of her subjects while her strength diminished.   In
the end, long before Britain was abandoned, the roads in the
outlying provinces were left to decay, and the sites of towns
were deserted.

In A.D. 1700 England still presented to the eye many of the
features she had shown in 1300.   She was still overwhelmingly an agricultural country, and at least three-fifths of the
population still earned their subsistence upon the land.   Hedges
were hardly to be seen except in Kent and Devon.   Villages
in the eastern corn-growing areas still had their great open
fields, almost a square mile in area, and divided into innumer-

able strips, of which a man might hold a scattered number, cultivating them according to the immemorial custom of the particular village community. The three-course cultivation was still general—usually wheat, rye, or mixed grain for winter corn; spring corn, barley, or oats; and fallow. Potatoes were hardly grown, and no roots. Beyond the fields was the waste land where the cottager fed his animals and took his fuel. England would still be exporting corn in the second half of the eighteenth century. Not long before 1700 Pepys had been complaining of the annual excess of her varied exports over imports, and wondering how long this drain upon the country's resources could continue. The chief density of population was still in the south. There was still a variety of classes in the village, and it was still in large measure self-sufficient both in its food and goods. Its craftsmen and its womenfolk supplied the bulk of its manufacturing needs. The roads between towns and villages were not usable for half the year except by pack-horse and pillion. There were no canals. In the towns there was no separation between a class of employers and a class of employed. The master employed a journeyman or two and had an apprentice about his house, all coming from the same social stratum and trained in the same school of apprenticeship. Scotland and Wales lagged far behind.

Society was still in a sense feudal. The Parliamentary representation had not altered since the Middle Ages, and would not be changed till 1832. Landlords nominated to a large extent the representatives of the boroughs, and a few of the county members. The towns were misgoverned under charters by narrow cliques. In rural England the landed gentry were the worthy justices of the peace, who constituted all that there was of local government. The clergy were of the same class, and prominent on the benches. There were no stipendiary magistrates anywhere.

Yet the world as a whole has always been moving forward along the same path at an increasing pace. It required the lapse of a million years of human history to reach civilization, and in the time-scale of humanity this was only the other day. Even from A.D. 1300 to 1700 there was steady advance.

For while the tired waves, vainly breaking
   Seem here no painful inch to gain,
Far back, through creeks and inlets making,
   Comes silent, flooding in, the main.

The old wasteful agricultural system could not maintain a denser population, but enclosures of various kinds, sometimes by local agreement, had been proceeding in small but increasing measure for several centuries. Ever since the invention of printing, improvements had been made in industrial technique. The spinning-wheel began to take the place of the distaff before the sixteenth century. Some inventions, such as the gigmill, were prohibited from use for fear they might put men out of work, and some were adopted contrary to law. The use of water-power for various processes, the use of coal in place of wood, steadily increased. There were other signs of progress! In the course of the sixteenth century the cost of living increased sixfold, and wages on the land only doubled. Making all allowances for growing cottage industries, it was a hard time for the poor. Elizabethan glory did not mean carnal comfort for them. And how subservient they were, on the whole! And how the Elizabethan legislation directed them and their labour! The country was not going to suffer again the inconvenience caused by the shortage of workmen in the previous century, when so many died of plague. It is true that statute provided for the assessment of wage-rates by the justices in accordance with the cost of living, but there were very few assessments as the cost mounted. By 1700 the folk in the villages who held no land except their gardens numbered some three-fifths of the local populace. By 1750, owing to a growing population and a static system of government by one class, there was a great, degenerate, drunken mob in the towns, whose reclamation an idle Church was content to leave to Wesley, and there was a growing landless community in the villages.

The main function of the law was generally acknowledged to be the protection of existing property rights, and at the first signs of disorder it hastened to come to the rescue of the landed gentry in whom lay the political sovereignty. At the beginning of the eighteenth century the law provided capital punishment for treason, murder, rape, arson of a dwelling-house, and a few other serious offences, some fifty in all. Thirty-three were added in the reign of George II, and by 1800 there were on the statute-book a total of some 200 or more Acts imposing the death sentence for an even larger number of offences. Every year many thousands of persons were arrested for debt and put under the charge of gaolers, to whom the prisons were farmed out to get what profit they could. Where food was allowed out of public funds it was little and atrocious. Yet to Blackstone and the bulk of his contemporaries in that static and classical age the law was the embodiment and perfection of reason and justice. Certainly criminal trials were fairer to the accused than anywhere abroad. The civil law was substantially unchanged by legislation, and, left to itself, developed slowly, gathering about it more and more technicalities, as law is apt to do at a static period. It was then, for example, that the English law of evidence grew up with its strange technical rules excluding hearsay evidence, save for defined exceptions. The refusals of individual judges to listen to evidence of what someone else had said became, by force of precedent, a rule that such evidence could not be given—a typical example of confusion of mind between what is expedient in a particular case and what the law demands or forbids.

And then in the middle of the eighteenth century the wheels began to turn quicker and quicker. Enclosure Acts came rapidly into the statute-book. Enclosure of waste and common, together with the growing of roots to keep cattle alive during the winter, and all the other improvements in agriculture that were being made by Coke and others, would get vastly more from the land, and give permanent employment on it to the man who lost his rights over the waste and common. The rural population became labourers. The justices of the peace largely abandoned the task, imposed by statute, of fixing wages in accordance with prices, and put the farm-hands on the rates as paupers. There was little in the way of proceedings to enforce payment of such rates of wages as were assessed, and wage rates were at the mercy of the landowners, who included the justices. Inventions came thick and fast. Yeomen and journeymen borrowed money and acquired workshops or mills, and the rural industries diminished and the movement to the towns grew fast. Yet, in spite of all, the nascent industries built up the strength that enabled England to defeat Napoleon. It was supporting a population increasing at a rate never known before. The population had doubled in the 250 years from 1500 to 1750. It doubled again between 1750 and 1821.[1] But the example of the French Revolution merely increased the anxiety of the ruling class for its possessions and privileges. And now, early in the nineteenth century, there began to form, in addition to the landed class, the two classes of employer and employed.

It was becoming an age—as it has been since in North America—which presented an almost unlimited vista of possible advancement and wealth for a young man of industry and enterprise, and it offered a similar vista to the nation which was leading the world in the industrial revolution. It was in the interests of an enterprising nation and citizen that restrictions in trade, internal and external, should be removed, and that meant free trade and a doctrine of *laissez-faire* and individualism. The clauses of Elizabethan legislation for the assessment of wages were repealed, and even Pitt's laws forbidding combinations of workmen. Industry had moved from cottage and workshop to powered factories at which hundreds of hands were assembled, thereby giving occasion for the association of workers in pursuance of their common interests. But it was long before trade unions could play an effective part in improving the conditions of working men, women, and children. In the 1830's their condition was too low, and their position too weak. Workmen were still on occasion being transported in their hundreds to the colonies for riot. The contest for power was between a privileged class of landlords and the middle class, and it was not till 1867, from the hands of Disraeli, that the whole of the middle class, together with the workers in the towns, received the franchise. The early improvement of the conditions of workers was effected not by the workers but by that growth of the social conscience which we have watched from the beginning of our story, and which,

[1] And again between 1821 and 1876.

in spite of apparent set-backs, has continued always to develop where self-interest does not cloud it. It was effected by such men as Owen and Disraeli and Shaftesbury with the support of the country gentlemen that formed the bulk of Parliament. It was the combined working of the principle of freedom from governmental interference and a growing and anxious care for the welfare of the worker who fell behind in the struggle for existence, that moulded England from 1868 to 1914. It was an age that coincided with England's leadership of the world, and an age of many-sided greatness in that country and its citizens. Indeed, the whole century from 1815 to 1914 was a period of remarkable and almost unbroken peace. The cry of " peace, retrenchment, and reform " served the country well, and from 1868 flowed a widening stream of well-considered legislation.

The passing of the Reform Bill of 1884 signified the transfer of political sovereignty in the State into the hands of all its citizens, of whom the vast bulk belonged to the working class. It was long before the results appeared. In the meantime the growing organization of the trade unions won some well-deserved and well-needed victories, but it was inevitable that when universal suffrage had had its full effect the days of the trade unions as a fighting force would be over. Their function would only remain as representative bodies who could be consulted as such by governments, and express to them the conditions and opinions of the industry, and could influence the legislation of the country either in that way or by their representative officers in Parliament. The sovereignty of the working class and the care for the underdog worked both to one end, a temporary struggle between that class and the rest for the transfer of the assets of the latter to the State, their elimination as a class, and the substitution of the State for them as employers.

Yet in these varying incidents of the past 250 years we can clearly see a continuation of the course of material progress and civilization that we have watched from the beginning of this book. We have watched a process of advance, at ever-increasing speed, in man's control of his environment, until it seems that all that remains unknown is the secret of exploding this planet. We have seen an ever-quickening tempo of change in the structure of society and in the law. With it comes an increasing adaptability of mankind to his altering environment, so that change is of the breath of his life. At the beginning of our story the Food-Gatherers were always unable to adapt themselves to the coming of the European and succumbed to the changes brought by him, sometimes before he had reached their vicinity. The Tasmanians, removed to a neighbouring island, clustered on the high ground gazing longingly at the familiar peaks of their home, and pined away. In the stage of the Late Codes we find today a rapidly increasing population in West Africa, and in South America it is chiefly in the Central Andes that the Indian population has grown.

There is a swiftly increasing population and density of population. The English figures are familiar. The population of the world, with its peoples of every stage of culture, has grown between A.D. 1900 and 1950 from about 1,200 millions to 2,000 millions ; and with its consequent rise in standard of living, its consumption of the world's food has probably multiplied fourfold, and its consumption of meat much more. States and empires have continued to increase in number and size, until the world consists chiefly of a few giants, each with populations between 150 millions and 500 millions. Only 5,000 years ago the population of the world was insignificant. The fields of uniform culture become larger and larger. Those who speak English as their mother-tongue total some 225 millions; and those who speak one of the languages formed from widening dialects of the Old Indo-European tongue (apart from many enclaves in Eastern Europe and Russia) stretch from Ireland to Vladivostok, and cover Australia and the bulk of North and South America and large parts of Africa and Southern Asia. There is an increasing strength of the central governing authority, as well in the United States as everywhere else. The State every year owns, manages, and directs a greater proportion of each growing country's assets, and owns vast powers to direct the life of the citizen. In this country it has already power to direct labour in peace time, and, generally speaking, strikes are illegal. It seems inevitable that before long it will be a common thing for the State to be empowered by means of the criminal law to punish idleness. Industrial organizations have grown to vast proportions and power, and the legislature of many countries in the Old World and the New puts curbs upon their freedom. The flow of legislation grows greater and greater, and such is its volume that it is necessarily enacted by ministers or their subordinates in accordance with principles laid down by representative assemblies. The volume of the criminal law, by which the State works its will, expands every day at an increasing rate. At the end of the Late Codes it embraced the main offences against order—first murder, and then adultery, rape, and theft, all of which were generally capital. Adultery has ceased to be an offence, and even murder is ceasing to be capital, and the number of inmates of prisons grows apace. But the total of criminal offences is now vast. It includes breaches of an unlimited number of ordinances and regulations. It includes even a great variety of acts of negligence, such as, in England, driving a motor-car without consideration for other persons using the road. Many of these offences are committed irrespective of any intention to do wrong. The criminal law tends to become the chief engine of good order in the State, as the State becomes the owner of more and more of the assets of the country. By the end of the period of the Late Codes justice had begun to be administered by professional judges and professional advocates and lawyers. It is now by slow degrees being taken out of their hands and administered by tribunals consisting (in England today) of an experienced chairman and two lay assessors, sitting in private, all appointed by a Minister, applying regulations made by him, and liable to dismissal by him without showing cause. Generally speaking, professional lawyers have no right of audience before these tribunals. The State gains a growing control over civil litigation, for it pays the fees of the advocate in State systems of legal aid.

The civil law has taken a path of which we have seen the beginnings. The increasing size and complexity of the life of the State and the increasing variety of the sets of facts that come before the tribunal, have produced ever wider and more general syntheses and legal conceptions. During the last fifty years we have seen three of them looming ever larger in the field of law and litigation. One is the contract—an agreement made by offer and acceptance. Whenever possible, any relation between the two parties is reduced to the terms of an implied contract between them, and the issue is, what have they impliedly agreed, and has the implied agreement been broken? The second conception is that of the trust: in a vast and growing number of cases a person is held to be a trustee of property for another on certain terms, and the issue is whether he has broken them. The third great conception is that of negligence or breach of duty. In the majority of cases covering the field of tort—that is to say, civil injury—the question of law is whether the one party was under a duty to the other, and what were the terms of that duty, and has he broken it? The civil law has, therefore, become simpler so far as law can be simple, in that it embodies wider and more general conceptions, and this is true of law in all civilized countries generally. Procedure is less important and is simplified as far as may be, and in England the technicalities of the law of evidence are fading away. With the growing modern interest in the mind and its processes, more and more questions are decided in accordance with the intentions of the parties.

Lastly, we observe a continuing increase in the scale of warfare. Even in the age of the Central Codes the more effective weapons of war were so costly that it was only the ruling class in the feudal State that could provide them. For centuries now only the State has had the means to do so, and finally the position is now reached when only one or two of the world's wealthiest States can provide them. The combatants in war are now the bulk of the world, and the whole of the energy of the State is bent upon it, and a growing proportion of its energy in times of peace. In the Late Codes, apart from the economic aims of war—for there is a growing pressure on the world's resources—there was the aim to spread the true religion. The influence of religion and the power of the Churches has much diminished. In its place grows a system of ethics in which duty to the State looms largest, and it seems likely that in the future whatever wars may be fought will be conducted between mighty groups of States fighting under democratic slogans to protect their economic interests or extend them.

Yet it is a thousand years and more since Wessex fought against Mercia, and within the boundaries of these vast and growing States internecine strife is rare. The birth-places of war grow, therefore, fewer. There is also, over the whole world, a general advance in knowledge and intelligence. While, therefore, the world seems likely to continue for long a dangerous place to inhabit, there is reason to hope for better things.

LIST OF ABBREVIATED REFERENCES

A.C. Code of Assyrian Laws relating to Women (Tablet A of Middle Assyrian Laws, in *The Assyrian Laws*, by G. R. Driver and Sir John Miles, 1935).

Aeth. The Laws of Æthelberht, in Attenborough, pp. 5 f.

Alabaster. E. Alabaster, *Notes and Commentaries on Chinese Criminal Law and Cognate Topics* (London, Luzac & Co., 1899).

A.P.S. *African Political Systems*, edited by M. Fortes and E. E. Evans-Pritchard (1940).

Arthasastra. *The Arthasastra of Kautilya* (trans. R. Shama Sastri, 1908-10).

Attenborough. F. L. Attenborough, *The Laws of the Earliest English Kings* (1922).

B.A.E.R. Bureau of American Ethnology, Annual Reports.

Bennett. W. C. Bennett, "The Andean Highlands: An Introduction," in *H.S.A.*, vol. ii, pp. 1-60.

Bird. J. Bird, "The Alacaluf," in *H.S.A.*, vol. i, pp. 55 f.

Cape Commission. *Cape Native Laws Commission, Cape of Good Hope Votes and Proceedings of Parliament*, Special Session (1883), Evidence.

C.H. *The Code of Hammurabi.*

C.H.I. *Cambridge History of India.*

Clapham. Sir John Clapham, *A Concise Economic History of Britain to 1750* (1949).

Cooper, "The Chono." J. M. Cooper, "The Chono," in *H.S.A.*, vol. i, pp. 47 f.

Cooper, "The Ona." J. M. Cooper, "The Ona," in *H.S.A.*, vol. i, pp. 107 f.

Cooper, "The Yahgan." J. M. Cooper, "The Yahgan," in *H.S.A.*, vol. i, pp. 81 f.

Crime and Custom. B. Malinowski, *Crime and Custom in Savage Society* (1926).

Curr, E. M. E. M. Curr, *The Australian Race*, 4 vols. (Melbourne, 1886-7).

Danquah. J. B. Danquah, *Akan Laws and Customs* (1928).

Davies. "On the Aborigines of Van Diemen's Land" (*Tasmanian Journ. Science*, vol. ii, p. 419).

Doke. C. M. Doke, *The Lambas of Northern Rhodesia* (1931).

Driberg. J. H. Driberg, *The Lango* (1923).

Durham. M. E. Durham, *Some Tribal Origins, Laws, and Customs of the Balkans* (1928).

E. & G. The Laws of Edward and Guthrum, in Attenborough, pp. 102 f.

331

E.A.L.   *East Africa Protectorate Law Reports*, Notes on East African Native Laws and Customs, vol. i, 1906, pp. 97–111; vol. ii, 1909, pp. 141–8; vol. iii, 1911, pp. 117–21.

Edictum Theoderici, in *M.G.H.*, Legum, Tom. 5.

Eshnunna.   Code of Eshnunna, found at Tell Harmal, published and translated by A. Goetze in *Sumer*, vol. iv, No. ii, pp. 63 f. (Sept. 1948).

Evans-Pritchard.   Prof. E. E. Evans-Pritchard, *The Nuer* (1940).

Fei, H. T.   Hsiao-Tung Fei, *Peasant Life in China* (Routledge, 1939).

Gaius.   *The Institutes of Gaius*, translated by J. Muirhead (1904).

Garcilasso.   Garcilasso de la Vega, The Royal Commentaries of the Incas, translated by Rycaut (1688), and by Markham (1869–71).

Germania.   Tacitus' *De Germania*.

Gold Coast Commission.   Report of the Gold Coast Commission on Native Courts, *Government Gazette*, Jan. 31, 1895, pp. 27–34.

H. & E.   The Laws of Hlothhere and Eadric, in Attenborough, pp. 18–23.

H.C.   The Hittite Code, translated into English by Walther, in *The Origin and History of Hebrew Law*, by J. M. P. Smith (Univ. of Chicago Press, 1931, App. IV).

Hobhouse.   Hobhouse, Wheeler, and Ginsberg, *The Material Culture and Social Institutions of the Simpler Peoples* (1930).

Hobley.   C. W. Hobley, *Ethnology of A-Kamba and other African Tribes* (1910).

H.S.A.   *Handbook of South American Indians* (Bureau of American Ethnology, Bulletin No. 143, vols. i–v, 1946–9).

Ine.   The Laws of Ine, in Attenborough, pp. 34 f.

Joyce.   T. A. Joyce, *Mexican Archæology* (1914).

Kirchhoff.   " Food-Gathering Tribes of the Venezuelan Llanos," in *H.S.A.*, vol. iv, pp. 445 f.

Krzywicki.   L. Krzywicki, *Primitive Society and its Vital Statistics* (1934).

Kuczynski.   R. R. Kuczynski, *Demographic Survey of the British Colonial Empire*, vol. ii (1949).

Les Bangala.   Van Overbergh and De Jonge, *Les Bangala* (Brussels, 1904).

Les Mandja.   F. Gaud, *Les Mandja* (Brussels, 1911).

Les Mangbetu.   Van Overbergh and De Jonge, *Les Mangbetu* (Brussels, 1909).

Les Mayombe.   Van Overbergh, *Les Mayombe* (Brussels, 1907).

Les Warega.   Delhaise, *Les Warega* (Brussels, 1909).

Lex Baiuvariorum, in *M.G.H.*, Legum, Tom. 3.

Lex Burg.   Lex Burgundionium, in *M.G.H.*, Legum, Tom. 3.

Lex Fris.   Lex Frisionium, in *M.G.H.*, Legum, Tom. 3.

Lex Rip.   Lex Ripuariorum, in *M.G.H.*, Legum, Tom. 5.

Lindblom.   G. Lindblom, *The Akamba* (Uppsala, 1920).

Lipit Ishtar. Code of Laws of Lipit Ishtar, King of Isin, in *American Journal of Archæology*, vol. li (1947), pp. 158–64; vol. lii (1948), pp. 426 f.

Lipkind. W. Lipkind, " The Caraja," in *H.S.A.*, vol. iii, p. 179.

Mair. L. P. Mair, *An African People in the Twentieth Century* (1934).

Man. E. H. Man, *The Aboriginal Inhabitants of the Andaman Islands*; ed. by A. F. Man (1932).

Meek, *Ibo*. C. K. Meek, *Law and Authority in a Nigerian Tribe* (1937).

Meek, *N. Nig*. C. K. Meek, *The Northern Tribes of Nigeria*, 2 vols. (1925).

Meek, *Tribal Studies*. C. K. Meek, *Tribal Studies in Northern Nigeria*, 2 vols. (1931).

Métraux, " The Botocudo," in *H.S.A.*, vol. i, pp. 531 f.

Métraux, " The Caingang," in *H.S.A.*, vol. i, pp. 446 f.

Métraux, " The Puri," in *H.S.A.*, vol. i, pp. 523 f.

Métraux, " The Tupinamba," in *H.S.A.*, vol. iii, pp. 95 f.

Métraux and Baldus, " The Guayaki," in *H.S.A.*, vol. i, pp. 435 f.

Métraux and Nimuendajú, "The Mashacali, etc.," in *H.S.A.*, vol. i, pp. 541 f.

M.G.H. Monumenta Germaniae Historica.

Nadel. S. F. Nadel, *A Black Byzantium* (1942).

Nimuendajú, " The Guaja," in *H.S.A.*, vol. iii, pp. 135 f.

P. & M. Sir F. Pollock and F. W. Maitland, *History of English Law before the Time of Edward I* (2nd ed., 1911).

Perham. Margery Perham, *The Government of Ethiopia* (1948).

Peristiany. J. G. Peristiany, *The Social Institutions of the Kipsigis* (1939).

Pozo, H. C. " Social and Economico–Political Evolution of the Communities of Central Peru," in *H.S.A.*, vol. ii, pp. 483–99.

Prescott, *Mexico*. W. H. Prescott, *History of the Conquest of Mexico* (new ed. published by Swan Sonnenschein & Co., 1890).

Prescott, *Peru*. W. H. Prescott, *History of the Conquest of Peru* (1847) (Everyman's Library Ed., 1924).

Primitive Law. A. S. Diamond, *Primitive Law* (2nd ed., 1950).

Radcliffe-Brown. A. R. Radcliffe-Brown, *The Andaman Islanders* (1933).

Rattray, *A. L. & C*. R. S. Rattray, *Ashanti Law and Constitution* (1923).

Robertson. A. J. Robertson, *The Laws of the Kings of England from Edmund to Henry I* (1925).

Roscoe. J. Roscoe, *The Baganda* (1911).

Roth. Henry Ling Roth, *The Aborigines of Tasmania* (2nd ed., 1899).

Routledge. W. S. & K. Routledge, *With a Prehistoric People* (1910).

Rowe. J. H. Rowe, " Inca Culture at the Time of the Spanish Conquest," in *H.S.A.*, vol. ii, pp. 183–330.

S.B.E. Sacred Books of the East.

Schapera, *Khoisan*. I. Schapera, *The Khoisan Peoples of South Africa: Bushmen and Hottentots* (1930).

Schapera, *South Bantu*. I. Schapera, *The Bantu-Speaking Tribes of South Africa* (1937).

Schapera, *Tswana*. I. Schapera, *Handbook of Tswana Law and Custom* (1938).

Seligman, *Pagan Tribes*. C. G. and B. Z. Seligman, *Pagan Tribes of the Nilotic Sudan* (1932).

Seligman, *Veddas*. C. G. and B. Z. Seligman, *The Veddas* (1911).

Serrano. A. Serrano, " The Charrua," in *H.S.A.*, vol. i, pp. 191 f.

Spencer and Gillen. Sir Baldwin Spencer and F. J. Gillen, *The Arunta* (2 vols., 1927).

Steward, " Native Population of South America," in *H.S.A.*, vol. v, pp. 655 f.

Talbot. P. A. Talbot, *The Peoples of Southern Nigeria*, 4 vols. (1931).

Temple. Sir Richard Temple, *Remarks on the Andaman Islanders and their Country* (1930).

Valcarcel. L. E. Valcarcel, "Indian Markets and Fairs in Peru," in *H.S.A.*, vol. ii, pp. 477–82.

Wagner. Günter Wagner, *The Bantu of North Kavirondo*, vol. i (1949).

Walker, C. H. C. H. Walker, *The Abyssinian at Home* (1933).

Walker, G. W. *The Life and Labours of G. W. Walker* (1862).

INDEX